Intramural Recreation

A Step-by-Step Guide to Creating an Effective Program

John Byl

Human Kinetics

Library of Congress Cataloging-in-Publication Data

Byl, John.
   Intramural recreation : a step by step guide to creating an effective program / by John Byl.
     p. cm.
   Includes bibliographical references and index.
   ISBN 0-7360-3454-4
   1. Intramural sports--Management. I. Title.
   GV710 .B95 2002
   796.04'2--dc21

                                     2002017194

ISBN: 0-7360-3454-4
Copyright © 2002 by John Byl

Acquisitions Editor: Amy N. Clocksin
Developmental Editor: D.K. Bihler and Myles Schrag
Assistant Editor: Lee Alexander
Copyeditor: D.K. Bihler
Proofreader: Pam Johnson
Indexer: Sharon Duffy
Permission Manager: Dalene Reeder
Graphic Designer: Robert Reuther
Photo Manager: Les A. Woodrum
Cover Designer: Keith Blomberg
Photographer (cover): Sara Rubinstein/UPA
Photographer (interior): Les A. Woodrum
Art Manager: Carl D. Johnson
Illustrator: Tom Roberts
Printer: Versa Press
On the cover: New York's Melanie Schoen throws a forehand in the Ultimate Players Association (UPA) mixed division championships.

Printed in the United States of America   10 9 8 7 6 5 4 3 2 1

Human Kinetics
Web site: www.humankinetics.com

United States: Human Kinetics
P.O. Box 5076
Champaign, IL 61825-5076
800-747-4457
e-mail: humank@hkusa.com

Canada: Human Kinetics
475 Devonshire Road Unit 100
Windsor, ON N8Y 2L5
800-465-7301 (in Canada only)
e-mail: orders@hkcanada.com

Europe: Human Kinetics
Units C2/C3 Wira Business Park
West Park Ring Road
Leeds LS16 6EB, United Kingdom
+44 (0) 113 278 1708
e-mail: hk@hkeurope.com

Australia: Human Kinetics
57A Price Avenue
Lower Mitcham, South Australia 5062
08 8277 1555
e-mail: liahka@senet.com.au

New Zealand: Human Kinetics
P.O. Box 105-231, Auckland Central
09-523-3462
e-mail: hkp@ihug.co.nz

I dedicate this book to my sister, Colleen.
Her faith in me when I was a teenager made this book possible.

Contents

PART III   The Program   177

Preface

"I loved going to school and coming home. I loved recess and lunch. It was the in-between part that got to me."
— John Byl

Intramural activities and events are organized to encourage students to participate in and build school community through fun physical activity. For most participants, they add fun to the love of recess and lunch time. Indeed, intramural activities were a highlight of my years in school.

In elementary school, I got to the schoolyard early. I wanted to be the first one at bat in softball. As I waited for my cohorts to arrive each morning, I wondered who would be the first to knock the ball over the street onto the church lawn. Later, while sitting at my school desk, I longed for morning recess and lunchtime, hoping for wild games of tag, knuckle-tearing games of street hockey, or our own variation of lacrosse, which amounted to throwing a tennis ball at a couple of boards standing on end.

In high school, I remember shooting a game-winning shot during a noon basketball game. I also recall accidentally body checking the 270-pound football coach and taking the ball away from him during a game of floor hockey. College intramural experiences also stand out in my memory. I remember being the first one to be dragged throught the mud at the front of my team in a tug-of-war across a muddy bog.

It was the joy of participating in these events in grade school and high school that encouraged me to study physical education. It was in college and university that I began to study the positive effects of play. It was in my teaching that I gave back to students what I had so much enjoyed when I was a student.

This book is about the part of school that so many students love the most—recess and lunchtime. From kindergarten, right through graduate-level university, students look forward to their time away from serious studies. More importantly, perhaps, students need these fun and active breaks during the day. These modifiers—*fun* and *active*—are the gist of intramurals.

This book is the result of two influences. The first is my love for intramurals, both as a participant and as a high school and university intramural director. The second is my recent tour of some intramural programs. I visited intramural directors at more than 40 schools, from grade schools to universities, and saw a lot of great ideas in practice. I knew these ideas should be shared. I also knew they should be presented in a comprehensive, sequential format that would help others create effective intramural programming.

Intramural Recreation: A Step-by-Step Guide to Creating an Effective Program is designed to help intramural directors and students revitalize student and staff interest in fun intramural activities. For those who are unfamiliar with the organization of intramural programs, this book will lead you step by step through the process of designing an intramural program. For experienced intramural directors, helpful tips and suggestions throughout the text should prove helpful in enriching your intramural program. At the very least, these ideas may help make your job easier.

Structure

The culmination of more than 20 years of teaching physical education, leading intramurals, and working with intramural participants and staff, this book is both practical and readily applicable. Organized as your typical textbook, each chapter begins with "Chapter Objectives," so you know right away what to expect. To avoid confusion in terminology, **key terms** are identified in bold and then defined. These terms are also included in a glossary at the end of the book. In addition to numerous examples, tips, suggestions, and ideas provided throughout, "Practitioner Perspectives" in every chapter present concrete examples of how intramural directors have tried to enrich their own intramural programs.

Each chapter ends with "Chapter Summary Exercises" and "Resources." These exercises provide the opportunity to review the contents of that chapter and are steps in completing a final assignment at the end of this book: preparing your own intramural handbook. "Resources" contains relevant publications, organizations, and Web sites that provide additional information for a more complete understanding of each chapter topic.

Structured to help you build your own intramural program one step at a time, this book is divided into three parts.

▶ Part I: The Idea
▶ Part II: The Plan
▶ Part III: The Program

Part I will help you focus on what you want your intramural program to be. Discussions in chapter 1 include the purpose, benefits, and history of intramural programs. Chapter 2, "On a Mission," leads you through the process of developing a clearly written mission statement for your intramural program.

Part II includes chapters 3 through 10, which present everything you need to know about planning an effective intramural program. Topics developed in chapters 3, 4, and 5 include defining program structure and leadership requirements; making the most of available facilities (from the gym, to the fields, to the parking lot); maximizing volunteer and student participation; and recruiting, hiring, and training program staff, officials, and volunteers. In addition, chapters 6 and 7 take you through the process of developing policies that will make your intramural program fair and safe for all. Promotional strategies to draw in participants are covered in chapter 8, and awards to celebrate intramural successes and individual achievement are discussed in chapter 9. The final chapter in part II, chapter 10, leads you through the process of developing an intramural budget.

Part III focuses on the program itself—that is, implementation and evaluation. Chapters 11 through 13 lead you through the process of creating the intramural programming you conceived in part I and planned in part II. Discussions include programming implementation, activity and event scheduling, and tournament and league selection. In addition, specific activity and event ideas are offered throughout. Chapter 14 presents effective tools for evaluating your intramural program. The final chapter, chapter 15, is the culmination of the entire book. Based on the discussion and exercises in every chapter, chapter 15 is an assignment that takes you through the steps of constructing a comprehensive intramural handbook.

When all is read and done, this book and the handbook you create will serve as practical guides for enriching people's lives through intramural activities. By helping you to provide vigorous, fun, inclusive, and safe activities, it is our hope that students—old and young, university and grade school—will treasure both their studies during class as well as their recesses, lunchtime breaks, and after-class activities. If we achieve that, we will have accomplished much.

Acknowledgments

Thanks to the campus recreation directors from the Ontario College Committee on Campus Recreation who shared many of their wonderful ideas with me. Also special thanks to the Canadian Intramural Recreation Association-Ontario board members (Andy, Carolyn, Herwig, Michelle, and Pat), who are an inspiration to kids and to me. Thanks to my daughter Judith for doing some of the initial editing.

I also want to thank the Ontario Ministry of Citizenship, Culture, and Recreation. It was in working on a related project to promote active living for Ontario college students that several of the ideas in this book came together. And thanks to Redeemer University College. It's a great place to work and provided me with the sabbatical that made writing this book possible.

I appreciate the staff at Human Kinetics for the support they have given me, and their encouragement of physical activity around the world. I owe special thanks to Amy for her confidence in this book and her encouragement in this project, and to D.K. for her editorial skills.

Thanks to my wife, Catherine, and my children Hannah (and Ryan), Judith, Matt, and Charis for their support during the writing of this book. I also want to thank God for putting all things together.

Finally, thanks to countless others who helped me on this project. Although I have acknowledged all the sources I know about, my files contained some anonymous papers, ideas, and notes. I would be happy to identify those sources in future editions.

Part 1

The Idea

As I mentioned in the preface, I liked intramural activities a lot as I went through school. While my enjoyment might justify my encouraging intramural programs and participation in my own university setting, however, it is probably not sufficient grounds to write a book that encourages and helps others develop great intramural programs. Thus, in addition to exploring the myriad benefits of intramural activities in any school setting—and what researchers have said about these benefits— chapter 1 also encourages you to recall your own intramural experiences.

Any idea needs a focus, and planning an intramural program is no different. In a formal program such as intramurals, this focus is achieved with a mission statement. Chapter 2 helps you to develop your own intramural program mission.

With a clearly conceived, focused idea and mission statement, you will be ready to develop an effective intramural program, the steps of which are developed in part II: The Plan.

Why Intramurals?

Since the arrival of television and personal computers, it seems that more and more students take less and less time for physical activity, instead lying on the couch or sitting at the keyboard. With increased cost for education, students seem more motivated to excel in their studies and hold jobs outside of school to pay for their education. Although watching television, working on a computer, doing well academically, and being gainfully employed are not necessarily bad, they do discourage active living. As campus recreation directors, our challenge is to offer exciting, accessible, innovative, and fun activities and information that encourage students to become more physically active.

Chapter Objectives

- ► Explore the purpose of intramural programming.
- ► Define the intramural terms used throughout this book.
- ► Explore the history of intramural programming.
- ► Identify the benefits of intramurals for students and educational institutions.

The Purpose of Intramurals

Intramurals is about people playing with people. It's about letting go of inhibitions and surrendering to the spirit of play. It's about physical activity and burning energy. Intramural activities should have an atmosphere of sweat and laughter. Participating in intramurals should not threaten egos, or make students look silly or feel uncomfortable. Intramurals can be about competition, but it is always about mass participation and fun.

Intramurals should be an opportunity to learn new skills or practice an existing skill learned in physical education. It should be an opportunity to play with friends and enrich friendships, and to make new friends. Intramurals is an opportunity to develop character, leadership, and sportsmanship in students. In short, an intramural program is a tremendous tool for enhancing students' lives—whether in grade school, high school, or university.

As an intramural director, then, it's important that you consider your students when devising your program. Let's look briefly at several specific purposes of intramurals.

Fun

Above all, an intramural activity or event should be fun for all participants. If intramurals is not fun and players are not enjoying themselves, they will not come back. There is nothing worse than a student excitedly joining an intramural soccer team and then having a miserable time at the first game. There are two components of fun: (1) joy of the moment and (2) satisfaction of the overall experience, which is what brings participants back for more.

As the director, it will be your job to ensure fun. Little things like officials showing up 15 minutes late and a shortage of necessary equipment at game time can dampen fun at the outset. During the activity, fun can be destroyed either by competition so excessive that participants dare not make a mistake, or overly aggressive play that results in injury. Problems like these prevent the carefree spirit of play. They ruin the joy of the moment and can reduce participants' satisfaction with the entire experience.

Physical Fitness

As mentioned above, intramurals is about physical activity. Physical activity, while a great reliever of stress and an even better mental distraction from the rigors of school, studying, and after-school jobs, also yields important health benefits. Among them: cardiovascular health, increased flexibility, and stronger bones and muscles. Certain types of formal exercise will also improve these functions, of course, but intramurals offers the benefits of physical fitness in an environment of play. There's nothing better than watching participants leave the floor or field rosy cheeked, physically drained, and excited for the next event. Even better if they walk away saying, "That was a real workout!"

Competition

Competition is usually thought of as rivalry, striving to beat an opponent. Competition can be a characteristic of an intramural event, certainly, particularly in team sports. In intramurals, however, competition is about participants challenging themselves to overcome obstacles. These obstacles can be momentary ("Susan is open and I need to pass the ball to her") or ongoing ("Let's see if we can win the championship").

Competition is also about focus. In a competition, participants must forget about grades, deans' lists, jobs, and other worries for a while and concentrate on the activity at hand. It does not matter if the game is part of an organized basketball tournament or a silly activity involving balloons and rubber chickens. Players must stay focused on succeeding.

Of course, intramurals should never be about winning at all costs. There is too much at stake, in terms of friendship, character, participation, and fun, for this to be the atmosphere of any intramural setting. As a director, then, it will be your job to ensure healthy, safe, and fun competition for all.

Character

Intramurals is an excellent opportunity to develop personal character, including winning and losing graciously, playing fairly, tolerating and encouraging less-skilled players, and watching out for others. If participants gain nothing else from their intramural experience, these qualities will serve them well throughout their lives.

Character also has to do with fun and competition. If games are too competitive, if the stakes are too high, and if players are overly aggressive with one another, participants will naturally respond in kind. As a director, it will be your job to develop an intramural program in which everyone can participate in fun, competitive play, which will lead participants to be fair, gracious, and encouraging of others.

Leadership

Innate to the structure of an intramural program is the opportunity for leadership. **Leadership** has been defined as stimulating and aiding groups to accept and formulate common goals and "to carry out effectively the measures leading to the attainment of those goals" (Kraus 1985, 25). In other words, leadership is the practice of helping a group of people know where they want to go and helping them get there. Leadership can be formal or informal. In an intramural program, formal leadership opportunities include being a team captain, a referee, and assisting the intramural director in running an event. Informal leadership opportunities include leading by example in playing fairly and encouraging others. As a director, it will be your job to initiate intramural activities and events that develop leadership opportunities for participants.

These purposes of intramurals have remained consistent over time, but the emphasis and organization of intramural programs has changed significantly. Before looking at a history of intramural programs, let's define some key terms.

Defining Our Terms

When discussing intramural programs, terms can get confusing. For example, some institutions use *intramurals* to refer to all recreational programs within the institution, while others use the term to include only the sport component of a recreational program. Some call a team not showing up for a scheduled game a "default," while others call this a "forfeit" and reserve the term *default* for those instances in which a team member has informed the intramural director

well enough ahead of time. Therefore, to ensure clarity in our discussion here, we'd best define our terms. (See chapter 13 for the working definitions of *default* and *forfeit*.)

Let's start with the basics. The term *intramural* is said to have been coined by A.S. Whitney, a Latin professor and member of the University of Michigan athletic committee, but *intramural* comes from two Latin words: *intra* meaning "within" and *muralis* meaning "wall." The translation of *intramural*, then, is "within the walls" of a school. Intramural activities typically include any in-school (or on-campus) activity, from team sport competitions to fitness classes for students. **Extramural** activities, on the other hand, would take place "outside the walls" of a school. Typically, extramural activities involve informal competition between schools. For our purposes, we're using **intramurals** and **intramural programming** to include all organized recreational and physical activities for students and other participants—whether grade school, high school, or university students—no matter where they take place. The term *programming* is also a verb, referring to the act of determining that programming.

Some institutions use the term **campus recreation** instead of *intramurals*. In other words, campus recreation includes any recreational events run on or off campus for students, faculty, and staff at educational institutions. At many universities, the campus recreation department is often responsible for implementing an intramural program. At many others, the intramural department is responsible for implementing all campus recreation. Thus, for simplicity's sake, we will use *campus recreation* and *intramurals* interchangeably. Finally, there's the issue of program versus programming. While intramural programming includes the activities and events, **intramural program** is the entire program itself, including the programming as well as the staff, volunteers, and procedures responsible for implementing that programming.

Next in the term-definition process comes the qualities of intramurals. While well known to most, for the purposes of this book, the definitions of *play* and *game* are specific to intramurals. In **play** participants are committed to amusement, enjoyment, and fun in an activity. In a **game** participants are committed to accomplishing a specific task (i.e., winning by scoring more goals than their opponents) and agree to overcome unnecessary obstacles or hindrances to accomplish that task (i.e., follow the rules of the game) (Suits 1973, 55). For example, it would be a lot easier to drop a basketball through the hoop while standing on a ladder perched against the backboard. The rules of basketball, however, do not allow the use of ladders. Thus, by participating in the game of basketball, players are agreeing to follow the rules.

Working with these definitions of *play* and *game*, then, we arrive at the different levels of game competition. As shown in figure 1.1, in a **playful game**, participants are more committed to the spirit of play than to winning. An example of a playful game might be one-on-one basketball where players don't keep score and try odd or unusual shots. Participants are equally committed to the spirit of play and to winning in **sport.** Many intramural events are played at this level. **Athletics,** the most competitive level, involves a greater commitment to winning. Athletics usually takes the form of between-school competitions and typically involves formalized practices, coaches, referees, records, rulebooks, historical team continuity, and so on. Some institutions refer to athletics as *varsity sport*. In general, the more formalized the game, the more athletic the event. (Byl 1994)

With these basic terms defined, we can now return to the discussion of different types of intramural programming. In addition to formalized intramural programming, two other school departments are devoted to physical activity: physical education and varsity athletics. **Physical education** is part of a school's curriculum and involves in-class instruction of physical activity. **Varsity athletics** is a voluntary program that offers highly formalized between-school competitions that are oriented towards winning.

It is important to be clear about how intramurals relates to physical education and varsity athletics. How we think they are related shapes our approach to intramural programming. For example, if athletics is the most desired outcome of a school's campus recreation program, intramurals will likely be either a recruiting program or serve as extra practice for varsity athletics. While varsity athletics enables the most able-bodied physical education students to refine their skills, this type of intramural programming is less than ideal because it will usually be limited to a select few. If physical education is more important, however—and this is the case at most schools, as it should be—the intramural program will strive to enable students to put the physical education curriculum into practice.

History of Intramurals

In early twentieth-century North America, schools provided opportunities for students to play informal games before class, at recess, and at lunch. Universities provided these games after classes and on weekends. Such play is evident in novels of that time period. In his 1912 novel *Stover at Yale*, for example, Owen Johnson describes hotly contested games between different classes, particularly between freshmen and sophomores during freshman initiation. Girls also played organized intramural games, as evidenced in early novels such as August Schwartze's *Vassar Studies* (1899) and the first two novels of Edith Bancroft's Jane Allen series, *Jane Allen of the Sub Team* (1917) and *Jane Allen: Right Guard* (1918).

Believe it or not, formalized game playing in an academic setting goes further back. Eric Stein (1985) provides an interesting look at the evolution of intramural activity since 1800. In many ways, intramural development across the U.S. is mirrored by intramural development at

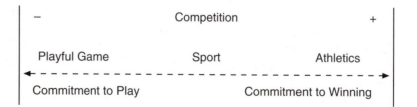

FIGURE 1.1 Levels of game competition. In a playful game, play is more important than winning. In athletics, winning is more important.

Princeton. Based on articles in *The Daily Princetonian*, Stein describes the period before 1800 as a time when university "sport" comprised such leisurely activities as walking, horseback riding, canoeing, and so on. Competitive matches and fast-paced movement were not part of institutional sport during this time period.

By the mid 1800s, competition emerged with informal "soccer" games between the students of East and West College at Princeton. The game involved kicking a ball downfield until it struck one of the college's walls, at which point the game would be over. In 1857, baseball entered the mix when Princeton freshmen and sophomores formed baseball clubs and challenged each other to a game. This "official" match is considered the first intramural event at a U.S. university. From then on, at the university level, male students organized many interclass competitions (Stein 1985).

Another sport tradition that developed around the mid 1800s was a "cane spree." The object was for one class to snatch walking canes from the other class. This activity, which quickly turned into an annual student event, tended toward the wild side. Students often played with little or no clothes on and, if they won, went on boisterous victory parades through town. Starting in the 1920s, Princeton's administrators tried to discourage cane sprees by introducing more structured events, including tennis, soccer, swimming, and volleyball competitions (Stein 1985).

The history of intramural organization follows a similar pattern. Michigan and Ohio State Universities were the first, in 1913, to create departments for intramural athletics as a response to the recreational demands of students. The year 1917 marks the first meeting of the Athletic Conference of American College Women. Organizers opposed women's intercollegiate athletics but valued every "girl" being on a team—an intramural team, that is. They didn't want a few female sport stars; they wanted every girl involved in some physical activity (Dudenyhoeffer 1997).

A forum for intramural professionals (mostly university employees) was not established in North America until 1950, when Dr. William Wasson organized a meeting of 20 African-American men and women intramural directors to found the National Intramural Association (NIA). The NIA extended its membership to females in 1971 (Hanniford 1992) and recognizing its broadened base in 1975, changed its name to the National Intramural-Recreational Sport Association (NIRSA). The Canadian counterpart to NIRSA is the Canadian Intramural Recreation Association (CIRA). CIRA was organized in 1977 when several intramural directors, financed by a brewing company, founded the organization. Today, both NIRSA and CIRA host conferences, publish magazines and other resources, and serve as a voice for intramural programs in their respective countries.

Grade and high school intramural programs and programming have not fared so well. Intramural games were a part of North American grade schools and high schools for much of the twentieth century, taking the form of organized lunchtime contests between students. During the last 40 years, however, intramural programming in grade and high schools has declined dramatically. The primary cause for this decline is the increased demand for and use of school busing, which limits after-school time for students. Another cause is athletics' rise in popularity and importance. Somewhere along the line, athletics—rather than playful games and sport—took priority, pushing intramural programs out of its way. Games that were organized over lunch periods and morning recess had to give way for athletic team practices. Finally, particularly in some Canadian schools, teachers often have neither the time nor the inclination to devote the extra work necessary for intramural programming.

Clearly, intramurals has played a role in North American schools, but it is a role that, at least at some grade levels, appears to be under some stress. As present and future intramural directors, you may one day be in a position to help revive the importance of this role and encourage the spirit of play in the school system.

As educational philosopher John Dewey wrote in *Democracy and Education*, "it is the business of the school to set up an environment in which play and work shall be conducted with reference to facilitating desirable mental and moral growth." This kind of growth would not happen by itself but rather should be assisted with careful supervision, he notes. "It is not enough just to introduce play and games, hand out work and manual exercises. Everything depends upon the way in which they are employed" (Dewey 1916).

Benefits of Intramural Activity

The way in which "play and games are employed," in Dewey's words, should be with an eye toward delivering the greatest number of benefits to the greatest number of participants. The specific benefits of involvement in intramurals are not well researched and documented, but the benefits of involvement in physical activity are. Because intramurals is largely about physical activity, it is both appropriate and helpful to look at these benefits. It is also helpful to consider how these benefits translate to other areas of participants' lives.

Clearly, students who are physically active feel better and tend to be healthier physically. But students who are involved in physical activity also tend to have a stronger commitment and a more positive affiliation to school and learning. As a result, they show higher academic achievement and greater post-secondary success. Those involved in intramurals from a young age are less likely to smoke, use drugs, or become pregnant as teenagers (Canadian Parks 1997).

Not surprisingly, the reverse is also true. Institutions that do not offer cocurricular activities such as intramurals tend to have more problems. School morale and academic achievement tend to be lower, and students tend to leave school at a younger age. Students are also more likely to become involved in crime and make more poor health-style choices such as smoking (Parks and Recreation 1999).

From the point of view of the school, then, a primary benefit of offering intramurals clearly lies in the health of its students—and not just physical health but also mental and emotional health. But this benefit goes further. By providing students with the benefits already described, the institution is sending the message that it cares about its students as more than grade point averages and statistics; it cares about them as people. In addition, providing intramurals also helps to shape positive school spirit, which is invaluable in student retention, participation, and even alumni interaction later on. And, when students are more committed to their school, vandalism decreases (Jandris 1980; Cappadonia 1970; Cohen 1991). A final, albeit institutional, benefit to offering intramurals lies in spotting and recruiting talent for varsity and other athletic teams. Coaches can observe students in action.

Put simply, can a school afford not to offer intramurals? It could probably be argued that if the time is not spent up front encouraging positive physical activity, the time will be spent later on picking up the pieces through discipline and other corrective measures. Let's take a look at the specific benefits of an intramural program.

Character

In the words of former Beardy's First Nation Reserve chief Rick Gamble from a Canadian reservation north of Saskatoon, "Sport is a character builder. Sport builds identity and camaraderie. You learn to win together and lose together. It's the game of life itself" (Cobb 2001). Although American mythology assumes that sport builds character, the literature gives mixed reviews on the topic (Lee 1986). If winning is the main purpose of the game, such a game does not build character (Chandler 1988). Furthermore, sport that encourages a "win at any price" ethic is conducive to aggression and violence, not good character (Vandyke 1980).

If players compete for the experience of participating in a game, however, positive character-development opportunities exist (Chandler 1988). Indeed, if program leaders such as referees, coaches, team captains, and even program directors model desirable behavior and discuss fairness, players are more likely to develop "good character" (Lee 1986). Thus, intramurals, which should de-emphasize winning and provide positive leadership about fair play, can be an important part of developing good character in students.

Leadership

An important component to leadership is self-esteem. Leaders have enough self-confidence to take the lead in something and are not afraid to take risks, to be in front of a group of people, and to help others succeed. A study of Canadian children aged 4 to 15 found that those who participate in organized physical activities tend to have higher self-esteem, interact better with friends, and be positive leaders. Inactive children, on the other hand, are four times as likely to have low self-esteem (Statistics Canada 2001). Consequently, inactive children are less likely to grow up to be leaders. Active students are also better able to cope with stress. They are more likely to have a social support structure in place and a higher sense of self-determination (Coleman and Iso-Ahola 1993). These children grow up to be leaders.

Intramural programs provide a wonderful opportunity to develop leadership qualities in students. In intramurals it is safe to experiment with and learn new skills because students' peers are in the same situation and also because intramural activity is about play, fun, and exploration. Even in this nonthreatening situation, however, teams need leaders, the program itself needs leaders, and games need referees. Thus, encouraging students to be physically active and participate in intramurals provides them with the opportunity to put their leadership skills into practice (Fabian 1982).

Fun

Everyone prefers fun to boredom, certainly. Intramural programming, if diverse enough to accommodate students' varied interests, can add some excitement and a welcome diversion to students' otherwise regimented school lives of study and learning. More important, perhaps, studies indicate that students who are more physically active experience less anxiety and depression and generally exhibit enhanced feelings of well-being (Cai 2000; Balady 2000). In fact, those involved in physically active leisure pursuits report much greater life satisfaction and a more positive outlook on the future than those who are inactive (Herzog and Rogers 1981; Statistics Canada 2001).

Educators have a responsibility to prepare their students for the future. Although education is not typically committed to providing fun for students, with so many advantages to adding fun to students' lives, can a school afford not to consider fun in its curriculum? That's where intramurals comes in. Well-implemented intramural programming, committed to encouraging fun as well as physical activity, can do a lot to improve the lives of participants (Hurtes et al. 2000).

Health

The health benefits of physical activity and fitness are well known. According to the U.S. surgeon general, "Significant health benefits can be obtained by including a moderate amount of physical activity . . . on most, if not all, days of the week. Through a modest increase in daily activity, most Americans can improve their health and quality of life" (U.S. Department of Health 1996).

Specifically, some of the health benefits of physical activity are listed here.

- ▶ Exercise has a positive effect on type 2 diabetes (Tudor-Locke, Bell, and Myers 2000).
- ▶ Physical activity increases bone mineral density (Drowatzky and Drowatzky 2000).
- ▶ Exercise has been found to be helpful in restoring overall health to obese children (Hunter, Gamman, and Hester 2000).
- ▶ Those who are physically active are less likely to smoke (Statistics Canada 2001).
- ▶ Physical exercise contributes to increased life span and lowered rates of heart disease (Froehlicher and Froehlicher 1991; Paffenbarger, Hyde, and Dow 1991).

Such health benefits can also be measured economically. The health costs of U.S. citizens 15 years and older was approximately 25 percent higher for those who did not exercise regularly compared to those who were physically active. In the year 2000, this translated to a savings of $76 billion in the U.S. (Pratt, Macera, and Wang 2000).

Those who adopt healthy lifestyle patterns early in life tend to stick to these patterns later on (Bailey 2000). Thus, intramural programs have a significant role to play in the physical health of their participants, not only in their present but also in their future lives.

Sociability

Strong, positive, and close social relationships with others are important to everyone, regardless of age or occupation. Studies have found that those who do not participate in physical activity are three times as likely to report having difficulties in their relationships with friends compared to those who are active (Statistics Canada 2001). On the positive side, those who are involved in physical activity feel freer to be themselves, freer to "let their hair down," so to speak (Kelly 1983). This freedom results in higher self-confidence and self-esteem, which as already discussed, leads to a promising future.

The Intramural Experience

The literature may document benefits of intramural activity, but what do the participants say about the benefits of intramural activity as they experience it? Following are four students' responses to this question. As an intramural director, it would be interesting to ask your own students this question from time to time.

"I have made countless friends and connections through intramurals. When you find yourself among 14,000 other students and are just a number to most people around you, finding a familiar face in the anonymous ocean of faces . . . is very comforting, especially when you're just starting there" (Gobhai 1996).

"Being involved in the intramural program means that all kinds of students who normally wouldn't interact in their day-to-day activities get to know each other and learn how to work with them in a team" (Antons 1999).

"Helping others become more involved in an intramural activity gave me the greatest sense of leadership and self-esteem" (Lam 1999).

"I decided to accept the position of Intramural Assistant Programmer. . . . I became a better organizer and met more people. . . . This invaluable experience has better prepared me for my future" (Johnson 1999).

Reprinted by permission of the Canadian Intramural Recreation Association. From the CIRA, 1999, "The intramural experience," *CIRA Bulletin* 25 (3):11.

Intramurals provides participants with a unique opportunity to meet others and develop positive friendships. In addition, it can help students learn how to relate to other people, including their peers as well as authority figures.

Achievement

Put simply, people who are physically active are higher achievers academically. Studies indicate that children between the ages of four and nine who participate in physical activities tend to have fewer difficulties in reading and math and have developed better study habits than those who do not rarely participate (Statistics Canada 2001; Alsager 1977). The benefits of physical activity go beyond school, however. Physically active adults tend to perform better and achieve more success at work (Balady 2000), and are better able to deal with higher levels of stress (Reich and Zantra 1981).

Skill development, which is a large part of any intramural activity, has also been shown to improve achievement. Studies indicate that skill development is important in the formation of self-image, self-esteem, and perceived self-competence (Kleiber and Kirshnit 1991; Iso-Ahola, Graefe, and La Verde 1989). Furthermore, research shows that those who try to match their skill level to the challenge at hand may be more likely to realize self-actualization (Csikszentmihalyi 1975).

Chapter Summary Exercises

Clearly, the benefits to offering an intramural program are many. Those described in this chapter are only a starting point, however. The following exercises will help you identify other benefits by recalling your own intramural experiences and features you liked in the programs you've participated in.

1. In small groups, discuss your intramural experiences in grade school, high school, and college or university. What are some of the benefits of these programs as you experienced them? Identify a specific benefit and provide examples for each. How do these benefits compare with those listed in this chapter?

2. Log on to the Internet and go to the following Web site: www.lin.ca. Do a search on the topic "children and benefits." Find (and document with full citation) one of the benefits for each of the six categories presented in this chapter (character, leadership, fun, health, sociability, and achievement).

3. Go to the Web site www.lin.ca/htdocs/cattofc.htm and read through the outstanding *Benefits Catalogue*. Find (and document with full citation) at least one new benefit that was not discussed in this chapter or mentioned in your group discussions.

4. NIRSA and CIRA were discussed in this chapter as key organizations in the history of intramurals. Peruse the Web sites of NIRSA (http://www.nirsa.org/) and CIRA (www.intramurals.ca) and find (and document with full citation) the key benefits of intramurals as they identify them.

References

Alsager, D. 1977. Intramural programming in Ohio high schools. Unpublished manuscript, Miami University, Oxford, Ohio.

Antons, J. 1999. The intramural experience. *CIRA Bulletin* 25 (3): 11.

Bailey, D. 2000. Is anyone out there listening? *Quest* 52 (4): 344-50.

Balady, G. 2000. *ACSM's guidelines for exercise testing and prescription*. 6th ed. Philadelphia: Lippencott Williams and Wilkens.

Bancroft, E. 1917. *Jane Allen of the sub team*. Akron, Ohio: Saalfield.

Bancroft. E. 1918. *Jane Allen: Right guard*. Akron, Ohio: Saalfield.

Byl, J. 1994. Coming to terms with play, game, sport, and athletics. In *Christianity and leisure: Issues in a pluralistic society*, edited by P. Heintzman, G. Van Andel, and T. Visker. Sioux Center, Iowa: Dordt College Press, 155-63.

Cai, S. 2000. Physical exercise and mental health: A content integrated approach in coping with college students' anxiety and depression. *Physical Educator* 27 (2): 69-76.

Canadian Parks and Recreation Association. 1997. *Benefits catalogue*. Ottawa: Canadian Parks and Recreation Association.

Cappadonia, P. 1970. Evaluation of vandalism during leisure time in all junior high schools of Utah County, Utah. Master's thesis, Bringham Young University, Provo, Utah.

Chandler, T. 1988. Building character through sport, and striving to win in sport: Values at odds or in concert? In *Persons, minds and bodies*, edited by S. Ross and L. Charette. North York, Ontario: University Press of Canada, 161-69.

Cobb, C. 2001. Recognizing impact of sports not rocket science: Common sense dispensed after national summit. *National Post* (April 30), A1

Cohen, A. 1991. Crime and punishment. *Athletic Business* 15 (10): 31-35.

Coleman, D., and S. Iso-Ahola. 1993. Leisure and health: The role of social support and self-determination. *Journal of Leisure Research* (25): 111-28.

Csikszentmihalyi, M. 1975. *Beyond boredom and anxiety: The experience of play in work and games*. San Francisco: Jossey-Bass.

Dewey, J. 1916. *Democracy and education*. New York: Macmillan.

Drowatzky, K., and J. Drowatzky. 2000. Physical activity and bone mineral density. *Clinical Kinesiology* 54 (2): 28-35.

Dudenyhoeffer, F. 1997. Life before NIRSA: A brief history of women's intramurals in the 20th century. *NIRSA Journal* 21 (2): 3-7.

Fabian, L. 1982. Leadership development through intramural sports. *NIRSA Journal* 6 (3): 18-22.

Froelicher, V., and E. Froelicher. 1991. Cardiovascular benefits of physical activity. In *Benefits of leisure*, edited by B.L. Driver, P.J. Brown, and G.L. Pederson. State College, Pa.: Venture Publishing, 59-72.

Gobhai, X. 1996. Thoughts on intramurals. *CIRA Bulletin*. 21 (7): 10.

Hanniford, G. 1992. Our past: Our heritage. *NIRSA Journal* 17 (1): 24.

Herzog, A., and W. Rogers. 1981. The structure of subjective well-being in different age groups. *Journal of Gerontology* 36: 472-79.

Hunter, G., M. Gamman, and D. Hester. 2000. Obesity-prone children can benefit from high-intensity exercise. *Strength and Conditioning Journal* 22 (1): 51-54.

Hurtes, K., L. Allne, B. Stevens, and C. Lee. 2000. Benefits-based programming: Making an impact on youth. *Journal of Park and Recreation Administration* 18 (1): 34-49.

Iso-Ahola, S., A. Graefe, and D. La Verde. 1989. Perceived competence as a mediator of the relationship between high risk sports participation and self-esteem. *Journal of Leisure Research* 21: 32-39.

Jandris, T. 1980. Possibilities and potentials: High school intramurals. *Journal of Physical Education and Recreation* 51: 48-50

Johnson, M. 1999. The intramural experience. *CIRA Bulletin*. 25 (3): 11.

Johnson, O. 1912 (Reprinted 1968, 1997). *Stover at Yale*. New Haven: Yale Bookstore.

Kelly, J. 1983. *Leisure identities and interactions*. London: Allen and Unwin.

Kleiber, D., and C. Kirshnit. 1991. Sport involvement and identity formation. In *Mind-body maturity: Psychological approaches to sport, exercise and fitness*, edited by L. Diament. New York: Hemisphere.

Kraus, R. 1985. *Recreation leadership today*. Chicago: Addison-Wesley.

Lam, L. 1999. The intramural experience. *CIRA Bulletin* 25 (3): 11.

Lee, M. 1986. Moral and social growth through sport: The coach's role. In *The growing child in competitive sport*, edited by G. Glesson. London: Hodder & Stoughton, 248-55.

Paffenbarger, R., R. Hyde, and A. Dow. 1991. Health benefits of physical activity. In *Benefits of leisure*, edited by B.L. Driver, P.J. Brown, and G.L. Pederson. State College, Pa.: Venture Publishing, 49-57.

Parks and Recreation Ontario. 1999. *Together with youth: Planning recreation services for youth at risk.* Toronto: Parks and Recreation Ontario.

Pratt, M., C. Macera, and G. Wang. 2000. Higher direct medical costs associated with physical inactivity. *Physician and Sportsmedicine* 28 (10): 63-70.

Reich, J., and A. Zantra. 1981. Life events and personal causation: Some relationships with satisfaction and distress. *Journal of Personality and Social Psychology* 41: 1002-12.

Schwartze, A. 1899. *Vassar studies.* New York: G.P. Putnam & Sons.

Statistics Canada. 2001. *National longitudinal survey of children and youth: Participation in activities.* Ottawa: Statistics Canada.

Stein, E. 1985. The first organized intramural event (1869): Princeton University's cane spree. *NIRSA Journal* 9 (2): 42-43.

Suits, B. 1973. The elements of sport. In *The philosophy of sport: A collection of original essays,* edited by R.G. Osterhoudt. Springfield, IL: Charles C. Thomas, 46-63.

Tudor-Locke, C., R. Bell, and A. Myers. 2000. Revisiting the role of physical activity and exercise in the treatment of type 2 diabetes. *Canadian Journal of Applied Physiology* 25 (6): 466-91.

U.S. Department of Health and Human Services. 1996. *Physical activity and health: A report of the surgeon general.* Atlanta: U.S. Department of Health and Human Services, Centers for Disease Control and Prevention, National Center for Chronic Disease Prevention and Health Control.

Vandyke, R. 1980. Aggression in sport: Its implications for character building. *Quest* 32 (2): 201-8.

Resources

Canadian Intramural Recreation Association (CIRA)
740-B Belfast Road
Ottawa, Ontario Canada K1G 0Z5
Telephone: 613-244-1594
Fax: 613-244-4738

Web site: www.intramurals.ca
E-mail: cira@intramurals.ca

Assists intramural directors in Canada. CIRA's mission is to encourage, promote, and develop active living and healthy lifestyles through intramural and recreation programs within the educational community. Also produces *Bulletin*, the quarterly periodical for its members.

Canadian Intramural Recreation Association-Ontario (CIRA-Ontario)
c/o Student Life
P.O. Box 2034
Hamilton, Ontario Canada L8N 3T2
Telephone: 905-575-2083
Fax: 905-575-2264
Web site: http://www.mohawkc.on.ca/external/cira/resource.html

Ontario chapter of CIRA. Produces *INPUT*, a quarterly newsletter for its members and offers other great resources by and for teachers. (Check out "resources" on its Web site.) Also provides a free, moderately active, listserv discussion group. (To join, E-mail ciraon@julian.uwo.ca.) The listserv is a forum where members can ask questions and offer solutions for problems related to intramural programs, particularly at the college and university level.

National Intramural Recreational Sport Association (NIRSA)
4185 S.W. Research Way
Corvallis, OR 97333-1067
Telephone: 541-766-8211
Fax: 541-766-8284
Web site: http://nirsa.org/
E-mail nirsa@nirsa.org

A nonprofit, professional organization dedicated to the establishment and development of quality intramural/recreational sports and fitness programs and services. Produces the semiannual *NIRSA Journal* and provides an active listserv discussion group to its members.

2

On a Mission

When someone is "on a mission," they know exactly where they're going and are focused on getting there. A lack of focus is exemplified by Alice in *Alice in Wonderland*.

> Alice . . . went on. "Would you tell me, please, which way I ought to go from here?"
>
> "That depends a good deal on where you want to get to," said the Cat.
>
> "I don't much care where—" said Alice.
>
> "Then it doesn't matter which way you go," said the Cat.
>
> "—so long as I get somewhere," Alice added.
>
> "Oh, you're sure to do that," said the Cat, "if you only walk long enough" (Carroll 1960, 62).

Alice will get somewhere, but clearly she is not on a well-thought-out mission. Likewise, to be effective, intramural programs must have focus.

Chapter Objectives

► Identify the focus of an intramural program.

► Develop an intramural mission statement.

► Understand the steps of developing an effective intramural program.

The Mission of an Intramural Program

As detailed in chapter 1, the benefits of an intramural program are many. Although intramural directors want to satisfy as many participants as possible, their programs cannot be all things to all people. Nor can one program do everything. It must have focus. And the best way to facilitate this focus is articulating an intramural mission statement.

Sometimes intramural directors are like Alice. They don't take the time to clearly map out a direction or focus of their programs. Without this focus, they will certainly get somewhere, perhaps even a great place, but neither they nor the program participants will know how to get there again.

A **mission statement** is a precise statement of what an institution wants its intramural program to be. A mission statement provides a direction for organizing and implementing a coherent, effective intramural program. Whatever the form, a mission statement should be simple, concise, and specific. The seven essential components of constructing an effective mission statement are listed here, followed by further explanation of each.

1. Start with a central theme. The statement should explain what the program is, what it stands for, and why it exists. This is the focus of your program.

2. Be realistic. The mission should push the program to new heights, incorporating fun and interesting activities, but it should also be attainable.

3. Keep it short and simple. Lengthy and overly complex or academic statements are not only vague and uninspiring; oftentimes they are not very useful. Keep the language simple and the statement short. You should be able to read it in 30 seconds or less.

4. Build excitement and inspire action. In addition to simplicity, word choice is important. Choose strong verbs and adverbs to communicate your mission. For example, verbs such as *inspire*, *excite*, and *laugh* are more powerful than *build*, *enhance*, and *initiate*.

5. Get others' input. Ask for ideas from all program staff and participants, including coaches, referees, officials, volunteers, supervisors, administrators, and students. It's also a good idea to look at other institutions' intramural mission statements. Your statement should reflect the intentions of everyone involved in the program, which requires that you take the time to understand everyone's thoughts, goals, and plans for the program.

6. Make it visible. Once completed, the mission statement should be posted for all to see. Use it on fliers, posters, and manuals, and advertise your mission on bulletin boards and other central locations throughout the school.

7. Revisit and evaluate. As with any plan, evaluation is key. A mission statement should be evaluated from time to time and adjusted as necessary, either to improve the message or to reflect more closely the purpose of the program.

Start With a Central Theme

A mission statement should explain what the program is, what it stands for, and why it exists. The following questions will help you identify a central theme, or focus.

▶ What central goals do your want your intramural program to achieve?

▶ Recalling the benefits of intramurals identified in chapter 1, what major benefits do you want your program to offer?

▶ Think back to an intramural program you participated in during grade school, high school, college, or university. What was the main focus of those programs? Is that the focus you want for your intramural program? Why or why not?

When identifying the focus of your program, it is important to identify and clarify all philosophical differences, definitions, and assumptions that may affect it. For example, you might want fun to be a central component of your program. Some students will think an informal, friendly game of unofficial volleyball—involving more catching and throwing than bumping and setting—is fun. Others, however, would find

Humming Along Without a Mission Statement

The State University intramural program was humming along. Jean Prophet, the intramural director, was pleased with the way her program ran each year. Recently, however, tensions were rising in some of the intramural leagues. In the volleyball league, for example, players were growing noticeably irritated with each other. Some wanted to play just for fun. They got angry when others spiked the ball or hit it too hard. The hard hitters, on the other hand, hated it when other players just passed the ball over the net on the first hit without setting it up for a big return.

Jean discussed the matter with her staff at their next meeting. Some staff thought volleyball should be played just for the fun of it. Others agreed with the hard hitters, saying that volleyball is only fun when the game is competitive and played hard. When she asked her staff what the purpose of the intramural program was, she received many different answers. It seemed staff members were operating with different assumptions and imposing those assumptions on their own part of the program.

Jean used the next few staff meetings to get everyone "on the same page." At the first meeting, she divided staff into groups of five and gave each group a flipchart and a marker. She then gave each group five minutes to answer the question, Why should students participate in intramurals? Groups were instructed to write down as many reasons as possible, and not to discuss (or cheer or ridicule) others' answers but simply to record everyone's thoughts.

Afterward, the groups pooled their answers while Jean recorded them on the blackboard. The rest of that meeting, and most of the following meeting, the staff discussed the pros and cons of each reason. During the third meeting, the staff prioritized the reasons and came up with a comprehensive list of the purposes of their intramural program. At the end of that meeting, Jean asked each staff person to write a mission statement that reflected the items on this list. The mission statement was to be realistic and simple, yet excite and inspire staff and participants.

The next meeting, everyone offered their mission statements while Jean recorded them on the blackboard. They used parts of each statement to write an intramural program mission statement. They determined that fun should be a key component of all intramural games but that different people defined *fun* differently. To accommodate these different views, they decided to create two intramural leagues: a recreational league and a competitive league. That way, the competitive players could join the competitive league and those interested in knocking the ball around for the fun of it could join the recreational league.

By taking the time to develop a mission statement, staff members were able to assess the focus of their program, identify the problem in the volleyball league, and come up with a solution that would prevent similar problems from arising in other leagues. In addition, they were able to create a mission statement that would focus the direction of their program in years to come. This mission statement, which follows, was printed on every intramural document and used in every promotional vehicle, from signup sheets and program handbooks to posters and the program Web site.

Intramural sports at State University is about Laughter:

Laughter
And
Unforgettably
Great
Hilarity
Through
Exciting and encouraging
Recreational games

such a game frustrating and want the game to be played "correctly," that is, using the official rules. The question then becomes, what do you mean by *fun*?

Brainstorming

To identify the focus of your program, it is often helpful to brainstorm. **Brainstorming** is a creative method of generating ideas. Usually a process of everyone calling out the first thing that comes to mind, brainstorming is useful for creating a mission statement because it gives an intramural director a large supply of ideas and possibilities. From those ideas, the focus of a program, specific words for the mission statement, and even action plans for implementation can be gleaned. One person can brainstorm, but a collaboration of five to twelve people is more effective. Other tips for effective brainstorming are listed here.

- The problems or questions need to be well defined. For example: What do we want to emphasize in our intramural program? What do we want students to get out of our program?
- Assign one person to write everyone's ideas and suggestions on a blackboard, flipchart, or other writing surface. Whatever the writing surface, it should be large enough that everyone can see it clearly from where they are sitting.
- Encourage everyone to suggest anything they think of that is relevant to the discussion. All ideas and suggestions should be written down, regardless of whether they are good or bad, obscure or obvious. Even the simplest or worst of suggestions might spur a great idea.
- At some point, ideas and suggestions will wane. That is the time to stop.
- Once all the suggestions have been written down, discuss the pros and cons of each. In assessing each suggestion, other ideas may be offered. Record them at the bottom of the list and then discuss the pros and cons of those as well.
- After the pros and cons have been assessed, prioritize the suggestions and eliminate the suggestions that don't fit.

Be Realistic

It's easy to spiral out of control when dreaming about and brainstorming an intramural mission. That's why part of the brainstorming process is assessment. The mission statement needs to be realistic. Don't be so grandiose that your mission is unattainable. Likewise, don't set your focus so low that you can achieve your mission with little or no effort. It is often helpful to start with your current resources and situation. Because every institution is unique in terms of staff talent, financial resources, and student needs, it's best that you consider these factors when assessing everyone's suggestions for a central theme.

Keep It Short and Simple

Now that you have a list of what you want to focus on in your intramural program, it's time to write the mission statement. You will likely have enough ideas to write several paragraphs, but a mission statement should be simple, concise, and specific. As a rule, the more specific the mission statement, the better your chances of achieving your mission. Keep the language simple and the statement short. You should be able to read your mission statement in 30 seconds or less.

That said, mission statements often need to be fleshed out beyond a single sentence. Many mission statements are a paragraph of three to four sentences. Another way to flesh out a mission statement is by supporting an introductory sentence or fragment with a short, bulleted list. For example: "Our intramural program will provide recreational activities that are fun and physically active by

- including as many participants as possible,
- offering activities that are fun and physically demanding, and
- developing administrative support to make the above possible.

Build Excitement and Inspire Action

The next step in formulating a mission statement is tweaking the language. Try to build excitement and inspire action by using specific, active verbs and phrasing. Mission statements should motivate your staff and attract volunteers and participants. For example, the Disney Corporation's mission statement is "to make people happy." In one punchy phrase, the mission statement clearly states a simple but specific goal. Every action of corporate staff and employees is designed to support this mission, from the way Disney treats its customers to the ventures it launches. As another example, the mission of this textbook is its title, *Intramural Recreation: A Step-by-Step Guide to Creating an Effective Program*. The contents of this book focus on helping intramural directors create an effective program.

If the mission statement is to inspire, it should be positive. Because intramurals should be a positive experience for all participants, it is important to develop a positive mind-set to intramural programming with a positive mission statement. Instead of "decrease inactivity," for example, "increase activity" phrases the mission positively. Likewise, to inspire program staff and participants, the mission statement should build some excitement. Again, the title of this book serves as an example. Which book would you rather read: *The Process of Developing an Intramural Recreation Program and the Procedures of Implementation* or *Intramural Recreation: A Step-by-Step Guide to Creating an Effective Program*?

Get Others' Input

In formulating and revising your mission statement, it's extremely helpful to seek others' suggestions, opinions, and ideas. It's also helpful to look at other institutions' mission statements. Your statement should reflect the intentions of everyone involved in the program, from staff and volunteers and officials to students and other participants. When looking at other mission statements, be sure to factor in your own resources and situation. For example, if your school has limited financial resources, it's probably not wise to start with the mission statement of an intramural program with millions in its budget.

Seeking feedback and suggestions from others will take time, just as the brainstorming component of identifying a central theme. This time is worth it, however. By listening to and understanding everyone's suggestions, goals, and intentions for your program, you will be better able to devise a realistic mission statement that will

embody the program you and your participants want.

Make It Visible

Once you formulate a mission statement that reflects what you want your program to be, and that builds excitement and inspires action, it's important to use it whenever and wherever possible. A mission statement should help recruit new participants and remind current participants of the purpose of the program. It should also communicate the essence of staff jobs. Using the example of Disney Corporation's mission statement again, "to make people happy" clearly communicates what everyone should be trying to do. From the engineers who design the rides to the street sweepers who keep Disney parks well kept, everyone in Disney's employ knows that above all else, their jobs are to make people happy.

While your intramural mission statement will not be as simple—indeed, it should be more specific—if it builds excitement and inspires action, it will make students and volunteers want to participate, and it will help motivate your staff. Use your mission statement on fliers, posters, manuals, bulletin boards, and other central locations throughout the school. (See chapter 8 for a detailed discussion of promotion.)

Another benefit of making your mission statement visible is that it will increase participants' feelings of ownership and accountability in the program. Seeing the mission often will remind staff and volunteers about what their focus should be. Otherwise, it becomes too easy to be careless or to forget about it. Students get lost in the details of the event or game, wanting to win or get the trophy rather than enjoy the experience and help build a program they can be proud of. Likewise, staff and volunteers may become so focused on their duties that they forget what those duties are intended to accomplish.

Revisit and Evaluate

The final component of constructing an effective mission statement is evaluation. As with any devised plan or goal, evaluation is necessary to modify or otherwise adjust things that aren't working. To remain effective, a mission statement must be evaluated from time to time, both from the standpoint of the program and the statement itself. If the program has changed due to an increase or decrease in resources, for example, the mission statement may need to be adjusted to reflect that. Likewise, if participants are leaning toward a different focus or the program leadership is shifting gears, the mission statement should serve as a guide for implementing that new focus or it should be revised if the new focus is to become the purpose of the intramural program. (See chapter 14 for a full discussion on evaluation.)

The Steps in Designing an Intramural Program

To climb Mount Everest, or even a small hill, one can only get there by taking one step at a time. Designing an intramural program is no different. That is, you must take one step at a time. Once you have conceived and written a mission statement that reflects the essence of your program, the following steps, taken in order, will lead you through the development of a comprehensive and effective intramural program.

1. Determine the structure of the program.
2. Define the leadership requirements for the program.
3. Determine how to recruit and train leaders to run the program well.
4. Formulate policies that will make the program fair for all.
5. Formulate policies that will make the program safe for all.
6. Develop promotional strategies to attract participants.
7. Determine how to celebrate participant success and achievement.
8. Consider financial resources and create a budget.
9. Devise activities that accomplish the program mission.
10. Become proficient at the use of leagues and tournaments.
11. Plan the details of each event.
12. Develop evaluation tools to assess and improve the program.

Sequence of Subsequent Chapters

As you have probably noticed, the remaining chapters in this book correspond with these 12 steps of creating a great intramural program. Each chapter provides both theoretical and practical suggestions for each step along the way. As in this and the previous chapter, the "Chapter Summary Exercises" section at the end of each chapter will help you review that step and make sure that you understand it well enough to proceed to the next step.

By the final chapter in this book, chapter 15, you will have proceeded through each step in devising an intramural program. This is an opportunity to put theory into practice. Using all the information and exercises in the book, you will be able to put together a program—and a program handbook—of your own.

Chapter Summary Exercises

This chapter detailed the steps of devising and recording a clear mission statement that communicates the focus of your intramural program and inspires participants to get involved. Now it's time to develop your own. Exercise 3 will lead you through the process of doing that, but first complete exercises 1 and 2 to clarify and structure that process.

1. The following mission statements are from an elementary school, a high school, and a university. While reading these statements, first identify the central theme. Then ask the following questions:
   ▶ Is it inspiring?
   ▶ Does it explain what the program is, what it stands for, and why it exists?
   ▶ Does the statement build excitement and inspire action?

The Intramural program should provide an opportunity for a large number of students to participate voluntarily in healthful physical activity (elementary school; Nova Scotia 1978).

Our main aim is to encourage and develop good character, fairness, and sportsmanship through games that are fun and enjoyable (high school; Kensington High School 1980-1981).

The mission of Queen's intramurals is to enrich the university experience for all students by providing quality opportunities for participation, healthy competition, and leadership in organized recreational activities. The overall aim is to provide widespread opportunities for the student population to participate and have fun with their peers in an athletic environment (university; Queens Intramurals 2001).

2. Go to the "recreation database" on the Leisure Information Network Web site (www.lin.ca). Then select from the following search options to find information about mission statements.

▶ Keyword search (search the title, abstract, author, language)

▶ Search by topic (if you just want to browse . . .)

▶ Full-text search (searches every unique word in every document)

If you use the keyword search to look for "mission statements," you will find several examples of mission statements that you can read online or purchase. The handbook *Organizational Planning: A Board/Staff Handbook for Women's Organizations,* published by Saskatchewan Women's Resources (www.lin.ca/lin/resource/html/jk57.htm), for example, contains some helpful exercises for developing a mission statement and is available online for free.

3. Using the information in this chapter, plus your responses to exercise 1, develop your own intramural mission statement.

▶ Begin by reflecting on your intramural experiences. Then form small groups and brainstorm ideas for a central theme.

▶ Once you have your central theme, determine whether you will write a one-sentence mission statement, a sentence or fragment with several bullets, or a short paragraph.

▶ Write your mission statement.

▶ Ask yourself, and others, Is it attainable? Does it inspire action? If you can answer affirmatively to both, you've got it. If it is not attainable or does not inspire action, revise your mission statement until it works.

References

Carroll, L. 1960. *Alice's adventures in wonderland.* New York: New American Library.

Kensington High School Intramural Department. 1980-1981. Kensington intramurals. Unpublished handbook, Burnaby, British Columbia.

Nova Scotia Department of Education. 1978. *Intramural programming: A public school guide.* Halifax: Nova Scotia Department of Education.

Queens Intramurals. 2000. *Intramural program overview.* [Online.] Available: http://www.phe.queensu.ca/athletics/phe/intramurals/policy/policyindex.html.

The Plan

To use a golf analogy, you cannot go from wanting to play directly to playing. You need to decide on such things as which course you'll play, the equipment you'll need, the people to play with, the rules you'll use, and the amount of money you wish to spend. Intramural programs are no different.

Part II takes you through the planning stages of developing an intramural program. Planning involves understanding the facilities available for the program and how you wish to organize participants. It also involves acquiring competent and trained staff and leaders, both paid and volunteer. The role of officials is an important aspect of a competitive intramural program. Thus, hiring them, training them, and compensating them is an important part of the planning process. Policies need to be developed to ensure fair and safe play for all. Then decisions need to be made concerning how to effectively promote the intramural program. Finally, the intramural director needs to know ahead of time what the anticipated program costs and revenues are. All of these items must be in place before any effective intramural program can begin, and they are all discussed in part II.

The Structure

Motivation, focus, and mission in hand, you are now ready to begin structuring the intramural program. The first part of that process is considering what you have available in terms of facilities and other resources such as equipment. Then you must determine the structure that will best facilitate your intramural participants.

As discussed in the previous chapter, your mission should serve as a guide. For this part of the planning process, it is important to revisit your mission and determine how facilities, resources, and organization structure will best facilitate that mission. If, for example, the intramural program mission is to revitalize fun and active movement, as opposed to encouraging competition and athletic achievement, then such things as rules are designed to equalize competition as much as possible to encourage participation, joy, and fair play—not victory. Do not get locked into seeing basketball lines and basketballs as requiring official basketball rules. A basketball court can serve many purposes and even a basketball game can be played with rubber chickens instead of basketballs. Be creative.

Chapter Objectives

▶ Assess available program resources.
▶ Explore creative ways of maximizing program resources.
▶ Consider various intramural structures.

Facilities

Obviously, for activities to be held, you will need a place to hold them. What may not always be obvious are your options. Most schools have a gymnasium, classrooms, and athletic fields, but what about stages, hallways, parking lots, or cafeterias? And what about facilities and resources beyond the confines of the school campus? Are there parks, hills, and forests nearby? What about gyms and other facilities in the community? To create a diverse and well-rounded intramural program, it is important that you, as an intramural director, be creative and resourceful in the early stages of developing your program by considering all facilities available to you.

Work With What You Have

On-campus facilities will likely be the most cost effective when you consider access to participants. If your resources and options are limited, in terms of options, proximity, and cost, do not lose heart. A gymnasium and a few playing fields can be enough for a great program. The important thing is to work with what you have and be positive and creative about it.

An intramural director for a small Ontario school bemoaned the fact that the school did not have a gym. But when asked what he did with students during the winter months, he excitedly reported that the winter activities included free skating and playing ice hockey on a nearby canal, and a winter carnival on the school soccer/football field and parking lot.

Recreational facilities vary by geographic region, topography, school size, and community economics, among other things. Indeed, intramural facilities range from no gym at all to large multisport complexes. Sizes range from small classrooms to double gyms. Even structures vary, ranging from new concrete or brick buildings to aging bubbles. Weight rooms are also disparate from institution to institution. Some schools have small and inadequately equipped or monitored weight rooms, while others have large, well-equipped weight rooms staffed by full-time fitness specialists. Large institutions have separate and well-designed weight rooms and aerobics studios, which appeal to the more self-conscious participants.

Whatever you have to work with, do not be discouraged. Instead, make the most of what you have at the present time and plan for the future. As part of planning your program, ask the question, Do existing intramural facilities need renovation or should new facilities be built? If your facilities are lacking, make improving your facilities a goal for your program. Then, after a few (or many, depending on the size of your goal) years of running a successful program, you may be able to renovate your existing facilities or build new facilities that will better suit your needs.

Use Alternative Spaces

As important as being positive and working with what you've got is being creative. Consider alternative in-school spaces beyond the gym. For example, some schools have a stage in the gym. Depending on its size, this stage can accommodate table tennis, foosball (table soccer), weight lifting, aerobics, wrestling, billiards, or quiet games such as euchre. Other parts of a school can also be used. Long hallways are ideal for shuffleboard, bowling, horseshoes, and floor hockey (if wide enough), as well as unusual events such as chair relay races. Classrooms lend themselves to quiet board games, instruction in yoga and aerobics, and so on.

Also consider outside school areas. Solid outside walls can be used for games such as handball and paddleball. Wooded campus areas with trails are great for orienteering, cross-country skiing, jogging, walking, paintball, and other outdoor activities. Parking lots make excellent surfaces for ball hockey and a host of other games played on asphalt. (For lots of asphalt game ideas, take a look at Pat Doyle's *Awesome Asphalt Activities* [1998].)

Work With Your Community

Once you've assessed your school's facilities, it's important to consider other available resources in your community. As Fred Batley learned (see "Intramurals Without a Gymnasium" on page 25), local resorts and bowling alleys may be willing to share their facilities (albeit usually at a cost). To create as broad and effective an intramural program as possible, consider what is available in your area. Swimming pools, fitness

Intramurals Without a Gymnasium

Fred Batley, the intramural director at Sir Sanford Fleming College in Peterborough, Ontario, had the unenviable task of running an intramural program without a gymnasium. This presented several problems, the first of which was how he could organize leagues for volleyball, basketball, indoor soccer, or any other activity. Rather than get discouraged, he visited some nearby schools and found a gym he could rent in the evening.

Another problem presented by the lack of a gymnasium was visibility. Without a gym, which is normally the center of intramural activity and promotion, how would students know about the program? Where would staff be able to interact with students and recruit new participants? For this problem, Fred came up with several solutions. The first was to locate the intramural program offices in the school's Student Life area, already a hub of student activity.

Fred's second solution was hosting a weekly intramural event. Wild Wednesdays were held every Wednesday at noon in the main lobby, through which students passed on their way to the cafeteria. (This location was ideal because it assured a lot of passersby.) Every week, new events were held and many prizes given away. Events included such things as a basketball free-throw contest (using a portable basketball hoop), a putting contest (using a green piece of carpet), and a hackey sac dribbling contest.

The third solution for increasing visibility was to offer regular intramural field trips. Fred visited nearby facilities to check out their schedules and see what he could arrange. In only a few visits, he was able to arrange monthly trips to a local ski hill and trips to different bowling alleys (every Thursday night and Sunday morning).

Clearly, trying to operate an intramural program without a gymnasium can be challenging. As Fred demonstrated, however, a little creativity can go a long way in offering a terrific intramural program. Always consider your options and turn them into opportunities.

clubs and gyms, courts for racquet sports, ice arenas, golf courses—these and other facilities are there to be used. If the cost of such facilities is too high, work with the facility management or ownership to see if certain discounts are an option. For example, some facilities offer student discounts (students save on admission or playing fees when they show their student cards), facility-rental discounts (to support their local educational institutions), and bulk ticket discounts (the school purchases tickets in bulk at a reduced rate and passes those savings on to students). If discounted fees are still too high, consider using free facilities such as community parks for Frisbee golf and cross-country running or skiing.

Also consider whether local facilities permit the intramural activities you wish to offer. If your intramural program mission is primarily geared toward fun, for example, it will likely involve goofy games and odd twists to traditional sport rules. In this case, you'll want to ask the facility if these variations are allowed. Take JJ Bowling (Byl 2002, p. 64), for instance, in which each frame is bowled differently. One frame the bowler bowls with her dominant hand, the next frame with her nondominant hand, the next frame with her left foot, and so on. This rule modification adds fun to the game, but bowling alley management may not permit such "improper" bowling decorum. Of course, if you rent the entire bowling alley, the management may be more amenable to new rules. You may even be able to offer more bowling variations, for example, glow-in-the-dark bowling. Be creative and work with local facilities to maximize the experience for your participants.

Size Up the Competition

When assessing the option of using community facilities, it is important to consider competition. If, for example, you want to offer weight-training and aerobics activities as part of your intramural programming and there are several nearby gyms that offer these same activities at an affordable cost to students, by including them in your intramural program you may be "reinventing the wheel." Likewise, there may already be a great badminton club close to the school that students regularly attend. If this club meets the needs of your students, there is no reason to compete with it.

Of course, if some students' needs are not being met, it may be wise to offer them an alternative through intramural programming. One such alternative is to offer a service that the badminton club does not. A second is to work with the badminton club to modify or add to its program so that it satisfies students' needs.

As you start to plan your program by considering your available facilities, ask yourself, Is there competition for this type of intramural activity? What about the entire program? For some institutions, particularly those in well-developed communities, launching an intramural program might be difficult because it may be in direct competition with well-established programs and clubs outside the institution. The bottom line is this: An intramural program should benefit as many participants as possible. If helping local clubs is the best way to do that, then do it.

Equipment

It is every intramural director's dream to have a large, well-stocked equipment room. Some live with that dream, but most have considerably less. As with facilities, intramural directors and staff need to be resourceful with what equipment they have, alternate uses of equipment, and consider other accessible equipment within the community.

Work With What You Have

Intramural directors should not allow a lack of equipment to discourage them and, in so doing, undercut the objective of having fun. Celebrate what you have and make the most of it.

A couple of bats, balls and bases, and you have a baseball game in the making. With a couple of soccer balls, and you have a couple of soccer games, a couple of basketballs and you have a couple of basketball games, and so on. It does not take nearly as much equipment to just play it as it does to teach these activities. Be resourceful in using what you have well.

Use Alternative Equipment

Be creative in adding more great equipment. If you have an old football, soccer ball, or volleyball with the cover half torn off, tear the whole cover off and save the bladder. The bladder will move erratically when throw or kicked, and is so light and soft that it will not injure anyone struck with it. Games of indoor soccer and indoor soccer-baseball are a riot with a bladder ball. Hula hoops are easily made from rubber piping purchased at the hardware store and beanbags are easily sewn together. All of these materials are inexpensive and add new and fun dimensions to an intramural program. Be creative in considering alternative equipment.

Work With Your Community

If you're short on basic equipment, your community probably has equipment available that can easily be borrowed or rented at reduced rates. A lot of students bring some of their own equipment from home, such as basketballs, soccer balls, bats, baseballs, baseball gloves, and so on. A lot of games can be arranged using equipment that students bring. Sometimes schools can share equipment. One school might have a set of lacrosse sticks and another a set of field hockey sticks. While one school does field hockey, the other can do lacrosse. Then they can switch equipment and each school gets to offer a new program. Other equipment, especially outdoor recreational equipment, can be rented at reasonable group rates. Such equipment might include rental of bikes, skis, or canoes. Be resourceful within the community to access additional equipment.

Program Structure

Once you have taken an inventory of available resources and considered your alternatives, it's time to think about how your intramural program will be structured. Like any organization, an intramural program needs some kind of structure to operate. Rather than the hierarchy of the program staff, however, *structure* in this case refers to how participants will be involved. If competition is to be part of your program, will leagues or tournaments better serve participants? Will special events, contests, or sport clubs be offered? What is the best time for different events? And how will participants sign up for intramural activities? These questions and issues are introduced in this chapter to help us develop a comprehensive understanding of how to plan intramurals. These topics are developed in greater detail in part III of this book.

As it should in every step of planning your intramural program, your mission should guide you in determining the organizational structure. For example, if your mission for intramural events is promoting competition, you would likely follow official rules rather rigidly, maintain up-to-date standings and post those standings in a conspicuous place, and award a substantial prize to the winners. If you mission for intramurals emphasizes fun, then you would likely use different rules and equipment to "level the playing field," weight the standings to reward participation, fun, and fair play on the court, and award prizes to the teams that most exemplified the spirit of fun in competition.

Leagues and Tournaments

Most intramural programs involve tournaments or leagues. In fact, tournaments and leagues are such an integral component of intramurals that an entire chapter (12) is devoted to the topic. For now, think of them this way. **Tournaments** are one- or two-day events in which teams or individuals compete. Tournaments usually involve **play-offs**, in which the highest-scoring teams or individuals compete to determine an overall champion. **Leagues** are competitions that run for a week or more, perhaps an entire school year. Leagues and tournaments are the most common method of organizing intramural sport competitions at the high school and university levels. In grade and junior high school, a drop-in approach is typically used.

Alternatives

In addition to leagues and tournaments, there are many other ways to involve students in intramural activities. Each will be discussed more fully in chapter 11, but it is helpful at this point in the planning process to begin thinking about the options. The most common options, introduced in the next few sections, include special events, contests, and sport clubs.

Special Events

Special events are usually one-day events, but they can also run shorter or longer. A lunchtime or after-school activity can also be a special event, for example. For our purposes, **special events** include any event that celebrates something (i.e., Thanksgiving or the winter season) or promotes the intramural program (e.g., an orientation activity or specially discounted group tickets to a local facility), or any event in which participants do something out of the ordinary.

For example, some schools organize games on orientation day or during the first week of school to promote intramurals. To celebrate winter or counteract "cabin fever," some schools organize a day of winter games and activities in January or a day of skiing at a local ski resort. To celebrate Thanksgiving, some schools hold an annual Thanksgiving Day Turkey Trot, a 5-mile (kilometer) run in which the winner is the one with the best time or the one who comes closest to that predicted finish time. This is just one example of a holiday special event, but any holiday can serve as the backdrop for a special event.

Contests

Contests are interspersed throughout the year to generate interest in an intramural program and to attract students who might not normally participate in competitive leagues and tournaments. Contests typically are brief promotional events, usually held somewhere other than a gymnasium. Some examples of contests include a lunchtime tug-of-war, a sock-shooting challenge before school (the shooter who shoots the most rolled-up socks into a portable basket in the main lobby wins, and all socks are donated to a homeless shelter), and a challenge to see who can Hula Hoop the longest. Finally, some schools use special events to generate interest in the intramural program. For example, a game like Sock It to Me (Byl 2002, p.4), in which players tuck one end of a sock in their waistbands and try to steal as many socks from other players as they can, could be run over a period of several days.

Special events usually revolve around a special day or theme, and although some of the activities are competitive, typically most activities are not. Contests are unique and usually brief competitive events used to promote intramurals in general and reach out to those not normally involved in intramural activities.

Sport Clubs

Sport clubs are another way to involve students in physical activity. A **sport club** usually comprises a group of individuals who join together voluntarily, in a formal or informal organization, for the purpose of participating in a particular sport. Sport clubs in educational institutions are typically student initiated and operated, and largely self-financed (Cleave 1994). For example, some students may want to learn and practice Tae Kwon Do, but due to financial reasons, the intramural program may not be able to provide that programming. Rather than forget about the idea altogether, students could decide to form a student club (methods of doing this vary from institution to institution), get a faculty advisor, and attend regular meetings. Once officially recognized as a club, the students might qualify for institution grants and/or student government aid (this also varies from institution to institution) to help with purchasing equipment or hiring instructors. The intramural program may also be able to help by providing facility time, administrative organization or services, and/or limited supervision.

Sport clubs can be formed for any activity of interest by a sufficient number of participants. Ideally suited to the sport club structure are interests and hobbies such as jogging, aerobics, cycling, orienteering, cross-country skiing, cross-country running, and any of the martial arts. While they are not technically part of intramurals, sport clubs can be publicized and promoted by program staff, which creates the appearance of a well-rounded intramural program that has something for everyone. (Sport clubs are more fully discussed in chapter 11.)

Timing

"Timing is everything," as the saying goes. In intramural programming, there are three factors to consider: (1) the best time to run an activity (when students are available); (2) the length of an activity (to capture and hold student interest); and (3) when the activities will be held throughout the year. Each of these factors is discussed in the following sections.

The Best Time for Intramural Activities

At grade and high schools, intramural activities are typically run over lunchtime or the noon hour. If students live close to the school building, some institutions have enjoyed success with before- and after-school programs, although fewer students are usually available at this time because of piano lessons, family commitments, bible study, and so on. Also, before- and after-school activities can be difficult to coordinate when the school gymnasium is occupied, which is usually the case at these times.

Many colleges and universities host intramural events throughout the day, although many students are reluctant to show up for early-morning activities. Some intramural directors go the extra mile and, at sign-up, ask students and teams when they are available and then schedule activities accordingly. This type of scheduling becomes difficult when a lot of teams have to be coordinated. One way to simplify the process of matching activity times with student schedules is to divide the teams into groups and assign times to each group. For example, if you had 16 teams, you could divide them into four groups (of four teams each) and schedule each group's playing time based on when they are available. Some students may prefer night games, while others might prefer morning or lunchtime or immediately after class. Play-offs, of course, would have to be scheduled far enough ahead of time that students could modify their schedules to accommodate the game(s).

Some colleges have found that hosting intramural activities between 4 and 7 p.m. works well. Close enough to the end of the students' classes, this time slot means that students do not have to come back to school to participate. Colleges with a large residence base often run their intramural activities from 10 to 12 p.m.

The late-evening hours accommodate varsity team practice times, so the gym is usually free. Plus, this time period is often considered "mid evening" by many college students.

The Length of Intramural Activities

Depending on the age of intramural participants, the length of intramural activities may be crucial. Younger students, for example, tend to get bored more quickly than older students. Likewise, energy levels naturally rise and wane throughout the day. These factors must be considered when planning the length of intramural activities.

Ideally an event should end at its peak. They should not be so short that participants are not satisfied and they should not be so long that participants get bored. In the last few years, intramural programming has moved away from long activities, such as semester- or year-long leagues. Instead, intramural scheduling is leaning toward shorter activity units (a unit being something like a two-week volleyball league, or three-week floor hockey league), some lasting as long as three to four weeks but many lasting only a weekend or an afternoon. University and college students do occasionally enjoy a semester-long league in a sport they are interested in, but that length of time is much too long for elementary students, who are more likely to lose interest in events that take that much time.

The Intramural Season

Planning an intramural season is like playing golf. Before a round of golf, a golfer begins to assess the course, plan some shots at various holes, take some practice swings, and make sure that all the equipment is ready to go. On the course, each hole has its own challenges. A golfer considers each shot by thinking about the successive shots required to get the ball in the hole. After each shot, a golfer evaluates the swing and the shot, and celebrates when it is done well. Throughout the game, a golfer makes adjustments according to certain variables such as a change in the weather, a broken club, and so on. In an 18-hole round, a golfer stops halfway through the course, taking stock of the game so far, mentally regrouping, maybe taking a break in the clubhouse for some refreshment, and developing a new strategy for the remainder of the course.

Like golfers, intramural directors must think about the season (assess the course), plan various activities and components of the program (plan some shots), try out a few ideas (take some practice swings), and consider their resources and facilities (make sure all equipment is ready). Then, throughout the planning process and season, intramural directors must think about upcoming activities (think about successive shots), all the while considering the program mission (to get the ball in the hole). After each activity (shot), as well as throughout the year (round of golf), intramural directors must evaluate, make adjustments, and celebrate successes.

The planning process is complex, to be sure. The following planning calendar will take you through the process of programming a year's worth of intramural activities. (See chapter 11's "Sample Activities for the Year," beginning on page 189, for specific activity ideas.)

July/August/September Before the start of the school year, it is important to review last year's program. This includes evaluating successes and failures, and making necessary adjustments. To begin, answer the following questions. (These questions, as well as the evaluation process itself, are discussed more fully throughout this book.)

- Do we need to revise our mission statement?
- What facilities are currently available?
- Have we adequately and fully used those facilities?
- Do our facilities need to be modified this year?
- Will other facilities become available during the year?
- Do we need to revise the structure of the program?
- What are our human resource needs?
- How will we ensure fair play?
- How will we ensure safety?
- How will we promote and celebrate program successes?
- How will the program be financed?
- Do we have adequate budgetary tools and procedures in place?
- What activities do we plan to offer?

- ▶ When and where will they be held?
- ▶ What type of events will we host?
- ▶ How will we measure our performance?

September/October/November At the start of the school year, you should have an overall plan developed—plus any immediate steps to begin the first activities and events. In other words, it's time to put planning into action. At this time, as well as throughout the year, it is important to deal with problems as they arise. This requires a procedure for recording and evaluating results.

December/January/February/March Mid year—usually the end of the first semester (or Christmas break for nonsemester schools)—is the time to take stock of the semester's intramural programming, celebrate the successes, make adjustments that will be helpful for the next semester, and prepare to implement the next semester's programming. At Easter break (for grade and high schools), it's a good idea to take stock again, readjust, and then implement the final portion of the intramural programming. It is often helpful at this time to ask the following questions about participation, staffing, and upcoming events.

- ▶ How did the participation numbers compare to last year?
- ▶ Was the spirit of participation positive or negative, encoruraging or discouraging, pleasant or nasty?
- ▶ Were participants satisfied with the activities?
- ▶ Were there any complaints?
- ▶ Were there any problems with program staffing?
- ▶ What needs to be done to get ready for upcoming activities?

April/May/June At the end of the school year, it's time to review and evaluate the year, which includes celebrating successes and making necessary preparations for next year. This year-end evaluation is a more comprehensive and formal evaluation. Thus, an entire chapter (14) is devoted to the subject.

- ▶ How did the overall specific event participation numbers compare to last year's?
- ▶ Overall, was the spirit of participation positive or negative, encouraging or dis-

couraging, pleasant or nasty? What about specific events?

- ▶ Were expected financial income and expense projections met? Why or why not?
- ▶ Have complaints or injuries raised concerns about specific areas of the program that need attention?
- ▶ What are staffing needs for next year?
- ▶ What must be completed to get ready for next year?

Sign-up

There are a variety of methods for organizing intramural sign-up, ranging from preseason team and individual sign-ups to last-minute team creation. These methods are outlined in the following sections. The guiding principle in deciding which method to use is as follows: (1) maximize participation (2) as simply as possible, (3) with equality of skill and playing level, and (4) be ready to reorganize teams as needed.

Whatever the specific program mission, intramurals is about mass participation (1). Organizational procedures should be developed to satisfy that requirement. Most intramural directors are busy, especially those at the elementary and high school levels who normally direct intramural activities on top of a full teaching load. Thus, whatever process gets the most people involved and is the most convenient to administer (2) is probably the best way to go.

When organizing competitive playing units, whether in the form of teams or individual opponents, equality of playing level (3) is important. If certain teams consistently dominate, players on weaker teams will likely not show up for games against the dominant teams. This is a surefire way to reduce participation, thus undermining a primary ingredient of the program. Because equal competitive ability is so important, you, as an intramural director, must reserve the right to restructure or reassign teams (4) if that would be helpful to participants.

Open Participation

The simplest way to organize intramural activities is **open participation**, an approach that specifies that grade levels for activities and attendance is open to anyone from that grade who wishes to participate. This method is commonly used in grade school intramurals. The following examples show a sample schedule for such a system, the first for a school with grades 1 through 5 and the second for a K-to-8 school.

Grades 1 through 5

Monday	Grade 1
Tuesday	Grade 5
Wednesday	Grade 3
Thursday	Grade 2
Friday	Grade 4

Grades K through 8

Monday	Grades 5-6
Tuesday	Grades K-2
Wednesday	Grades 7-8
Thursday	Grades 3-4
Friday	Open Gym (or make-up if there was a holiday)

The open participation system works best when participation numbers are unknown. In other words, if you don't know whether 10 or 60 students will show up, it's best to use open participation. Using this approach requires that you must able to quickly modify the activities to maximize participation. If the activity is floor hockey and 48 kids show up, for example, you could have teams of 24 and six on the floor at a time. To make sure everyone gets to play, you can signal a line change every 30 seconds.

Open participation also includes free, or unstructured, gym time. During free time, participants can sign out a basketball and play a pick-up game at one of the nets with a few buddies while others play different games in other parts of the facility. A **pick-up game** involves a few students who show up, want to play, and organize themselves into an informal game. For example, if six students show up for free gym time, sometimes called "open gym," they might decide to play a game of three-on-three basketball. They divide themselves into two teams, determine the rules, sign out a basketball, and begin to play. Because of the liability issues (namely, negligence, adequate supervision, and risk management), which will be discussed in chapter 7, these players need to be supervised by employees of the educational institution, but this supervision does not require any organization or planning before or after the free gym time.

There are two advantages for using open participation. The main advantage of open partici-

pation is that students are free to attend or not attend. If they want to come one week but not the next, no problem. From the school's perspective, another advantage of open participation is the lack of administration. There are no league schedules to prepare or promote and no standing to keep. The disadvantage of open participation has to do with meaningful participation. If a lot of students show up, allowing everyone enough play time may be difficult. Thus, the pressure is on the instructor to be prepared with games that can accommodate a few players as well as many.

Houses and Home Rooms

Another relatively simple way to organize intramural activities is the use of houses. A **house** is an organizational unit to which participants are assigned by dividing the student body into several large groups. Students are first organized into houses and then compete as house teams, or in the case of individual sports (such as badminton), compete as individuals representing their house teams. In a high school, for example, there might be four junior houses (grades 9-10) and four senior houses (grades 11-12). When a house is scheduled to compete, anyone from that house is encouraged to participate. For certain special events, some schools allow students to participate with their friends from other houses.

In grade and high schools with student populations under 500, it is common to organize students into houses. Based on a student list, students are randomly assigned one of four houses in which they will compete during the year. These house lists can also be generated from registration lists, by birth date, surname, home rooms, or geographical location. House lists should be balanced by gender, grade level, and competitive level (see "Inclusion" in chapter 6). Thus, intramural directors should be ready to scrutinize these lists and make any adjustments necessary.

The house system has advantages and disadvantages, some more obvious than others. The advantages are that students have the opportunity to meet their peers and create new friendships, and the administration is simple. Because students will likely be grouped with house team members they do not know, and because they will be playing with students who share their interests in a particular sport or activity, the house system presents an ideal opportunity to develop new relationships and friendships. On the administrative side, a house system is easy to structure ahead of time. Whether planning a tournament, league, or special event, an intramural director can count on four teams playing.

The disadvantages of the house system also have to do with friendships and administration. Because students are randomly assigned to houses, friends might not be on the same team. Thus, if a game is scheduled when a player could be hanging out with friends, the player may be tempted to hang out rather than play in the game. This, of course, erodes the central principle of intramurals: maximum participation. Along the same lines, students might feel reluctant to contact other house teammates they do not know, and therefore choose not to participate. On the administrative side, while a house system is relatively easy to organize ahead of time, it can take a lot of energy and time to maintain. For example, keeping each house involved and organized requires staff time and student leadership to maintain and develop interest and excitement for the students toward their house.

Similar to the house approach, some high schools use home rooms as houses. That is, each home room is a separate house. Home rooms generally meet first thing in the morning for school announcements and comprise students from different grades within the school. The advantages and disadvantages are similar to the house system. One additional advantage of this system over the house system, which is typically random, is that communication is simplified. Because students meet in home room every morning, schedules and other details can be easily announced. This system also has an additional disadvantage. Because home rooms usually consist of 40 or fewer students, house teams will have fewer available players. Thus, if not enough students are interested in playing for a home room team, those who are interested will not get to participate. Of course, home rooms can be combined to solve this problem.

Team and Individual Sign-up

As opposed to the random nature of the house and home room system, team and individual sign-up allows participants to sign-up with their friends. Most high schools and universities use an individual or team sign-up, or a combination of the two. The advantage of team sign-up is that when students sign up as a team, they

have a sense of ownership. They feel connected to one another and, thus, encourage their teammates to show up. This results in greater camaraderie during the game and also fewer cancellations. The primary disadvantages to team sign-up lie in competitive level and inclusion. When athletic students sign-up as a team, lopsided matches result, and shy or less-skilled students may not be invited to sign-up. (A sample team sign-up sheet is shown on figure 13.1 on page 217.)

These disadvantages can be prevented with individual sign-up. In individual sign-up, everyone who wants to participate signs up on the activity sign-up sheet. Those who wish to be team captains indicate this on the sign-up sheet (see figure 13.2 on page 218). From there, the intramural director can either invite team captains to a closed-door meeting to select their teams or assign students to teams and appoint team captains. The individual sign-up approach makes it easier for timid students to submit their names. All students who sign-up, regardless of popularity, personality, disposition, or athletic ability, get to be on a team.

The best way to ensure competitive equality, of course, is for the director to assign teams by spreading out the best players over several teams. While the most fair, however, this method may result in students dropping out or not showing up for games if they don't get to play with their friends. When team captains select their own teams, it is more likely that friends will get to play on the same team, but lopsided matches and dominant teams will be the result.

On the administrative side, the individual sign-up approach is simple. Once players are divided into teams, competitions are scheduled and players are informed of the schedule. Because students may not know their teammates, it is important to make sure that team captains feel comfortable communicating with all their players—not just their friends.

Some high schools and colleges use a slightly different approach to team and individual sign-up. Rather than sign-up as a team or individual for only one activity, students sign up for an entire semester or academic year. The same team then competes in all intramural activities. Not all students are interested in every sport or activity, so in this case, teams must comprise at least 15 students. It is necessary to have a large enough team of players so that sufficient numbers of players are present for each game. If a team sign-up is used, friends will be playing together and will encourage one another to show up. If individual sign-up is used, students will get to know one another over the year and develop new friendships. Administratively, this approach is reasonably simple. The teams either organize themselves, or are organized at the start of the season, and the intramural director can count on a certain number of teams for most activities.

A final variation to team and individual sign-up is the use of departmental teams. Like company sport teams, department faculty and students can form teams to compete. Individuals or teams from each department sign up for intramural activities and then compete throughout the season. For example, the engineering school, business school, and nursing school could each have its own team. The advantages to this system include (1) greater team commitment and unity, particularly in the case of interdepartmental rivalries; and (2) familiarity between departmental students, and (3) decreased likelihood for scheduling difficulties since students in similar departments take classes at similar times and have similar breaks. Disadvantages include competitive equality and those instances when a student has friends on another departmental team.

Chapter Summary Exercises

This chapter outlined the basic structures of an intramural program, namely, the different types of facilities available and structural considerations about the timing of events and grouping of participants. The following exercises will help you review the contents of this chapter. In the next chapter, we will look at the structure of the organization itself.

1. What can you do with a hallway? Picture the hallway immediately outside of your classroom. Now select an age group of students. What intramural activities or events could you hold in that area?

2. Visit some facilities in your community. Could any of these be used for intramural activities? Prepare an outline of how you would go about renting or using those facilities. What questions would you ask the management? What other factors should you consider?

3. Take a few minutes to review your list of intramural activities you enjoyed in grade school, high school, and college. Now try to recall how you signed up. Did you like this sign-up method? Did it seem fair? Were you on teams with your friends, or were teams randomly assigned? Were you or other team members excluded? What would you do differently if you were the intramural director?

4. Use your answers in exercise 3 to describe the competitive playing units you plan to use for your own program. Describe why you chose these over the others.

References

Byl, J. 2002. *Co-ed recreational games: Breaking the ice and other activities.* Champaign, IL: Human Kinetics.

Cleave, S. 1994. Sport clubs—More than a solution to shrinking dollars and growing demands. *NIRSA Journal* 18 (3): 30-33.

Doyle, P. 1998. *Awesome asphalt activities.* Hamilton, Ontario: CIRA-Ontario.

Resources

Athletic Business Publications
Customer Service Department
P.O. Box 807
Fort Atkinson, WI 53538-0807
Telephone: 920-563-1761
Fax: 920-563-1704
Web site: www.athleticbusiness.com

Publishes *Athletic Business,* a free monthly journal about the business side of athletics, including such intramural-related topics as facility planning, equipment recommendations, legal issues, event administration, product reports, fitness center problems and solutions, and risk-management ideas.

AthleticSearch.com
Web site: www.AthleticSearch.com

Allows a free back-issue search, by topic, title, and author, of the Momentum Media Sports Publishing journals *Athletic Management, Coaching Management,* and *Training and Conditioning.* It also provides links to suppliers of intramural-related products by product category.

If you want information on weight room lay out, effective positioning of a control (welcome) desk, suggestions about new equipment, or examples of new facilities, you'll find a lot of useful informantion in these journals.

The Leadership

It has been said that there are three kinds of people: those who make things happen, those who watch things happen, and those who wonder what happened. Intramural program leaders are the ones who make things happen for intramural participants. Whether these leaders are students or staff, volunteers or paid employees, care must be demonstrated in selecting them and helping them to fulfill their responsibilities. In this chapter, we first define the different types of leaders in an intramural program. Then we look at how to recruit, organize, train, and manage those leaders to effectively implement a great intramural program.

Chapter Objectives

- ▶ Learn the importance of volunteers and paid staff, and the benefits both bring to an intramural program.
- ▶ Explore the most important aspects of recruiting paid and volunteer staff.
- ▶ Understand the process of hiring and managing paid and volunteer staff.
- ▶ Examine how to assist volunteer and paid staff in fulfilling their responsibilities.

What Needs to Be Done?

To satisfy the mission of your intramural program, there are many factors that need attending to. Programming needs to be planned, activities organized, events promoted, schedules prepared, officials trained, and budgets calculated. Although at times it may be tempting to do everything yourself, most intramural directors have neither the time nor the know-how to implement these crucial components without help.

A day in the life of intramural directors is busy. They are often trying to organize special events on the one hand and answering the phone with the other hand, only to be interrupted to answer a question from a student before rushing off to the gymnasium to solve a problem that has just been reported. They cannot do the job alone and must rely on the help of others, either paid staff or volunteers.

The Intramural Director

In North America, physical education teachers typically run elementary and high school intramural programs. After all, intramurals is a natural extension of physical education. In fact, most grade and high school teachers take on extra duties, volunteering for a variety of student activities including choir, theatre, photography club, yearbook committee, and chess club, among others. If such activities are popular and the program is run well, two or three teachers may be assigned to help out. For these types of activities, including intramurals, teachers typically volunteer for these assignments. As unofficial intramural directors, their compensation is the appreciation of students and a break on other school committee work.

In the college and university setting, the intramural director and staff are usually paid. At small institutions, the director may also do other jobs, such as teaching part time. Paid staff oftentimes do other work for the college as well, although some are employed directly by the student association. Recently small institutions have resorted to contracting out the intramural director's position to a local YMCA or, in some cases, to a private for-profit management team that runs the facility and much of the programming. For the purposes of this text, we will assume a director is in place to implement the intramural program.

As intramural budgets have decreased in recent years, the position of intramural director has changed significantly. These directors are now doing more work with less support staff. As one frustrated director reported, "Receiving a return phone call from me is less likely than winning a lottery!" He simply doesn't have time to get everything done.

Introduction to Councils

A tool intramural directors use to get everything done is various councils. For example, an **intramural council** is a group of students (volunteer or recruits) who help lead and implement intramural programs at many institutions under the direction of the intramural director. Whether in a grade school or university setting, an intramural council can provide invaluable assistance to the intramural director. Taking on the role of advisor, the council often informs the intramural director of the kinds of activities and events students most appreciate. They also take on the role of event conveners and help organize and implement many specific events and leagues. An intramural council presents superb leadership training for students, providing them with the opportunity to understand group decision making, event planning, event implementation, and event evaluation and follow-up. Intramural directors often use intramural council meetings as opportunities to provide hands-on leadership training. Student intramural councils will be discussed more fully later in this chapter.

Another council that may also be of assistance to intramural directors is an institution's parent council. Parent councils are helpful in gaining parent's perspectives about how the intramural program is going as reported at home by the students. They are often involved in various fundraising projects and should be approached for additional funding for special intramural events. Some of the parents may also have useful expertise to offer, such as clinics in such areas as officiating, leadership, and marketing.

The Intramural Department

An intramural department can be large or small, often depending on the size of the institution and the intramural program. The department can be as small as one teacher who volunteers to lead occasional lunchtime games, or it can be large with many paid staff members (each of whom has paid and/or volunteer assistants) responsible for each programming unit, such as intramural leagues or marketing. The latter is typical at large universities. Whatever the size of the department, it is important that every position be clearly identified and that all responsibilities be clearly defined and assigned.

Organization

An excellent tool for organizing individual jobs and responsibilities is the flowchart. Flowcharts are helpful not only in defining various responsibilities within an organization but also in understanding how each position is related to others. When devising your departmental flowchart, you'll likely go through several drafts. Rest assured, however, creating a flowchart is not busy work. It is extremely important when it comes to implementing your intramural program.

Figure 4.1 is a simple flowchart for a typical high school intramural program. It shows the positions as well as the hierarchy of the department. The flowchart in figure 4.2 represents a

university intramural program and is therefore more detailed. It lists each activity and component of the intramural program, everything from sports, fitness, and dance to membership, marking, and a resource library.

The Structure

As shown in figure 4.1, the top of the line is the school board, board of regents, or other governing body. If the governing body of the institution does not want to support an intramural program, it will be extremely difficult for a director to run an effective and lasting program. Simply put, the governing body is in the position to make or break intramurals at any school. If the board wants an intramural program, it must provide, or instruct the school principal or president to provide, the staff and resources required. When a governing body does not support the hiring of additional people trained in physical education or reduces staff morale by increasing the workload of already overworked intramural directors, running an effective intramural program becomes extremely difficult, if not impossible.

Unfortunately, as school budgets and community commitment to school programs wanes,

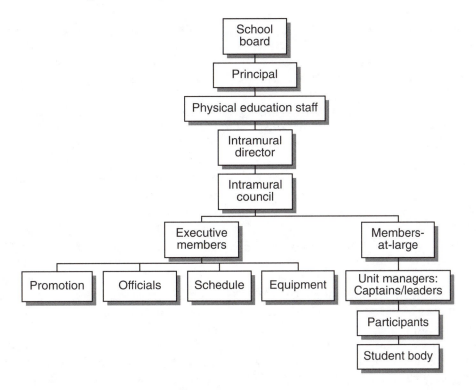

FIGURE 4.1 High school intramural department flow chart.

Campus Recreation

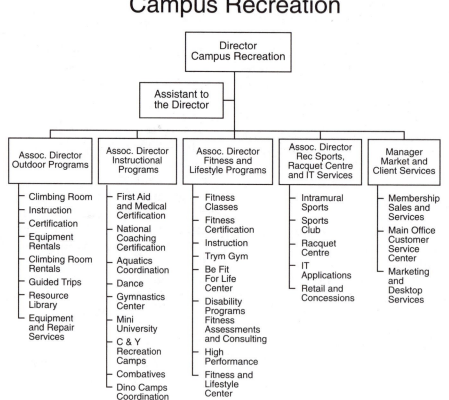

FIGURE 4.2   University intramural department. This flow chart is modeled after the University of Calgary campus recreation department, but most university intramural departments have a similar structure.

the instances of school boards cutting programs like intramurals is all too common. The good news is, intramural directors can play a role in educating school board members on the importance of physical activity and help to sustain intramural programs. As directors, you can seize this opportunity by speaking formally or informally to school board members. Share your program mission and the excitement of intramural participation by inviting board members to give away prizes or be otherwise involved in the program so that they can experience the fun of intramurals firsthand.

Moving down the flowchart, then, the school principal or president is the next key position. Also in a position to make or break an intramural program, school principals have the choice of supporting intramural staff, which sometimes involves recommending that the governing body give the matter more attention, or not. Principals are also usually the ones who assign committee responsibilities, so they have the choice of keeping intramural programs on the table or letting them slip through the cracks. School principals

can also get involved in intramurals, participating by dressing up with a student on Twin Day (students dress as similarly as possible) or leading students on the Thanksgiving Day Turkey Trot. Principals are also in a position to work personally with parent and teacher councils to provide financial and other assistance to teachers in organizing and offering intramural activities.

In larger institutions, intramural directors do not usually report directly to the principal or president but rather to an intermediary such as an athletic director, the physical education department chair, or someone in student government. It is important for intramural directors to maintain good working relationships with these superiors, during the good times as well as the tough times when directors will need their support.

As mentioned earlier, the intramural director is often assisted by an intramural council, which is made up of members-at-large, a student representing each grade, and members who are elected or appointed, who volunteer, or who are fulfilling senior physical education requirements by participating in the council. The positions of council members, which may be paid or unpaid, involve reviewing last year's recommendations; planning intramural activities, formats, time lines, and modifications for the new year's activities; and implementing these plans.

The rest of the intramural positions shown on figures 4.1 and 4.2 vary from school to school. The remainder of this chapter outlines typical intramural positions and responsibilities, which are listed here. Then, we will look at the roles of volunteers in an intramural department.

- ▶ Intramural director: Oversees entire program, including marketing, finances, and facility and equipment needs.
- ▶ Associate director: Responsible for implementation, staffing, training, and staff certification in specific program areas such as tournaments, leagues, and marketing.
- ▶ League conveners: Responsible for successfully implementing a specific league.
- ▶ Head officials: Responsible for recruiting, training, managing, and evaluating officials.
- ▶ Front line staff: Perform daily program administration, including face-to-face contact with participants, instructors, officials, and equipment room monitors.

Volunteers

Given the budget constraints at most schools these days, hiring additional help is usually not an option. Thus, volunteers are often a director's only available personnel resource. Indeed, many organizations rely on volunteer help. In the year 2000, for example, Canadian volunteers donated a total of 1.11 billion hours. That's the equivalent of 578,000 full-time jobs. Calculated at $30,000 per year per job, volunteers saved Canadian organizations more than $17 billion dollars (Canadian) (May 2000). In addition to the financial benefits, of course, volunteers also bring a passion for what they do. In an educational setting, volunteers serve as great intramural ambassadors.

Student Volunteers

Student volunteers are particularly beneficial to an intramural program. Peers can positively influence the intramural experience for participants.

Student volunteers know their peers, what interests them, what motivates them, and how to "persuade" them to join intramural activities. A few years ago at Redeemer University College, for example, Student Life staff (university staff responsible for student life on campus) organized a bowling evening and about 10 people signed up. The next time, Student Life asked a student to organize the event and he filled more than 20 lanes (80 people)! Students understand each other. They know what to emphasize and how to promote the events. Student volunteers can help out with administration, promotion, rides, officiating—anything, really. They are a great resource in any institution's intramural program.

Students also benefit from the arrangement. By volunteering for many of the roles in running an effective intramural program, students gain valuable leadership skills and training. For example, delegation of work, accountability for doing what is assigned, speaking to a group of peers and leading them through an activity, setting priorities, and planning an event. The key for intramural directors is to select these student leaders carefully, then take the time to guide them and develop their talents and leadership abilities.

Roles

Of course, the younger the students, the less responsibility they should be assigned. At the elementary and high school level, students can do announcements, take attendance, monitor outdoor equipment, officiate, and myriad other activities with a little instruction and supervision. Older students (grade 4 or above) can help teach some of the games to younger students (grades 1 through 3). To assist in game instruction, the same intramural activities can be taught in physical education classes so that these students will be familiar with and excited about participating in these games.

At the high school and college levels, students can do practically everything to make an intramural program exciting and effective. More can be expected of students at this age, since they are more mature and can work independently. College and university student volunteers, can even run and supervise programs. Many students at this age are certified in certain sports and activities—for example, aerobics or martial arts—and can run specialized classes for participants.

With some regularly scheduled training sessions, peer leaders are an invaluable resource to intramural directors. They are resourceful and creative, and they are often more aware of the broader context of campus life and how an intramural program can fit into it than older, paid program staff. In short, the greater the number of students involved in intramural leadership, the less paternalistic and more participant centered the program. Plus, student volunteers will save intramural directors an enormous amount of time.

Intramural Council An excellent way to use student volunteers is having them participate in the intramural council. Different schools approach the formation of this council differently. One elementary school, Public School 44, welcomed everyone who wanted to join and, lo and behold, more than 100 students showed up. Although this particular school makes it work, a council of this size is usually too unwieldy to be effective. Another option for council formation is to handpick a few students for the council and fill the remaining positions with students recommended by teachers. This assures high-quality students, but some who want to participate may be left out. Some schools hold elections for intramural council positions. While a great way to excite kids about the intramural program, this method has a downside. Namely, students may elect the most popular person, not necessarily the best leaders for the council.

Whatever the selection method, before the council holds its first meeting or conducts its first activity, it is a good idea to get council members committed to the task at hand: building an effective and fun intramural program that all students will enjoy. One way of doing this is having student council members sign a contract that they are committed to making the intramural program great.

The Leadership Challenge

"It took me the first four years of teaching to learn about the leadership potential of our students. Students should not be simply used as 'gofers' and equipment chasers. They are capable of planning, creating, and implementing entire intramural programs—at any grade level.

"In my first year of running the school's intramural program at a K-to-8 school, I spent countless hours setting up team signup lists and tournament draws on the computer. I used incredible computer graphics and fancy colors, and boy, did that intramural bulletin board look great! In my second and third years, I turned this planning and organizing over to the athletic council. I found it hard to let go and allow the students to find their way through the planning process. But I had to trust that the leadership activities I put the students through from September to mid-November would pay off.

"When all was done, the schedules were posted for three-on-three volleyball, the referees were assigned, the equipment setup crew was appointed, and I didn't do one ounce of work! Of course, their signup sheets didn't look as professional as mine and they didn't use a ruler to draw the tournament layout, but it was a start. The student body had no problem understanding who played on what day and the athletic council made sure that announcements were on the P.A. every morning. All I did was show up in the gym to supervise and keep peace.

"Our athletic council would meet once a week for the first few months and then once every month for the remainder of the year. The students began to plan activities—sometimes inventing games I'd never seen before—to use during our intramural lunch period. Besides, who better knows what's good for kids than kids themselves? I learned a valuable lesson from my students: By allowing them to plan, organize, implement, and officiate the program, it is possible to establish a fantastic intramural program enjoyed by all students" (Peng 1997).

Reprinted by permission of the Canadian Intramural Recreation Association. From S. Peng, 1997, "The leadership challenge," *The Leader* 5 (4):1.

So what does an intramural council do? As introduced earlier, intramural councils are a group of students (volunteers or recruits) who help with the leadership and implementation of intramural programs at many institutions. Of course, directors will need to assist the council in accomplishing these tasks. In grade schools, directors should hold weekly meetings to discuss upcoming events, delegate responsibilities, and provide instruction. These three components of a meeting can come together quickly and easily. For example, say you have an upcoming awards banquet. One of the things to be decided is what should be awarded and how. The intramural director could have students on the council define the award criteria first, and then go about the process of nominating and selecting students who will receive the awards. Other decisions could involve what the award will look like, who will buy or make it, and who will present it at the banquet. At this age level, and perhaps at all age levels, even the simple task of giving an award can be a tremendous learning opportunity for students on an intramural council.

At the high school level, juniors and seniors lead intramural activities as part of their physical education requirements—the class itself takes on the roles of an intramural council. For example, students take turns (individually or in small groups) organizing six-week intramural units on an activity of their choice. The physical education teacher leads the first six-week unit to show the students how to teach a unit, and usually provides instruction on the organization of intramural activities throughout the program.

At the university level, the role of student council members can include all of the responsibilities discussed so far—and may be even larger. Many colleges have a **student intramural association** or athletic association. Basically it's a student-run group that plans and implements an intramural program or activity as a way to take responsibility for a segment of campus life. These associations are usually financed by the students themselves, either out of pocket or as part of their **student fees** (flat fees charged to pay for intramurals, recreation, athletics, and other programs). When overseeing the formation of such an association, intramural directors should try to ensure that the association adequately represents the student body, in terms of gender, skin color, race, grade level, area of study, and other characteristics.

An intramural program can benefit tremendously from these associations. For starters, these associations often increase participation in the program. Student leaders know which activities are of most interest to other students, which times and days of the week work best for their peers, and which advertising and promotional techniques will be most effective for attracting participants. In addition, student leaders can advise the intramural director on the direction of intramural activities, help in the administration of intramural programming, participate in the budgeting process and assign financial priorities, and organize forums and other feedback opportunities for students.

Like an intramural council, students interested in being in these associations may apply for the post, be appointed by the intramural director, or campaign and be elected by the student body. Also like an intramural council, too large a group makes for an ineffective association. An association should have up to 10 students. In addition to two directors (one male and one female), association posts can represent such areas as outdoor recreation, finance, promotion, officiating, scheduling, and administration. To maintain their position on the association, student members should be required to maintain a minimum grade point average and be active members of the council. The institution's registrar can inform the intramural director when a council member's grades have dropped below the minimum required, or the intramural director can ask the registrar for a monthly update. Meetings should be held every other week and attendance should be mandatory.

For students studying recreation, the opportunity to be on an intramural council or association is an invaluable training experience and looks great on a resume. It demonstrates a student's interest, initiative, and experience providing leadership in a recreational setting. To reward those students who are simply there to help, most schools provide incentives. Some universities, for example, provide council members with T-shirts containing the intramural program logo, access to the intramural office computer, their own space (or office) to work on intramural duties or private study, free passes to community events, an honorarium for their time, and sometimes even an allowance or stipend for time spent running events.

In the end, both the students and the program benefit. The students get valuable training in leadership and organization, and they get to have fun. The program benefits from students' fresh ideas and perspectives. And, the institution benefits because an intramural council or association made up of students will help to create an effective intramural program that will include more students. In other words, involving students in intramural leadership is a win-win situation.

Note: Sometimes the relationship between student government and an intramural association or council can become adversarial. For example, student government may schedule a dance on a certain day and the intramural association may schedule a major tournament that same day. Likewise, the intramural council may decide on a weekly bowling night, only to find out that student government has planned a weekly co-ed barbecue for the same night. The students suffer because, clearly, some students might wish to attend both events. And the events suffer because attendance will likely be reduced at both. There is also the competition for attendees that ensues. Such a scenario can be prevented if an alliance can be built right away. For example, perhaps the two groups could work together: the intramural council planning a late-afternoon bowling event followed by the student government's barbecue. As intramural directors, you can do a lot to encourage this alliance. It is important to step above the petty politics and develop positive relationships with both groups, demonstrating the benefits of cooperation to the student body.

Student Officials   Another way students can contribute to an intramural program is by officiating as referees and umpires. At some high schools, seniors enrolled in physical education classes officiate as part of their course requirements. Some programs use varsity players as officials. These students are usually knowledgeable about the game, respected by their peers, and benefit from learning what it is like on the other side of the whistle. Paying varsity players to officiate is also an option—and is often used as a means of fund-raising for the varsity team (their earnings go to the team), but the intramural director must make sure these athletes call the games well.

A less common option for recruiting student officials is having each team provide a referee, called **peer officiating**. Student officials are appointed for an entire contest or tournament and must be selected either before or immediately following their team's first game. Because student officials preside over other teams' games, this practice is usually fair. But some additional supervision may be required.

Team Captains   In intramural competitions, students can volunteer to be team captains. Team captains act as a liaison between the intramural director and the players. As discussed in the previous chapter, team captains are often the ones who take a leadership role in putting an intramural team together. In the case of houses, teams can elect their own captains.

Team captains are responsible for

▶ signing up the team and paying any registration fees;

▶ confirming the eligibility of team players;

▶ representing the team at meetings;

▶ distributing schedules and other correspondence to team members;

▶ advising team members of league or tournament rules;

▶ ensuring that team members uphold the spirit of the intramural program (which should be prominent in the program mission statement);

▶ advising team members of a facility's rules (e.g., valid student ID needed for admittance);

▶ advising team members of the intramural program rules (e.g., proper game attire);

▶ obtaining necessary equipment and distributing it to teammates;

▶ filling out game sheets before games;

▶ checking weekly standings and scores, and notifying staff of any errors; and

▶ coordinating scheduling with team members.

It's a big list, and a lot of responsibility, which is why volunteering to be a team captain affords students the opportunity to develop important leadership qualities and experience. Given the enormous responsibility of being a team captain, intramural directors would be wise to appoint team captains themselves or to oversee the selection process.

Staff Volunteers

School staff and faculty, including teachers, administrative workers, and staff from other departments, also make excellent staff volunteers for an intramural program. They may be difficult to recruit, however. School faculty members are often given insufficient time to develop their own curriculum, much less volunteer for extra duty. The demands on teachers are many, and they are increasing. Although the importance of education is given plenty of lip service in most parts of North America, certain segments of society are becoming increasingly vocal about diminishing the role of the teacher. Especially in certain areas of Canada, such undervaluing is destroying the morale of teachers and diminishing any excitement or enthusiasm to do more than required.

To make matters worse for intramural departments, some school districts have few physical education specialists, meaning fewer teachers in the schools have any training or experience in physical activity and physical education. Nevertheless, colleagues are a great resource for intramural directors. It may take some work to get colleagues aboard and keep them there, but their support and assistance is invaluable.

Roles

School staff and faculty can play diverse and important staff roles in an intramural program. Most often, time-consuming fund-raising is their charge. But their involvement can be much broader. School faculty, for example, could coordinate house (or home room) teams. Faculty and staff could serve as mentors or instructors in their areas of expertise. For example, art and media teachers and assistants could help out with marketing suggestions. Perhaps certain staff members are students themselves and can use intramurals as the forum to complete a practicum. Or perhaps student teachers are on the faculty and would be willing to add to their teaching experience. If someone is studying to be a teacher, being an advisor for an intramural club (skiing, one of the martial arts, aerobics, and so on) or a supervisor for a few intramural events might satisfy some of the requirements.

As with any volunteer, when a faculty or staff member is willing to volunteer, intramural directors need to be as specific as possible about the tasks and responsibilities involved, including the time commitment and the resources that volunteer will have at his or her disposal.

Recruiting Volunteers

So if volunteers are so difficult to get, how do you get them? First and foremost, as intramural directors, you will do well to keep in mind that recruitment is an ongoing process. As Susan Ellis writes in *The Volunteer Recruitment Book*, "Recruitment is a constant, year-round process of keeping your organization's name and its available volunteer opportunities in front of people" (1994, 102). Satisfied volunteers can be strong advocates for the intramural program and persuasive partners for future volunteer recruitment. Probably the best recruiter is a satisfied volunteer who encourages others to join.

Before going about the task of recruiting volunteers, however, several things need to be in place within the intramural program. First, there should be an obvious need for the volunteer. Do not seek volunteers and then simply assign busy work to keep them occupied. The work they are assigned needs to be meaningful. Second, honor their requirements about the amount of time they are willing donate. There's nothing more frustrating than volunteering to work a few hours a week only to be given a task that requires double or triple that time commitment. Third, liability issues relating to volunteers must be resolved. These issues involve such factors as waiver forms, which are discussed more fully in chapter 7. Fourth, there must be a system in place to train volunteers, in terms of both the mission and goals of the intramural program and the specific role the volunteer will serve.

Once these items are in place, how do you get volunteers to join? Intramural directors should do a few things. First, make sure that your program is good enough that volunteers will want to get involved. Second, utilize volunteers' talents as completely as possible and make them feel comfortable. Third, plan to keep at it. As Ellis points out, volunteer recruitment is an ongoing process. Finally, check out some of the research on volunteering. Find out what motivates people to volunteer and then channel your volunteer recruitment accordingly. According to one study (May 2000), people volunteer for the following reasons.

- To help others and contribute to the community.
- To use skills in a new setting.
- To gain work experience.
- To find new friends and form new relationships.
- To develop a sense of accomplishment and self-worth.
- To learn new skills.
- To challenge themselves.
- To contribute to a cause they hold dear.
- To gain recognition for their abilities.
- To help improve the quality of a community.

Interviewing Volunteers

Volunteers for intramurals will typically come from within the walls of the institution. That means, intramural directors will often know the volunteer candidates personally. Familiarity will make the interview more comfortable, certainly, but intramural directors should still adhere to a structured interview. Avoid the temptation to chat with student and faculty volunteer candidates. The interview should be a forum to assess whether a candidate's skills are suited to the job. In the intramural program setting, this will involve gaining an understanding of how a volunteer can best contribute to the program.

Myriad books are available on interviewing and hiring employees, and specific interviewing tips are offered later in this chapter (see "Interviewing Staff" on pages 49-52), so we will not go into much detail here. Because volunteers are a unique component of an intramural program staff, however, the following criteria will help you conduct an effective interview and hire the right volunteer for the job.

- Is this candidate familiar with and enthusiastic about the intramural program?
- Does this candidate have a good relationship with students?
- Does this candidate have particular skills that are uniquely suited to the intramural program?
- Is this candidate self-motivated, flexible, and creative in work?
- Will this candidate need training or assistance? In what areas?
- Does the candidate's schedule fit the needs of the intramural program?

Hiring Volunteers

Far too often, particularly in small institutions, volunteers join an intramural program informally. Responsibilities are explained over a conversation and commitments are made with a handshake. Because volunteers will be representing the institution in some cases, particularly at the university level, it is a good idea to formalize the hiring process. As will be discussed in the next section, training is always a good idea. Class times and training schedules should be communicated to volunteers when they are hired. Likewise, any intramural property given to volunteers should be recorded. This information can be included on a volunteer contract, like the one shown in figure 4.3.

Emphasize the important role the volunteer has in terms of promoting a positive intramural experience for all participants, and express your appreciation for the volunteer's willingness to help. Remind the volunteer that if things do not work out for the volunteer or for the institution, and things cannot be worked out positively, that is "sufficient cause" to relieve the volunteer of his or her duties or for the volunteer to leave on his or her own. These factors may have to do with the volunteer experience not being what was expected, or the volunteer not following through with commitments by not submitting necessary work on time, dealing inappropriately with others, or any other ways being undependable.

Because volunteers will likely run across confidential information—for example, documents that deal with discipline cases, phone numbers and addresses of participants, and so on—volunteers should also sign a confidentiality agreement, shown in figure 4.4. Finally, volunteers should also be made aware of the institution's policy on harassment and the program's safety and fair play policies. These are explained in chapters 6 and 7.

Volunteers should also sign a consent form warning the volunteer of potential risks of involvement in intramural programs, and protect-

Volunteer Contract

(For children under legal age of consent, parent/guardian must sign.)

Name _____

I consent to perform the duties listed below at _____ [institution], hereafter referred to as The Institution.

Day(s):_____

Time:_____

Location:_____

I agree to abide by the rules and policies at The Institution and to participate in all necessary training.

Date of training: _____

If for any reason I am unable to be at the program at the designated time, I will notify the program supervisor at least 48 hours in advance.

Program Supervisor:_____

Phone:_____

I have received the following property in exchange for volunteering. I agree to return this property upon the completion of my volunteer experience.

___T-shirt   ___Manual   ___Badge   ___Other _____

I agree that this contract may be terminated either by myself or The Institution staff for sufficient cause.

Volunteer signature _____

Date _____

FIGURE 4.3   Sample contract for intramural program volunteers.

ing the institution from any claims resulting in injuries while the volunteer is involved in the intramural program.

Managing Volunteers

Besides inadequate pay, the most common complaint of employees is not knowing what is expected of them. Volunteers, although not paid in the first place, are no different. They must understand their responsibilities, and this includes knowing others' responsibilities in the department. There's nothing more frustrating to a volunteer than not knowing what everyone else does and whom to go to for help or support. Another complaint, both of employees and volunteers, is not feeling appreciated.

You and your staff have a responsibility to volunteers. As intramural directors, set a good example for departmental staff. Thank volunteers for their time and their help, and do all you can to let them know they are a valued part of the program. Volunteers should be treated as more than free help for menial labor. If that is the attitude of the intramural director, few volunteers will sign up. Keeping volunteers happy on the job and making them want to come back year after year (with a few friends, we hope) will

Confidentiality of Information

During your work with _____'s [institution] Intrmaural Program, you may have access to confidential information. You may not discuss or misuse this information in any way. In the event of any breach of confidentiality in your area, the intramural director may suspend your placement immediately pending an investigation. If it is found that you are responsible for the breach of confidentiality, your placement may be terminated immediately.

Signature _____

Name _____

Date _____

FIGURE 4.4 Sample confidentiality agreement.

benefit your program. Use the following basic standards to organize your volunteer program (May 2000).

- Treat volunteers as coworkers, not free help for menial jobs or tasks no one else wants.
- Whenever possible, assign tasks based on volunteers' personal preferences.
- Also consider volunteers' temperament, education level, and skills when assigning duties.
- Create a comprehensive training program to help make volunteers feel part of the intramural team.
- Devise a fair and comprehensive system of supervision.

As much as you have a responsibility to volunteers, they also have a responsibility to you and to the intramural program. Don't fall into the trap of keeping volunteers who underperform simply because they are working for free. As directors, you must be able to count on all program participants—not just paid staff. As outlined earlier, volunteers will interact with other program participants, including personnel, players, officials, and so on. They should be reminded that they represent the intramural program to these participants. If they do their work well and positively represent the program,

everyone benefits. If they don't do their work or create a negative impression to participants, the intramural program will suffer.

Use the following components of a volunteer's contribution to instruct and manage your volunteer pool. Volunteers should

- be sincere in the offer of service;
- be loyal to the program and staff;
- maintain the dignity and integrity of the program;
- understand their jobs;
- carry out their duties promptly and reliably;
- accept guidance and respect departmental decisions;
- maintain a smooth working relationship with staff and program participants; and
- contribute to their own supervision with self-evaluation and a willingness to ask questions.

Paid Staff

If the task of running an effective intramural program were not complex, a book like this one would not be necessary. In truth, an intramural program is multifaceted and complex, and it requires a staff that has a broad range of expertise and is capable of dealing with many tasks.

For these tasks and broad expertise, suitable candidates must be recruited, interviewed, and then hired. This section outlines how to put together an effective intramural staff.

Roles and Responsibilities

In addition to the key position of intramural director, who oversees the entire program, the basic functions in need of staffing include program development, officiating, promotion, budgeting, tournament and league coordination, and event management. In small institutions one person can do most or all of these, but in large institutions several people are needed. Because the specific job requirements of each function vary from program to program, and will depend on the facets of the program, the strengths of existing staff, and the resources available, it is impossible to delineate every intramural job here. Instead, the following suggestions will help you clarify the roles and responsibilities of your intramural program staff.

Job Descriptions

Let's start with a story that underscores the importance of proper job descriptions. It's about four people named Everybody, Somebody, Anybody, and Nobody.

> There was an important job to be done, and Everybody was sure that Somebody would do it. Anybody could have done it, but Nobody did it. Somebody got angry at this because it was Everybody's job. Everybody thought Anybody could do it, but Nobody realized that Everybody wouldn't do it. It ended up that Everybody blamed Somebody when Nobody did what Anybody could have done.

Name confusion aside, it is crucial that staff—paid and volunteer—have clear job descriptions to ensure that all facets of the program are covered and that individual staff members are not overextended. Staff members need to know exactly what their responsibilities are. These responsibilities should be developed in conjunction with the entire staff, seeking input as necessary, and then written down as formal job descriptions in staff orientation and training manuals. If created responsibly and used consistently, job descriptions form the basis of ongoing and annual employee evaluation. (Also be sure to measure and evaluate the effectiveness of training procedures.) Chapter 13 provides checklists to ensure the successful completion of various intramural events. These checklists may be helpful in developing the specific job responsibilities of the staff.

As a rule, job descriptions should include six main components: job specifics, purpose, qualifications, essential functions, additional responsibilities, and principle accountabilities. Figure 4.5 shows an example of a head official's job description. The first component includes position title, supervisor, classification or level of the position (if necessary for compensation), the department, the division within the department, and the date the position (and job description) was created. The second component deals with the purpose of the position. This should only be a sentence or two and should clearly and concisely state the essence of the job. The third component lists the qualifications for the job. Minimum qualifications should be listed, but preferable degrees or training may also be included. The fourth component is the meat of the job. That is, essential functions and duties of the position are listed. Additional or unusual duties can be added in the fifth component, additional responsibilities, but essential functions should be limited to the basic job. The sixth component is highly specific, listing exactly what an employee must accomplish to perform his or her duties satisfactorily.

Recruiting Staff

So how do intramural directors find qualified intramural personnel? Although this section is intended to help directors recruit suitable candidates, it will also help students seeking jobs to better understand the recruitment and hiring process. Some of this information may be helpful for recruiting volunteers as well.

The first thing to determine is the type of person you are looking for. Essentially, intramural directors look for leaders who can relate well with people, are self-motivated, can solve problems creatively, and can accomplish tasks efficiently while having fun. In a recent informal poll of colleges and universities, intramural directors were asked what they specifically looked for in intramural staff. The findings are listed, from the most often reported to the least often reported, with the percentage of respondents indicating that criterion in the left column.

Intramural Program Job Description

Title: Head Official

Supervisor: Intramural Director

Classification: Level 3

Department: Campus Recreation

Division: Intramural Programming

Created: 1 January 2002

Position purpose: The head official oversees the recruitment, training, certification, and evaluation of all officials, as well as the assigning of all officials to games.

Job qualifications: The head official must hold current certification in two sports and have refereed at least 40 intramural contests.

Essential functions: The head official

- is responsible for all policies, procedures, and programs relating to officiating. These include, but are not limited to, recruiting, training, safety, evaluation, and compensation.
- will ensure that all documentation for officials is available and properly filed.
- will develop recruitment strategies for high-quality intramural officials.
- will identify training topics, ensure a high standard of training, and maintain accurate training and certification records.
- will ensure that officials are certified or qualified to an acceptable level of proficiency for officiating.
- will assign all officials to different levels of competition according to their certification and qualifications.
- is responsible for communicating the Intramural Mission Statement and other relevant intramural program policies and procedures to all officials.
- will develop and implement an evaluation system for all officials.
- is responsible for identifying problems with the intramural program or participants, reporting problems reported by all officials, and seeking remedies for these problems.

Additional responsibilities: The head official will attend official meetings of the intramural staff and contribute in other areas of the intramural program as needed.

Principal accountabilities: The head official is accountable for the following results:

- Recruiting an adequate number of high-quality officials
- Ensuring that all officials are certified or qualified to officiate
- Ensuring that all officials are adequately trained
- Ensuring that all officials are aware of the institution's safety procedures and will do their part to ensure safe games for all participants
- Ensuring that all games have the correct number and level (competency) of officials
- Ensuring that all officials are appropriately compensated for their work
- Evaluating officials and the officiating program

FIGURE 4.5   Sample job description for head official.

73%	Strong interpersonal skills in communication
73%	Self-motivation, flexibility, and creativity
45%	Realistic attitude and honesty
45%	Efficient organization and effective time management
45%	Competency, responsibility, and accountability
36%	Courage (to be a change agent) and problem solving
36%	Dedication and determination
36%	Role model and maturity
27%	Sense of humor
27%	Nurturing and encouraging of others
18%	Vision of future
18%	Goal orientation
9%	Lifestyle

Most of these criteria can be ascertained in an interview. Before the interviewing process is begun, however, an intramural director must determine the qualifications necessary for the job and schedule interviews with candidates who possess the skills or have the experience that will best match the requirements of the position. As is often the case with most professional jobs, networking, word-of-mouth, and newspaper advertising start the process. From there, the flood of resumes ensues.

A resume is the most common method used to assess and understand the qualifications of job candidates. Resumes typically include the candidate's name, street (and E-mail) address, and telephone number. From there, resumes can differ dramatically. Some are brief and to the point, contained to one page, while others can be several pages long and contain narratives of each job held and type of experience gained. It is helpful when a candidate includes a statement of long-term (and sometimes short-term) objectives, a summary of related jobs, educational background, and several references. A list of job-related achievements can also help a director assess candidates. While many directors wait to check a candidates references until after an interview, it may be informative and save some time to check a few references before inviting a candidate in for an interview.

Note: Student candidates will often have less-impressive resumes, but they can be an excel-lent staff resource for most intramural programs, especially those that offer formal training. Students studying recreation leadership, for example, are often hired to organize certain events or activities, or even certain facets of the intramural program. Some students do this work to fulfill a required program practicum; others simply want the experience. It would be wise for grade and high school intramural directors to tap into this resource.

Interviewing Staff

Once you have candidates that appear to have potential, it's time to schedule an interview. An interview is like any presentation. The opening few minutes set the stage for what follows and makes the audience comfortable. The next few minutes set the stage for what is to come, plot development or general information. The body of the presentation is the climax, when general points are sharpened and amplified. The final few minutes are the conclusion, an opportunity to summarize the presentation. The following suggestions will help you maximize the interview experience.

► Pay attention to your first impressions. Although it seems unfair to many candidates, interviewers often jump to a conclusion within the first few minutes and then spend the rest of the interview confirming this first impression. That means, anything that creates a negative impression from the outset will likely set the tone for the entire interview. If a candidate is late or uninformed about the job, for example, the interview will likely not go smoothly. Appropriate attire also tells something about the candidate. Be on the lookout for candidates having a flimsy handshake, chewing gum, and being unwilling (or unable) to look you in the eye. These are telltale signs that a candidate may not be comfortable working with people.

► Try to start on time. If the candidate is late for an interview, you've got to wonder if they'll be on time for work.

► Ask questions that will evoke personal and specific responses. If you want to know how a candidate would respond to a difficult situation, ask. For example, "How would you handle a student who was mad about the officiating after losing a play-off game? What would you tell the player?" Contrast that with the following question: "What would be a textbook way of dealing with an irate participant?" Without being specific and relating the question to the candidate, you're bound to get speculation, which is not very helpful in assessing the person's qualifications.

▶ Try to ask open-ended questions rather than those that invite a simple "yes" or "no" response. For example, rather than ask, "Have you ever run a special event before?" Ask the candidate, "What kind of special events have you run? Which did you enjoy most?"

▶ Use brief questions and ask only one question at a time. Rather than question the candidate about the pros and cons of separate rules for girls' sports, how it has changed, what direction these rules will likely go in the future, and what is fair to girls and to boys, it may be more helpful to ask for some examples of situations in which separate rules for girls and boys are appropriate, or how female participation numbers can be improved.

▶ Cut the chitchat. While a dialogue or conversation can be helpful in getting to know a candidate, it should not take over the interview. Limit your own remarks and let the interviewee speak. Using the example in the previous point, you may be tempted to provide others' opinions about where girls and boys sports rules will go in the future. Just ask the question.

▶ Save the delicate questions (i.e., why an interviewee left a previous job) for the end of an interview. This will help to ensure that neither you nor the candidate are flustered from the beginning but instead have been able to feel comfortable throughout the interview. It may also save some time, since you will not need to ask these questions if the rest of the candidate's responses have alerted you to the fact that he or she is not suitable for the job.

▶ Give candidates time to think through their responses. Don't hurry them unnecessarily; allow them the time to collect their thoughts. Then, once they start talking, don't interrupt. Interrupting or cutting them off sends a message that you are not interested in what they are saying. That said, however, if a candidate is talking too much or is needlessly going into lengthy responses and stories, be prepared to step in and steer the interview to the next question.

▶ Don't ask questions in a way that suggest a right or wrong answer. For example, "It has been my experience that men will always play ball hockey roughly. It's part of the game, and it's a part of what makes a man a man. What do you think?" This type of question does not leave much room for a candidate's own opinion.

▶ Be prepared to ask a candidate to elaborate. For example, if you ask, "How would you handle a student who was mad about the officiating after losing a play-off game?" and "carefully" is the candidate's response, a simple "And?" might encourage more detail. You might also ask, "Can you elaborate on that?" or, "Can you give some specific examples of what you would do?" Of course, one-word and inappropriately brief responses like this should also clue you in on how the candidate communicates with others.

▶ End the interview by asking candidates to summarize their relevant experience and interest in the position. You might ask, "If we were trying to decide between hiring you or someone with similar abilities, why should you get the job?" or, "What are two characteristics we should remember about you?"

▶ Also briefly mention the salary, vacation, and other benefits, and ask the applicant if he or she has any questions about these.

Using these suggestions for structuring and steering an effective interview, then, the following questions will help you plan the areas to be covered.

▶ "Why did you apply for this position?" Will the candidate be able to handle the responsibilities? Does he or she really understand what the position is? Finally, is the candidate committed enough that training him or him will be worth the time and money?

▶ "What is your greatest strength?" A candidate might be especially suited for a specific part of the program or certain tasks and responsibilities. For example, an applicant may possess excellent communication or writing skills and would be ideally suited for writing or proofreading promotional posters and other departmental documentation. Or perhaps a candidate is highly social and would be great at orientation events and large group activities.

► "What is your greatest weakness?" No one is perfect, certainly. Although intimidating for many job applicants, this questions is extremely important. It will help you assess where training and/or extra help will be required. It will also enable you to determine certain situations to avoid. For example, if a candidate is easily intimidated, running a competitive indoor soccer league would probably not be the most appropriate job.

► "What are your interests?" Does the candidate have a full and balanced life? Is he or she a couch potato? Is the candidate involved or interested in any of the intramural activities? These considerations are certainly important if you want staff members to serve as role models for active living. Likewise, some candidates may have some unique interests that could be of benefit to the intramural program. A candidate with an active interest in photography, for example, could significantly contribute to the production of visually appealing promotional materials.

In addition to these general questions, be sure to ask candidates specific questions that relate to the exact position being interviewed for. For example, "What have you done in the past that will be particularly helpful in this job?" Say you're looking for a head official. You have five applicants, all of whom have similar backgrounds on paper. The best choice will probably be the candidate who can explain the problems she's encountered with officiating and some of the quick, effective, and unique solutions she created.

Problem Solving

Rather than use a traditional interviewing approach, another option is to place the applicants in several groups and have the groups solve a problem. Such problem-solving sessions are invaluable in assessing applicants' leadership skills (you may also want to review the criteria identified by intramural directors on page 49). The details of the response are not as critical as the way each candidate deals with other group members.

The following three scenarios are examples of problems and challenges you can pose. No answer is right or wrong, but we have provided one potential solution for each scenario. *Note:* These scenarios are set at the collegiate level, since colleges and universities are the most likely institutions to hire intramural staff.

Scenario 1 You have 48 teams signed up for an opening weekend (Friday night beginning at 6:00 p.m., and all day Saturday) softball tournament. You have two unlit diamonds and a soccer field. How would you successfully implement this tournament?

You could calculate the number of hours available to compete and the number of games required. In terms of available hours, you might schedule Friday's session for 6 p.m. to 8 p.m. (2 hours) and Saturday's session for 8 a.m. to 8 p.m. (12 hours), for a total of 14 (2 + 12) hours. Using the two softball diamonds and soccer field as playing areas, there are three playing fields. If games lasted 40 minutes, 63 games could be played in 14 hours. For the number of games required, you could divide the 48 teams into groups (pools) of three totaling 16 pools. If the three teams in the pools each played each other (A plays B; B plays C; A plays C), this would require three games per group for a total of 48 (3 x 16) games. If this pool play was followed by a single-elimination playoff, that would require 15 additional games, for a total of 63 games. In other words, the schedule would work perfectly.

From the specifics of game numbers and times, the rest of the implementation process would involve the following:

► Schedules would need to be communicated to the teams so they know when and where they play.

► Umpires need to be recruited and assigned.

► Safety considerations for converting a soccer field into a softball diamond, such as the location of the goal posts in relation to the baseball diamond.

► Revenues and expenses need to be projected.

► Event promotion needs to be considered, refreshments thought about, and awards (trophies or other recognition) planned.

Scenario 2 The student senate wants campus recreation to organize some activities on Saturday afternoon as part of orientation week. The event will be followed with a barbecue and dance. How would you successfully implement this event?

The options here are endless. When posing this questions to candidate groups, watch for leaders to emerge. The applicant who steers the group into outlining the process of implementation (i.e., planning who will attend, how many to expect, how to promote the event, how to gather activity suggestions, and so on) will be an excellent addition to your staff.

Scenario 3 The weight room on campus is being underutilized. How would you increase student use of this room?

Again, watch for leaders to emerge. Candidates should identify and assess the problem first, then come up with solutions. Identifying the problem may involve interviewing current users, students who stopped using the weight room, and those who do have never used it. Identifying the problem may also involve interviewing school staff who work in the vicinity. Solution approaches might include conferring with other intramural directors in similar situations, reviewing relevant studies on the topic, and brainstorming.

Hiring Staff

Once you have an eager and suitable candidate, it's time to extend an offer. The employment offer should be delivered in person (or over the phone) and be followed up by a formal letter stipulating the conditions of employment. This letter, also called an **employment contract**, commits a hiree to perform his or her work responsibilities and outlines the role of the institution and program staff. An employment contract, like the casual employment contract shown in figure 4.6, should spell out the following:

► Start date and time, and where the hiree should report on the first day.

► Specifics of the job, including the position title, to whom the hiree will report, and so on.

► Compensation package, including salary, lunch and break times, vacation time,

health benefits, sick leave, and so on (if applicable). Or refer the hiree to school or program manuals and handbooks that outline these terms of employment.

► All relevant manuals/handbooks enclosed, including program mission statement and a job description (see page 48).

Training and Management

In managing intramural staff and volunteers, one of the most important roles of the intramural director is to ensure that staff members have the opportunity for professional growth. In addition to skill development, professional growth includes participation in all areas of decision making and program improvement. It's best to think of every intramural staff person as a leader (thus the title of this chapter), a team player who is working on behalf of the intramural program to satisfy participants' needs. To help staff members accomplish this mission, leadership training is important.

Intramural directors should create formal training opportunities. Staff and intramural councils should set aside some time in meetings to learn about brainstorming, leadership styles, time management, communication, teamwork, decision making, conflict resolution, problem solving, evaluation, and recognition. CIRA and other intramural organizations provide excellent resources to help directors incorporate student leadership training into the programs (see "Resources" at the end of this chapter), and there are plenty of books on just this topic.

Note: Training programs do not have to become another item on your "to do" list. While many intramural directors might conduct staff training themselves, plenty more have senior students hire and train their own staff or develop a mentor training system in which an experienced staff member mentors a rookie. In many cases, experienced staff and students understand the specifics of a job better than an intramural director. Such mentor and peer training is an invaluable component of any training program. For one thing, trainees often feel more comfortable learning from their peers. Also, the process of mentoring and training others is great leadership training in and of itself.

Letter of Casual Employment Offer

PERSONAL AND CONFIDENTIAL

Date _____

Name _____

Address _____

_____

Dear _____:

This letter will confirm an offer of casual employment with _____ [institution] (hereafter referred to as The Institution) reporting to _____ [supervisor name]. Your employment will start on _____ [date] and end on _____ [date]. Your employment may be terminated at any time at the sole discretion of the supervisor.

You will be paid an hourly rate of $_____. Your work hours will be _____ a.m. to _____ p.m., or as modified by The Institution from time to time, with a minimum of one-half hour unpaid lunch for every 5 continuous hours of work. Your pay includes 4 percent vacation pay and will be subject to deductions required by law.

As a casual employee of The Institution, you will not be eligible to enroll in The Institution's benefit plans and you will be paid only for time worked.

You will be responsible for assisting The Institution's intramural office in the role of _____ [job title], which consists of the following duties:

-
-
-
-
-

[list all job duties]

Should you have any questions concerning your employment, please contact _____ [supervisor] at _____ [phone number/E-mail].

You may accept this offer by signing the duplicate copy of this letter enclosed and returning it to me on or before _____ [date].

Sincerely,

[your signature]

_____ [printed name]

_____ [title]

_____

I have read, understand, and accept the offer of casual employment as outlined above.

Date _____   Employee signature _____

Adapted, by permission, from J. Kestner, 1996, *Program evaluation for sports directors* (Champaign, IL: Human Kinetics), 45-52.

FIGURE 4.6   Sample casual employment contract.

Autonomy

It is important to give staff and volunteers the authority to make decisions in their own areas. They should not have to run to you every time there is a problem. Doing so is frustrating for them and may be frustrating for you, particularly when several other fires are waiting to be put out. First and foremost, understand that mistakes will be made. Likewise, everything will not be done as you would have done it yourself. Nevertheless, giving your people the authority and autonomy to do their own jobs as they see fit empowers staff and volunteers to take the ball and run with it, be creative in seeking solutions to problems, and gives everyone a sense of ownership and control in their job. The bottom line: staff and volunteers need to be encouraged to make their own decisions and not be afraid to make a mistake—unless, of course, the safety of participants is at risk.

Goal Setting

An excellent way to assist staff and volunteers in taking ownership of their jobs is goal setting. Just as setting goals is important to athletes working toward a winning season or important competition, goal setting is important for staff and volunteers working to create an effective intramural program and satisfy the program mission. Supervisors should periodically sit down with staff and volunteers to help them formulate and monitor their goals. This can be done at the beginning or end of a season or event, or after a formal evaluation (discussed later in this chapter).

The process of goal setting includes identifying specific tasks to accomplish or areas to work on, refining and prioritizing those tasks or areas, and planning the actions or steps required. It is also helpful to determine a time by which those goals should be achieved. Then, on that predetermined date or shortly thereafter, supervisor and staff or volunteer again sit down and review the goals, acknowledging progress and identifying new goals to achieve.

The process of professional goal development involves four steps, outlined by Jim Kestner in *Program Evaluation for Sport Directors* (1999). The first step in developing goals is to identify important areas for professional growth such as developing budgeting skills, or sharing successes with colleagues. The second step is to develop specific goal statements for the areas identified

in step 1. The third step is to identify actions that will accomplish the goals in step 2. The fourth step is outlining supervisor actions that will enable the employee to successfully accomplish his or her goals.

The following questionnaire illustrates the process. An intramural director would ask an employee to answer the following questions, which would help him set goals for the coming year. As he thinks about his goals, he would consider areas of his performance that he would like to strengthen, as well as areas he would like to learn more about. Once he responds to all the questions, he and the intramural director would sit down to discuss his goals and figure out a way to accomplish them.

Step 1: Identify areas for professional growth. List four areas of your professional responsibilities that you would like to improve during the coming year. For example, develop budgeting skills, learn new activities, and share successes with colleagues from other institutions. Thinking about your own responsibilities, which areas would you like to improve?

1. _____
2. _____
3. _____
4. _____

Step 2: Identify specific goal statements. Examine each of the areas you identified in step 1, and use the space below to rephrase each of your responses in the form of a goal. The more specific you can make your goal statements now, the easier it will be able to judge your achievements. For example, if you wrote "share successes with colleagues from other institutions" in step 1, you might write the following goal statement: "to volunteer to lead a workshop on budgeting at the upcoming intramural/physical education conference."

1. _____
2. _____
3. _____
4. _____

Step 3: Identify actions to take in pursuit of goals. For each of the goals you wrote in step 2, list two specific actions you could take to reach them. Following the example used in step

2, you might list these actions: Goal 1, action 1: "Decide which successes I would most like to share." Goal 1, action 2: "Contact NIRSA to see if I can lead a workshop at its upcoming conference."

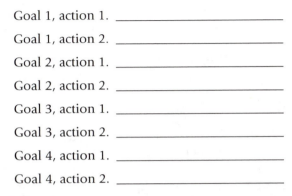

Goal 1, action 1. _____

Goal 1, action 2. _____

Goal 2, action 1. _____

Goal 2, action 2. _____

Goal 3, action 1. _____

Goal 3, action 2. _____

Goal 4, action 1. _____

Goal 4, action 2. _____

Step 4: Identify ways that your supervisor can assist you in the pursuit of your goals. For each of the goals identified in step 2, list two actions that your supervisor could take to assist you in reaching your goals. Again following the example in step 2, you might list these actions. Goal 1, action 1: "Suggest which program successes the administrator feels would be best shared with others." Goal 1, action 2: "Provide time and money to prepare and present the material."

Goal 1, action 1. _____

Goal 1, action 2. _____

Goal 2, action 1. _____

Goal 2, action 2. _____

Goal 3, action 1. _____

Goal 3, action 2. _____

Goal 4, action 1. _____

Goal 4, action 2. _____

Communication

Job satisfaction, autonomy, sense of ownership, feeling proud of one's accomplishments and professional development—any and all aspects of a job are affected by communication. As intramural directors, it will be your job to keep the lines of communication open with staff and employees. Information must flow freely between all concerned to ensure that nothing is forgotten, everyone feels included, and all program participants are getting a rewarding intramural experience. Regularly scheduled meetings are invaluable aids in keeping communication open within a department. Informal chitchats, keeping your office door open, and eating lunch or going for coffee breaks together are also helpful.

Communicating in person is usually best but, unfortunately, is not always possible. To ensure that no one is left out, another way to keep everyone "in the loop" is distributing regular memos on the goings-on in the department, including recent successes and events, and what to look forward to. Computers are enormously helpful in this regard. In particular, group E-mail and electronic message boards (i.e., listservs) ensure that all staff and volunteers will get the information they need.

Listservs are also excellent communication tools, although used primarily by intramural and campus recreation directors. Users pose a question, suggestion, or concern on a listserv, and others may offer feedback, ideas, or other input. In Canada, CIRA-Ontario offers a free listserv (ask to be added to the list by E-mailing ciraon-requesr@julian.uwo.ca). In the U.S. and elsewhere, NIRSA offers a helpful listserv reserved for its members (www.nirsa.org or general email nirsa@nirsa.org).

Time Management

With the myriad responsibilities and "to do" items these days, time management is crucial for everyone. In the intramural setting, encourage volunteers and staff to set long-term, weekly, and daily priorities. Long-term projects should be broken up into identifiable and manageable steps, accompanied with a realistic timeline. There are many major projects which intramural directors and their staff and volunteers would like to do but these too need to be ranked in order of priority.

Over the years, thousands of time-management resources have become available on the market. Daybooks and electronic calendars have proven particularly effective. Key events can be recorded, including the steps to be completed by certain dates. Key contacts can be cross-referenced, along with notes about conversations, necessary follow-up, and so on. The features of such tools are far too numerous to elaborate here. Whatever the system you choose, be sure to use it efficiently and to its full potential, and encourage staff and volunteers to do the same.

Conflict Resolution and Discipline

Whatever the caliber of your staff and volunteers, conflict will arise. As directors, it will be your job not only to resolve conflict and institute necessary discipline but also to maintain an atmosphere in which conflict is seen as a natural result of working together and is resolvable. Positive conflict and heated discussions are healthy and can move an organization forward. For example, conflict is often the result when someone suggests a different way of doing things. While the tension this creates can be uncomfortable, more often than not, exploring this new approach is useful, if not to find a better procedure then at least to reinforce the current way of doing things.

In terms of personal conflicts, however, it is best that they be resolved quickly and professionally. Rather than concentrate on the other person, both parties need to focus on the issue(s) that caused the difficulty. As the director, you may have to step in and make sure that both parties listen to the other's concerns and ideas, and not take any of the comments personally. The following suggestions for dealing with interpersonal conflict may prove helpful.

1. Get emotions under control, then immediately deal with the conflict.
2. Be honest.
3. Use "I" messages instead of "you" messages.
4. Use active listening to promote understanding.
5. Seek a win-win solution, if possible.
6. Always try to resolve conflicts in private.
7. Honor confidentiality.
8. Always treat each other with courtesy and respect.
9. If the tension isn't resolved, agree to disagree.

Without undergoing the study of psychology, you may find yourself in hot water every now and again when it comes to dealing with interpersonal conflict. The following may be helpful. It's been said that we all judge our peers using three, simple, universal questions (Murray 1995):

▶ Can I trust you?
▶ Are you *really* committed?
▶ Do you care about me?

In the end, it's best to keep your staff and volunteers focused on the task at hand: accomplishing your program mission. That means, any tensions that develop in an intramural setting should be about developing ways to improve the experience for participants. If staff members know that their colleagues care for them and that any suggestions made are meant to benefit the program, healthy discussion and disagreement on improving the intramural program is possible.

Relationships

A significant part of effective management of staff and volunteers is to respect them as people. An intramural director does well to remember that tournaments and sign-up days are important, but so are staff and volunteer birthdays, anniversaries, and other important life events. Indeed, having positive relationships with colleagues is integral to job satisfaction. According to a 1983 study of volunteer firefighters, subjects stated that they joined the organization predominately for "service reasons, but friendships and social interaction were more influential in their decision to remain with it" (Brudney 1990, 162).

Take the time to get to know your people. Personal announcements could be incorporated into periodic meetings, or you can even assign someone in the office to keep track of birthdays and other important celebrations in the lives of your staff and volunteers. In the end, the more involved your people feel, both with one another and with the program, the higher their job satisfaction and performance.

Recognition

Likewise, take the time to recognize and acknowledge significant contributions of staff and volunteers, including scheduled periodic celebrations. According to Tracey Mann (1999), manager of Volunteer Regina and United Way of Regina, recognition should be an ongoing and frequent occurrence within your organization, not just an annual event. In other words, don't wait until April to recognize a volunteer whose project was completed in October.

According to Mann (1999), the most meaningful recognition will come from staff, volunteers, or participants directly impacted by the person's efforts—for example, a team recognizing or thanking the team captain. According to Mann (1999), meaningful recognition will also respect an individual's personality, interests, and preferences. If an individual is uncomfortable with public recognition, don't hold a school-wide ceremony or place his or her picture in the local newspaper. Although personalized recognition will take a bit more time and effort to coordinate, an individualized trophy or other award will be a lot more special than one of 20 wall plaques presented each year. Most important, of course, remember to say "thank you" often (Mann 1999).

Evaluation

Constructive feedback is important to the development of staff and volunteers in an intramural program. As staff and volunteers improve their work, the intramural participants benefit. Feedback should be both informal and formal, but the evaluation should always be formative. **Formative evaluation** is any kind of evaluation that is used to help a person improve. To be most effective, formative evaluation should take place once every few months. To use the analogy of a round of golf, the score you receive at each hole is an evaluation of your performance on that hole and provides an incentive for the next hole.

There are two types of formative evaluation, informal and formal. **Informal evaluation** is a nonsystematic collection of data for the purposes of measuring performance and making improvements to the intramural program. This type of evaluation usually takes the form of feedback and is often offered as an aside. It can come during or after an event, in the morning or at the end of the day—any time feedback is appropriate. Informal evaluation is typically based on observation and can take the form of "I like the way you explained the rules," "You seem a little tired today," "That poster looks great," or "The standings are running a little behind—can you update them soon, please?" Informal evaluation helps keep staff and volunteers on their toes and running an effective intramural program. **Formal evaluation** is the systematic collection of data for the purposes of measuring performance and making improvements. When it comes to evaluating staff, this systematic data collection should include observation at fixed times using specific criteria such as job descriptions.

Staff and volunteers should be evaluated using both types of formative evaluation. First, spontaneous and frequent informal evaluation should be used to let them know how they are doing, perhaps on a daily basis, and keep them functioning to the best of their ability. Second, they should have periodic formal evaluations. A formal evaluation should be used as an opportunity to thank staff and volunteers for their specific contributions as well as to help staff and volunteers maintain their present level (if already excellent) and improve their performance (if needed).

Before looking at methods of evaluating staff and volunteers, it is important to emphasize that an evaluation is an opinion. To be effective, it should involve the staff person's or volunteer's input. Also, it should include an appeals process. For example, if a supervisor is dissatisfied with an employee's work, that employee should have the option of turning to you, the director, for more confirmation of the supervisor's evaluation or more feedback. A formal appraisal should also provide an opportunity for program managers to learn how they can assist staff and volunteers. Finally, every institution should have a policy about how long evaluations are kept in an employee's or volunteer's file.

Evaluation Tools

As in any service industry, it is important to get feedback from customers. In the case of intramurals, the customers are participants, including students, players, and team captains. Others who contribute may also be fellow staff or volunteers, including officials, directors, or conveners—anyone who works or has contact with the staff person or volunteer being evaluated. An efficient way of gathering this information is using an evaluation form. Using the same form for each source of information—as well as from year to year—is helpful for comparison.

When designing an evaluation form, according to James Kestner (1996), there are five key program areas:

▶ Safety assurance
▶ Duty proficiency
▶ Administrative competence
▶ Professional development
▶ Motivation

Figure 4.7 provides a sample participant's evaluation form for a league or tournament convener. A **convener** is responsible for running an event, including special events, leagues, and tournaments. Typically they supervise all games they are responsible for and ensure that events run well. Such a questionnaire should simply ask if the staff person or volunteer does or does not meet a certain criteria, permitting some space for additional remarks. Figure 4.8, a sample supervisor's evaluation form for a league or tournament convener, is more comprehensive. It assesses areas about the convener that only a supervisor is aware of: administrative competence and professional growth, and it allows for more detailed evaluation by providing numbers rather than "yes" or "no" options.

Meetings

As mentioned, intramural directors need to keep participants and staff informed and involved in the development of an intramural program. One effective way of doing this is with meetings. Meetings differ in purpose and attendance. A meeting can be an opportunity to distribute and clarify information such as playing rules, discuss items of concern such as increasing female involvement, or plan an activity such as Winterfest. Meetings can be held for staff to assist in event and program planning. Meetings can be held for team captains to inform them about game rules and schedule changes, and to seek their input on improving an activity or event. Volunteer meetings can be held for the sole purpose of getting feedback on the volunteer program. Committee meetings can be held to work out the details of specific events or policies. Departmental meetings can be held to discuss employment practices, program specifics, and so on.

Whatever the purpose or attendance of a meeting, it should be run efficiently and effectively. The following tips will help you organize and run effective meetings.

▶ Distribute an agenda and other relevant documents well in advance. Everyone should come prepared and have an idea of what will be discussed ahead of time.

▶ Start on time. Nothing is more frustrating than assembling for a meeting, after scheduling it into an already packed day, only to sit and wait for stragglers to arrive and be seated. If certain people are late, start without them.

▶ Appoint a chair or someone to lead the meeting, including the discussion and decision-making process.

▶ Have someone record what is said and decided at the meeting. Often called the "meeting minutes" or simply "minutes," this record should be typed up and distributed after each meeting.

▶ Stay focused. Meetings have a habit of quickly spiraling out of control. The more people involved, the longer it can drag on. Distributing an agenda—and then sticking to it—will help keep meetings on track.

▶ Summarize action steps. Before you adjourn the meeting, summarize what needs to be done and who needs to do it.

▶ Adjourn promptly. Participants should know when the meeting is over and when socializing (which often ensues after a meeting) begins. People are busy. Don't take up more time than required simply because no one is certain when to leave a meeting.

Chapter Summary Exercises

Recruiting, hiring, training, and managing staff or volunteers is a complex and involved process. Having competent staff and procedures in place to help them develop makes for a great program, to be sure. It will also make your job as an intramural director easier. The following four questions will help you review the contents of this chapter and apply it to your intramural program.

1. Do you remember school staff (teachers, secretaries) volunteering for intramural activities at schools you attended? If so, what did they contribute? If not, why do you think they did not want to be involved? Also note some highlights of staff involvement in an intramural program. After reflecting on your responses, how would you run these programs differently to attract volunteer help?

2. Draft a departmental flowchart that would suit your institution. Determine how many different posititons and people you need and arrange them in a hierarchical format according to who reports to whom.

3. Set up a mock interview for an intramural staff position and ask fellow students to play

Evaluator name: _____	Name of convener: _____		
Is enthusiastic	Yes	No	Not sure
Observation:			
Maintains self-control	Yes	No	Not sure
Observation:			
Models principles of sport conduct	Yes	No	Not sure
Observation:			
Enforces policies consistently	Yes	No	Not sure
Observation:			
Provides adequate notice when making schedule changes	Yes	No	Not sure
Observation:			

(continued)

FIGURE 4.7 Participant's evaluation form.

Attends to participants who disrupt the activity	Yes	No	Not sure
Observation:			

Emphasizes safety during participation	Yes	No	Not sure
Observation:			

Appears well organized	Yes	No	Not sure
Observation:			

Appears knowledgeable about the activity	Yes	No	Not sure
Observation:			

Evaluator, please indicate

Gender_____ Grade/year_____ Major_____

Adapted, by permission, from J. Kestner, 1996, *Program evaluation for sports directors* (Champaign, IL: Human Kinetics), 45-52.

FIGURE 4.7   *(continued)*

Supervisor name: _____	Name of convener: _____
Safety	**1 = very bad; 5 = Very Good**
Inspects equipment for hazards Observations:	1 2 3 4 5 Not sure
Removes hazards from contest area Observations:	1 2 3 4 5 Not sure
Adapts to environmental (i.e., weather) hazards appropriately Observations:	1 2 3 4 5 Not sure
Warns participants of inherent risks of activities Observations:	1 2 3 4 5 Not sure
Allows adequate warm-up prior to contest Observations:	1 2 3 4 5 Not sure
Matches participant skill levels Observations:	1 2 3 4 5 Not sure
Attends to injured participants quickly Observations:	1 2 3 4 5 Not sure

(continued)

FIGURE 4.8   Supervisor's evaluation form.

Duty Proficiency	1 = very bad; 5 = Very Good
Displays enthusiasm Observations:	1 2 3 4 5 Not sure
Interacts with participants in a professional manner Observations:	1 2 3 4 5 Not sure
Remains poised in unexpected situations Observations:	1 2 3 4 5 Not sure
Demonstrates adequate knowledge of activity Observations:	1 2 3 4 5 Not sure
Administrative Competence	1 = very bad; 5 = Very Good
Manages conflict effectively Observations:	1 2 3 4 5 Not sure
Follows through with promises (prizes, officials, etc.) Observations:	1 2 3 4 5 Not sure
Professional Growth	1 = very bad; 5 = Very Good
Interacts with colleagues in a professional manner Observations:	1 2 3 4 5 Not sure

FIGURE 4.8 (continued)

Interacts with participants in professional manner   1 2 3 4 5 Not sure

Observations:

Attends required meetings   1 2 3 4 5 Not sure

Observations:

Submits budgets on time   1 2 3 4 5 Not sure

Observations:

Keeps accurate records   1 2 3 4 5 Not sure

Observations:

Conducts effective meetings with coaches and officials   1 2 3 4 5 Not sure

Observations:

Keeps administrators appropriately informed   1 2 3 4 5 Not sure

Observations:

Takes responsibility for actions   1 2 3 4 5 Not sure

Observations:

Supervises staff (officials) appropriately   1 2 3 4 5 Not sure

Observations:

Adapted, by permission, from J. Kestner, 1996, *Program evaluation for sports directors* (Champaign, IL: Human Kinetics), 45-52.

FIGURE 4.8   *(continued)*

the candidates. Develop a sample job description and then create an outline for the interview. Have your classmates observe the interview, then have them vote on which candidate they would hire for each position. Which leadership skills did each candidate demonstrate? Following the interviews, ask for feedback about how you led the interview.

4. Have small groups of students discuss the problem-solving scenarios in this chapter (pages 51-52) while the rest of the class observes. Then vote on whom they would hire for certain positions. Which leadership skills did each of the participants demonstrate?

5. Select a staff member who supervises others, and develop five ways they can encourage those they are supervising.

References

Brudney, J. 1990. *Fostering volunteer programs in the public sector.* San Francisco: Jossey-Bass.

Ellis, Susan J. 1994. *The volunteer recruitment book.* Philadelphia: Energize.

Kestner, J. 1996. *Program evaluation for sport directors.* Champaign, Ill.: Human Kinetics.

Mann, T. 1999. Volunteer recognition. *Recreation Saskatchewan* 26 (8): 3

May, S. 2000. Volunteering—Back to basics. *Profile* (June/July): 3

Murray, C. 1995. Dealing with conflict. [Online]. Available: www.lin.ca/lin/resource/html/bramp3.htm.

Peng, S. 1997. The leadership challenge. *The Leader* 5 (4): 1. Used by permission of the Canadian Intramural Recreation Association.

Resources

Books

Perry, H. 1999. *Call to order—Meeting rules and procedures for non-profit organizations.* Owen Sound, Ontario: Big Bay Publishing.

Offers a simplified approach to running meetings.

Robert, H., S. Robert, and W. Evans, eds. 1991. *Robert's rules of order newly revised.* 9th ed. New York: Perseus.

The most common "rule book" for effective and formal meeting procedures. There is also a Web site for *Robert's Rules of Order* (www.robertsrules.com/).

Web Sites and Organizations

Bloomington Parks and Recreation
401 N. Morton Street, Suite 250
Bloomington, IN 47404
Phone: 812-349-3700
Website: www.city.bloomington.in.us/parks/
E-mail: parks@city.bloomington.in.us

Canadian Association of Student Activity Advisors
Web site: http://www.casaa-resources.net/

A great resource for leadership ideas. Its mission is to promote and develop student leadership and activities within Canadian high schools. The Web site offers helpful resources, newsletters, and links, as well as an excellent section to share ideas for grade and high schools.

Canadian Intramural Recreation Association (CIRA)
740-B Belfast Road
Ottawa, Ontario Canada K1G 0Z5
Telephone: 613-244-1594
Fax: 613-244-4738
Web site: www.intramurals.ca
E-mail: cira@intramurals.ca

Offers members a quarterly newsletter for student leaders (*The Leader*). Also offers three practical student leadership guides that provide practical information, activities, and worksheets on how to start a leadership group and develop leadership skills, including teamwork (*Elementary Teacher's Guide*, 1999; *Secondary Guide*, 1998; and *Post-Secondary Student Leadership Development Guide*, 1998).

EffectiveMeetings.com
http://www.effectivemeetings.com/

A fun, lively Web site offering advice on effective meetings in the workplace, advice that can just as easily be applied to intramural meetings, plus an opportunity to get a free subscription.

The Leisure Information Network
www.lin.ca

Provides sample job descriptions for program positions (not to mention postings in the field of recreation). Also offers excellent guidelines on working with volunteers (do a keyword search on "volunteers" and "guidelines").

TxServe
http://www.txserve.org/

A Texas-based organization designed to strengthen volunteerism. Its Web site provides great information and links to important information about effectively leading volunteers and using them in an intramural program.

The Officials

They're the people on the court or ice rink or field in black-and-white stripes, or the ones in black with large pads covering their chests behind home plate. They are often loved by one side and loathed by the other, or vice versa, at any point in the game. They are heckled, jeered at, argued with, screamed at, and ridiculed. Nevertheless, they are critical to a successful, effective intramural game. Why? Officials are often the only ones working on the front lines to ensure safety and fun in a competition. As intramural directors, then, it will be your job to attract competent officials to your program, and then keep them. This chapter will help you do just that.

Chapter Objectives

- ▶ Explore different ways to create an official-friendly program.
- ▶ Understand the key components of officiating.
- ▶ Learn how to attract, manage, and evaluate intramural officials.

The Role of Officials

Think back to your own intramural experiences. Do you remember pick-up and other informal games on the grade school playground or in the high school or college gym? They probably worked fine without a referee. Games like these are meant to be a playful game, emphasizing the spirit of play and fun, and that's how participants probably played it. Indeed, if all players cooperate, that's how intramural games should be played.

Intramural pick-up games of basketball, recreational volleyball, and Ping-Pong should work without referees. In fact, students calling their own games develops honesty, cooperation, and personal responsibility. Sometimes, the presence of officials simply places the responsibility for adhering to the rules on someone else's shoulders, and it seems to encourage arguing about calls. Besides, officials cost money, and organizing and training them takes time. So if intramural participation is about fun, why not have all games self-officiated? Because in practice, games do not always work well without officials.

Many games, even playground games, break down when no one is enforcing the rules. Children get nasty and aggressive toward each other. Players new to the game or sport are often less familiar with the rules. Spirits and adrenaline run high when more is at stake, such as in playoff and championship games. When bodies are bumping into each other, players are quick to anger. Sometimes equipment is used improperly, resulting in damage to the equipment or injury to participants. In other words, officials play a key role in intramural games, particularly competitive sport and athletic games. They not only protect the safety of the participants but also ensure a fair and enjoyable experience for all.

Officials also benefit by participating in intramurals. Officiating provides the opportunity to make new friends. It develops such leadership qualities as patience, self-confidence, and the ability to deal with stressful situations, make tough decisions, and deal with criticism. These skills are helpful not only in one's career but also in life. By participating in intramurals, officials also benefit physically, especially in sports such as ice hockey and soccer, which provide an excellent opportunity to stay in shape. Not

only that, but they get the best seats in the house, so to speak, enjoying a close-up view of the game and getting to feel the excitement of the players. For those who love the sport they are officiating, these benefits alone would be enough. But officiating provides other important opportunities—namely, the opportunity to give something back to a sport or an organization they love, earn partial course credits for refereeing (if they are students), and earn some pocket money.

There are a variety of officials in intramurals. A league convener oversees the entire league, including the officiating. The officials include the referees (in sports like basketball and soccer) or the umpires (in sports like baseball) who ensure that the game is played by the rules. If a league has many referees or umpires, the convener may select a head official or head umpire to oversee the officiating. Referees and umpires serve as major officials, and those that assist by keeping score or watching the lines serve as minor officials. The major focus of this chapter is to assist major officials in doing their jobs well.

As described at the beginning of this chapter, refereeing isn't always easy. Public critiques of an official's work can be harsh: "What?! Are you blind?" "Read the rulebook, why don't you!" and "Are you in a hurry to go home?" Public scrutiny alone can impel some officials to quit, and often not even to try it. But there are other reasons. The top three complaints from referees are:

▶ verbal abuse from participants,

▶ little reward for hard work, and

▶ lack of support from the administration.

Creating an Official-Friendly Program

The good news is, as intramural directors, you can do a lot to make the experience of officiating more positive. For starters, ongoing training does much to make officials feel more competent and comfortable on the court, field, or rink. In fact, training will likely reduce the number of bad calls they make and, subsequently, the verbal abuse they suffer. Supporting officials is also important, in terms of providing professional uniforms and acknowledging and reward-

The Role of Competent Officiating in an Intramural Program

Mr. Arbiter ran an intramural basketball program, but participation numbers had steadily decreased over the last few years. As he sat in the gymnasium watching two intramural games on separate courts, he wondered why. His thought process was interrupted when one of the games stopped.

Two players began shouting about what did and did not constitute a foul. Soon several teammates stepped in to stop the fight that was about to erupt. Mr. Arbiter walked over to the players, calmed them down, and explained the type of foul in question. Play resumed after a two-minute interruption.

As he went back to his seat, Mr. Arbiter resumed his thought process. Maybe a lack of advertising had decreased participation, or maybe it was just that students were not interested in basketball anymore. He had just sat down when the same group of players stopped play again. Frustration high and tempers flaring, they were trying to resolve another difference of opinion. At that point, Mr. Arbiter decided to referee the rest of that game. Some of the players disagreed with a few calls, but for the most part, the rest of the game went smoothly. At the end of the game, several players asked Mr. Arbiter if he could referee their next game.

As he was driving home, he went through the evening in his mind. He recalled how frustrated the players were before he stepped in. He thought to himself, "There is no way I would want to play in a game like that." Then he remembered how much the players enjoyed the game after he started to referee. "Aha!" It dawned on him why participation numbers might be down.

The next day at school, Mr. Arbiter found a couple of referee shirts. He asked a few players from the advanced league if they would like to be referees. He told the students that he would train them and, if they got good enough, hire them to be scorekeepers for varsity games. Several students accepted his offer. After some basic training in officiating, these students officiated the intramural basketball games, and ended up making some extra money as varsity scorekeepers.

Mr. Arbiter attended several of the officiated basketball games and noticed that the spirit of competition improved significantly when officials were inserted onto the basketball court. Players were happier, there were fewer stoppages in play, and everyone enjoyed the game. It was too early to tell, but Mr. Arbiter was convinced that with this new climate on the court, more people would get excited about intramural basketball. He anticipated that his participation numbers would begin to climb again. Even if the numbers didn't improve, however, Mr. Arbiter took comfort in knowing that the experience for the participants would be much better than it had been.

Reprinted by permission of the Canadian Intramural Recreation Association. From M. Boyles, 1996, "On officials, fair play, and otherwise sunny days," *CIRA Bulletin* 22 (3):3-5.

ing their contributions. Many officials participate in intramurals for the love of sport. But even in these situations, it is wise to reward them. In addition to formal compensation, rewards can include such incentives as participation points, a pizza party at the end of a season, an officials club, free access to the gym or a monthly "officials gym time," special awards at annual banquets, certificates of participation, gift certificates for local restaurants or theaters, discount tickets to local events, and so on.

Training

Whether you use volunteer student officials or hire professionals, all officiated activities and games—not to mention your intramural program—will benefit if you offer training in officiating. Training will help officials competently and prudently enforce the rules while maintaining a fun, rewarding experience for all participants. Having two or more officials at all intramural events will best enable the officials to make the best calls. To teach referees how to work well together, consider offering clinics and instructional seminars on such topics as common courtesy to fellow officials, effective positioning, and individual responsibilities when working on a team. In addition, the basic standards of officiating should be taught to all officials when they join your program and throughout their tenure.

What are the essential ingredients of officiating training? The following criteria are generally considered to be most important. Officials must

- know the rules;
- be confident in their decision making;
- be consistent;
- be decisive in their calls;
- position themselves effectively on the court, rink, or field;
- use proper and authoritative signals when making a call;
- be objective; and
- maintain a professional appearance.

Know the Rules

To be effective, officials must know the rules. As explained in chapter 1, rules define a competitive game. Thus, officials need to know the rules if the game is to be played as it is intended. Intramural directors can help officials in this regard by

- keeping the rules simple;
- providing a copy of game rules to each official prior to a game;
- explaining and demonstrating rules to officials;
- posting official rules prominently in or near the playing area (a central intramural bulletin board is also an ideal location for prominent posting of official game rules);
- distributing copies of the rules to team captains at the start of each season; and

- testing officials on and off the court.

This last suggestion—testing officials on their knowledge of the rules—should be part of an overall training or official-certification program. If they do not pass, they do not officiate.

Be Confident

Referees need to be poised and confident in their decision making. If aggressive or overly tense players excite an official, consistency and calmness are unlikely to occur. This situation only adds to the tension of a competitive game. As the game heats up, officials must stay cool. When officials "lose their heads," their judgment is blurred and their calls will be questioned or criticized more often. Officials who fly into a rage will lose respect from players and negatively affect the game. You, as intramural directors, can assist your officials by encouraging them to

- enforce penalties calmly and with confidence;
- give players a warning and then penalize them for unsportsmanlike behavior (e.g., foul language, taunting, and threatening with violence); and
- use positive self-talk.

Be Consistent

Consistency is something players value highly in officials. Players need to know where the referee "draws the line," both figuratively and literally. For example, the size of the strike zone in baseball typically varies from official to official. It cannot, however, vary from player to player. If the strike zone is four inches above and below one batter's shoulders and waist, it cannot be eight inches above and below the next batter's shoulders and waist. Likewise, if an umpire puts up with abuse from one player or team captain, team morale and players' attitudes will likely plummet if the same type of language results in another player's being thrown out of the game.

As intramural directors, you can help your officials to be consistent in their calls by encouraging them to

- think about the rules before the start of game;
- defining ahead of time what they will and will not tolerate;

▶ apply their decisions fairly and evenly; and

▶ remain focused and relaxed.

Be Decisive

Being decisive is another important criteria for an official. An official who hesitates is lost. A delayed or indecisive call makes a referee appear uncertain. In fact, hesitation usually increases the number of infractions and results in an official losing control of the game. Officials must make the calls on time. On the other hand, being too hasty can also lead to problems. For example, in baseball it may appear that a runner is out, a call is hastily made when the ball contacts the glove, but the ball falls out of the glove, making the runner safe.

Likewise, changing a call based on jeers or cheers of participants and spectators is never a good idea. A referee's credibility is completely shot if he does not "call it as he sees it." If spectators and players realize they can sway a referee's decision, they will be more boisterous and make the task of officiating even more difficult.

As intramural directors, you can assist your officials in being decisive by encouraging them to

▶ be quick but not hasty in their calls;

▶ use authority without grandstanding; and

▶ learn the rules of the game so they are confident in their decisions.

Position Effectively

Effective positioning is an official's best bet for making accurate calls. If there is a close call at first base and the official was approximately 3 meters from the bag, for example, players will be less likely to question the call than if the official were 5 meters away and didn't hustle to get into a better position. You, as intramural directors, can assist your officials to position effectively by encouraging them to

▶ practice positioning on their own or during team practices;

▶ hustle throughout the game;

▶ anticipate where the play is going but not anticipate the call; and

▶ when they are in position to do so, call them as they see them.

Use Proper and Authoritative Signals

An official should signal calls with authority but not with pomposity. Signals can be made with a whistle, voice, gesture, or a combination of the three. Signals should be sharp, unhesitating, and unhurried. For example, a crisply blown whistle gives the perception that the official meant the call, not that the call was a guess. As intramural directors, you can assist your officials in using signals properly and authoritatively by encouraging them to

▶ learn the signals;

▶ practice voice projection so that a call is firm and loud enough to be heard (but not obnoxiously so); and

▶ build self-confidence so that they are certain about their calls and, thus, authoritative when they make them.

Be Objective

Officials must be objective. Officials must not be influenced or be perceived as being influenced by factors other than the way the game is being played. Officials are human beings. Their objectivity can be affected by such things as personal relationships with players or a personal stake in a game, grudges or memories of bad experiences with certain players or teams, and even personal crises or circumstances in their own lives. You, as intramural directors, can help your officials remain objective by

▶ not assigning them to games in which their objectivity might be compromised (e.g., refereeing an interdepartmental game between colleagues);

▶ not discriminating against players on the basis of race, gender, or other personal characteristics;

▶ encouraging them to call the game as it is played, not as they think it should be played or want it to be played;

▶ getting to know them and being sensitive to what is going on in their personal lives; and

▶ offering stress-management classes or training so that they are not affected by the score, the time remaining, or players' reactions and behavior.

Maintain a Professional Appearance

The saying that perception is reality holds true in most of life's settings and circumstances. Intramural competitions are no different. An official's appearance will influence participants' opinions of the official, the event or game, and even the intramural program itself. As intramural directors, you can assist your officials in maintaining a professional appearance by

- providing professional uniforms;
- enforcing dress codes and standards of appearance (i.e., hair length, jewelry, appropriate attire in addition to the uniform provided, and so on); and
- modeling a professional appearance yourself, thereby reinforcing the importance of positive image to the clients.

People Skills

You may recall past intramural experiences when a referee knew the rules but did not have good people skills, or the opposite, of a referee with good people skills not knowing the rules. In both cases, the result is participant frustration.

Some officials may be technically knowledgeable and proficient at officiating a sport, but if they lack interpersonal skills, they will run into many difficulties. Indeed, according to Jason Geiger, the intramural and recreational assistant director at the University of North Carolina at Charlotte, "Customer relations are probably the most important role of the official" (Geiger 1997, 13).

A good official knows how to relate to players, team captains, spectators, and fellow officials. In addition to providing training in these areas, intramural directors can also help officials to improve their people skills in general. Talk to them about showing respect by being amiable, cooperative, patient, and understanding in an emotional environment such as a competitive game. Teach them to be wise and diplomatic. The following areas should be discussed often with officials. Better yet, incorporate these skills into your officiating training program. Officials should

- answer *reasonable* questions before, during, and after a game (this means that some questions do not have to be answered). They should be approachable and recep-

tive to such questions but not let unnecessary or questions designed to stall a game bog down the action.
- be diplomatic when tensions rise and the game heats up. If players become irritated, as will often be the case in a competitive or aggressive game, or when there is a lot at stake, officials must avoid adding fuel to the fire.
- maintain a professional distance from players. Officials must avoid getting into arguments at all costs, both to stay calm themselves and to keep the game moving.
- not tolerate any form of abuse. A certain amount of anger is healthy, as long as it is expressed respectfully. Empower officials to nip unsportsmanlike conduct in the bud by ejecting players immediately.
- be patient with, or ignore, spectators. Remind officials that spectators do not always know the official game rules, may be biased toward (or against) a team or invested in the outcome of a game, and may even delight in antagonizing officials. Teach them stress and anger management as well as conflict resolution to deal with these situations.

Minorities

In terms of being objective, a referee cannot allow a person's gender, skin color, or any other factor affect her officiating. The official cannot allow herself to harass or discriminate against anyone for any of the above reasons, and not allow the players to do so either. Any players, coaches, or spectators who harass anyone on account of such things as gender or skin color should be removed from the playing area and a report written up about the nature of the harassment.

Compensation

As mentioned in chapter 4, people will continue to do something if the benefits outweigh the costs. For officials, the benefits include getting to participate in a sport they love, being involved in a physically active hobby, forming new friendships, and so on. Nevertheless, some institutions pay their officials, particularly at the collegiate level. Most universities use a graduated pay scale for officials, with pay depending on their experience, the number of training clinics they have attended (some of these clinics are mandatory for intramural officials, and some intramural programs pay officials to attend these clinics), and official certification. Other institutions use a different pay scale for each sport, with compensation depending on the potential for injury, necessary preparation, length of games, physical requirements of the game, time between games (in the case of a tournament), skills required (such as skating in ice hockey), and evaluation ratings (discussed later in this chapter). Some institutions also offer bonuses at the end of a season, usually based on participants' evaluations. Finally, many institutions provide a travel allowance for off-campus games.

The compensation you offer to officials will depend on your intramural budget, of course, but it's important that you plan for this ahead of time. It is wise to establish a pay scale that is consistently applied to everyone based on their certifications, experience, and the type of sport being officiated. Having higher pay for those who are certified officials and have more experience encourages those who do not have their certification to acquire it, and for those who have experience to continue to referee. The benefit of this pay scheme is that it provides incentives for referees to improve themselves. The benefit to the program is that participants should experience better officiating.

Official Duties

Before we discuss the specifics of where to find officials, how to recruit them, and specific official evaluation techniques, it's best to get an idea of what an official does. The following sections explain an official's duties in detail, including specifics of ensuring safety, dealing with players during the heat of a game, and handling overly aggressive or abusive players.

Safety Management

First and foremost, officials are on hand to protect the safety of participants. It is therefore important for intramural directors to help officials understand their role in preventing injuries and help effectively deal with injuries should they

occur. For a more detailed look at developing safety policies, see chapter 7.

To prevent injuries, officials should do a quick check before each game to make sure that the playing area is safe. This includes looking for such hazards as potholes and broken glass on an outdoor field, large bumps or cracks in the ice, obstructions or debris on the court or field, and so on. Ensuring that adequate protective padding is provided, such as on volleyball poles and soccer nets, is also part of a pre-game safety check. Should an official deem the site unsafe, they must be empowered to delay the game until all hazards have been removed.

Officials should also observe the players before a game. If any players are under the influence of drugs or alcohol, they should not be allowed to compete. Likewise, mandatory safety equipment should be checked before a game, including shin guards, body padding, helmets, and proper footwear. Players should be asked to remove any jewelry that could potentially injure someone, including necklaces, watches, dangling earrings, hair combs, and so on. Rule 4 Section 2 Article 4 of the *National Federation of State High School Associations 1999-2000 Rule Book for Soccer* states: "Players shall not wear jewelry with the exception of medical bracelets or medical metals. Metal medals and medical bracelets must be taped to the body with medical data visible" (Flanery 1999, 15). The *NCAA Soccer Rulebook* is even more specific, disallowing any and all "jewelry such as earrings, chains, charms, and hairclips" (National Collegiate Athletic Association 1999, 27).

Weather can also be a safety risk. Thus, officials should stop an outdoor game when the threat of lightning or other severe weather is imminent (see chapter 7 for more detail on lightning policies). Even in the case of heavy rain, an official may need to make a judgment call to stop the game because the water is making the contest unsafe. Indoor playing areas also carry the potential for player injury. When participants fall and leave sweat on the floor, or when water is spilled, for example, these areas should be wiped up before play resumes.

During the game, of course, officials must be on constant watch for potential hazards and unsafe play. They also need to use the whistle efficiently to stop play immediately. If a whistle is not blown soon enough, injuries may occur.

To use and example from ice hockey, a player may be clearly off-sides and sees the referee making the call, she lets up a little in anticipation of the call only to receive an unsuspected body check from an opposing player who is playing till the whistle blows. Officials should also control rough play. Players may be so focused on the contest or may be so inexperienced at competing in the game that they unintentionally play dangerously. Stopping play and calming everyone down or imposing minor penalties may solve the problem. Intentional unsafe or unsportsmanlike behavior, however, should be immediately penalized. If continued, the offending player should be ejected from the game. When training your officials in safety management, teach them to err on the side of safety.

Of course, safety management also includes officials watching out for themselves. Before games such as soccer, floor hockey, and basketball, which require a lot of running, officials should warm up by stretching before the game. Wearing suitable footwear is also advisable. When officiating in such sports as ice hockey, officials should wear a protective helmet. When officiating in a warm environment, officials should ensure that they eat a low-fat, high-protein meal a couple hours before game time, wear cotton or other breathable clothing, and consume adequate amounts of water before and during the game. When officiating in the sun, officials should wear a hat and sunscreen, and perhaps sunglasses, and in breaks in the action, officials should seek out shade. Effective positioning during a game will also ensure their personal safety. Most important, perhaps, officials should be encouraged to take care of themselves physically by undergoing physical conditioning and stress-reduction training.

Even with all these preventative measures, injuries will still occur. As intramural directors, it will be your responsibility to train your officials in emergency first aid and procedures. While officials should not be expected to be medical experts, providing basic training in first aid is helpful. Likewise, equip them with bandages and proper medical supplies so that they are prepared. An important part of basic medical training is crisis training. When under acute stress, as would be the case in the event of serious injury, for example, it is not uncommon to panic, hyperventilate, feel dizzy or faint, experience tunnel vision, and even lose touch with reality. Officials should be educated about these symptoms and be told how to regain their composure. In many cases, simply breathing into your cupped hands for a moment, which increases the level of carbon dioxide in the blood, is enough.

A medical training program is beyond the scope of this book, of course. Instead, plan and incorporate basic medical training into your officiating training. You might contact a local clinic or hospital about conducting a monthly or semi-annual seminar for officials. At the very least, should a participant be injured in a contest, an official's first responsibility is to stop play immediately to prevent further injury. Then, officials must contact properly trained medical personnel immediately. Because time can be critical in certain injuries, it is extremely important that officials be trained in basic emergency response and know the location of the nearest telephone. Then, officials should be prepared to do the following.

- Ensure that the injured person is safe and comfortable.
- Do not move the injured participant until the injury has been diagnosed and medical personnel are sure that moving the participant will not aggravate the injury.
- Although it is not their responsibility to apply first aid, if no one else is available, officials should administer first aid to the best of their ability (this ability will be improved with training).
- If an injury is life threatening, ensure adequate breathing and apply direct pressure to the bleeding area. Then get help, stay calm, and think clearly. If possible, appoint someone else to call or go for help.
- Delay or cancel the game if necessary.
- Create space around an injured participant and prevent others from crowding the victim.

After the incident (once the injured party has been attended to) or after the game (if it is continued after an injury), officials should complete an accident report form like the one shown in figure 5.1 and return it to the intramural office. Outlining all necessary information should problems develop later, this form provides space

Accident/Incident Report Form

(In the case of accident or injury, please complete and submit within 24 hours to Human Resources)

Name: _____ Date of Birth (M/D/Y): ___/___/___

Current Address: _____ Telephone: (H) _____

_____ (W) _____

Check all applicable:
Staff/Faculty ____ Guest/Member ____ Student ____ Male ____ Female ____

Check off the type of activity you were engaged in when the injury took place

Recreational (includes squash, weights, aerobics, general gym) ____ Varsity ____

Intramurals ____ Club ____

Date of the incident (M/D/Y): ___/___/___ Time of the incident: _____ am/pm

Location of the incident: _____

Describe the nature of the incident/injury and exactly how it occurred:

_____

_____

_____

Were you taken to the hospital? Yes ____ No ____

If Yes, which hospital? _____

Is follow-up care/treatment required? Yes ____ No ____

If Yes, please describe: _____

Witness name: _____ Recreation staff on duty: _____

Telephone: _____ Signature: _____

Signature: _____

_____ _____
Signature of individual filling in report Date

FIGURE 5.1 Sample form to report accidents or injuries.

to describe the accident and the injury, record actions taken, and provide relevant information about the injured party and any witnesses present.

Dealing With Inappropriate Behavior

One of the best ways to prevent injury, of course, is stopping inappropriate behavior before it escalates into a hazardous situation. It is your job, as intramural directors, to help your officials reduce the potential for violence in a game and also help them to deal with violence should it occur. The first step is creating a positive, nonconfrontational atmosphere by officiating effectively, fairly, consistently, and so on. Officials must listen to players. If a player reports that another player is "elbowing me all the time," and the official responds, "I'm here to call the game, not baby-sit," the official will be inviting players to take "the law into their own hands."

Officials should observe players and immediately warn or penalize players who are taunting other players. This includes observing body language, gestures, glaring or other aggressive stares, and overly excited or sporadic movement. If certain players are determined to cause trouble, an official may be able to defuse the situation with diplomatic humor, a firm warning, a minor penalty, a cooling-off period, and perhaps a yellow warning card. Officials should not provoke players or look for reasons to issue such a card, however. Ultimately, if the players persist in obnoxious behavior, officials should not hesitate to issue a red card and eject the offending players from the game.

If a game starts to get rough, officials can also stop the game and talk to the team captains. Team captains can be warned that the game will be stopped unless their players calm down and can be given up to a minute to talk to their teams. The game can be restarted if the official feels the participants have sufficiently calmed down. If the game starts to get out of control again, the official may need to call the game and report the incident to the person in charge (i.e., a convener or the intramural director). In such situations, officials should not make any statements to players other than declaring that the game has been called and the decision of the game is in the hands of the convener.

If there is a fight, officials should eject offending players immediately. If officials are close enough to the offending players just before a fight erupts, a sudden whistle or a loud "Cool it!" may provide sufficient time for the officials to get between players before any fists are thrown. Once a fight has begun, however, officials should not try to step in and get between fighting players. Instead, officials should first isolate the fight by having all other players go back to their benches. Then it may be helpful to enlist the team captains to separate the players (always approaching them from behind and pulling their arms back). After a fight, offending players should be escorted from the playing area one at a time.

Player Abuse

In the case of fights, hostility or tension, and aggression between players, officials often become the target. At best, they are likely to be called names; at worst, officials could be attacked physically. Indeed, one of the major reasons officials quit is that they have suffered player abuse. Such abuse typically evolves out of a game that gets out of control, which usually evolves out of ineffective or lack of officiating training. One of the best ways to protect officials from player abuse, then, is to strictly adhere to disciplinary standards for the program (Geiger 1997, 14).

What can officials do to dissuade unsportsmanlike behavior that oftentimes escalates into player abuse? According to Mike Boyles (1996), there are four steps.

Step 1: Educate. Offer your officiating staff instructional clinics and training about interpersonal skills during the game. For example, teach them to first recognize problem situations and deal with them before they become a larger problem. Then teach them techniques for dealing with a difficult situation or an abusive participant. Shouting back at a participant will not help alleviate the situation. Likewise, educate officials about respect: As Doc Rivers, veteran player of the Los Angeles Clippers and current coach of the Miami Magic, says, "A referee who shows respect gets respect."

Step 2: Advocate. Develop a program that advocates fair play and sportsmanlike conduct. The University of Calgary, for example, rewards sportsmanship and fair play instead of winning. Rather than award prizes for winning a league, the "best sports" get prizes. In fact, the program is called Fair Play. Throughout the season, teams are rated according to how well they adhere to Fair Play standards, which are posted prominently and communicated to all participants at the start of each season. Teams with a fair play rating of at least 3.25 (out of a possible 5), for example, are eligible for playoffs regardless of their standing in the league. To ensure consistent results, team captains and officials determine Fair Play points after each game. (See chapter 6 for a complete discussion of fair play.)

Step 3: Discipline. Along with advocating sportsmanship and fair play in your program goes the task of discouraging and disciplining bad sportsmanship and inappropriate behavior. To do that, you must have disciplinary policies and procedures in place. Disciplinary procedures must be documented and consistently followed. Of course, disciplinary policies must also allow the flexibility for officials to use discretion. For example, removing a hothead for a portion of a game is preferable to ejecting that player at the first sign of frustration. Likewise, developing a rapport with players will help to alleviate animosity during the game.

Disciplinary procedures should be progressive. For example, if players on a particular team habitually engage in unsportsmanlike conduct, it may be neccssary to suspend them, or their team captain, for a portion of the season. Such consequences are sure to get players' attention. It is also wise to incorporate a formal appeals process into disciplinary policies. Players should not feel victimized or that they have been singled out unfairly. (See chapter 13 for a full discussion of suspensions, including the appeals process.)

Step 4: Reward. In any competitive setting, participants are working toward a goal. In the case of intramural competitions, that goal is usually the championship trophy. As explained in step 2, the University of Calgary rewards teams for sportsmanship and fair play—not winning. This reward system lets players know at the outset what they should be striving to achieve. Rewards can include such items as intramural T-shirts, plaques, discount tickets, and so on.

Officiating and the Law

Officials have a legal responsibility to provide a safe game for participants, which is outlined in chapter 7, Policy II: Safety. They also have certain rights. For example, officials have the right to wear a beard, even if your dress code or standards of professional appearance discourage the practice. In certain cases, officials have been awarded monetary damages for defamatory comments made by a participant or physical injury they suffered while officiating. The details and considerations of these legalities are beyond the scope of this book. Thus, it is a good idea to get the advice of legal counsel in planning the officiating component of your intramural program. It may also be helpful to draw up a contract between officials and your institution.

Official Recruitment

Now that the roles and general responsibilities of an intramural official are understood, it's time to figure out how to recruit competent officials to your program. As explained in chapter 4, students often volunteer to officiate their favorite sports. In addition, however, you will need other places to recruit officials. Some schools ask that each team provide an official. The risk with this approach is that the officials may not be of the highest caliber. In sports such as ice hockey, a weak official may contribute to players getting injured. Having teams provide their own officials needs to be used with considerable discretion. Other schools form an officiating club to attract and train potential student officials. Some schools cannot get enough competent officials from within the school system and turn to state and provincial referee associations. These associations provide certified officials and will probably provide the safest conditions for players, but they will usually cost more to hire than students.

As explained at the beginning of this chapter, creating an official-friendly program is a surefire way to recruit competent, eager officials. That may not be enough, however. To attract competent officials, you'll need to promote your program. Advertise in local sports clubs, throughout the school, in student and local newspapers, and so on. Word-of-mouth advertising is also extremely helpful. Officials talk to one another. Hearing about what a great program you have will likely bring qualified officials to your door. (See chapter 8 for a complete discussion of promoting an intramural program.)

Providing incentives and rewards also helps to attract competent officials. If you are using a house system, for example, you could award a participation point each time a house member officiates a game. Select an "official of the week" (or month or year) and publicly thank or recognize that official's effort on an intramural bulletin board or other display case located centrally in the school. Statements of thanks in the school newspaper and at the awards banquet also provide incentive for officials.

When hiring officials, be sure they are made aware of the mission statement for your intramural program. This will help them officiate in a manner that supports the goals of the program. Provide them with pre-game and postgame checklists (figures 5.2 and 5.3) and review the contents with the new officials. Give the officials other relevant paperwork including such items as an officiating schedule, compensation schedules, and any relevant rulebooks. Inform them who is supervising their work should they need to speak to someone about concerns they have with their work or the intramural program.

When officials are assisted in doing their jobs well, they are more likely to stay on as officials. Conveners or head officials should train officials as outlined in the preceding part of this chapter. They should also be helped in setting personal goals to improve their officiating skills and given opportunities for professional growth through attending officiating clinics. If possible, it is helpful to encourage officials to dialogue with each other. Creating a listserv just for officials may be one way to do this. Perhaps of greater importance to officials than regular employees is instruction in conflict resolution. Chapter 4 provides several important suggestions that should be stressed with officials. Be sure to recognize the general contributions that officials make as well as the exceptional contributions that some officials make (most games refereed in the season, top official as rated by the participants, or the official that took the most training in a season).

Official Positions

Officiating entails more than standing on a court and blowing a whistle. Officials need to get things ready before a game, accomplish certain functions during the game, and perform several duties after a game. These responsibilities vary by the type of official and are identified in the next two sections by position: major officials and minor officials.

Major Officials

Major officials such as referees and umpires do not begin their responsibilities at the first whistle nor end at the final whistle. Rather, referees are usually responsible for such things as checking that the playing site is safe and that everything is ready to start the game on time and in a positive manner. To help referees understand and accomplish their specific duties, it is helpful to provide them with checklists like those shown in figures 5.2 and 5.3. These forms outline each responsibility and action required to accomplish it.

Minor Officials—Timers and Scorekeepers

Timers and scorekeepers also contribute to the overall success of an intramural competition. Typically one person can carry out the timing and scorekeeping responsibilities for an intramural contest. Such a person's responsibilities, outlined in figure 5.4, include gathering necessary equipment before the game, keeping track of the score, handing in equipment after a game, completing the game sheet (see figure 13.3), distributing official evaluation forms to players, and turning in the results of the game to the appropriate intramural staff.

Code of Ethics

Regardless of official position, there is a standard of conduct for all officials. Published by the U.S. National Association of Sports Officials, the code of ethics shown in figure 5.5 provides some important guidelines for officials. As intramural directors, it will be your job to communicate these standards and ensure that your officials follow them. It would probably be a good idea to provide a copy of this code to all official hirees.

Pregame Checklist

Responsibility	Action/Consideration	✓
Arrive early	Depends on the game, but 15 minutes early is usually desired.	
Check facility	Is playing area safe?	
	Are there any special rules? (If the team does not meet intramural standards [e.g. if the team does not have enough women for a co-ed game], the official must cancel the game and award a forfeit to the offending team.)	
	Is all necessary equipment on hand?	
Observe participants.	Are participants competing at the same level? Observe for different levels and ensure everyone's safety by your calls (sometimes stopping play even when there is no foul in order to avoid injury).	
	How important is the game (play-off, championship, etc.)?	
	Have players adequately warmed up?	
	Are team lists (score sheets, etc.) in order?	
Define officiating responsibilities.	If more than one referee will be officiating, have responsibilities been clearly defined?	
Meet with team captains.	Review game rules.	
	Explain consequences of unsportsmanlike behavior.	
	Tell them how much time is left until game time.	

FIGURE 5.2   Sample referee pre-game checklist.

Post-Game Checklist

Responsibility	Action/Consideration	✓
Ensure spirit of intramural program.	Encourage participants to shake hands, but remember that players may be volatile after an intense game.	
	Be available for handshakes with team captains and/or participants.	
Complete necessary paperwork.	Complete score card, adding comments if necessary.	
	Complete accident or injury report if necessary.	
	If a player was ejected from a game, write a brief report summarizing the cause of the ejection.	
Review and evaluate.	Meet with other referees to discuss what went well and what, if any, mistakes were made.	
	Celebrate successes and learn from mistakes.	

FIGURE 5.3   Sample referee post-game checklist.

To increase accountability and reinforce your commitment to these standards, you may also want to have all officials sign a statement that they've read and will adhere to this code.

Official Evaluation

As discussed in chapter 4, formative evaluation improves both the program and intramural staff, offering them the opportunity to develop leadership skills and improve job performance. The same is true with officials. Constructive evaluation provides feedback on their performance and gives them the opportunity to improve. Because players are the ones to interact with officials, it's usually helpful to get their input when evaluating officials. League and tournament conveners and other officials should also complete an evaluation to add peer review to the process.

A sample official evaluation form is shown on figure 5.6. A representative from each team should complete it after each game. The process

of filling out these forms will not only increase participants' sense of ownership and involvement with the program but also reinforce the multidimensional aspect of officiating. In addition, having players evaluate officials will communicate the message that officiating is treated seriously by your organization.

Note: If teams submit these forms only when they wish to criticize an official, you should discard them. Above all, you want a fair, comprehensive critique.

If there are concerns about certain officials being insufficiently sensitive to inclusion issues you may wish to have several people, representing the affected group, complete the evaluation form.

The criteria to be evaluated include those identified throughout this chapter as the characteristics of an effective official (consistency, proper positioning, knowledge of the rules, and so on). The overall evaluation is probably the most important criteria on the evaluation form, but the other characteristics provide focus for

Timer and Scorer Responsibility Checklist

Responsibility	✓
Pick up pencil, clipboard, and game sheet from the intramural office 15 minutes before the game.	
Ask team captains to have team members print their full names (and uniform numbers, if applicable) on the game sheet.	
Compare the number of participants with the sheet. If a discrepancy exists, rectify the situation.	
Sign out and set up the clock if required.	
Assign pinnies and other equipment as necessary.	
Run the clock according to game requirements.	
Record penalties as reported by the referee (player name, number, offense, time of penalty, and penalty expiration time).	
Inform offending player of penalty expiration time.	
At the second offense, warn players that a third penalty will result in game misconduct.	
Inform referees of any player accumulating three minor penalties in a game.	
Record goals and assists (including player name, number, and time of goal).	
At the end of the game, summarize any difficulties or game highlights.	
Give team captains official evaluation forms.	
Sign the game sheet and have the referee do the same.	
Return the game sheet and equipment to the intramural office.	

FIGURE 5.4   Sample checklist for intramural scorers and timekeepers.

CODE OF ETHICS:
National Association of Sports Officials

ARTICLE I   Sports officials must be free of obligation to any interest other than the impartial and fair judging of sports competitions. Without equivocation, game decisions which are slanted by personal bias are dishonest and unacceptable.

ARTICLE II   Sports officials recognize that anything which may lead to a conflict of interest, either real or apparent, must be avoided. Gifts, favors, special treatment, privileges, employment or a personal relationship with a school or team which can compromise the perceived impartiality of officiating must be avoided.

ARTICLE III   Sports officials have an obligation to treat other officials with professional dignity and courtesy and recognize that it is inappropriate to criticize other officials publicly.

ARTICLE IV   Sports officials have a responsibility to continuously seek self-improvement through study of the game, rules, mechanics and the techniques of game management. They have a responsibility to accurately represent their qualifications and abilities when requesting or accepting officiating assignments.

ARTICLE V   Sports officials shall protect the public (fans, administrators, coaches, players, et al) From inappropriate conduct and shall attempt to eliminate from the officiating avocation/profession all practices which bring discredit to it.

ARTICLE VI   Sports officials shall not be party to actions designed to unfairly limit or restrain access to officiating, officiating assignments or association membership. This includes selection for positions of leadership based upon economic factors, race, creed, color, age, sex, physical handicap, country or national origin.

FIGURE 5.5 Sport officials ethical codes.

Reprinted with permission from the National Association of Sports Officials. For membership information contact NASO, 2017 Lathrop Ave, Racine, WI 53405; phone 22-632-5448; www.naso.org.

Intramural Official Evaluation

1 = Unsatisfactory, 2 = Satisfactory, 3 = Good, 4 = Excellent

Official names	Official #1 _____	Official #2 _____
Overall performance	1 2 3 4	1 2 3 4
Decisiveness	1 2 3 4	1 2 3 4
Knowledge of rules	1 2 3 4	1 2 3 4
Court or field positioning	1 2 3 4	1 2 3 4
Effective use of whistle and signals	1 2 3 4	1 2 3 4
Demeanor	1 2 3 4	1 2 3 4
Consistency	1 2 3 4	1 2 3 4
Integrity	1 2 3 4	1 2 3 4
Hustle	1 2 3 4	1 2 3 4
Attire and appearance	1 2 3 4	1 2 3 4
Interaction with participants	1 2 3 4	1 2 3 4

Comments: _____

_____

Evaluator name: _____

Team name: _____

Team played against: _____

Date: _____

FIGURE 5.6 Sample official evaluation form.

evaluating the official's strength and weaknesses. The scale (1 to 4), ranging from unsatisfactory to excellent, enables evaluators to be precise. At the bottom of the evaluation form is a place for evaluators to provide their names and information about the game or event. This information is important because an official's supervisor may have questions about the evaluation.

If players fear retribution or other consequences of completing an honest evaluation of officials, you may want to provide an evaluation box in the intramural office where players can turn in their evaluations after the game. Some schools offer on-line evaluation of officials. This type of evaluation is more anonymous than completing an evaluation form under the watchful eye of an official (although participants must identify themselves to submit the form), certainly, but it may not be representative of all participants. To view examples of on-line evaluation forms, visit the following two Web sites: www.indiana.edu/~recsport/forms/offeval.html and www4.gvsu.edu/hrw/intramurals/official_evaluation.htm.

Chapter Summary Exercises

Well-trained, competent officials can benefit your intramural program enormously. In addition to providing a safe arena in which to compete, they can help keep the game moving, which increases the enjoyment for all. Answer the following questions to ascertain the role officials will play in your intramural program.

1. In your past intramural experiences, did some games work better with an official and other games not work with an official? What made the difference?

2. Envision two referees officiating an intramural play-off game of basketball. All of a sudden, two players collide. One referee blows the whistle to stop play. One of the players complains that she can't feel her feet and is experiencing sharp, shooting pains in her knees. The other referee tells the team captain to move this player off the court so that play can resume. Based on the guidelines in this chapter, what should the first official do?

3. Outline the components of a comprehensive officiating program. Be sure to start with your program mission, and then include such areas as training, safety, and evaluation.

References

Boyles, M. 1996. On officials, fair play, and otherwise sunny days. *CIRA Bulletin* 22 (3): 3-5.

Flanery, T., ed. 1999. *National Federation of State High School Associations 1999-2000 rule book for soccer.* Indianapolis: National Federation of State High School Associations Publications.

Geiger, J. 1997. "Count it!" Officials that don't miss the call. *NIRSA Journal* 21 (3): 12-14.

National Collegiate Athletic Association. 1999. *NCAA soccer rulebook.* Indianapolis: National Collegiate Athletic Association.

Resources

National Association of Sports Officials (NASO)
2017 Lathrop Avenue
Racine, WI 53405
Phone: 262-632-5448
Web site: www.referee.com

An excellent source on officiating, offering helpful sport quizzes, newsletters, and other information. "Favorite official links" on the Web site contains many helpful organizations and sources of information on a wide variety of sports.

Yahoo
520 North Bridge Road
#05-01 Wisma, Alsagoff
Singapore, 188742
Web site: asia.yahoo.com/Recreation/Sports/Officiating

Offers information about officiating specific sports.

About.com
1440 Broadway
New York, NY 10018
Phone: 212-204-4000
Web site:volleyball.about.com/sports/volleyball/msubofficialr.htm
Web site: ussoccer.about.com/sports/ussoccer/msub17.htm?once=true&

Offers information about officiating volleyball and soccer.

Policy I:
Fair Play

Clearly written and comprehensive policies are crucial to any successful, effective intramural program. Effective policies essentially define many components of the program, including its mission and what is required to satisfy that mission. In this chapter, we will look at the role of policies in an intramural program and begin the process of creating a fair play policy. In the next chapter, we discuss the role and importance of safety policies.

Chapter Objectives

► Understand the development and role of policies in an intramural program.
► Define *fair play*.
► Understand the concepts of inclusion and sportsmanship.
► Learn how to apply fair play principles to an intramural program.

Developing Policies for Intramural Programs

As introduced, **policies** are formal, written declarations, based on the mission statement, that define the parameters necessary to achieve the program's goals. Indeed, the process of developing an intramural policy starts with mission. If it is your mission that all students participate, or at least as many students as possible, for example, you'll want to formulate inclusion and fairness policies that address discrimination having to do with race, gender, disability, and so on. If your mission is promote safe, fun activities, you'll want policies in place that reduce the risk of injury and other harm. (Most likely, you'll want to develop safety and inclusion policies in your intramural program, which is why we concentrate on these topics in this and the next chapter.)

Working with your mission, you should also consider risk when developing intramural policies. For example, what risks are inherent in certain activities? If competitive leagues are part of your program, how high is the risk of injury? Is there a chance certain populations will get left out (e.g., women, minorities, and people with disabilities)? You'll also want to consider legal issues when defining your intramural policies. Are there state, local, or national laws that come into play? Finally, you'll need to plan the steps necessary for implementing the policy and ensure that everything is in place.

The key components of designing a policy, then, include the following.

► Have a well-defined mission statement.
► Identify risks that may require a policy.
► Incorporate local, state, and national laws.
► Devise the procedures necessary for implementing the policy.

When developing your policies, keep in mind that they should be written for the participants, staff, and volunteers. In other words, policies should be written so that every leader, student, staff member, volunteer, and so on will understand them. They should also be written within the context of your program. That is, the motivation and justification for the policy should be included in the policy itself. For example, in the case of an inclusion policy, it would be wise to briefly explain the marginalization of certain groups in society, including minorities, women, and so on.

In addition, policies must be specific. For example, it is not enough to suggest that women *should* be included in all intramural activities. Rather, an effective inclusion policy should spell it out: "Either gender must constitute at least 2/5 of all co-ed teams. In other words, on a five-person team, two participants must be male, two must be female, and the fifth can be of either gender."

To be clear, policies should identify whether they apply to just the intramural program or to the entire institution. In this regard, it is helpful to include such information as whom the policy affects, who will enforce it, and how it will be enforced. Using the inclusion example in the previous paragraph, the phrase "all co-ed teams" takes care of the first element. As for who will enforce it and how it will be enforced, another sentence could be added: "If there are not enough females on a team at the start of the game, the major official will cancel the game [or tournament or event] and the offending team will get a forfeit."

Finally, policies must be publicized and used consistently to be effective and if they are to be considered in all aspects of an intramural program. It is not enough to have a well-written policy on the books. If participants do not know about it, or they know about it but are not induced to think about it, a policy will quickly become moot.

Role of Policies

Particularly in the cases of inclusion and discrimination, the role of policies in an intramural program is central. Written policies will help to implement and ensure that the mission is accomplished in the day-to-day operations of the program. By being specific, clear, and thorough in formulating policies, and you will increase the likelihood of succeeding at your intramural mission.

For example, if not enough women are coming out for intramurals, then a policy that every team has one woman on the floor at all times is one step in the direction of increasing women's participation. A policy that requires the intramural council to have representative from different grades or departments in a school ensures broad representation on the council. A policy that states that intramurals rewards fair play more than winning means that awards for fair play need to be more significant than those for winning a league or tournament. Policies are ways of ensuring that the mission of intramural programming is carried out.

Fair Play Defined

To develop a fair play policy, of course, you must first be clear about what *fair play* is. Fair play, also called "sportsmanship" at some institutions, is essential to any effective intramural program. For our purposes, the concept of **fair play** is not only about the standards of sportsmanship—playing within the rules, both the letter and the spirit of the rules, and respecting others, all others—but also about inclusion. If intramurals is about fun and active movement for all, then promoting an attitude of fair play is clearly critical to the success of the program.

In September 1992, the Committee of European Cultural Ministers, as part of the European Cultural Co-operation of the Council of Europe, adopted a code of ethics entitled "Code of Sports Ethics Fair Play: The Winning Way." According to this document, *fair play* is defined as follows:

> Fair play is defined as much more than playing within the rules. It incorporates the concepts of friendship, respect for others, and always playing within the right spirit. Fair play is defined as a way of thinking, not just a way of behaving. It incorporates issues concerned with the elimination of cheating, gamesmanship, doping, violence (both physical and verbal), exploitation, unequal opportunities, excessive commercialization, and corruption (European Cultural Co-operation of the Council of Europe, 1992).

Considering the myriad factors and issues in this definition, it is clear that fair play should be a central issue for intramural directors. In fact, the concept of fair play should be at the very core of the program. According to the committee,

> The basic principle of the Code of Sports Ethics is that ethical considerations leading to fair play are integral, not optional, elements of all sports activity, sports policy and management, and apply to all levels of ability and commitment, including recreational as well as competitive sport.

> The primary concern and focus is fair play for children and young people, in the recognition that children and young people of today are the adult participants and sporting stars of tomorrow. The code is also aimed at the institutions and adults who have a direct or indirect influence on young people's involvement and participation in sport. The code embraces the concepts of the right of children and young people to participate and enjoy their involvement in sport, and the responsibilities of the institutions and adults to promote fair play and to ensure that these rights are respected (European Cultural Co-operation of the Council of Europe, 1992).

The Components of Fair Play

Because fair play is a multifaceted concept, it is helpful to break it down into components. First, it's important to note that fair play is the responsibility of everyone, from program staff and participants to the intramural director and leadership. The type of program, the age of participants, the specific activities engaged in—every participant and facet of your program should model and emphasize fair play. Because this book is intended for intramural directors and students studying recreational education, we will focus on the two groups with the most immediate impact on an intramural program: intramural leaders and participants.

According to Fair Play—It's Your Call! (1994), Fair Play Canada's manual for coaches, there are five principles of fair play.

1. Give everyone an equal chance to participate (referred to in this text as "inclusion").

2. Respect the rules.

3. Respect the officials and their decisions.

4. Respect opponents.

5. Maintain self-control at all times.

In essence, these five principles can be grouped into two components: inclusion and sportsmanship. In the following sections, these two components of fair play are discussed first from a program perspective and then from the perspective of who plays a role in achieving it.

Inclusion

Inclusion is a spirit of equality. In an inclusive program, everyone feels welcome and encouraged to participate regardless of personal characteristics such as age, gender, disability, fitness level, race, ethnicity, and so on. If an intramural program wants to be inclusive, it must ensure that everyone has an equal chance to participate. It is, of course, the law in most countries that no one can be denied access on the basis of gender, race, skin color, and disability. Adding fitness level and age to the mix is clearly appropriate in an intramural setting.

Unfortunately, North American culture has not been, and is not, as inclusive as one would hope. In a study of federal- and state-run recreational areas and parks, researchers found that 94 percent of the users surveyed identified themselves as "white, not Hispanic" (Academy of Leisure Sciences 2001). Clearly these numbers do not represent current population demographics. *Trying to play together: Competing paradigms in approaches to integration through recreation and leisure* recounts the recreational experiences of 12 people with disabilities as they tried, and failed, to participate in sport (Human Services Institute 1992). Reports and tales like these do not speak well of intramural inclusion on this continent.

So what does achieving inclusion entail? Much like the discrimination laws in society at large, intramural inclusion encompasses such characteristics as race, skin color, gender, ethnicity, and disability. Because the nature of intramurals is physical activity, however, two additional characteristics should also be included: age and fitness level. These are discussed in the following sections, after a brief explanation of the essence of inclusion, equal opportunity.

Equal Opportunity

A key part of inclusion in intramurals is **equal opportunity**, which is simply ensuring that everyone has the opportunity to participate. Equal opportunity is achievable through a variety of means. As intramural directors, you should try to accommodate participants' schedules and resources, ensure equal playing time, modify the rules of traditional games to "level the playing field," and offer nontraditional games to make your programming accessible and inviting for all participants.

Try to schedule games when they will be convenient for participants. Holding intramural football games when the varsity football team practices is probably not a good idea. In finding out why participants are not showing up, it is important to ask whether the timing of intramural events is a problem. Financial resources may also prevent some students from participating. Whenever possible, try to make intramural activities affordable (free is best). Of course, communicating game times and schedules is included in accommodating participants. If players don't know when and where events are to be held, the chances are high that they won't be able to participate. (Promotion is more fully discussed in chapter 8.)

Equal playing time must be a part of all event and contest structure. In softball or baseball, for example, make each inning one rotation through the entire team's lineup. For volleyball, when th serving team loses service , the server goes to the bench and a new player comes on in her place. In addition, maximize actual playing time by minimizing stoppages in play. For example, in indoor soccer and hockey, limit substitutions at breaks in the game—the breaks just get longer—and require that substitutions be made only on the fly. In basketball, maximize playing time by giving the offense one point and the ball at the sideline in the case of defensive non-shooting fouls. For a defensive shooting foul, the offensive team gets two points and the defensive team gets ball on the end line. For an offensive foul, give the defensive team the ball on the sideline—don't waste players' time by having them stand around and watch one person throw two free throws.

To "level the playing field," consider modifying the rules of traditional games so that all participants can play. Simple rule modifications encourage fun and active participation by all and discourage violence and potentially dangerous injury. For example, the rules of hockey can be altered to discourage high sticking (keep sticks below the waist) and aggressive play (players are expelled from the league if they get three penalties in one game). (The topic of safety is fully discussed in chapter 7.)

Nontraditional events are also a great opportunity equalizer. Some schools have had success with activities such as boot hockey (floor hockey without the sticks, and using a tennis ball that is advanced toward the goal by players kicking it), Frisbee golf (golf using targets, Frisbees are thrown at the targets and each throw counts for one swing), and blind volleyball (volleyball with a tarp hanging over the net so opponents can't see one another; no spiking or overhand serves are allowed). Table 6.1 lists some modifications to traditional intramural sports. By changing a few rules of a game, or even the equipment used, sport and intramural activities can become inviting to all.

Age

The structure of intramural activities should accommodate special requirements of the participants. In other words, rules and play should reflect participants' developmental levels. This is particularly important when it comes to intramurals for young children. As intramural leaders, you should understand the different needs of various age groups, and not simply treat children as small adults. Let's look at some of the unique characteristics, abilities, and interests of these age groups. Do recognize that children in the same grade, especially in grades 5-10, can be as much as four years apart from a maturational level. The characteristics that follow are average features of the different age groups.

Children in kindergarten through grade 3 tend to be individualistic, have low skill and high energy levels, tire quickly. However, leading them through fun games and providing playground equipment for lunchtime enjoyment are welcomed by these children.

Children in grades 3 through 5 are capable of more complex hand-eye coordination, have a longer attention span, and are interested in group activities. Games for these children can be more complex and of longer duration. They may have some interest in an intramural league as they enjoy informal games of pick-up basketball, skipping, and baseball.

Grades 6 through 12 are extremely peer conscious and, thus, typically enjoy "hanging out" and being spectators. That said, they do enjoy fun activities as long there is no fear of embarrassment. These kids will play games with intensity but are wary of getting too sweaty. They like organized activities and enjoy league and tournament play unless they lose frequently and,

thus, are continually near or on the bottom of team or individual rankings. These students like playing with peers, namely, students in their own grades. With preferences such as these, good leadership will go a long way in this age range. As grade and high school intramural directors, you may want to group students by grade level. Of course, there is no rule against having fun with this grouping. For example, identify grade 8 as the "rookies," grades 9 and 10 as the "semipros," and grades 11 and 12 as the "pros."

College and university students enjoy meaningful relationships with peers, are fitness conscious, and may pursue outdoor and high-risk activities to test physical competency. In general, they compete to have fun, stay fit, and be with their friends, although they usually do not have as much time as high school students to "hang out." Specifically, undergraduates tend to participate for social reasons, while graduate students tend to participate for **personal enhancement** such as improving fitness, enjoying time with friends, and taking a break from their studies (Smith 1995, 42). Most college students will rise to the challenge of trying to win a game and try a new activity. They enjoy fun games and competitive leagues if they are well organized.

Gender

As explained earlier, intramurals has long history of male involvement. Females, however, have been and continue to be under represented in leisure and sport activity. In Canada, for example, girls are slightly less likely to participate in organized activities than boys between the ages of 6 and 11. By age 14 to 15, however, according to Statistics Canada's 2001 national survey, one in five girls indicated they were not participating in any activity, compared with about one in 10 boys (Statistics Canada 2001). In Australia, male participation in sport is far greater than female participation. This disparity is seen in the hierarchy of national sporting organizations as well. Only 11 percent of women are national presidents of these organizations, and women constitute less than 25 percent of their executives (Lundy 1999). Yet since 1948, Australian women have won 40 percent of Australia's Olympic gold medals, even though they have competed in only a quarter of all events!

TABLE 6.1 Modified Sport Games

Competitive	Recreational Twist	Description
Lacrosse	Scoop ball	Lacrosse played with plastic scoops. The basketball backboard is the goal—no goalies are needed.
Water polo	Inner tube water polo	Regular water polo rules apply, except players sit in inner tubes while playing.
Swimming relays	Gym "pool" relays	Competitors lie on scooters using swimming strokes to advance down the "pool" (designated by gym/court lines).
Bowling	JJ Bowling	Players bowl differently for each frame: bowl with right hand, left hand, forward between legs, backwards between legs, pushing ball with feet, pushing ball while lying in stomach, etc. (Byl, 2002)
Golf	Glow ball golf	Night golf using florescent balls.
Best ball	Team golf	Players hit their own ball, first from the tee and then from the spot where the best hit landed. Each best ball counts as 1 stroke.
Volleyball	Beach volleyball	Regular volleyball using a large beach ball.
Flag football	Fishball	Flag football using a large rubber fish instead of flags.
Floor or ice hockey	Boot hockey	Regular hockey using no sticks and a tennis ball. Wearing boots, players pass and score by kicking the tennis ball into the goal.
Indoor soccer	Bladder soccer	Indoor soccer using the bladder of a soccer ball.
Four-goal soccer		Soccer using four goals and four teams instead of two. The team with the fewest goals scored against it wins.
Softball	Two-pitch softball	Teams provide their own pitcher, who pitches a maximum of two pitches per player. Teams can have as many players on one base as will fit. Everyone gets to bat once an inning.
European handball	OCE ball	Like basketball but without dribbling. Players use a volleyball and try to score into a floor hockey goal. Players may not run with the ball, must pass or shoot the ball within three seconds of catching it, and are not allowed inside the basketball three point shooting arch.
Table tennis	4-player table tennis	Players see how long they can keep the ball in play. One player hits the ball and goes to the side of the table, while another person hits the ball, then goes to the other end of the table and hits the ball. . . . If this is too easy, then make sure the ball goes off the end of the table before it can be played.
Basketball	Scooter ball	Players sit on scooters and score by shooting a rubber chicken into the hoop. No moving with the scooter is permitted when you are holding the rubber chicken

Such gender inequities are also seen in the intramural arena. Typically, female intramural staff run fitness classes or are behind the scenes, serving such functions as equipment room attendant and office assistant. Their male counterparts, however, get to be on the front lines, serving as officials, gymnasium attendants, and maintenance aids (Gaskins 1996). Despite the passage of Title IX in 1972, an act prohibiting discrimination in educational institutions on the bases of gender, research indicates that "Title IX has had little influence on the field of intramural-recreational sports" (Tharp 1994, 29). To take a look at Title IX and several articles dealing with the impact of Title IX, visit the following Web site: http://www.ed.gov/pubs/TitleIX/title.html.

Specifically, this act requires that programming satisfy at least one of three tests—though ideally it would be great if an institution could pass all three tests. The three parts of the tests are as follows:

Part I: Substantial proportionality. This part of the test is satisfied when participation opportunities for men and women are "substantially proportionate" to their respective undergraduate enrollments.

Part II: History and continuing practice. This part of the test is satisfied when an institution has a history and continuing practice of program expansion that is responsive to the developing interests and abilities of the under represented sex (typically female).

Part III: Effectively accommodating interests and abilities. This part of the test is satisfied when an institution is meeting the interests and abilities of its female students even where there are disproportionately fewer females than males participating in sports (Riley 1997).

The question is, then, how can intramural directors involve women more in intramural activities? Research shows that female university students participate in intramurals to meet new people, get together with friends, develop or maintain fitness, and have some fun (Smith 1995, 42; Proescher 1996). Keep these interests in mind when planning your intramural activities. In addition, try to involve females in your program leadership whenever and wherever possible. Their voices need to be heard as you plan and develop your program.

As indicated above, female involvement is less of a problem in grade school, but as soon as females enter high school, they become self-conscious. Feeling socially and physically awkward is the result of male and female adolescence, of course, but teenage and older girls tend to feel this more strongly than their male peers. In current Western society, women are defined by their bodies, specifically, how they measure up to the "beauty ideal," which for most females is thinner than is healthy. This poor body image affects females more than it does males and partially explains why females are less likely to participate in high school and collegiate intramurals.

With this in mind, using body image and fitness can be a powerful motivational tool to increase female involvement, but be careful of the body images you portray in your promotion. Do not use the discomfort and insecurities of females to goad them into participating in your program. Instead, concentrate on the health benefits of fitness and offer skill-development clinics. If you have a large number of highly skilled female athletes at your school, you may want to consider offering some activities for males, some activities for females, and some for both.

If your budget doesn't allow for an equal number of male and female games or events in each programming area, you may want to offer open events. An **open event** is open to either male or female participants, but teams are not required to have a specified number of males or females. That means, women are permitted to participate in men's activities and men are permitted to participate in women's activities. Understand, however, that without adequate skill instruction and development, modified rules to equalize play, and a clear sexual harassment policy that is enforced (see "Harassment" later in this section), females will likely opt out of male activities.

To equalize play, consider applying some of the same programming discussed under "Equal Opportunity" earlier in this chapter. Specifically, try to ensure equal playing time, consider rule modifications to "level the playing field," and offer nontraditional games or activities that will accommodate the interests of females. These programming considerations are particularly important when planning co-ed activities. For example, in a co-ed swimming race, have males wear shoes or make it a team event with equal numbers of females and males on each team. In co-ed basketball, double all female-scored points and/or do not allow males inside the key. For co-ed games that involve passing, such as soccer, hockey, and basketball, institute a rule that the ball (or puck or whatever) must be passed to a female before a team can score.

Females have another disadvantage when it comes to participating in intramurals: safety. Particularly at the high school and university levels. Safety may be a concern for many females. Many school grounds and recreational centers are open to the public and inadequately lit, thus making females feel unsafe when going to or leaving the facility, especially in the evening. Such issues as public transportation to facilities, lack of suitable changing rooms and toilets, lack of privacy, and access to childcare may also prevent females from participating in intramural activities. Ensuring safety and providing suitable facilities should be a basic part of your program planning. If parking ramps and lots are far away from the recreational facility or are inadequately lit, rectify the situation by taking them up with the school's governing body. In addition, consider developing a buddy system for female participants, or offer security at your events. (See chapter 7 for more discussion on safety.)

In summary, whenever and wherever possible, you as intramural directors should strive to balance your program by gender. Organize intramural events and activities to maximize participation and make the experience positive for every participant, male and female. If your current budget doesn't allow for male and female leagues and teams in every activity, institute some rules to equalize play. Then use the success of your program to institute gender equality in future years. And always educate staff, volunteers, and participants about sexual harassment. After all, everyone has the right to be treated with dignity and respect.

Harassment   Although people are harassed about more than their gender, this section is included here because gender or sexual harassment is one of the most common types of harassment. Simply put, **harassment** consists of one or a series of bothersome comments or conduct that is known or might reasonably be known to be unwelcome or unwanted, offen-

sive, intimidating, hostile, and/or inappropriate. The Ontario Human Rights Code specifically prohibits harassment on the basis of race, ancestry, place of origin, skin color, ethnic origin (including language, dialect, or accent), citizenship, creed, sex, sexual orientation, disability, age (18 to 65), marital status, family status, the receipt of public assistance, and record of provincial offenses or pardoned federal offenses. The United States does not have a Human Rights Code, though organizations have encouraged the United States to adopt the 1948 Code of the United Nations, it can be found at www.undhr50.org/UDHR/udhr.htm. Examples of harassment, in both Canada and the United States, include but are not limited to the following:

▶ Gestures

▶ Remarks

▶ Jokes

▶ Taunting/teasing

▶ Innuendo

▶ Display of offensive materials/pornography

▶ Offensive graffiti

▶ Threats

▶ Verbal or physical assault

▶ Unfair imposition of academic penalties

▶ Stalking

▶ Shunning or exclusion

▶ Unwelcome/unwarranted attention or comments

How can you, as intramural directors, protect your participants—and staff and volunteers—from harassment? First, you must create a comprehensive harassment policy. This includes a zero-tolerance approach. A harassment policy can be as simple as a brief statement explaining harassment and stating that it will not be tolerated. Or it can be a lengthy document outlining all types of harassment and detailed definitions of each, along with preventative measures, rules of conduct, and disciplinary procedures should harassment be engaged in.

Canadore College in North Bay Ontario created such a policy and then added the following three-step procedure for promoting its policy and dealing with infractions.

It's Policy

At Public School 44, the intramural program was having a difficult time getting girls to come out to compete. Jan Bennett, the intramural director, wanted this corrected. She invited any interested girls to attend a meeting to discuss improving female participation in intramurals.

Seven girls came to the meeting. Their discussion was lively and two general themes emerged: more activities should be developed that focused on fitness activities in a social setting, and existing programming and structure made it difficult for girls to get on a team. For the time being, Jan decided to focus on the second concern.

When Jan advertised volleyball signup the next week, she included photos of women playing on the posters and on the signup sheets. In her public announcements, she encouraged girls to participate and encouraged teams to solicit girl members. Inspired by the discussion at the meeting and Jan's interest in including girls, two of the girls who attended the meeting "forced" their way onto one team. Aside from them, however, no girls were on any of the other teams.

Sitting at a stoplight on her way home from school the day after volleyball signup, Jan grew irritated. She wondered why she had to wait for the light to turn green; there were no cars coming from either direction, so it would be perfectly safe to cross. Nevertheless, she didn't cross. The law stipulated that drivers must wait for the green light, even though that doesn't always seem to make sense. Then it struck her. To include more girls in her intramural program, female participation had to become "law." The boys might not understand the law at first, but the law would improve the program for everyone.

Indoor soccer was the next activity to be planned. In previous years, Jan had averaged around 12 teams, and the league was fairly successful. Teams played with a goalie and four players on the floor, and they usually had substitutes. To institute the new intramural "law, Jan wrote on the signup forms that two girls and two boys must be on the floor at all times.

As she predicted, the boys did not receive this new law graciously. Instead, many of them boycotted the event, resulting in only five teams signing up. Jan's resolve was unscathed. She ran the league for five teams, added a pizza party for the team that demonstrated the most sportsmanlike behavior, and rewarded the captain of the team that dressed most like soccer players with a cool sweatshirt.

Jan maintained her resolve for the rest of the school year, sticking to her new policy of gender equity on teams. Enrollment on other activities that year was down, but eventually things changed. A year later, soccer league signup was back up. In fact, 22 teams signed up!

In this case, it took more than a new attitude and a simple announcement to change things. It took policy.

Adapted, by permission, from J. Byl and J. Vanderwier, 1995, "Encouraging fair play in college intarmurals," *CAHPERD* 61 (2):26-27.

1. Make the harassment policy available to everyone by distributing a harassment brochure to all program participants prior to their first game.

2. Have all employees and volunteers sign a form indicating that they have been informed and understand the importance of the harassment policy (see figure 6.1).

3. Notify all staff, volunteers, and participants of the following complaint procedure.

During any or all stages of resolution, either party may be accompanied by a support person, who may be a co-worker, friend, recommended volunteer or a union representative. This person's role is to give support by listening, consulting and ensuring a fair process is followed. He/she does not advocate on behalf of the complainant or play any other role in the process. In no way can he/she obstruct the process.

Following consultation with a college harassment advisor, the complainant may decide to:

► Take no further action, in which case the matter will be closed;

► With a witness present, make the respondent aware that his/her behavior is disturbing to the complainant;

► Have the advisor intervene on his/her behalf; in which case the advisor will attempt to resolve the problem;

► Request mediation (attempt to reach a settlement with the help of a third party);

► Make a formal complaint through the College policy;

► Seek legal counsel and/or file a complaint under the Human Rights Code, 1981.

Disability

To be truly inclusive, intramural programming must involve people with disabilities. This is more than mission, however. In the U.S., it is the law and in Canada it is part of the Human Rights Code. Section 202 of the Americans With Disabilities Act, passed in 1990, states:

> Subject to the provisions of this title, no qualified individual with a disability shall, by reason of such disability, be excluded from participation in or be denied the benefits of the services, programs, or activities of a public entity, or be subjected to discrimination by any such entity.

In the context of an intramural program, however, how is this accomplished? To start, it's important to involve people with disabilities in your program planning. Specifically, they should be involved "in redefining criteria by which success (or normality) is measured" (Phillips 1992, 217). That means, involve people with disabilities in significant leadership and advocacy roles, both to represent an inclusive organization and to plan activities that the disabled can participate in. In general, you can involve them in three key ways: offer accessible facilities; appeal to them in your intramural promotion; and offer exciting and fun games by modifying existing game rules and/or creating new rules to include them.

Harassment and Discrimination Policy

I hereby acknowledge that I have been informed of, received, and understand
_____'s [institution] Harassment and Discrimination Policy.

As an employee of _____ _____ [institution], I am aware of the importance and the seriousness of this policy. I understand that everyone has the right to be treated with dignity and respect, consistent with _____'s [institution] mission statement, which provides for "an environment of trust, equality, and mutual respect."

Employee signature: _____

Employee name: _____

Date: _____

Supervisor signature:_____

FIGURE 6.1   Sample harassment policy acknowledgement form.

Because accessibility is legally required at public facilities, including learning institutions, we will not spend a great deal of time on this subject. If your school building is new, chances are good that your intramural facilities are already accessible. If your buildings are older, however, or if they were inadequately designed, you as intramural directors should take responsibility for evaluating what is needed to make your activities accessible. Wheelchair ramps, for example, are located in most school buildings, but they may be so far removed from the facility that access becomes difficult and/or frustrating for students in wheelchairs. Perhaps the governing body of your institution could add additional ramps, or perhaps you could relocate certain intramural activities so that physically disabled participants would not feel left out. *Note:* this also includes making your intramural activities accessible and welcoming to spectators in wheelchairs.

When promoting intramural activities, be sure to encourage those with disabilities to participate. Use visual images of disabled participants on program and event posters and fliers. Structure your sign-up sheets and other program documents so that people with disabilities will not feel left out. This applies particularly to any illustrations that might be used on such forms. Invite them to participate by posting schedules, announcements, tournament results, team standings, and so on in a central location where people with disabilities are sure to see them. Above all, remind your staff, volunteers, leadership, and participants about the importance of including everyone by integrating them where possible and positively accommodating them with various rule changes when necessary.

The best way of including people with disabilities is to fully integrate them in your intramural activities (Wilhite and Kleiber 1992, 8). If you already have high participation among disabled students, all the better. In some activities, there is no need to make any changes to accommodate a person with a disability. In baseball, for example, players with a hearing deficiency are able to participate. In other sports and activities, and in the case of severe disability or deficiency, however, you will likely need to change the rules to create equitable competition. Badminton and tennis rules for example, explain how able-bodied players can compete against those in a wheelchair (International Badminton Association; National Capital Wheelchair Tennis Associaton 1995).

In many cases, you will have to be creative about the best way to accommodate everyone. A helpful resource in this regard is *Palaestra,* a journal that provides a forum for sport, physical education, and recreation for those with disabilities. One way to include people with disabilities is creating new games that "level the playing field" by equalizing the participants. These new games may involve different activities, different rules, and different equipment. For example, physically disabled students may find it easier to play volleyball with a beach ball or other large, light ball. Reducing the size of the playing area may equalize play for blind students or those in a wheelchair, or using such equipment as towels and noodles may increase a physically weak or slow participant's reach in tag. The following tips, grouped by disability, will help you make your intramural programming accessible to people with disabilities. Don't stop there, however. Try to think of other ideas and involve your disabled students in the process. Like the voices of women, the voices of the disabled should be heard when planning your intramural activities.

For those in a wheelchair:

▶ Offer activities such as wheelchair basketball, a game open to all students but everyone plays in a wheelchair. If many participants show up—enough that line changes would be too frequent and interrupt the flow of the game—have all players start on the court seated in a chair (a wheelchair or classroom chair). Players must remain on their chair and pass to one another.

▶ Hold a basket-shooting contest in which everyone is seated in a wheelchair at the foul line.

▶ Use scooters in any number of games: indoor hockey, basketball, football, soccer, and so on. Able-bodied players play on scooters, and those in a wheelchair play in their wheelchairs. In addition to equalizing play, the use of scooters makes for an entertaining game (particularly to watch).

For those with an amputated arm or leg:

▶ Require all participants to compete using one limb. For example, hold a high jump contest hopping on one leg.

▶ Have participants time how quickly they can do something (tie their shoelaces or other two-handed activity) with one hand.

▶ Offer a game of one-arm basketball or volleyball (players secure the other arm to their waists using a belt, rope, or other material).

For those who are blind:

▶ Try blind soccer played in pairs. One partner is blindfolded and does all the kicking, while the seeing partner directs the blindfolded partner where to move and when to kick.

▶ Play blind Ping-Pong. Using a ball with a bell inside, blindfolded competitors see how long they can sustain a volley (no net is needed).

▶ Try Goalball, a game in which none of the players can see (participants can be blind or blindfolded or wear ski goggles that are painted over so that no light can enter). Played on a volleyball court, goalball involves some setup. At either end of the court, place a net 1.5 yards (meters) high across the court. Then mark the playing area with tactile lines (tape over string or thick tape such as duct tape), as shown in figure 6.2. Feeling these lines with their hands or feet, players can use these lines to orient themselves on the court.

Players are positioned between the goal line and the front team are and use a hollow rubber ball (basketball size) with bells inside to score goals by throwing the ball from their side of the court into the opposing team's net. Only three players from each team are allowed in the playing area at a time (teams usually have a few substitutes). The ball must contact the floor before crossing the overthrow line. Defensive players try to stop the ball from rolling or bouncing toward their net by using their feet and hands. Return shots must be thrown within eight seconds of controlling the ball, and no player can throw the ball more than twice in a row. The game runs for two seven-minute periods (International Paralympic Committee 2001).

Fitness and Skill Level

Because participation in intramurals should be maximized, programming should cater to the broadest base of people—not a select group such as varsity athletes. Indeed, some intramural programs do not allow varsity athletes to participate in intramural activities. Others, not wanting to exclude anyone, allow varsity athletes to participate but limit each team to having only one varsity player. If alumni are permitted to participate in intramural activities, the same rules for athletes are usually applied to ex-athletes. Otherwise, a team of ex-varsity basketball players, for example, would dominate the intramu-

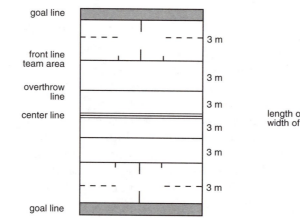

FIGURE 6.2 Goalball court.

ral basketball league. Many schools apply this rule only to athletes wanting to compete in their particular sport; other schools limit varsity athletes to one per team, regardless of the varsity team they played on.

To make sure that participants of poor or moderate levels of fitness and skill feel welcome, there are a few things an intramural director can do, such as change the competitive structure of intramural programming and/or change the activities. As discussed in chapter 1, the level of competition is a function of players' commitment to play versus winning and formality. In addition to "leveling the playing field" for all participants, equalizing play (changing the game objective, rules, or equipment used) can help to emphasize the spirit of play over winning, and thus make your activities fun for all participants. For example, rather than hold a traditional bike race, which involves going fast and getting to the finish line first, why not hold a contest in which participants see who can ride 1 yard (meter) in the slowest time without falling over? Likewise, change basketball rules so that players only get points when shooting underhand. This drastically changes the nature of the game. On the equipment side, in addition to the suggestions given earlier, using the bladder of an old soccer ball is a fun way to change the nature of soccer. Bladder balls move erratically, which makes the game extremely entertaining to play and watch. In the end, with such game modifications, all students—the athlete and nonathlete, the fit and the out-of-shape—leave the game feeling happy, exuberant, and excited for the next event.

Included in the level of fitness and skill is the topic of weight. As intramural directors, how can you get over- and underweight or frail students to participate? The first step is to create a nonthreatening, fun program, as explained earlier. The next step is to be inclusive in your planning and promotion. Just as the voices of women and the disabled should be heard when designing your intramural activities, so should the voices of the frail and overweight. Ask for their input and include them in the decision-making process. Then, when it comes to promoting your activities, including these students can be as simple as featuring them on posters and other intramural visuals, and inviting them to participate by using language they will relate to.

Another idea is to consider developing activities at different competitive levels. For example, create two leagues for each activity: a recreational league for less-skilled and unfit players and a competitive league for competitors with well-honed skills and fine-tuned bodies. Because the structure of an event or activity tends to dictate its nature, you must predefine the competitiveness of each league, contest, or game and then plan accordingly when developing each program. The competitiveness of each activity will be determined by such factors as the rules, team requirements, promotion, and even awards. If the stakes are high, such as when the victor is awarded a prestigious trophy, for example, competition will likely be higher.

Race, Skin Color, and Ethnicity

The color of people's skin, the language they speak, and their nation of origin ought to make no difference in their involvement in intramurals. Unfortunately, studies show mixed reports on racial and ethnic integration. In one study, students of color who attended predominantly white institutions frequently perceived the intramural environment to be hostile, while their white counterparts experienced less hostility in interracial environments (Helm, Sedlacek, and Prieto 1998).

This doesn't have to be the case. In a report from another study, this one at the University of Maryland in College Park, Maryland, one student noted that playing on a multiracial volleyball team gave "different perspectives on individuals and, I guess, their interest in the game and approaches in playing the sport. One kid lived in Japan when he was younger and had a different perspective on how the sport is played. Basically it made the whole sport more interesting and gave different perspectives" (Cotton, Kelley, and Sedlacek 1999).

As an aside, it is worth noting that William Wasson, the founder of the National Intramural and Recreational Sport Association, was African American. In the fall 1994 issue of the *NIRSA Journal*, which was devoted to the history of NIRSA, Peter Graham, long-time intramural advocate at the University of Massachusetts in Amherst, noted that NIRSA "constitutes visible evidence that men and women, black and white, majority and minority can jointly perceive common goals and work toward their attainment in a spirit of cooperation and harmony—a spirit sadly lacking in many segments of our society" (Graham 1994, 21). Let's hope Graham is correct when it comes to intramurals.

Intramural programming should not reflect a "leisure apartheid," as one paper suggested (Academy of Leisure Sciences 2001). Instead, intramural directors would do well to listen to the voices of minorities to better understand how to integrate your intramural programming and ensure that the needs of all people are met.

Sportsmanship

The second component of fair play is sportsmanship. Called "fair play" and "sportsmanlike conduct" by many, **sportsmanship** refers to how a game is played. Sportsmanship, which seeks meaningful participation for everyone, requires that all participants respect the rules, respect the officials and their decisions, respect their opponents, and maintain self-control at all times. The following sections discuss each of these requirements and suggest ways of ensuring that sportsmanship is developed, encouraged, and included in your intramural program.

Respect Rules

Game rules are intended to keep everyone on the same page, so to speak. If some participants follow the rules but others do not, the result is likely to be chaos and frustration. To make intramural activities a positive experience for all, intramural directors would be wise to consider the following suggestions.

▶ Encourage participants, particularly young children, to devise their own games with their own rules, including their own incentives and sanctions for fair or unfair play. This helps them to take personal responsibility both for their actions and for the success of the game or activity.

▶ Hold team meetings with team captains prior to the start of league play. These meetings should reinforce the mission of sportsmanship in the intramural program and serve as a forum to explain, discuss, and demonstrate the rules.

▶ Hire and train officials to know the rules of each game they are officiating.

▶ Discipline or eject participants who flagrantly violate the rules.

Respect Officials and Their Decisions

Officials should serve as ambassadors of the intramural mission. To help them do that,

▶ train officials to respond consistently, decisively, and assertively;

▶ develop an evaluation and rating scale for officials, correlating their compensation to this ranking;

▶ give officials credibility by providing professional uniforms and equipment;

▶ support officials in their jobs, including expelling or otherwise disciplining players who argue with their decisions;

▶ post game rules for all participants to see and schedule enough time before games so that officials can highlight important rules for players; and

▶ require officials to attend team captains' meetings.

Respect Opponents

Without an opponent, there is no competition. Although fierce competition should be discouraged in most intramural activities—unless, of course, you have a separate competitive league—a little healthy competition can be fun for participants, and it usually adds excitement to the game. Encourage participants see their opponents as partners in the cause of fun and active movement, not obstacles in the way of getting the prize. This will require walking a fine line, but the following suggestions (Byl and VanderWier 1995) should help.

▶ Remind participants, and team captains at captains' meetings, of your intramural mission: for example, in chapter 2 the last part of the mission statement at State University stated that intramural contests are to be "exciting and encouraging recreational game." Players need to encourage other each other, on their own team and the competition.

▶ De-emphasize winning and encourage the spirit of play.

▶ Prevent or curb hostility by assigning two players who are disrespectful of each other to the same team.

► Do not permit verbal abuse of any kind. It may be helpful also to remind players of your institutional harassment and discrimination policy.

► At the beginning and end of a game, encourage all participants to shake hands or give "high fives."

► Encourage participants to congratulate all players on good plays, regardless of which team a player is on.

► Reinforce the golden rule: encourage participants to treat all players as they would want to be treated. That means, participants should not interfere with, bully, or take advantage of any player, opponent or teammate.

► Discourage behavior such as showing off and always trying to get the most points or penalties. Remind players that the goals of the game are to have fun, improve their skills, and feel good.

► Demonstrate the importance of sportsmanship—and your commitment to it—by rewarding sportsmanship, either in place of winning or in addition to winning. Involve participants in the process by having one team award a member of the opposing team and vice versa at the end of every game.

Body Contact Because a lack of respect for opponents is often at the root of body contact, which all too often becomes aggressive and excessive, a word of caution is warranted. Institutions at all levels experience many problems with rough games such as basketball and hockey, in which body contact is part of the game. If participants have difficulty treating their opponents respectfully in these games, it may be necessary to remove some of the physical contact. In touch football, for example, diving, setting picks, and blocking are not allowed, yet the game is still enjoyed by thousands. Hockey can also be played as a noncontact sport. One way to reduce contact in hockey is to limit the number of players on the ice. Rather than five players and a goalie, have only three players and a goalie. With fewer players on the ice, participants will not be as likely to come into physical contact. Plus, they will tire more quickly and, therefore, be less likely to get into rough or overly physical play.

Maintain Self-Control at All Times

Clearly, intramural directors, officials, staff, and even team captains cannot control participants. Players must be responsible for and control themselves. The best way to ensure that participants maintain self-control is to spread the message that self-control is the responsibility of each individual and then set up policies that enforce it. For example:

► Provide officials and players with game rules and standards of conduct before the start of each activity or game.

► Alert team captains that they should be on the lookout for their teammates losing control or behaving in an unsportsmanlike manner. Like officials, team captains can be given the discretion to insist that a player take a break or sit out of a game.

► Have team captains sign a "Spirit of Competition" agreement like the one shown in figure 6.3. This agreement identifies the key points of sportsmanship and, perhaps more important, places the responsibility for sportsmanship on the team captain by having him or her sign it. Directors may want to take this agreement one step further by alerting team captains that their entire team could be suspended for a game (or a tournament) if their players are habitually aggressive or violent.

► Train officials on handling players who may be losing control. For example, officials can be trained in the following sequence: (1) give a time out or suggest that the player take a break; (2) impose a minor penalty, (3) impose a second penalty, and then warn the player that another offense will mean being ejected from the game; and (4) eject the player.

This last one, training officials how to handle out-of-control players, is especially important. Ejecting players from a game should be used sparingly but consistently. The following behavior should result in player ejection.

► "Mouthing off," swearing or using profanity, or using other inappropriate language toward a player or official.

Spirit of Competition
Captain's Agreement

Captain's Name/ID# _____
(Please print)

Team Name/Sport _____
(Please print)

I agree to and will education my teammates on the following.

- That the true essence of sport is to strive for personal achievement and excellence through full and honest effort.
- To be committed to participating in sport with integrity, and to striving to win only by legitimate means.
- Pledge to learn, understand, and adhere to both the written rules of my sport, including the eligibility and conduct terms, and the accepted rules of fair play.
- Believe that violence and physical intimidation are harmful to sport and refuse to use such tactics.
- Understand that officials, teammates, and opponents are all integral to sport and are worthy of my respect.

It is my responsibility, as a captain, to maintain self-control of myself and my teammates. We will accept officials' decisions without argument, play with intensity but without animosity and behave graciously in triumph or defeat.

_____
Signature

_____
Date (day/month/year)

Fair Play – it's your response-ability!

FIGURE 6.3 Intramural team captain fair play agreement.
Courtesy of Ontario College Athletic Association, 1185 Eglinton Avenue East, Suite 505, North York, Ontario, Canada, M3C 3C6. Phone: 416-426-7043.

- ▶ Deliberately mistreating or damaging equipment (i.e., breaking hockey sticks and throwing bats).
- ▶ Initiating a flagrant violation with the intention of hurting someone.
- ▶ Fighting, which in intramural sport includes the intention to throw a punch (this typically results in a four-month suspension from intramural activities).

Sportsmanship and the Law

There is no law endorsing or enforcing sportsmanship, certainly, but there are laws against violent behavior. For example, assault and bullying. Thus, as intramural directors, you need to prevent violence by developing and enforcing policies to discourage it.

Many institutions have a zero tolerance policy on violence. The most common type of violence in an intramural setting is, of course, fighting. In developing a violence policy, then, first you must determine what constitutes a fight. For the safety of all participants, staff, and volunteers, including officials, it's wise to state that violence includes fighting before, during, or after an event or game. From there, your definition of *fighting* will likely vary. Some institutions include throwing a punch (i.e., not necessarily making contact) in the classification of fighting. Others go as far as including taunting or provoking a fight. However you define *fighting*, make sure your definition is clear to and understood by everyone.

Once you formulate a violence policy, you must put into place procedures for enforcing it. The typical punishment for fighting in intramurals is a four-month suspension from all intramural activities. For less-severe infractions, this could be limited to the rest of the season in a certain activity. For more-severe and habitual infractions, you may want to expel the offender from all intramural participation. *Note:* Some institutions reduce the length of or lift the suspension if the offender completes an anger-management course. These are usually offered by local community organizations such as public health departments and continuing education departments of hospitals.

Suspensions from intramural activities appear to go against the mission of intramurals. But remember, most mission statements maintain that intramurals is for everyone. If violent behavior goes unchecked, other participants are robbed of fun and are discouraged from participating. Thus, to protect the safety and enjoyment of many, it is best to discipline or suspend a few. (See chapter 13 for a full discussion of suspensions, which includes a suspension notification form in figure 13.4 on page 228.)

Fair Play: The Policy

Now that the components of fair play have been defined and understood, what to do next? That is, how do you go about developing a fair play policy? Fortunately, the process is fairly simple and straightforward. It involves the following seven steps.

Step 1: To begin, understand that a fair play policy must be comprehensive in design and consistent with the stated mission of your program. Considering the components of inclusion and sportsmanship presented in this chapter will be a good start to creating a comprehensive fair play policy. From there, research the topic more thoroughly. (Visit the European Cultural Cooperation of the Council of Europe Web site [http://culture.coe.fr/Infocenter/txt/eng/espcod.htm] for an example of a fair play policy.)

Once you thoroughly understand the topic and have a good idea of what your fair play policy should include to fit the needs of your program, revisit your mission statement. Does it include the essence of fair play (sportsmanship and inclusion)? Although "inclusion" and/or "sportsmanship" may not be specified, it is likely that the principle is there. If your mission statement contains "for as many students as possible" (or "for all who want to participate" or a similar phrase), for example, the words imply the essence of fair play.

Step 2: Once you are fortified with a solid understanding of and a commitment to fair play, the second step is evaluating your current program. Of course, if you are designing a program from scratch, you won't have anything to evaluate. You will, however, have something to consider in creating your program. Measurements of inclusion are best taken by looking at participation numbers. How many males and females show up for activities? Which ethnicities are represented? How many people with disabilities participate? Measurements of sportsmanship are easily gleaned by attending a few events or activities or games. Are participants enjoying themselves? Do fights erupt often? Do players leave the field feeling invigorated and energized or hostile and angry?

Step 3: If you find problems—specifically, inequities in participation or flaring tempers during games—it's time to find out why. Seek out students and representatives from under-represented groups. Ask them why they don't participate, or if they know of any barriers that would prevent their peers from participating. Like the activities themselves, true inclusion necessitates shared awareness, shared commitment, and collaborative decision making. Likewise, poll participants to determine whether sportsmanship is alive and well in your program or something sorely lacking. Officials may also have some useful observations to add. For example, perhaps the stakes are too high at certain games or in certain leagues.

Step 4: Armed with this information—the more specific, the better—you can begin the process of formulating your policy. This stage of policy formulation is largely planning. Much like the process of writing your mission statement, explained in chapter 2, planning a fair play policy starts with prioritization. Work with the problems and solutions you identified in steps 2 and 3, making a list of all problems and specific strategies to resolve them. Depending on the number of problems you find, it may be helpful to start big and work your way down. For example, it would be extremely inefficient, if not completely ineffective, to work on promoting your program to people in wheelchairs if the facilities are not accessible.

Step 5: Once you have a plan in place, it's time to begin to implement that plan by writing your fair play policy. Write a comprehensive statement describing your intention. You can outline your plan for achieving total inclusion and uniform sportsmanship in this policy, or you can simply specify the policy requirements. As was explained above, specifics are important. Do not note that all people, regardless of age, gender, skin color, race, and so on, should be included in intramural activities and leave it at that. Give the numbers: "all co-ed teams must comprise 2/5 of either gender" or "at least one

minority must be on every team that competes in the volleyball league."

Step 6: By having a formal, written fair play policy in place, you will now be able to physically implement your plan. First and foremost, it's important to understand that achieving total adherence to your policy will take time. Indeed, this is why it is so important to incorporate fair play into your mission statement. As you and your staff go about the day-to-day operations of your intramural program, your mission statement will serve as an active reminder of what you're striving for. Specific implementation strategies have been offered throughout this chapter and are partially summarized in the next section, "Putting Fair Play Into Practice."

Step 7: As is the case with all goal setting, to be effective, the creation and implementation of a fair play policy requires constant monitoring and periodic evaluation. If your policy is specific, it should be fairly simple to monitor simply by using participation statistics and attending some activities. Participant questionnaires (see figures 14.1 and 14.2 on pages 237 and 238) are also helpful. (The topics of monitoring and evaluation will be discussed more fully in chapter 14.)

Part of the evaluation process is revision. Because the makeup of your student body—indeed, society at large—is fluid, the inclusion component of your fair play policy will likely change over time. For example, maybe your current plan includes ways to attract more African Americans to your program. At some point, we hope, you will have achieved that goal. Or perhaps another minority will represent a larger percentage of the student body and will have to be targeted. In addition, when one group feels welcome, often a different group feels excluded. The sportsmanship component of your policy may also be in need of revision at some point. If, for example, your participation numbers drop and do not recover after eliminating the competitiveness of certain intramural sport activities, you may want to consider creating a competitive league to get former participants back. As intramural directors, you will need to continually work at encouraging and incorporating fair play—for the sake of your program, certainly, but more importantly for the sake of those who will benefit by being involved in fun, active movement with others, namely, program participants.

Putting Fair Play Into Practice

Fair play is about more than creating inclusive and fair policies and practices. Leaders, officials, and participants all need to take responsibility for doing their part. The following sections identify some of the ways these three groups can put a fair play policy into practice.

Leadership

As intramural leaders, you will have an important role to play in making fair play a reality. In addition to devising policies and enforcement procedures, you should publish fair play guidelines, create promotional campaigns to communicate the principles of fair play, and support further research into the topic. The following are practical suggestions to help you in the process.

▶ Publish clear, comprehensive fair play guidelines.

▶ Emphasize the joy of participating over winning.

▶ Raise awareness of fair play within your intramural program with a fair play promotional campaign. A poster from just such a campaign is shown in figure 6.4. You can involve participants in this campaign by holding a contest to see who can come up with the best fair play slogan, poster, or other promotional tool. (To model the emphasis of participating over winning, of course, you should probably

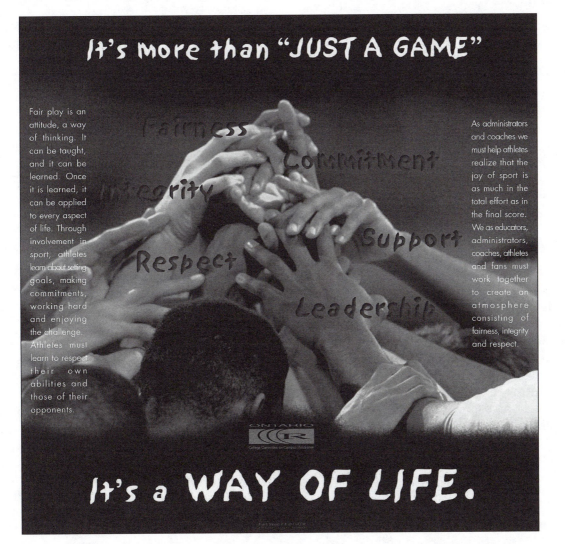

FIGURE 6.4 Fair play poster.
Courtesy of Ontario College Athletic Association, 1185 Eglinton Avenue East, Suite 505, North York, Ontario, Canada, M3C 3C6. Phone: 416-426-7043. Art work by Kristine Verbeek.

give an award to every submission and perhaps a special prize to the top three entries.) Then, place all the entries on the walls near the gym or in another central location as a reminder of the importance of fair play.

▶ Establish fair play awards to reward respect and sportsmanship (more on this to come in chapter 9).

▶ Support all staff and participant attempts to promote fair play, such as pregame fair play talks.

▶ Research the topic of fair play to expand your understanding and generate new ideas for encouraging fair play in your program. For example, keep abreast of journals and even newspapers as they discuss problems in sport and suggest solutions.

▶ Monitor and evaluate the impact of your fair play initiative by measuring violent penalties and paying attention to referee's reports on the games. (Evaluation is discussed in chapter 14.)

▶ Plan to keep at it. Fair play, like any intramural endeavor, will take time to develop fully. Work with your evaluation results to incorporate more fair play initiatives into your program from year to year.

Officials

Being on the front lines with participants day in and day out, officials have a unique opportunity to encourage and enforce fair play in all intramural activities. As intramural directors, you will have the responsibility to help them do so. The first step is ensuring that all officials are adequately trained and prepared to officiate. As explained earlier in this book, there's nothing more likely to inflame aggravation and frustration than an inconsistently and/or incompetently called game.

In addition to offering basic training in the rules of those sports they will be officiating, you will also need to explain rule modifications, unusual equipment or play, and other ways you have built inclusion and sportsmanship into intramural programming. For example, if gender equity is a requirement for all teams in a baseball league, officials must know this ahead of time and be trained in what to do if teams show up without enough male or female participants.

Finally, you can provide officials with ways to enforce your standards of fair play. For example, ask officials to rate teams on their adherence to fair play rules during a competition. (Team captains can also participate, each captain rating the players on the opposing team.) A simple scoring system can be used in such evaluations: a team earns one point if players' fair play attitudes were commendable, earns zero points if their attitudes were simply okay, and loses one point if their attitudes were poor (Varley 1994, 7). Officials then turn in their evaluations after each game and the intramural director or other intramural staff person keeps track of these points throughout the season. If a team ends the regular playing season with a negative score, it is disqualified from the play-offs. And if two teams are tied in the standings, the team with the highest fair play score is ranked ahead of the team with the lower fair play score.

Participants

Of course, participants are really the ones on the front lines. More than anyone else, at times it seems players represent the tone and standards of an intramural program. In other words, intramural leadership can devise fair play standards and policies, and officials can encourage and enforce these standards and policies. But if spectators continually see players antagonizing one another and notice that people with disabilities, women, and minorities rarely if ever participate, the notion of fair play will be little more than an ideal certain people pay lip service to.

The bottom line: all participants must approach intramural activities with the spirit of fair play, including sportsmanship and inclusion. During sign-up and registration, participants should adhere to inclusion policies and try to encourage minorities, females, people with disabilities, and other populations underrepresented in intramurals to get involved. Before games and activities, team captains should meet with officials and other participants to introduce themselves and discuss last-minute instructions. The rules of respect (rules, officials and their decisions, and opponents) and self-control should be posted prominently in all in-

An Athlete's Prayer

I thank you, O god, for giving me a body that is specially fit and strong, and for making me able to use it well.

In my training, help me not to shirk the discipline, which I know that I need and that I ought to accept.

In my leisure, help me never to allow myself any indulgence that would make me less fit than I ought to be.

When I compete with others,

Help me, win or lose, to play fair.

When I win, keep me from boasting; when I lose, keep me from making excuses.

Keep me from being conceited when I succeed, and from being sulky when I fail.

Help me always with good will to congratulate a better athlete who beat me.

Help me to live so that I will always have a healthy body and a healthy mind.

—*Source: unknown.*

tramural facilities, and players should follow them. If players are unsure about an official's call, they can ask their team captain to politely ask for an explanation. Participants should compliment one another for demonstrating fair play and not encourage or otherwise condone actions that violate fair play principles. Above all, participants should set a good example by treating others the way they wish to be treated themselves.

Chapter Summary Exercises

Having considered the importance of policies for maintaining and developing fair play, it is time to consider developing your own policies. In addition to the suggestions throughout this chapter, the following three exercises will help you.

1. Visit a playing field or gym at a grade school and high school (ask permission from the principal), as well as a university during lunchtime. Take notes on what children of different ages are doing. Can you identify age-specific characteristics? Are their noticeable examples of inclusion or exclusion?

2. Recall your own intramural experiences. Describe situations in your experience at grade school, high school, and college where there was evidence of exclusion. What was, or what should have been, done to rectify the situation?

3. Spend some time thinking about sportsmanship as it was defined in this chapter. Then start to develop your own ideas of how you would incorporate sportsmanship into your intramural program. List specific elements you want to include, and outline procedures for enforcing each element.

4. Using the steps outlined in this chapter, as well as the prioritization and revision process outlined in chapter 2 in developing your mission statement, formulate a fair play policy that includes both inclusion and sportsmanship components. For each component of your policy, be sure to list specific strategies for accomplishing and monitoring it.

References

Academy of Leisure Sciences. 2001. White paper #2: Leisure apartheid. [Online]. Available: www.eas.ualberta.ca/elj/alswp2.html

Americans with Disabilities Act. 1990. Public law 101-336, July 26, 1990, 104, Statute 327. [Online]. Available: http://janweb.icdi.wvu.edu/kinder/pages/ada_statute.htm.

Byl, J., and J. VanderWier. 1995. Encouraging fair play in college intramurals. *CAHPERD Journal* 61 (2): 26-27.

Cotton, V., W. Kelley, and W. Sedlacek. 1999. Situational characteristics of positive and negative experiences with same race and different race students. [Online]. Available: http://www.naspa.org/resources/complete.cfm?ID=1&display=full.

European Cultural Co-operation of the Council of Europe. 1992. *Code of sports ethics fair play: The winning way.* Europe of Cultural Cooperation. [Online]. Available: www.culture.coe.fr/Infocenter/txt/eng/espcod.htm.

Fair Play Canada. 1994. *Fair play—It's your call!* Ottawa, Ontario: Fair Play Canada.

Gaskins, D. 1996. A profile of recreational sports student employees. *NIRSA Journal* 20 (3): 43-77.

Graham, P. 1994. The old and the new, the past, present, and future of the NIA. *NIRSA Journal* 17 (1): 21-22.

Helm, E.J., W. Sedlacek, and D. Prieto. 1998. The relationship between attitudes toward diversity and overall satisfaction of university students by race. *Journal of College Counseling* 1: 111-20.

Human Services Institute. 1992 *Trying to play together: Competing paradigms in approaches to integration through recreation and leisure.* Cambridge, Mass.: Human Services Institute.

International Paralympic Committee. 2001. Goalball. [Online]. Available: www.lboro.ac.uk/research/paad/ipc/goalball/goalball.html.

Lundy, K. 1999. *Community vs. elite sport: The elusive balance.* Sydney, Australia. [Online]. Available: http://www.katelundy.dynamite.com.au/access&.htm.

Phillips, M. 1992. The experience of disability and the dilemma of normalization. In *Interpreting disability: A qualitative reader*, edited by P. Ferguson, D. Ferguson, and S. Taylor. New York: Teachers College, 213-32.

Proescher, L. 1996. Participant satisfaction in intramurals. *NIRSA Journal* 20 (3): 20-24.

Riley, R., and N. Cantu. 1997. *Title IX: 25 years of progress.* [Online]. Available: www.ed.gov/pubs/TitleIX/part5.html.

Smith, S. 1995. Personal meaning in intramural basketball. *NIRSA Journal* 20 (1): 36-44.

Statistics Canada. 2001. *National longitudinal survey of children and youth: Participation in activities.* Ottawa: Statistics Canada.

Tharp, L. 1994. The effect Title IX has had on intramural sports. *NIRSA Journal* 19 (1): 29-31.

Vanden Boor, M. 2000. Ultimate medical dodgeball. *CIRA-Ontario Input* (March): 6.

Varley, Jane. 1994. Campus recreation protest and conduct board. *CIRA Input* (December): 7.

Wilhite, B., and D. Kleiber. 1992. The effects of Special Olympics participation on community integration. *Therapeutic Recreation Journal* 26 (4): 9-20.

Resources

Books, Periodicals, and Videos

Byl, J. 2002. *Co-ed recreational games: Breaking the ice and other activities.* Champaign, IL: Human Kinetics.

Presents numerous games and ideas for equalizing competition.

Canadian Rehabilitation Council for the Disabled. *Sharing the Fun: A Guide to Including Persons with Disabilities in Leisure and Recreation.* [Online]. Available www.lin.ca.

A practical guide about enabling people with disabilities to participate in community leisure and recreation. Made available through The Leisure Information Network.

Palaestra.
P.O. Box 508
Macomb, IL 61455
Telephone: 309-833-1902
Web site: www.palaestra.com

Published in cooperation with the United States Paralympic Corporation of the United States Olympic Committee and the Adapted Physical Activity Council of the America Alliance for Health, Physical Education, Recreation and Dance. This journal is about encouraging sport, physical education, and recreation forum for people with disabilities.

Recreation Nova Scotia. 1999. *Inclusion: A Sense of Belonging.* [Online]. Available: www.lin.ca.

Video and presenter's guide offering a candid discussion among teens about inclusion Made available through The Leisure Information Network.

Organizations and Web sites

Active Living Alliance for Canadians with a Disability (ALACD)
720 Belfast Road, Suite 104
Ottawa, Ontario, K1G 0Z5
Telephone: 613-244-0052
Toll-free: 1-800-771-0663
Fax: 613-244-4857
Web site: www.ala.ca

Provides resources for offering inclusive active-living programs for Canadians with disabilities.

Americans with Disabilities Act Document Center
Web site: http://janweb.icdi.wvu.edu/kinder/index.htm

Explains the legal requirements for accommodating people with a disability. There are also additional links to information, networks, and job accommodations.

The Arc
National Headquarters
1010 Wayne Avenue, Suite 650
Silver Spring, MD 20910

Phone: 301-565-3842
Fax: 310-565-5342
e-mail: info@thearc.org

For more information on integrating those with mental disabilities, check out the helpful Web site at the The Arc, (http://thearc.org) especially the sections dealing with integration in recreation.

Canadian Association for the Advancement of Women and Sport and Physical Activity (CAAWS)
N202-801 King Edward Avenue
Ottawa, Ontario, Canada K1N 6N5
Phone: 613-562-5667
E-mail: caaws@caaws.ca
Web site: www.caaws.ca

One of two leading organizations promoting women in sport in Canada and the United States. CAAWS encourages girls and women to get out of the bleachers, off the sidelines, and onto the field by offering conferences, grants, newsletters, and public lobbying.

European Cultural Co-operation of the Council of Europe
Web site: http://culture.coe.fr/Infocenter/txt/eng/espcod.htm

Offers an example of a fair play policy, including who the key players are.

International Badminton Association
4 Manor Park
Mackenzie Way
Cheltenham, Glos, United Kingdom GJ51 9TX
Phone: 44-011-1242-234904
Fax: 44-011-1242-221030
E-mail: info@intbadfed.org

For more information on badminton for disabled people, particularly the rules, (http://www.worldbadminton.com/ifb_laws.html#a5).

The Leisure Information Network
1185 Eglington Avenue East, Suite 502
Toronto, ON Canada M3C 3C6

Phone: 416-426-7176
E-mail: info@lin.ca
Web site: www.lin.ca

Publishes *Active Living Alliance*, which focuses on active living through physical education that maximizes opportunities for students with a disability.

National Capital Wheelchair Tennis Association
880 Wellington Street, Unit 4
Ottawa, ON Canada K1N 6K7
Phone: 613-569-7632
Fax: 613-569-8507
E-mail: ncscd@magma.ca

For more information on wheelchair tennis and particularly the rules see: http://ww.magma.ca/~ncwta/trules.html

National Center on Physical Activity and Disability (NCPAD)
1640 West Roosevelt Road
Chicago, IL 60608-6904
Phone: 1-800-900-8086
E-mail: ncpad@uic.edu
Web site: www.uic.edu/orgs/ncpad/

Encourages persons with disabilities to participate in regular physical activity by gathering, evaluating, and disseminating information on physical activity and disability science. NCPAD offers a variety of resources, including fitness and health professionals and research on disability and physical activity.

Women's Sports Foundation
Eisenhower Park
East Meadow, NY 11554
Phone: 516-542-4700
E-mail: wosport@aol.com
Web site: www.womenssportsfoundation.org/templates/index.html

The other of two leading organizations promoting women in sport in Canada and the United States, providing resources, grants, and action opportunities for women in sport.

Policy II:
Safety

Providing a safe intramural environment should be a primary concern for intramural directors. No one likes to see a participant get hurt, but safety doesn't stop there. If participants perceive a risk of injury, they will likely refrain from participating. Worse still, if participants do get injured, there is a potential for costly and unpleasant lawsuits. A lot of problems can be alleviated by ensuring adequate staffing, both quantitatively and qualitatively. Quantitatively a program needs an adequate number of staff and officials to run and supervise the events. Qualitatively a program needs an adequately trained and prepared staff.

Note: Much of the discussion in this chapter involves legal matters. This discussion is not intended as legal advice, just suggestions worthy of consideration when planning a safe intramural program. When setting policy or drafting documents, it is important that you seek professional legal advice to ensure that all program documents and activities adequately protect the participants and staff.

Chapter Objectives

▶ Define the legalities related to intramural programs.
▶ Learn how to develop intramural safety policies.
▶ Understand the role of program leadership and participants in providing a safe intramural program.

Legalities:
Defining Legal Concepts

Let's define a few terms. As you read these definitions, think about how they might apply to intramural situations. To begin, there is a certain level of care that intramural directors, staff, and volunteers have a responsibility to administer. This **standard of care** is simply the basic standard "a reasonably prudent" individual would expect under the same or similar circumstances. **Professionals**, those who participate in a field for material or other gain or for their livelihood, are held to a higher standard of care because of their training and expertise, a standard largely determined by the profession itself or by other professionals in similar circumstances. In the intramural arena, this standard of care is ensured with adequate supervision. For the purposes of this discussion, then, **supervision of participants** in the context of intramural safety, is the keeping of order in a game or activity, stopping of fights and other hazardous conduct, and general protection and assurance of safety for all program participants.

If a reasonable standard of care is not present or if intramural personnel fail to act prudently, they are deemed negligent. Negligence is the most common violation brought against intramural professionals. Put simply, **negligence** is doing something a reasonably prudent person would not do, or not doing something a reasonably prudent person would do, under similar circumstances. Because what is a reasonable standard of care varies—as explained above, professionals are held to a higher standard of care—so does negligence vary. Indeed, children are not held to the same level of accountability as adults. According to "age of negligence" statutes, a person is incapable of negligence up to the age of seven and an "unlikely" contributor to negligence between the ages of seven and fourteen. In other words, people can only be found negligent if they are 14 or older.

If something goes wrong and results in damage or injury, the injured party can seek compensation. A **tort** is an injury to another person or to property, which is compensable under the law. Categories of torts include negligence, gross negligence, and intentional wrongdoing. **Gross negligence** is conduct so reckless as to demonstrate a substantial lack of concern for whether injury results, while **intentional wrongdoing** is the intent to do harm. To justify a legal tort claim, an act (or inaction) must satisfy four elements: (1) There must be a legal duty of care to another person and (2) a breach of that duty; (3) the **claimant**, the person filing for compensation, must have suffered damages; and (4) the damages must have been proximately caused by the breach of duty. Once these elements have been satisfied, if the proceedings find for the claimant, that obligation is a liability. **Liability** is legal responsibility for injury or damage to another. If found guilty the defendant may need to pay or make restitution.

In court, various labels indicate various people's roles in the proceedings. The **plaintiff**, or claimant, is the injured party who files a claim in court. The **defendant** is the one who is being sued or charged and must defend him or herself against the plaintiff's claims. An **appellant** is someone who loses in court and appeals the court's decision to a higher court. An **appellee** is the one who wins in court proceedings and against whom the appellant appeals.

Courts can award various damages to a plaintiff. **Actual damages** are the actual costs directly related to the injury (medical expenses, lost wages, and so on). **Speculative damages** comprise costs the injured party will likely suffer as a result of the injury (future income, future life opportunities, and so on). **Punitive damages** do not relate to a plaintiff's costs but rather are imposed to punish a defendant, in the hope of preventing the violation from being repeated. Punitive damages are the type of damages awarded in defamation cases. **Defamation** includes verbal (slander) or written (libel) communication that is false and holds the subject of the statement up to public ridicule.

A trial can end in several ways. First, a judge may make a **summary judgment** when there is no dispute about the facts of the case and case law is directly applicable. In such cases, judges find for the plaintiff or defendant and mete out an appropriate judgement. Second, the plaintiff and defendant may settle. A **settlement** is a reward or solution both parties agree to before or during a trial. Third, the trial can run to its completion, in which case a judge or jury finds for the plaintiff or defendant and awards damages. Finally, a case can be dismissed by a judge before going to trial. Dismissals are issued when a case is fraudulent or specious on its face.

Put simply, litigation should be avoided in every way possible. In your intramural program, the buck will stop with you. It will be your responsibility to ensure that all intramural staff, volunteers, and participants consider safety and reduce the likelihood of damages to persons and property. One way to do that is **risk management**, which is simply the process of limiting dangerous, harmful, and hazardous situations. Whatever steps you take to ensure safety, however, many intramural activities have some inherent risk. You can protect yourself, the institution, and the program by explaining these risks to participants—and having them sign a statement that they understand these risks— before they engage in an activity. This is called **assumption of risk**. To inform participants of risks inherent in intramural activities, many programs use consent forms and waivers. A **consent form** is an authorization, usually signed by a parent or guardian, permitting a child to take part in some activity. When participants sign a **waiver**, they agree to waive their right to seek damages from the intramural department, its staff, and the institution should they be injured while participating in an intramural activity or event.

Legal Forms

Consents, waivers, disclaimers, and assumption of risk paperwork can protect you, your program, and your institution from being sued. As noted at the beginning of this chapter, these forms are included to provide an example. They are not meant to replace legal advice.

Waivers can be used to indicate the inherent risk in intramural activities and waive the right of a participant to sue should he or she be injured while participating. Waivers can be long and formal or short and informal. They can be stand-alone documents that participants sign, or they can be a paragraph or two included on team or individual signup sheets. In addition to preventing lawsuits, the two primary purposes of a waiver are to (1) explain the risks of an activity and (2) get participants to agree to assume those risks. The following suggestions will help you in drafting a clear waiver that will likely stand up in court.

1. Include a title. To make sure participants understand what they are signing, a waiver needs a descriptive title such as "Waiver and Release of Liability," or other similar title, that is conspicuous (in large, bold type, perhaps in an upper case, colored, or underlined font).

2. Make the writing clear and understandable.

3. Specify who is relinquishing their rights to sue and whom the waiver protects.

4. Specify the inherent risks of the activity.

5. Have participants sign the waiver to acknowledge that they know and understand the risks of the activity but are voluntarily agreeing to participate despite those risks.

Note: In the case of minor children, a waiver signed by parents does not relieve anyone of legal liability. It does, however, enable a parent or guardian to keep a child from participating. In addition, including a section for parents to complete about any physical or other limitations of the child is helpful if program staff should know about these limitations. Finally, it is important to realize that even well-written waivers are not upheld in all states. Protect yourself by having the school attorney examine and finalize your waiver form.

Figures 7.1 and 7.2 show samples of waivers, short and long respectively. Notice how the inherent risks of the program are carefully explained and how the signee takes personal responsibility for these risks. The longer form identifies some of these risks in greater detail. Both forms also relinquish the rights of heirs or executors to sue the institution at a future date. The longer form also builds into it an agreement against harassment and the rights of the institution to use photographs or video clips of the signer for purpose of promotion.

These waivers should be signed when participants sign up for intramurals and individual intramural activities. Thus, it is helpful to indicate participants' acknowledgment and signing of this waiver right on the sign-up sheet. Sign-up sheets typically also include student name, student number, and a phone number in case of an emergency, as shown in figure 7.3 for team signup and figure 13.2 for individual sign-up.

Informed Liability Release

In consideration of the opportunity provided by _____ [institution] to participate in its Intramural Program, I do hereby voluntarily and with full understanding forever discharge, waive, release, and hold harmless _____ [institution] from any claim that may arise from any injury or illness I sustain while participating in any Intramural Program activity/event, including any injury or illness resulting from the gross negligence or tortuous activity of _____ [institution], its officers, directors, employees, agents, or volunteers. This includes returning from any activity or event related to my program membership. I specifically assume any and all risk inherent in said activity/event related to my program membership. I certify that I am presently and will continue to be properly trained and prepared for all activities or events in which I choose to participate.

I have read the above Informed Liability Release. I understand its contents and all implications, and I voluntarily agree to be bound by said Release, in whole and by each of its parts.

Name _____

Signature _____

Date _____

FIGURE 7.1 Example of short waiver.

The small text in the signature box, "Agree to waiver," is there to remind participants that they have also signed a waiver. In the case of students under the age of 18, many schools require parents to sign both a consent form (see figure 7.4) and a waiver.

The inherent risks of each intramural activity or event should also be reinforced on the intramural department's Web site, program materials, handbooks, and other appropriate communications, including rule sheets distributed to team captains before each game. These messages will likely be shorter than the comprehensive waivers presented in figures 7.1, 7.2, and 7.4, certainly, but they will serve as a helpful reminder. An example of an abbreviated statement detailing participants' assumption of risk is shown in figure 7.5.

Waivers, consents, hold harmless agreements, assumptions of risk—the legalities can be daunting. Luckily, there's no rule against having fun with this part of your intramural program. Indeed, Tennessee Tech showed a sense of humor by posting the following (Tntech 2001):

Q: While slam-dunking the ball in a basketball game, I got my leg caught in the rim and consequently broke my little toe. The intramural director refused to reimburse me for medical expenses. Since I'm female, can I claim sexual discrimination and negligence and sue the university for a million bucks?

A: Nope. When you sign the roster for each sport, you also sign a release agreement that releases the university from any responsibility for your injury. Besides, every player has an equal opportunity to break their little toe on the rim.

In the end, the fear of being sued can paralyze some intramural programs, not to mention thwart creative programming. It need not. The reality is that millions of students, young and old, participate safely in intramural and recreational activities around the world. The challenge for intramural directors is to continue to provide fresh and interesting programming that is as safe as possible for the participants. That largely entails minimizing the risks, which is the topic of the next section.

Assumption of Risks and Personal Responsibility

In consideration of the services of _____ [institution] Intramural Sports Program, the _____ [institution] Board of Regents, their officers, agents, employees, and all other persons or entities associated with it (collectively referred to as Intramural Sports Program), I agree as follows.

Although the Intramural Sports Program has taken reasonable steps to provide me with appropriate equipment and skilled staff so that I can enjoy this activity for which I may not be skilled, I acknowledge that this activity is not without risk. Certain risks cannot be eliminated without destroying the unique character of this activity. The same elements that contribute to the unique character of this activity can cause accidental injury; loss or damage to my equipment; illness; and in extreme cases permanent trauma or death. The Intramural Sports Program does not want to frighten me or reduce my enthusiasm for this activity but deems it important for me to know in advance what to expect and to be informed of the inherent risks. The following describes some, but not all, of these risks.

Intramural Sports Program activities take place both in and out of doors, where participants are subject to a variety of risks. Participation in "contact" and "noncontact" activities varies and includes such actions as running, jumping, passing, kicking, catching, and physical contact with others. Falling, slipping. sliding, tripping, bumps, bruises, cuts, abrasions, contusions, dislocations, broken bones, pulled muscles, fatigue, and sunburn can potentially be a part of this participation.

I am aware that the Intramural Sports Program activities include risks of injury or death to teammates and myself. I understand that the description of these risks is not complete and that other unknown or unanticipated risks may result in property loss, injury, or death. I agree to assume responsibility for the inherent risks identified herein as well as those inherent risks not specifically identified. My participation in this activity is purely voluntary, and I elect to participate in spite of and with full knowledge of the inherent risks.

I acknowledge that engaging in this activity may require a degree of skill and knowledge different from other activities and that I have responsibilities as a participant. I acknowledge that the Intramural Sports Program staff has been available to fully explain the nature and physical demands of this activity as well as the inherent risks, hazards, and dangers associated with this activity.

I have read and understand the information sheet and handbook provided by the Intramural Sports Program. I am aware of the level of exertion required to participate in this activity and have the necessary skills as listed on said sheet and handbook. I have verified with my physician and other medical professionals that I have no past or current physical or psychological condition that might affect my participation in this activity, other than that described on the attached health statement form (if applicable). I authorize the Intramural Sports Program to obtain or provide emergency hospitalization, surgical, or other medical care for me.

I understand that the laws of the state of _____ [state of institution] govern this Assumption of Risks and Personal Responsibility statement. I certify that I am fully capable of participating in this activity, without causing harm to others or myself. Therefore, I (or my parents or guardians, if I am a minor) assume full responsibility for bodily injury or death, loss of personal property, and all expenses that result from those inherent risks and dangers identified herein, those inherent risks and dangers not specifically identified, and those that result from my negligence in participating in this activity. I am responsible for reading the current intramural handbook and sports rules, and I agree that I will abide by all rules, policies, and procedures. I also agree to pay any related fees or penalties associated with my team's participation in this activity as outlined in the intramural fee policy.

I acknowledge that racial epithets, anger-motivated outbursts, demeaning, degrading and derogatory remarks, homophobic comments, and intimidating actions are unacceptable. I agree that I will not participate in said behavior during participation in the Intramural Sports Program because it is contrary to _____'s [institution] fair play as well as its Intramural Sports Program policy. I also agree that any spectators associated with my participation in this activity and/or in attendance at this activity will be held to the same standard as participants.

I hereby grant full permission to record my participation in this activity, including photographs, motion pictures, radio, videotape, E-mail, Web and Internet, and other media known or unknown. I also grant full permission to publish and/or use such recordings—no matter who recorded them—in any manner for publicity, promotion, advertising, trade, or commercial purposes without reimbursement.

I acknowledge and understand that, at all levels, playoffs may be scheduled at any time, including any day of the week, and I will be prepared to play.

I (or my parents or guardians, if I am a minor) have read, understand, and accept the terms and conditions stated herein and acknowledge that this agreement shall be effective and binding upon myself, my heirs, my personal representatives, my estate, and all members of my family.

Name _____

Signature _____

Date _____

FIGURE 7.2 Example of long waiver.

Sign-up Sheet

Student signature	ID #	Phone #	Emergency contact	Contact number
Joe Black (Agree to waiver)	234-45-678	317-555-9286	Sharon Black	317-555-9477
(Agree to waiver)				
(Agree to waiver)				
(Agree to waiver)				
(Agree to waiver)				
(Agree to waiver)				
(Agree to waiver)				
(Agree to waiver)				
(Agree to waiver)				
(Agree to waiver)				
(Agree to waiver)				
(Agree to waiver)				
(Agree to waiver)				
(Agree to waiver)				

FIGURE 7.3 Intramural program sign-up sheet.

Liability Release for Children Under 18

Activity _____

I am the parent/legal guardian (circle one) of the child named below. I recognize that because of the inherent hazards of this activity, my child may sustain some injury. In the event that my child is injured and my spouse or I cannot be contacted, I give my permission to the attending physician to render such treatment as would be normal and agree to pay the usual charge for said treatment.

I hereby release _____ [institution] and its employees, agents, and assigns for any and all claims for personal injury and/or property damage that may arise from or be in any way connected to the named child(ren)'s participation in this activity. I understand that this release applies to both present and future injuries, and that it binds myself, my spouse, and the named child(ren), as well as the heirs, executors, and administrators of each of these persons. I have read this release and understand all of its terms. I sign it voluntarily and with full knowledge of its significance.

Signature _____

Printed Name _____

Date _____

Relationship to child _____

Please list all children for whom the above waiver applies.

_____

_____

_____

In case of emergency, please contact:

Name _____

Phone _____

Relationship _____

FIGURE 7.4   Consent form.

Assumption of Risk

By voluntarily participating in _____ [institution] Campus Recreation programs, all participants assume risk of injury. _____ [Institution] does not accept responsibility for injury or loss incurred by any person participating in activities organized and administered by the Campus Recreation program.

Each participant is responsible for having his/her own medical, dental, and hospital coverage. Information about insurance providers is available from _____ [health services department].

To ensure personal safety, participants should follow these guidelines:

- Have annual physical examinations.
- Warm up and cool down slowly (10 minutes before and after each activity).
- Wear proper safety equipment (footwear, eye protection, helmets, and so on).
- Check equipment to ensure that it is safe and in good repair. (Report any unsafe equipment to the activity supervisor.)

FIGURE 7.5   Assumption of risk reminder.

Safety Policies

So how do intramural directors go about ensuring the safety of participants? As was the case with fair play, the best way is to develop procedures and policies. The word *safety* means different things to different people, certainly, and thus the components of a safety policy will vary from institution to institution. Colleges and universities will likely include a policy on alcohol use, for example, while it would be neither necessary nor appropriate for a grade school to have such a policy. In this section, we consider the various components of a comprehensive safety policy, including player eligibility, officials' responsibility, attire, competitive level, emergency procedures, lightning, blood, alcohol, and facility security.

Eligibility

Any students of an institution are usually eligible to participate in intramurals. Chapter 11 discusses the inclusion of others as well, such as alumni, faculty, and staff. Students should not be discouraged from participating in intramural programs on the basis of GPA, gender, or other factors. However, for the safety of the participants, they must be physically well enough to withstand the physical demands of participation. That means, they should have an annual physical to make sure they have no conditions that will limit their ability to participate. A common procedure at Canadian and some U.S. institutions is for potential participants to complete a health questionnaire before they are permitted to participate. One such questionnaire, called *Par-Q & You*, has been prepared by the Canadian Society for Exercise Physiology and is supported by Health Canada. The questionnaire asks a series of questions, including those listed here. To view the complete questionnaire, visit the Canadian Society for Exercise Physiology Web site (www.hc-sc.gc.ca/hppb/paguide/parq.html).

1. Has your doctor ever told you that you have a heart condition that limits your ability to participate in physical activity?
2. Do you feel pain in your chest when you engage in physical activity?
3. In the past month, have you had chest pain when you were not doing anything physical?
4. Have you ever lost your balance because of dizziness?
5. Have you ever lost consciousness?

6. Do you have a bone or joint condition that could be exacerbated by participating in physical activity?

7. Are you currently taking doctor-prescribed medication for high blood pressure or a heart condition?

8. Do you know of any reason why you should not participate in physical activity?

Officials' Responsibility

If officials do their jobs effectively, fairly, and with obvious concern for the welfare of all participants, the likelihood of anyone getting injured—and the likelihood that the intramural department or attending official will get sued—is greatly reduced. It is important for officials to keep the game under control without becoming "whistle happy." The type of control needed is the control any prudent person would exercise. In the case of litigation over perceived negligence, the principal question a judge will ask is the following: "Did the negligence of the defendant cause or aggravate the injury in question?" If it did not, the participant (claimant, or plaintiff) cannot sue the official. To avoid litigation, then, officials should heed the following suggestions.

1. Officials should consistently enforce the rules of the game as they are written and as they are intended. If officials do not routinely penalize "illegal" acts (i.e., game offenses such as fouls), which usually lead to rougher and more aggressive play and precipitate an injury, they may be held partly or wholly accountable for the injury.

2. Pointing out a hazard and working around it is not enough. The hazard needs to be removed before the game starts. To ensure safe playing areas, officials should complete pregame facility safety checklists (explained in chapter 5; also see figures 7.6, 7.7, and 7.8 on pages 121-123). If the grounds or facilities create an unreasonable risk of injury, and if officials agree to begin the game anyway but with certain modifications to the rules, officials may be partially liable if an injury occurs because of these modifications. *Note:* This also includes protecting fans. If fans are sitting too close to a batter and could get hit by a ball or bat, for example, officials should warn the fans to move further away before the game.

3. Play should be suspended when participants are at risk of hurting themselves or others. This includes a player being hurt, exhausted, outmatched, intoxicated (see "Alcohol" on page 119), or wearing inappropriate attire. Officials' responsibilities in this regard will vary according to the present danger and according to the normal standard practiced and required in the sport.

4. Officials should exercise restraint with participants who are out of control. First, of course, officials should try to alleviate the situation and gain control. If that is not possible, however, and a participant assaults an official, the official should not strike back. Instead, officials should write down what occurred, check to see if a video was taken of the event and obtain a copy of it, and get all relevant information about the incident, including names of the assailant, name and contact information from any witnesses, and the score sheet—particularly if a previous incident occurred in the same game. If officials lose control themselves by striking back or otherwise participating in a confrontation, they may be sued.

Attire

As discussed in chapter 5, proper attire will help make an intramural activity or game safe and fun for all. Participants should not wear any jewelry, including dangling earrings, necklaces, rings, and so on. Likewise, clothing with buckles, protruding metal or other objects, or anything else deemed potentially dangerous in sport or other activities should not be allowed. Participants should wear shoes that give adequate traction and protection—that means, no bare feet or sandals in most activities. Depending on the level of competition, spikes should not be allowed in outdoor soccer, flag football, baseball, and softball.

In many activities, particularly the rough sports of hockey and football, protective padding and equipment is necessary. This equipment should either be provided by the institution or players should be required to supply their own. Whatever the source, players should not be allowed to participate without necessary protective equipment. Some institutions also require that players wear eye protection in certain intramural activities. When formulating attire policies, you will need to consider the activities, the level of competition, normal game conduct and play, and so on.

General safety requirements such as the wearing of jewelry should be noted in any general information about intramurals as well as in sport specific rules. In addition, sport-specific rules should also note the specific attire requirements for that activity. In a sport such as floor hockey, the rules might state: "Attire: for everyone's safety, players are not permitted to wear any jewelry while participating. Clothing must permit freedom of movement and not be a threat to others—therefore, clothing may not include belts with large buckets or other items that have protruding metal or other objects. For your own safety, you must wear eye protection provided by the institution."

Competitive Level

Proper administration goes a long way toward reducing the potential for injuries in intramurals. As intramural directors, you will have the responsibility to ensure that players and teams in leagues, tournaments, games, and other activities are evenly matched. In one intramural program, a large, unskilled indoor soccer player signed up for an intermediate soccer league. Because he was outmatched, he overexerted himself during a game, lost his balance, and fell onto a small player who had the ball. The small player broke his leg. This accident was not the result of improper rules or procedures. It is important, however, because less-skilled players often sign up for intramural activities and find themselves in "over their heads."

In devising your sign-up procedures, it's important that you create a procedure for conveners, administrators, and even officials to assess the skill level of all participants. To encourage players to improve their skills, you can offer clinics and other instruction. To help officials and conveners assess participants' competitive level, you should observe players competing and ask students well before the beginning of a league if anyone wishes to participate in a developmental clinic for the next league sport. These clinics would review the basics of the rules and skills of the sport. You should also develop procedures for disqualifying players whose skills are not advanced enough to compete at the level of the

game. Since intramurals should not discourage participation, the director should make sure that other opportunities for involvement are available. Offering a sport at different competitive levels is one way of doing this.

In a men's badminton game I observed novices were competing against experienced badminton players. One of the novice players (Novice 1) returned the bird to the middle of the opposing court. His partner (Novice 2) stayed at the net. One of the experienced opponents (Expert 1) smashed the bird back to the novice team, hitting Novice 2 in the eye. More-experienced players would have protected their face and eyes by holding up their racquets or moving back away from the net in anticipation of the smash. Being relatively new to the sport, however, Novice 2 had no idea what was to come and, as a result, lost all sight in his left eye. While an extreme example, this underscores the need to match players by competitive level. This can be accomplished by setting up tournaments that minimize such mismatches and creating separate leagues for different abilities, as discussed earlier in this book.

You may also want to consider modifying some game rules to minimize body contact and other potentially hazardous action, particularly in recreational leagues and activities. In recreational floor hockey, for example, players could be instructed to avoid body checking and high elbowing. Rather than let players dig the ball out from along the wall, officials could blow the whistle and have a face-off. To make sure players keep their hockey sticks below the waist at all the times, a high-sticking rule could be imposed: any infraction—even celebrating a goal—and the ball goes to the other team.

Emergency Procedures

At this point in the discussion, it is important to understand that injuries will occur in intramurals. There is nothing you can do that will prevent all accidents. (This is why the assumptions of risk, waivers, and consent forms are so important.) There is, however, a lot you can do to ensure that injured participants get the medical attention they require as quickly as possible.

1. Be sure to get emergency contact information on all participants when they sign up (see figures 7.3 and 7.4 on pages 112 and 113), and provide this information to game and event conveners and officials (see figure 13.3).

2. Be sure that the emergency procedure, including relevant phone numbers and first-aid information is posted prominently at all activities and events.

3. Provide first-aid equipment and training to all intramural staff, officials, and team captains. Supervisors should be trained in CPR and first aid.

4. Communicate to all program staff and officials that safety is part of their job. (You should also include safety responsibilities in all job descriptions.

5. At the beginning of each game or activity, tell all participants who they should go to in the event of an accident or injury. For younger children, supervisors and medically trained personnel should wear identifiable and brightly colored backpacks with appropriate first-aid supplies and a cell phone (to make emergency calls).

6. Reinforce emergency procedures often by holding periodic practice emergency drills.

An emergency plan should be simple and easy to follow. According to Ian McGregor (1997), with experience as a director of athletics and intramurals at several universities and an expert on the topic of risk management, suggests that there are two steps in developing an emergency procedure policy.

First, find out what needs to be done. Think through various emergency situations and identify what should be in place before an emergency. Consider communication from the site, emergency equipment on hand, evacuation should it be necessary, the availability of medical personnel, and who will do what by answering the following questions:

- Is a phone on site and accessible? (If not, consider providing cell phones to conveners, officials, and other program staff in attendance.)
- Are first-aid kits available?
- How will participants evacuate the facility?

- Will emergency response teams be able to find the facility?
- Are intramural staff medically trained or adequately certified in CPR?
- Who will take control at the accident scene?
- Who will call for help?

At this step it's also important to specify what information will be needed before, during, and after an accident or other emergency. For example, emergency contact information should be available, and officials and conveners should have accident report forms on hand. Many institutions require that all injuries be recorded on the game score sheet.

The second step, of course, is delegating these responsibilities and then ensuring that staff are adequately trained to carry out the emergency procedure. Training can consist of informal clinics for officials, team captains, and other intramural staff, as well as formal medical classes for certain key personnel. A local hospital or clinic may be willing to train staff for a small fee.

Even with a comprehensive emergency plan in place, intramural directors and their institutions do get sued from time to time. The reason: something went wrong. It's as simple as that. For the well-being of all participants, any injury should prompt a closer look, both at the incident and at the emergency policy. What contributed to the injury? Will further policy development or refinement in anyway minimize the risk of such an injury reoccurring? These are called **safety audits** and are an important component of an overall safety policy. Let's consider the following two scenarios.

Scenario 1. A college student was injured when he jumped on a hammock that was part of an obstacle course. The student suffered a painful knee injury and filed a lawsuit against Johnson and Wakes University. He claimed that he had to go through the obstacle course and that the university failed to provide adequate lighting, thereby allowing a dangerous condition to exist. In addition, he claimed that the university failed to provide adequate supervision. In defending itself, the university argued that the student assumed the risk and was responsible for this action. A jury agreed and refused to award any damages to the plaintiff (Appenzeller, 1994).

Although the university was not forced to pay damages, because the plaintiff had signed an assumption of risk, the intramural director and staff should carefully look at the obstacle course to see if it could be made safer.

Scenario 2. A college student was tackled during a flag football game. In arguing his claim before a judge, the student contended that the injury to his shoulder resulted in "limited motion, permanent weakness, and permanent scarring." He argued that his opponent negligently tackled him during the flag football game and thus caused his shoulder injury. The defendant—in this case, the student who made the tackle—argued that the plaintiff assumed the risk of injury when he voluntarily agreed to play the game and also that he was comparatively negligent by assuming risk of injury by voluntarily choosing to play. A Louisiana jury disagreed, however, and awarded $99,000 in compensatory damages to the plaintiff (Appenzeller, 1994).

This example underscores the key role of three people in making a safer intramural program. First, players must play within the rules of the game to create a safe experience for everyone. Officials should remind the players at the beginning of the game of the key rules and the mission of intramurals as being fun recreational activity for all. Second, officials must make sure that they call rule violations so that participants are not injured. (Officials can also help by reminding participants of the key rules of the game and why these rules are there.) Third, the intramural director should consider how policies or procedures should be changed in order to reduce the risk of such an injury occurring again.

Lightning

"Lightning kills a pitcher." "Lightning kills a canoeist." Headlines like these appear far too often. To protect intramural participants, any school should have a bad weather policy (and possibly a lightning detector) in place. Such a policy should be unambiguous. That is, there should be no wavering on the call. Part of this bad weather policy should include the following sentence: "If there is any lightning in the sky, the game is off." The bottom line: a life is worth more than a game.

Blood

To reduce infections caused by another person's blood, your institution should also have a blood policy. Typically, if participants are bleeding or have blood on their clothes, they should be immediately removed from the game or event. The general concern here is to protect both the participant who is bleeding and his or her fellow participants—not to mention intramural staff, volunteers, and officials—from secondary contamination. The specific concerns are about spreading the hepatitis B virus and acquired immunodeficiency syndrome (AIDS) caused by human immunodeficiency virus (HIV). *Note:* This spreading occurs when someone is bleeding. Participants should not be restricted from competing merely because they are infected with HIV. To protect participants from blood infections, the NCAA (2000a) has developed nine guidelines.

1. All wounds must be covered.
2. Necessary equipment and/or supplies important for compliance with universal precautions should be available to caregivers.
3. An athlete who is bleeding must have the bleeding stopped and covered.
4. All involved in the contest (officials, captains, players, spectators) have a responsibility to report bleeding.
5. Personnel handling acute blood exposure must take universal precautions such as wearing latex gloves.
6. Any surface area with blood needs to be thoroughly cleaned with an appropriate decontaminate.
7. Sharp instruments such as scalpels need to be properly disposed of.
8. Any clothing that has blood on it needs to be handled and laundered to avoid secondary contamination.
9. All intramural personnel should be trained in basic first aid and infection control.

In NCAA basketball, the blood rule (which could be applied to intramurals in general) is as follows: "Rule 5. Section 9. Article 9. [The official] suspends play when a player incurs a wound that causes bleeding or has blood on his/her body

Striking Out

It was the championship intramural floor hockey game at Hunter High School. The two teams, the Batteries and the Stampers, had met twice before and both won a game each. Batteries teammate Joe was a particularly tenacious player. When his check had the puck, Joe would give her no room to move. Given this and other overzealous play, Joe had been getting under Stampers teammates' skin all game. When Joe got the puck, the Stampers captain, Chris, yelled to her teammates to take Joe out.

It didn't take long for the tension to break. Stampers forward Jim had the puck on his stick. Tenacious Joe tried to check him but missed and inadvertently slashed Jim across the ankle. Jim had finally had enough and swung his stick at Joe, striking him in the face and knocking out his two front teeth. Everyone soon realized that this had gone too far. The game was immediately stopped, the championship game was left undecided, and Joe was taken to the emergency room where they stitched his cut lip. This was followed shortly thereafter by a trip to a dentist for two crowns.

Joe's parents were upset—rightfully so—by what had occurred. Fueled by anger and a little encouragement from friends, they turned around and sued nearly everyone involved. They sued Jim for striking Joe. They also named Chris, the team captain, in the lawsuit for inciting Jim to "take Joe out." Finally, Joe's parents named the intramural director in the suit for failing to provide competent officials.

The intramural director had trouble sleeping the night he heard about the lawsuit. He lay awake wondering if he, Jim, and Chris were in fact negligent, and how he should have done things differently.

What do you think? Are the intramural director, Jim, and Chris all negligent? If you were the intramural director, what would you do differently next time?

---

caused by blood from another player's wound. The official shall stop the game at the earliest possible time and instruct the player to leave the game for attention by medical personnel. A player with blood on his or her uniform shall have the uniform evaluated by medical personnel. When medical personnel determines that the blood has not saturated the uniform, the player may immediately resume play without leaving the game. When medical personnel determines that the blood has saturated the uniform, the affected part of the uniform shall be changed before the player shall be permitted to return" (NCAA 2000b).

Alcohol

When it comes to intramural activities—any intramural activity—alcohol and safety don't mix. Players under the influence of alcohol do not have as much control over themselves as they need in intramural activity. They are clumsier and are more likely to lose their balance and hurt themselves, or they might injure another player by falling or losing control of a stick or bat. When under the influence of alcohol, they tend to be more irritable and less easily appeased and therefore more inclined to violent activity. Put simply, allowing participants to drink alcohol before a game is asking for trouble. In fact, many institutions do not allow players to participate even if the scent of alcohol is on their clothing.

In designing an alcohol policy, it is important to be specific. Start with the policy and then formulate consequences to enforce it. For example: Individuals who are intoxicated or otherwise smell of liquor will be asked to leave the facility. If said individuals create a disturbance when asked to leave, their entire teams will be forced to forfeit the contest and may be subject to further disciplinary actions from the recreation department or the institution. If a player violates the policy a second time, said player will be expelled from all intramural activities for one year.

Facility

It is important that intramural facilities be safe for participants. A lot of personal safety measures involve the presence of staff. Positioning a receptionist at the entry to the facility who controls access with electronic entry provides some control over the people who enter. Failing electronic access, some facilities require participants to sign in as a means of tracking who is in the facility. Video cameras in the hallways and weight rooms is another tool that increases personal safety of the participants and also tends to reduce vandalism. Providing the opportunity for females to request security guards to walk them to their cars following intramural events is another helpful occasion to create a safe intramural environment for all. It is also helpful for staff to have quick access to security through two-radio or cell phones. Should there be an emergency, intramural staff can quickly contact campus security, local police, and ambulance services. Each of these security measures helps to protect the personal safety of all participants and reduce vandalism.

Facility Audits

Obviously, a facility should be designed with safety in mind. To describe such safety features goes beyond the scope of this book, but they would include adequate space around competition areas and keeping protruding objects (e.g., stages, light fixtures and switches, and other equipment and furniture not related to the contest) away from the playing area. More often, however, you and your staff will be responsible for ensuring the safety of an existing facility. The easiest and most effective way to make sure that a facility is safe and ready for play is to conduct safety checks. These checks, also called **audits,** involve a regularly scheduled and thorough site review to critically evaluate facility safety hazards and protective equipment.

Before each game, event, or other intramural activity, the convener and major official should inspect the area for any potential hazards and complete a checklist. Sample safety checklists are shown in figures 7.6 (ice arena), 7.7 (outdoor field), and 7.8 (gymnasium). Each checklist serves two purposes: they (1) force the convener and major official to make sure that everything is safe and ready for competition, and (2) demonstrate to a judge, should you be named in a lawsuit, that you have done everything possible to provide a safe facility. In most tort cases, you will be required to prove that you have done everything possible to prevent injury and be able to show that proper instruction was given, that equipment and facilities were adequately maintained and safe, and that supervision was adequate and competent.

In addition to these checklists, it's also a good idea to develop specific procedures and logs for cleaning, maintaining, and repairing equipment as per manufactures' recommendations. You might check with the legal department at your institution about these standards of care and enlist their help in designing a form that best suits your needs.

As shown on figures 7.6, 7.7, and 7.8, these checklists should include six main areas: playing surface, fixtures, lighting, emergency procedures and equipment, regulation equipment, and details of check-off. Let's take one at a time.

Playing Surface The playing surface must be free of any hazardous debris, including sharp objects like glass, hard objects like stones, or slippery areas like water puddles or grease marks. There should also not be any protruding objects such as uneven ice in an arena, or badminton and volleyball plugs that have not been correctly inserted on a gym floor. Lines should be clearly marked so that players know where the boundaries are. On an outdoor field, there should be no dangerous holes on which players might trip and sprain an ankle.

Fixtures Fixtures need to be properly installed and padded to avoid injuries. For example, volleyball posts need to be securely positioned and completely padded. That way, if players inadvertently collide with the pole, they will be protected. Fixtures on the edge of the playing area also need to be padded and secured. In ice hockey, the doors to the penalty boxes and players' benches need to open freely and close securely. In indoor soccer, any protruding objects such as wall plugs for the basketball scoreboard need to be recessed into the wall or padded if they protrude out from the wall.

Lighting Lighting safety has two components. First, lighting must be adequate so that players can see one another as well as where they are going. If the playing area is too dark, bumps and collisions could result in injury. In the case of

Arena Safety Checklist

This checklist must be completed prior to every day of a tournament or game.

✔ = Everything is good

X = Needs repair (discuss in comments sections)

N = Not applicable

Playing surface

_____ Ice surface free of debris   _____ No ice build-up along the boards

_____ Ice surface thickness adequate   _____ Lines clearly marked

Fixtures

_____ No loose, uneven, or rough boards

_____ Safety glass properly secured

_____ No jagged edges on net frame

_____ No holes in netting

_____ Doors to penalty boxes and players' benches open and close freely

Lighting

_____ All ceiling lights working   _____ Exit lights working

Emergency equipment

_____ Telephone and emergency numbers accessible

_____ First-aid kit complete and accessible

_____ Emergency procedures posted

Regulation equipment

_____ Yes _____ No

Comments _____

_____

_____

Official's name (please print) _____

Official's signature _____

Date: _____

FIGURE 7.6 Sample ice arena safety checklist for officials.

Field Safety Checklist

This checklist must be completed prior to every day of a tournament or game.

✔ = Everything is good
X = Needs repair (discuss in comments sections)
N = Not applicable

Playing surface

_____ Field surface free of debris (especially broken glass)

_____ Lines clearly marked

_____ No dangerous holes or bumps

Fixtures

_____ Posts/ bases secure

_____ No holes in netting

Emergency equipment

_____ Telephone and emergency numbers accessible

_____ First-aid kit complete and accessible

_____ Emergency procedures posted

Regulation equipment

_____ Yes   _____ No

Comments _____

_____

_____

Official's name (please print) _____

Official's signature _____

Date: _____

FIGURE 7.7   Sample outdoor field safety checklist for officials.

Gymnasium Safety Checklist

This checklist must be completed prior to every day of a tournament or game.

✔ = Everything is good

X = Needs repair (discuss in comments sections)

N = Not applicable

Playing surface

_____ Surface free of debris (including water and excessive dust)

_____ Volleyball/badminton post plugs inserted correctly

_____ Lines clearly marked

Fixtures

_____ Boards, posts, and nets proper and clean

_____ Cables, pulleys, screws, and so on working and safe

_____ Proper (standard) safety matting in place

_____ Players protected from protruding objects on the walls (bleachers, switches, plugs, and so on)

_____ Players' benches safe distance from playing area

Lighting

_____ All ceiling lights working

_____ Exit lights working

Emergency equipment

_____ Telephone and emergency numbers accessible

_____ First-aid kit complete and accessible

_____ Emergency procedures posted

Regulation equipment

_____ Yes _____ No

Comments _____

_____

_____

Official's name (please print) _____

Official's signature _____

Date: _____

FIGURE 7.8 Sample indoor gymnasium safety checklist for officials.

an emergency, exit lights should be in working order. Second, all lighting must be fitted with appropriate safety screens in case a bulb is broken. Safety screens ensure that broken bulb pieces do not fall down onto the playing surface, and possibly hit a player on the way down.

Emergency Procedures and Equipment
Emergency equipment must be readily available and staff must be clear on how to proceed in the event of an emergency or injury. As explained earlier, emergency procedures should be posted prominently, a telephone should be accessible, and intramural staff and officials should be well practiced in following emergency action plans.

Regulation Equipment Regulation equipment should be used for traditional games so participants know what to expect in the way it will feel, move, bounce, slide, and so on. Balls need to be properly inflated and sticks and other equipment need to be in good repair. When nontraditional equipment is used, participants need to be made aware of the unique features of the equipment and given the opportunity to experiment with the equipment to become familiar with it.

Details of Check-Off Last but not least, each checklist must be dated and signed so that everyone knows who completed the safety check and when it was completed. This is important should a lawsuit occur. It will not be enough to report that "someone" did a safety check at "some time" during the intramural season, but you don't know who or when.

Putting Safety Into Practice

Everyone has a role to play in the administration and implementation of safety policies. You, as intramural directors, will oversee the development and implementation of that policy as well as how participants practice, support, and sustain it. But practicing safety is also the responsibility of intramural leaders, officials, and participants. In the following sections, we will discuss the role of each intramural position in ensuring a safe intramural program.

Intramural Directors

The development and implementation of safety policies are primarily the responsibility of the intramural director. To develop policies that

will work and benefit all program participants, it will be important to get the input of your program staff and volunteers. From there, you must stand behind the policies and enforce them. The most effective way of doing that is ensuring that all personnel are aware of and knowledgeable about all safety concerns, issues, and procedures.

In addition, new staff should be told of their safety responsibilities as soon as they are hired, preferably in their job descriptions. For example, program directors are usually responsible for regular safety audits, implementing a risk-management plan, and developing and implementing a detailed emergency action plan (Cooper 1997), while officials are primarily responsible for facility audits.

Leaders

As explained in chapter 4, intramural leadership includes staff, conveners, and instructors. These leaders are typically the front-line folks who are the implementers of the policies. They must know and understand all the policies, promote adherence to them, and deal with violations to the policies as they occur. These policies were developed for the safety of all and it is the leaders who are most directly involved in putting the policies into practice.

Conveners need to ensure that safety checks are properly done prior to each game, make sure regulation equipment is available, and that staff are aware of emergency procedures.

Officials

Officials wield the big safety stick: "suspension." By having the authority to toss a player out of the game, league, or program immediately at the time of offense, officials can do a lot to ensure that safety policies are followed. That said, effective officials will often be able to diffuse volatile situations and remove potential hazards before safety is compromised. For example, an official can gently take a player who smells like alcohol to the side and say, "You smell like alcohol. For your protection and everyone else's, I cannot let you play tonight." Likewise, it will probably be the official who senses that certain players are getting a little hot under the collar and, thus, can suggest that the game be stopped for a few minutes so that hotheads can calm down and teammates can encourage each other to better model the conduct of fair play.

Officials also have an important role when it comes to implementing facility and playing area safety policies. As mentioned earlier, officials are usually the ones who complete facility audits and safety checklists prior to each game. Minor officials should also keep an eye out for safety, making sure their scoring and timing tables are far enough away from the playing area, and alert the major officials to potential problems as they perceive them (perhaps smelling alcohol on a player, noticing a player bleeding, or some equipment that has broken).

Participants

Of course, participants are ultimately responsible for their own safety. This includes having regular medical checkups and taking care of themselves physically. In addition, they must take personal responsibility for their own actions. They must be warned about the safety policy and then accept the consequences if they violate the rules.

Players need to accept their responsibilities for the safety of others as well. They need not wear clothing that will not injure others. They need to leave the playing area when they notice they are bleeding. They need to know better than to drink alcohol before intramurals. They need to also pay attention to hazards that may develop during a game, such as unsafe equipment, water on the floor, or noticing another player who is injured. A player needs to report any of these things to the official to ensure safety for all. Finally, participants can be encouraged to play safely by adhering to the rules of sportsmanship, which should be included in your fair play policy (see chapter 6). Such things as respecting their opponents, respecting the officials and their calls, and maintaining self-control at all times will go a long way in ensuring a safe, rewarding intramural experience for all.

Chapter Summary Exercises

A safe intramural program is one in which participants can experience the most fun and participate with the least fear. The following two exercises will assist you in reviewing the concepts of this chapter and beginning the process of formulating your own safety policy.

1. Walk through the recreational facilities at your institution and note physical precautions that have been made to make the facility safe. Then take another walk-through, this time noting potential hazards.

2. The following five scenarios are real accidents. Based on your knowledge and understanding of safety, answer the following questions for each scenario.

▶ Do you believe there was negligence in any of these cases?

▶ What policies and procedures should be in place to reduce the risks of these accidents occurring?

Scenario 1. A grade 9 student was killed when a heavy, wooden-framed handball net tipped and struck him on the head. (These particular nets are so heavy that they require four to six people to carry them.) The nets had fallen before, and the gym teachers warned students not to play around them because "they might fall." This particular student was reportedly swinging on the net's crossbar.

Scenario 2. A high school teacher was driving a van carrying six high school students on their way to a tournament at a neighboring town. While traveling down a two-lane highway, the van crossed the centerline and smashed head first into a transport truck. All the people traveling in the van were killed instantly.

Scenario 3. A van carrying a kindergarten class to an outing at a local park swerved out of control. Most children were wearing their seat belts, but there were more children than seat belts in this van. (State law permitted extra passengers not to wear seat belts.) When the van rolled, every child not wearing a seat belt was killed.

Scenario 4. An intramural college soccer game was scheduled. A student official surveyed the field and spotted a few potholes in the playing area. Before the game began, the official informed the players of the potential danger when playing in that part of the field. During the game, however, as two players rushed for a ball in the "dangerous zone," one of them stepped into a pothole and broke his leg.

Scenario 5. A high school hosted its annual intramural track-and-field meet. One of the events was the javelin throw, with a clearly marked area in the infield identified as the target zone. Just to the side of this zone, the long jump was in action. The next javelin thrower in line was given the okay by his supervisor. He threw the javelin, but it rolled off his hand, headed out of bounds, and struck a long-jump volunteer (who was measuring jumps) in the back of the leg. The volunteer student was taken to an emergency clinic for stitches. For the next several weeks, the student experienced a lot of pain and was not able to work (a part-time job) for 10 days after the injury.

References

Appenzeller, H. Student tackled during flag football awarded $99,000. 1994. *From the Gym to Jury*. 6 (1): 6.

Appenzeller, H. College student injured on obstacle course. *From the Gym to Jury* 6 (1): 6.

Cooper, N. 1997. Will the defendant please rise: How effective is your risk management plan? *NIRSA Journal* 21 (2): 34-41.

McGregor, I. 1997. Emergency response planning: Are you prepared? *NIRSA Journal* 21 (3): 24-25.

National Collegiate Athletic Association (NCAA). 2000a. *Guideline 2H: Blood-borne pathogens and intercollegiate athletics.* [Online]. Available: http://www.ncaa.org/sports_sciences/sports_med_handbook/2h.pdf.

National Collegiate Athletic Association (NCAA). 2000b. *2001 men's and women's basketball rules and interpretations*. Indianapolis: The National Collegiate Athletic Association. Tennessee Tech. 2001. Handbook. [Online]. Available: www.tntech.edu/www/acad/honors/handbook/chap6/chap6.html

Resources

Books

Barnes, John. 1988. *Sports and the law in Canada.* Toronto: Butterworth.

A highly useful book for anyone called upon to litigate a sports-related personal injury.

Dougherty, N. D. Auxter, and A. Goldberger. 1993. *Sport, physical activity, and the law.* Champaign, IL: Human Kinetics.

This book will help the reader find the legal knowledge they need to manage programs effectively and avoid legal problems in an U.S. context. It also includes 68 real cases which illustrate the concepts discussed in the text.

Organizations

Center for Sports Law & Risk Management
6917 Wilglen Dr.
Dallas, TX 75230
Telephone: 214-987-1766
Web site: www.ithaca.edu/sslaspa/links.htm

Publishes *From the Gym to the Jury,* an informative publication offering information on legal trends and risk management strategies for those involved in intramurals, physical education, and athletics. Find additional court cases related to intramurals, physical education, and varsity athletics on its Web site.

Society for the Study of Legal Aspects of Sport and Physical Activity (SSLASPA)
Thomas H. Sawyer, Executive Director
5840 South Ernest Dr.
Terre Haute, IN 47802
Telephone: 812-237-2186
Fax: 812-237-4338
E-mail: pmsawyr@scifac.indstate.edu

Publishes the *Journal of Legal Aspects of Sport* (JLAS), a peer-reviewed and copyrighted professional journal intended to meet the needs of sport law educators and to serve as a forum for legal issues related to clubs, fitness, health and wellness, physical activity, recreation, and sport. Also produces a quarterly newsletter (SSLASPA Newsletter), provides a resource list, and hosts an annual conference for members.

8

Promotion

As any intramural director will report, the best and most fun activity in the world can be planned and it can be staffed with superb personnel and hosted in the greatest facility with the finest equipment, but if no one knows about it, no one will attend and the event will be a huge failure. For successful, effective intramural programming, participants must participate—and lots of them. To get them to do that, they need to be told about the events and activities, and when and where to show up. In other words, if you want participants to participate in your intramural program, you will have to promote it effectively.

Chapter Objectives

► Understand the basics of promotion.
► Identify existing resources in promoting and advertising an intramural program and its programming.
► Learn how to use those resources to produce effective promotional materials.

Effective Promotion

First, let's start by defining terms. Although the concept of promotion is clear to most people, the specifics of promotion can be sketchy. For the purposes of this book, **promotion** is any activity or specific result of that activity that raises people's awareness about the intramural program, including specific intramural activities and the benefits of participating. For example, intramural promotion would include such things as program Web sites, bulletin boards devoted to intramurals, posters, celebrations to hype the program or a certain activity, intramural calendars, and so on—anything that raises awareness about the program. **Advertising**, a component of promotion, is a specific promotional tool for raising people's awareness that typically involves media. For example, running advertisements (also called "ads") in a local or student newspaper, on a Web site, or in a local sporting magazine or newsletter would all be examples of advertising. With these definitions under our belt, then, let's proceed.

Promotion has three major functions. First, it creates awareness. This can be as simple as making students aware that there is an exciting intramural program at their school. Second, it informs. This is more specific than raising awareness. After making students aware that there is an intramural program at their school, for example, it becomes necessary to inform them how to participate. This information includes such things as specific activity or event times and locales, the benefits of participating, and so on. Third, effective promotion elicits a response. Using our running example, then, an effective promotional campaign would encourage (if not compel) students to act, that is, to go to the intramural director and sign up for an activity.

Before we look at how to effectively develop and use various promotional tools, it is helpful to look briefly at some important and common characteristics of effective promotion. *Note:* These characteristics apply both to promoting a program in its entirety and promoting specific activities and events.

The Details

First and foremost, effective promotion communicates the nitty-gritty details. How do partici-

pants join? Where do they go? What do they do? If an event, what will it be? Where will it be held? When? Who is eligible to participate? This type of information is essential if you want to attract a high number of participants. There's nothing more frustrating than being excited about something and not knowing where to show up or what to do in order to participate. Because this information is key to effective advertising, this topic is discussed more fully in the "Advertising" section later in this chapter.

Inspiration

Effective promotion draws participants in by inspiring them. If you want to entice students to join the intramural volleyball league, for example, they will need to know when, where, and how to do so, but they will also need to know why. What need or desire will joining the intramural volleyball league satisfy? Beer and soda advertisements are an excellent example of inspiration. These ads never talk about where it is available or even how much it costs; they feature friends having fun together. The motivation behind this type of advertising has been well documented and involves simple psychology and human behavior. People see something they like and want to look like the people in the ads or do what they are doing. Thus, by seeing attractive people having fun while drinking soda or beer, viewers will buy that soda or beer in order to be attractive and have fun. While a simplistic explanation, this is the gist of advertising in the Western world. And believe it or not, it works. Ad executives count on it to the tune of billions of dollars each year.

Inspiration can also be achieved with well-written materials. A catchy slogan, brief or personal statements that appeal to would-be participants, and other writing strategies and formats can go a long way in enticing students to join. For example: "Intramurals: A Fun Place to Play"; "Go Active—Intramurals"; and "No Barriers. Just Fun." Inspiration needs to be inspiring, of course, but it should also be accurate. In other words, don't oversell the program. While most viewers have come to expect the hype and exaggeration of national advertising, it can backfire when it comes to small or local promotion. If, for example, students show up at an event with overly high expectations, they may be disappointed and not show up for future events. If the event exceeds their expectations, however, they will likely return. For example, if you merely promote a great baseball league and then deliver a well-run, enjoyable season of baseball, players and spectators will be satisfied. If, on the other hand, a celebrity throws the first pitch at the championship game, which is followed by an outdoor barbecue and music, players and spectators will be surprised and delighted, and they will likely come out next year to see what you have planned next.

Consistency

Think of a couple driving across the country. They become hungry and begin to look for somewhere to eat. What do they look for? If they are like most people, they look for familiar restaurant signs. McDonald's serves as an excellent example of consistency. In addition to offering a consistent product, name, logo (think of those golden arches), slogan ("We love to see you smile"), and mascots (Ronald, the Hamburglar, and so on) also build familiarity. When our traveling couple sees the familiar logo on a sign or a billboard advertisement, past experiences come flooding back: "Oh! I love their fries! Let's eat there." Or "They have fast service. Let's go there so we can get back on the road before 7." McDonald's and other large corporations know that consistency creates recognition, and therefore familiarity and comfort and, in the case of our cross-country travelers, patronage.

This same strategy should be applied in designing your intramural promotion. Whatever visual image, slogan, logo, and so on you use, it should be a consistent feature on all promotional materials. In the intramural context, consistency might be achieved by one or a combination of the following: a photographic image, a program logo, a slogan, a mascot, or even color. If your school already has a mascot and school colors, which is usually the case, achieving consistency in mascot or color will be that much easier. For example, you could feature the school mascot in an intramural T-shirt on all program promotion, or you could add an intramural color to your school colors.

Visual Appeal

If the promotion is visual (i.e., it will be seen rather than heard), it should catch people's eyes and draw them in further to see what it's about. This visual appeal is usually achieved with color and photographs or other visual images. The name of the game is getting people's attention. Once you have their attention, they will be more likely to read on.

Use of Color

Bold or bright colors divert the eye. As you've probably noticed when looking at a newspaper or magazine, the eye will immediately cross over the black and white and go right to any color on the page. Thus, it's a good idea to use color in promotional materials whenever possible. If you were promoting a volleyball league, for example, contrast the appeal of a black-and-white photograph to that of a color photograph, featuring a white volleyball against a blue sky or even brightly colored uniforms. In addition to using color rather than black-and-white photographs, using color in the text, logo, and design is effective as well. A bright orange "Sign Up Now!" is sure to capture some attention. Once people have stopped to look, many will read the text to find out the what, when, where, how, and so on.

Use of Photographs and Visual Images

The adage is true: a picture is worth a thousand words. This is especially true of intramural promotion. Using our volleyball example, a poster that features students playing volleyball will attract far more people than a typed or handwritten note containing information about volleyball signup. Not only will photographs grab people's attention, but if these photographs feature interesting subjects, they will most certainly be scrutinized further. In the context of intramurals, pictures of fellow students are usually effective. Passersby look closely to see if they or their friends are in the photos. Photos of peers also elicit the "people watching" response in most students.

Visual images can often communicate other components of effective promotion discussed in this section—inspiration, in particular. Look at the collage of visual images used in figure 8.1. Each of these photos inspires active living, which

FIGURE 8.1   Active Living campaign poster.
Courtesy of Ontario College Athletic Association, 1185 Eglinton Avenue East, Suite 505, North York, Ontario, Canada, M3C 3C6.
Phone: 416-426-7043. Art work by Kristine Verbeek.

is the mission of this particular program (see chapter 11 for more details). The upper-right photo of the tennis player in a wheelchair, for example, will inspire people with disabilities to join. Those who want to get in shape will likely find the upper-left and lower-right photos inspiring. The center and lower-left photos will probably appeal to students who want to have fun and who enjoy sports. Even the background, a beautiful blue sky, is appealing to those who crave time away from their offices or computers, those who long for clean air, free movement, and recreation.

Now try to imagine writing about these concepts. Clearly, it would take too long. Even if you did come up with the right phrases (e.g., "sick and tired of sitting in your office all day?"), chances are good that readers would not walk away from a text poster feeling as inspired as they would walking away from this Active Living poster. The same goes for intramural promotion. More than likely, the best way to capture and communicate the spirit of a game, activity, or event is with visual images.

Illustrations and clip art also fall under the category of visual images, of course, but unless you have an illustrator, artist, or computer graphics person on staff, photographs will most often be the most accessible visual images (see the next section, "Design"). Indeed, to get appropriate photographs for promoting your intramural program, you need only attend a few games and events. You'll also need a camera, of course. Polaroids are great because they are developed immediately, but the quality tends to be poor and they are more expensive. Regular cameras also work. In this case, it is best to use 12-exposure film so that the photographs can be developed quickly while spirits from the event are still high. Finally, digital cameras are rapidly becoming affordable and easy to use. What's more, if you have the equipment available, taking digital photographs and downloading them to your program Web site (if you have one) costs nothing.

If none of these options are doable, you may want to consider forming a partnership with your school photography and/or computer club. Student photographers could attend intramural activities and shoot the highlights. (They may also be able to develop the film for you.) Com-puter club members could scan photos for use on the program Web site or other promotional materials. Such collaboration will not only reduce the workload of intramural administrators and office workers but also spur interest in the intramural program.

Photographs and other visual images can be used in a variety of ways. They can be displayed on the bulletin board following an event, used on the program Web site, put together into a collage for posters and other promotional materials, blown up and used as posters themselves, and even put together in a pictorial "hall of fame" display somewhere on campus. Clip art and other graphics available in most computer software packages make an excellent addition to intramural materials for promotional and even administrative uses. Photos, logos, and other graphics can also be used on T-shirts and recognition plaques.

Design

Designing promotional materials may seem daunting at first. After all, in addition to having expertise in physical movement, staff management, and other aspects of running an intramural department, intramural directors may not be experts in psychology and graphic arts. Thus, it may be necessary to seek help. In many cases, particularly at the high school and college levels, this help may just be down the hall. Talk to some of the marketing, advertising, and graphic arts faculty and students to see if they might be of assistance. Perhaps a student or group of students is looking to do a practicum or simply practice what they have learned in class. In such cases, helping with the promotion for the intramural program makes for a win-win opportunity.

Timeliness

Whatever your promotional vehicle—bulletin board or poster, flyer or newspaper article, still photo or video, Web site or word of mouth, or a combination thereof—timeliness is crucial when it comes to specific activity promotion. In other words, promotion should be current. Students' enthusiasm and momentum is quickly deflated when, for example, they go to check the bulletin board or Web site for tournament standings and find they are not up to date. The same is true for trophies. Looking at trophies in the display case on which recent winners of the last few years have not had their names engraved makes these rewards less desirable and decreases students' respect for the overall program.

Audience

The final, and perhaps most important, characteristic of effective promotion is appealing to the intended audience, also called the **target audience**. Indeed, advertising and marketing executives spend millions researching the habits, interests, and characteristics of potential customers. Such research and its application are beyond the scope of this book. Instead, a brief explanation will serve this discussion.

Using the model of transtheoretical stages of change is helpful in understanding how to promote effectively. This model, in adapted form, describes the stages people go through in implementing any change in their lives. For our purposes, of course, the change being encouraged is going from inactivity to activity by getting off the couch and participating in intramurals. The transtheoretical model has six stages. In general, effective promotion will move would-be participants from one stage to the next.

Stage 1 Precontemplation. People in this stage have not even thought about participating in intramural activities or fitness classes at your institution. Anything that one does to promote the existence of intramural programs and fitness classes will help. This can include demonstrations, posters, announcements, advertisements in student newspapers, or presentations to large first-year classes. People in this stage need to be made aware that programs exist.

Stage 2 Contemplation. People at this stage recognize and begin to think about the need to change. Promotion for contemplators should focus on the supports in place for intramural involvement, including instructional clinics and developing a partnering or mentoring system for beginners. A parterning or mentoring system involves encouraging individuals to seek out nonparticipants, invite them to get involved, and take them through such things as the steps of signing up, showing them where the change rooms are and where the gymnasium is, explain-

ing the rules and procedures of an intramural game, and just being available for them if they have questions. Showing how much fun everyone is having, despite their level of fitness, age, or skill, is also effective for reaching this group.

Stage 3 Preparation. People at this stage are close to getting involved. They are beginning to focus on the possibilities rather than on what seems impossible. Thus, promoting intramurals to this group of people is most effective when the possibilities are emphasized. For example, promotions for this group should reemphasize the fun and satisfaction that people experience from intramural activities and inform the people in the preparation group how easy it is to sign up and get involved.

Stage 4 Action. People at this stage are beginning to take action. And, they are likely to succeed if a plan, support from others, realistic goals, and rewards are in place. Intramural promotion to this group should highlight the rewards of involvement in intramurals, particularly prizes for participation.

Stage 5 Maintenance. Vigilance is needed in reaching people at this stage, as these people are involved in intramural activities and committed to continue coming out, but their allegiance can easily be lost if the intramural experience is not satisfactory. If the program remains organized and positive, they are likely to stay. Promoting intramurals to these people should feature ongoing possibilities, including the many options available for higher levels of activity, and provide encouragement for continued involvement.

Stage 6 Permanence. At this stage, activity and participation are so ingrained that the rewards of participation need no longer be emphasized. In other words, these people just need to be told when and where activities and events are taking place and they'll be there (Velicer et al. 1998).

When promoting an activity or event or program, then, it is important to consider your audience. The most effective message will vary depending on what stage they're at. In addition, audience characteristics such as fitness level, socioeconomic and ethnic background, race, age, and recreational interests should be considered in constructing promotional messages. If at all possible, intramural directors would be wise to design different advertising for different cohorts—that is, assuming there is a large enough audience to make the effort worthwhile. The following sections examine some of these characteristics for grade school, high school, and university students and list some effective types of promotion for each level.

Grade School

Students in grade school are looking for fun lunchtime experiences. They are more visual than verbal, and they are more captivated by a demonstration than by reading. They also love to see teachers having fun demonstrating and participating in intramural events. "Live" promotion (see page 134) is the most effective vehicle for this age group. For example, an intramural director or other staff member could come to a school assembly dressed as a funny-looking baseball player or soccer star and talk about how excited she is for the baseball or soccer season next week because she is such a great player. At this age, the crazier the demonstration, the more memorable the event. Sometimes principals get into the act by volunteering to kiss a pig if a certain number of students sign up for intramurals during the next month. Video promotion (see page 135) is also highly effective for kids at this age. They are captivated by television and computers, and these media provide and excellent tool for exciting them about intramural events.

High School

High school students are very peer conscious (as indicated in Chapter 6) and always appreciate a good challenge. Thus, promotion should appeal to their sense of adventure and competition. Promoting an upcoming event or activity, or the program itself, can be as simple as hosting a battle of the sexes or a competition between students and faculty. Using the P.A. system (see page 135) to build up hype before an event is sure to get high school students talking about it. Even those who opt out of participating will likely attend the event as spectators, which may increase participation at future events.

College and University

Crazy gimmicks and simple challenges are less effective at the collegiate level, although some universities host silly intramural activities that are highly successful. University and college students are more sophisticated, they know what they like, and they are fitness conscious and enjoy having fun with friends. Thus, word-of-mouth promotion, a type of "live" promotion (see page 135), and sophisticated print promotion (see page 135) such as a clean and professional-looking poster that lets students know how to sign up for events is probably the most effective. Including key dates on college daybooks is also effective, as are intramural calendars that provide contact information for all aspects of the intramural program (see page 139). By this age, most students are already involved in intramurals and simply need to be told when events are happening and how to get involved.

Types of Promotion

Armed with a clear understanding of the components of effective promotion, then, it's time to focus on the specifics. There are a variety of ways to promote intramurals. There is "live" or personal promotion such as presentations to classes and word-of-mouth promotion, P.A. announcements, and videos. There is print, including posters, fliers, newspapers, and other print publications. The computer is a medium in and of itself, offering the use of Web sites and E-mail as promotional options. There are also bulletin boards and sandwich boards. Advertising on television, in newspapers, or on calendars is another promotional opportunity. Clothing and gadgets are also promotional options, depending on the budget. Finally, there are special promotional activities or events that demonstrate the joy of intramural participation. These types of promotion are explained in the following sections.

The following event was both promotional and a promotion itself. Every one looked forward to the event each year and when people spoke about intramural events, this was always a highlight. Adding excitement to the daily announcements by inserting predictions made people more attentive to the announcement and more eager to watch the game to see what the outcome would be. The student newspaper provided another media to promote the event, and pictures made the article inviting to read. The trumpet-led processional caught the attention of any students lingering in the halls and signaled that the event was going to begin. Because

Jimmy the Greek Predicts Big Win for Faculty

It was an annual tradition at Chatham Christian High School. The best table-tennis faculty member challenged the reigning table-tennis student champion. Jimmy the Greek predicted the outcome in daily announcements during the week before the big event. The outcome was always in the faculty's favor. By noon on Wednesday, the table was set up at center court in the gym. No other activities were permitted in the gymnasium during the hour.

Announced by a trumpet prelude, the faculty member rode into the gym on the shoulders of two other professors. The paddle, carefully carried and presented on a pillow by another teacher, led the procession into the gym, through the crowd of students who came to watch, and finally to the table. At the table was a very nervous student competitor waiting beside her overly excited student coach, who was trying to keep the player focused. After grand introductions, the contest began.

In previous years, the students rarely won. They were often overwhelmed by the attention and found the fanfare distracting. Thus, prior to this year's tournament, the school newspaper featured the event. Student reporters surveyed their peers as well as the teachers, asking everyone who they thought would win. Pictures from previous tournaments accompanied the article, along with the evocative caption, "Will the staff ever be dethroned?"

Adapted, by permission, from "Nobody Listens," *The Cabbage Game*, 1999, the Canadian Association of Student Activity Advisors.

the event was such a success each year, there was never any trouble getting people to sign up for the annual intramural table tennis tournament, which ended with a staff member playing the student winner.

"Live" Promotion

Person-to-person, face-to-face, or even voice-to-voice—personal interaction is an effective way to promote intramurals. Because these formats are "live" or active, and because they involve humans interacting with humans, they have a dynamism and energy not present in other types of promotion. Real voices of real people are heard giving testimony to or displaying the spirit and excitement of an intramural program.

"Live" promotion includes presentations, P.A. announcements, and videotape, which are discussed in the following sections. Word-of-mouth promotion is also included in this category. It is the personal nature of these promotions that makes them effective. This type of promotion also enables personal interaction. To promote an upcoming dance, for example, a small ninth-grader volunteered to be taped to the wall at a major exit. This student had promotional flyers in his hands, which he handed to passersby who stopped to take a look. Although this particular promotion has nothing to do with intramurals, it does illustrate how effective personal promotion can be. As Conlon comments in telling the story, "It drew a crowd and was a great one-time advertisement" (Conlon, 1999).

Presentations

Clearly, it would be far too time consuming to speak to every potential participant one-on-one, face-to-face. The spirit of such personal interaction can be captured in a presentation instead. Presentations offer students the opportunity to ask questions, and they offer the presenter the opportunity to gauge reactions to the program and address particular concerns. In addition, presentations allow program staff to reach groups of potential participants rather than individuals one at a time, saving valuable time in the process. Finally, presentations yield an energy all their own. Would-be participants excited by what they hear can help recruit others in attendance.

The opportunities to give presentations are numerous, particularly at schools. Students are, in some respects, a captive audience, since they are on campus anyway. Ask fellow teachers and professors to allow five minutes of class time for a brief presentation about intramurals. Home rooms, classrooms, central corridors before school and between classes, and the cafeteria during lunchtime allow access to many students at one time. To reach even larger numbers of students, make a presentation during an introduction at a school assembly. Such presentations are especially helpful for first-year or new students at large institutions.

Word of Mouth

Once a successful intramural program is underway, participants are the best promoters of the program. Students listen to and are influenced by their peers. Take advantage of this free promotion by encouraging program participants to spread the word. You, as intramural directors, can also help in this regard. Talk with students in the halls or in the cafeteria. Make yourself available and interact with students often. You might even consider setting up a station in the cafeteria or central corridor where students can stop by for a free-flowing discussion about campus recreation.

P.A. Announcements

Many grade schools and high schools use the public address (P.A.) system to make general announcements to the entire school. These announcements are usually made at the beginning of the day, but lunchtime and the last period work well too. If your school has a P.A. system, take advantage of it. Announce upcoming intramural activities and events, and promote the program throughout the year.

These announcements should grab students' attention, of course. Set your announcements apart from the humdrum of typical P.A. announcements by communicating the spirit and energy of your intramural program. For example, have announcers predict the outcome of upcoming games, or have team captains challenge each other. You could even produce a 30-second commercial type of announcement, complete with sound effects such as music or a cheering crowd, and play that over the P.A. system a few times the week before a big game or event. The possibilities are many.

Videos

One need only look at the billion-dollar movie industry or recall the fun of watching a wedding or other event on video to understand the appeal of moving pictures. This appeal can be used in promoting an intramural program. For example, videotape a key game or a silly event to promote the fun. Participants reliving these moments will rush to sign up for more (if they haven't already), and nonparticipants will see what they are missing. The worst-case scenario is that students will simply enjoy the videos and echoes of laughter will be heard around the school.

If your school has an audio visual department, get those students involved by enlisting their help with videotaping and editing. Encourage their creativity by hosting a contest or other type of event in which students put together several different videos using the same footage. Then broadcast their tapes in prominent locations throughout the school. For example, play the videos at award banquets or season-end parties and in the hallway near the gymnasium, intramural office, or intramural bulletin board. To promote a specific activity or league, compile the highlights from a season or game and play it at activity sign-up or registration.

Print Promotion

In addition to "live" promotional tools, the print medium is an effective way of communicating with people. In some respects, it's more effective that face-to-face promotion. For starters, the message—be that a poster, flier, bulletin board announcement, or newspaper article—is permanent. That is, print promotion is in its location 24 hours a day (until you take it down, of course), and students can read it on their own time.

When it comes to print promotion, you'll have lots of competition for students' attention. Thus, the characteristics of effective promotion are especially important—visual appeal and consistency, in particular. It may be helpful to take a look at magazines such as *Sports Illustrated*, or *Runner*, or other sport and fitness magazines and see what techniques they are using to promote their products. The following sections explain the most common types of print intramural promotion: posters; bulletins, newsletters, and fliers; and newspaper articles.

Posters

As explained in the discussion about figure 8.1, colorful and dynamic posters will get student's attention, get them into the spirit of an activity or event, and explain where to get further information or sign up. From there, effective placement becomes crucial. High-traffic areas are best, including the school entrance or lobby, gymnasium, well-traveled hallways, and residence buildings. Posters can also be effective in classrooms, especially for the bored student whose eyes drift during a lecture. Another excellent location is in the washroom (inside the stalls or near the sinks), since students may have some free time to read.

Bulletins, Newsletters, and Fliers

Weekly or monthly bulletins or newsletters can be excellent tools for updating participants on the progress of current events, including scores and standings of various leagues and tournaments, but they are also an opportunity to promote upcoming events. Promotional fliers are effective in this regard as well. Students can pick them up and read them at their leisure.

In addition to specific program activities and results, however, bulletins, newsletters, and fliers are excellent tools for inspiring students to be active. For example, in your monthly intramural bulletin, you could suggest some healthy places to eat in town, tips on how to tune up a bicycle in the spring, recommended warm-ups and stretches to prevent injury, and so on. You could even offer basic instruction in a particular sport or exercise each month and then tie that activity into your intramural programming season. You can provide additional resources as well, offering students access to all intramural equipment, facilities, and programming. For example, direct readers to helpful Web sites (including your own) that focus on healthy living.

Newsletters, bulletins, and fliers should be widely distributed. It is not enough to make them available in the gymnasium and intramural office. Supply them on tables in the cafeteria and near checkout at the school store, stock them in wire racks at all school entrances, and ask the school nurse or health workers to distribute them. In addition, seize the opportunities of your school's distribution system. At most colleges, for example, students have mailboxes they check every day or at least several times a week.

Student and Local Publications

Most high schools and universities have student newspapers, written by and for students. Because the information contained in these publications is directly related to them, students often read them cover to cover. Student newspapers can be a key source of free promotion for an intramural program. For one thing, their readership is the exact group of people you're trying to reach: your target audience. Local publications are also useful in promoting an intramural program. Typically, local publications publish movie guides, band appearances, and other information students seek in filling their spare time. Thus, especially at the college level, these publications enjoy a high student readership.

Reliable, knowledgeable, and sympathetic sports writers can do much to enhance interest in your intramural program. In fact, if these writers could be a part of the intramural council, all the better, since they would be well acquainted with your mission, goals, and intramural events. Get to know the sports writers and encourage their participation in intramurals. In fact, you might want to talk to the publisher about assigning an intramural writer who could attend key events and games and then report on the highlights and fun. In addition, keep student and local sports writers abreast of upcoming events and ask them to encourage students to participate.

Computer Promotion

The computer is taking an increasingly more dominant role in the lives of students. Many students are regularly on chat lines and searching their favorite Web sites for hours each day. With its immediacy and high-speed interaction, the computer is an integral part of young people's lives. Plus, the computer offers low-cost updating and last-minute alteration, a benefit not seen in traditional print promotion, which is permanent once published. Thus, as intramural directors, you would be wise to utilize this tool of communication. The main components of computer promotion are Web sites and E-mail, each of which is discussed in the following sections.

Web Sites

As alluded to throughout this book, having your own intramural Web site is a good idea. A Web site will minimize confusion and eliminate the difficulties of participants not being clear about specific aspects of the program. A Web site should provide all relevant information about your program, including your mission and purpose, important events and dates and locations, sport and other participation rules, eligibility and a comprehensive outline of all intramural activities offered. It should feature the characteristics of effective promotion, including color, photographs, and other components of visual appeal described earlier in this chapter.

The first consideration, of course, is access. If your school does not have the capability of hosting its own Web site, there are many sport organizations on the Internet that will allow intramural directors to display a Web site for free on their site, including www.esportsdesk.com and www.active.com.

Once you have access, the next consideration is ability. In some universities, the sports information or computer services department will take charge of setting up home pages for the intramural department. Some even employ full-time Webmasters for the athletic area. If your school has no such assistance in place, however, fear not. Creating your own Web site is not difficult. In fact, numerous software packages make the task relatively easy. Microsoft FrontPage is one of the best. Its "wizards" will put together most of a site for you and guide you through the process of launching the site in a simple, straightforward manner. In two days, an intramural director can use FrontPage to put a Web site together and launch it. Netscape also offers a fairly straightforward Web-publishing program, although it requires more user expertise than FrontPage. Claris HomePage and Adobe Pagemill are inexpensive software programs that allow you to set up your own Web sites, including such components as images, text, and tables. HomePage is a user-friendly program that lets you create Web pages by pointing and clicking on icons. If you are already familiar with Hyper Text Mark-up Language (HTML), you can use HomePage to author a Web page quickly. The program does have limitations, however, including weak frame control, the apparent impossibility of text wraps and limited HTML menu. Fortunately, you can directly edit the HTML of you HomePage files and preview your work-in-progress in a browser (such as Netscape) (Claris HomePage 2001). Adobe Pagemill is similar to HomePage. Those beginning with Pagemill benefit from reading a 50 page handbook to get them started (Mendelson, 2001). If your site will be limited to one page, Word, Publisher, and WordPerfect offer some help.

When designing your Web site, the best advice is this: simpler is better. If you effectively promote your program using other promotional tools, as described throughout this chapter, those interested in intramurals will visit your site to get the details and see what the program is all about. Directors should make their sites as visually appealing as possible, all the while not forgetting that those visiting the site are most interested in reading the information, such as schedules, standing, and rules. Carefully plan the site on paper first, outlining a map of the site, and then decide how many pages and links you will need. From there, the process is simply assembling and launching each page. Once a page is up, it takes only a moment to switch to "editor view" and add any changes or updates. Web-design software will lead you through the process of adding page links and other devices that enable visitors to easily navigate the site. Each page should have a "home" button so that users can get back to the home page. Otherwise, particularly on larger sites, users may get lost.

Once you get going, you may decide to add more pages, links, and banners. It is also helpful to add a hit counter on each page to help you decide if your effort is worth the trouble. A hit counter counts the number of times someone visits the web site. If an intramural director is putting a lot of work into developing and maintaining a site and no one is visiting it, either the effort is not worth it, or people do not know about the site. Knowing how many times people visit the site is also helpful when convincing advertisers of the worth of advertising on your site. Include E-mail links in each section to encourage interaction between site visitors and intramural staff. These links are particularly useful in evaluating your program, specific activities, and your Web site. (See chapter 14 for a full discussion on evaluation.)

E-mail

Many schools communicate with their students online. And the number is rising every day. Because E-mail is so efficient in terms of access and timing, institutions are beginning to understand the benefits of having student-wide E-mail. In fact, many colleges are already offering ISP (Internet Service Provider) services to students and alumni. These institutions often have an E-mail distribution list that goes to all students who are online. If used judiciously, such a distribution list can be an effective way to communicate to a lot of students. However, most people online today do not appreciate receiving junk E-mail. Many, in fact, delete these messages without even reading them. Thus, intramural directors would be wise to not send too many E-mail messages that are not relevant to all students.

Another E-mail option is available to intramural directors. Listservs enable specific communication to a large number of people simply by sending one message that automatically goes out to a group of people. Listservs can be done simply by using a group E-mail. When new people are added to the main list, the director sends a note out to the group, and when people want to send a message to everyone, they can simply respond with "reply to all." There are other programs available (Majordomo, for example) that permit a director to subscribe interested staff and student to an intramural listserv. Participants send messages addressed to the list serve address and the message goes to all subscribers. Intramural directors can develop a specific intramural listserv for anyone who wants to read about updates and discuss intramural matters. All team captains should be put on such a list.

Location, Location, Location

While not traditionally considered promotion, the location of the intramural office, including the director's office, is vital. Put simply, the higher the daily traffic, the better. Ideally, intramural offices should be located near both the gym (or other school recreational facility) and student government offices. If your school layout does not support such a location, in addition to promoting your program and activities, you'll also have to promote your location. For example, put up arrows in the hallways: "This way to fun and active living" or other messages to get students' interest and encourage them to find you. Be creative and have fun with it. Your goal is to make the program visible.

In addition, make yourself and your staff available to participants. This is also achieved easily with a central office location. Interact with as many students as possible during the day. As mentioned above, word-of-mouth promotion and personal interaction are key. Visit the cafeteria during lunchtime and make the rounds. Encourage students to ask questions and invite individuals to participate and register.

Bulletin and Sandwich Boards

Because they are typically located in high-traffic areas around campus, bulletin boards are an invaluable tool for intramural promotion. In the case of sandwich boards, which are mobile, they can be moved to high-traffic locations. For example, if you want to attract commuter students to an event, a sandwich board could be placed at one (or a few) of the main entrances near the parking lot. Likewise, if an event is geared toward weightlifters and students who work out, it could placed near the weight room. Before using sandwich boards, be sure to check out whether fire regulations allow their use inside the building.

The characteristics of effective promotion are important when it comes to bulletin and sandwich boards. Timeliness, for example, is crucial. Keep bulletin boards updated. Students will soon learn that if they want up-to-date information on intramurals, they can go to these specific boards. These boards should also grab the attention of passersby. Use bold colors and dynamic posters and advertisements that are visually appealing and are quick and easy to read. The following components make for an effective bulletin or sandwich board.

▶ Large, colorful heading: "**INTRAMURAL PROGRAM**"

▶ Slogan, mascot, or other tool that builds familiarity through consistency (see "Consistency" section on page 129) and communicates the purpose of intramurals

▶ Current events

▶ Schedule of activities

▶ Relevant rules

▶ Up-to-date contest results

▶ Referee schedule

▶ Upcoming events (who, what, when, where, and why)

▶ Photos of participants in action

A great way to draw people to a bulletin board and heighten students' interest in the current season or your program is to post a weekly riddle. If the riddle is related to the current season or is sport specific, all the better. For example, during the intramural baseball season, try the following riddle.

Q: What is the least number of pitches that a pitcher can throw in one nine-inning game? Which team would win and by what score?

A: The least number of pitches that a pitcher can throw in one game is 25, pitches thrown by the visiting pitcher, and the home team would win 1 to 0.

Explanation: The least number of pitches a pitcher can pitch in an inning is three (each batter hits the first ball and it flies out). The visiting team always bats first, followed by the home team. Thus, the fewest pitches the home pitcher could pitch would be 27 (3 outs × 9 innings). But because the visiting pitcher pitches second, she would only need to pitch eight innings, meaning 24 pitches (3 outs × 8 innings), plus one pitch in the bottom of the ninth (for a total of 25 pitches), when the batter hits a home run and wins the game 1-0.

Another option is to involve participants in bulletin and sandwich board upkeep. For example, if students are divided into houses (see chapter 3), give each house a portion of the intramural bulletin board, or a board all their own, to update and promote intramural activities. Houses could use their team logo and colors and add their own announcements, team pictures, and other interesting items. To keep students inspired to produce the best-looking board, hold a contest. At the end of a season or the school year, award the best-kept bulletin boards. With this approach to bulletin and sandwich boards, students take ownership of their board (or portion of the board) and often create more interesting displays than an intramural director or staff might have time for.

Daybooks and Calendars

Many schools, from the elementary school through the university level, offer their students daybooks or calendars. Daybooks often provide a separate page for each week of the year with plenty of room for students to write down daily assignments and notes to themselves. School calendars, which are typically monthly, contain such important dates as holiday and semester breaks, orientation weeks, and special events. If your school offers student calendars and daybooks, talk to the department responsible for these scheduling tools about adding key intramural dates. In addition, be sure that intramural program information is included in the school information section. It is here that you should include your program mission, specific activities and services offered, and how to contact intramural staff and coordinators.

Of course, another option is printing your own intramural calendar or daybook for students. Canadore College in North Bay, Ontario, for example, produced the calendar shown in figure 8.2. The cover, a photo collage featuring team pictures, participants in a pyramid, and specific activities offered such as skiing and white-water rafting, communicates the fun of the program and provides students with a useful scheduling tool. Inside, each month lists scheduled intramural activities and advertises specific events (see figure 8.3 on page 141).

Clothing and Intramural Memorabilia

Clothing and other intramural memorabilia provide great prizes and give-aways, and they present important promotional opportunities. People appreciate receiving a T-shirt, hat, sweatband, or other memorabilia at an orientation event or as a prize for being the "fair play" winner at an intramural event. Inscribed with "Intramurals" and perhaps an important phone number or dates of upcoming events, these prizes become walking billboards for the intramural program. I remember wearing a shirt given out to participants in an active living challenge. The shirt read, "I accepted the challenge." It happened, with some regularity, that people asked what challenge I had accepted. This meant describing the intramural program through which I had won it. I had a free T-shirt and the intramural program accomplished some great advertising. Queen's University had some fun with one of its T-shirts, as well. On the front was "School makes you Sweat, Cry, and Worry." On the back, "We just make you Sweat—Queen's University."

FIGURE 8.2 Intramural calendar.
Courtesy of Canadore College, Campus Recreation, North Bay, Ontario.

Advertising

When asked why they do not participate in intramurals, students from a variety of institutions report that they often did not know the dates, times, and places of events until it was too late. That's where effective advertising comes into play. As explained at the beginning of this chapter, advertising is a specific promotional tool that raises awareness about an activity, game, instructional class, or event. Also as explained earlier, advertising typically involves such media as local or student newspapers, Web sites, magazines, and newsletters. There are other available advertising vehicles, however. You can advertise on bulletin or sandwich boards, on place mats for use on cafeteria tables, in student daybooks and calendars (see figure 8.3), and even print T-shirts advertising a spe-

cific event or activity and distribute them at registration and activity sign-up (if the budget is available).

As defined at the beginning of this chapter, advertising is a specific promotional tool to raise awareness of an event or activity. Thus, effective advertising contains the nitty-gritty details: the who, what, where, when, and how of the activity or event. These details are clearly explained in figure 8.3.

- ▶ What: "Snofest," including airbands, ball hockey, a fashion show, bowling, billiards, a free lunch, and so on
- ▶ When: February 4 to 8
- ▶ Where: Commerce court
- ▶ Who: Everyone
- ▶ How: Register at PAC office

FIGURE 8.3   Advertisement from Recreation & Leisure Guide 2000–2001.
Courtesy of Canadore College, Campus Recreation, North Bay, Ontario.

Like effective promotion, effective advertising is visually appealing and inspires action. In the "Snofest" advertisement in figure 8.3, for example, photos of some of the fun are included: students arm wrestling, riding a tricycle, and jumping into an inflatable pool. The caption "We dare you!" inspires students to participate in "the famous polar bear dip" by appealing to their sense of adventure, not to mention nerve. Finally, a specific invitation is offered to team captains in the way of a special "captains' rules meeting" the week before the event, and entices them to come by offering free pizza.

In addition, effective advertising aims at a target audience. The ads should be as inclusive as possible. If the only people on the pictures for the ads are athletic types, those who are overweight may not want to participate for fear of embarrassment. If the only people on the pictures are white, or male, or able-bodied, then those who are not white, are female, or have a disability may feel unwelcome. If you want certain people to come out to your intramural program, demonstrate that in the advertising. In the case of the "Snofest" ad in figure 8.3, the Canadore College intramural staff considered audience in placing its advertising. The ad appeared in its annual intramural calendar, which is distributed to all students on the first day of classes. Wanting to reach as many students as possible, the ad appears in a publication that all students receive and/or have access to. That's what reaching a target audience is all about.

The "Snofest" advertisement, of course, is just one example of advertising in one type of publication. There are many advertising vehicles available, including radio and television, print media, the computer, and others, each of which is described in the following sections.

Radio and Television

Because network advertising is out of the reach of most intramural departments, given the cost of the air time and producing high-quality ads, local cable channels and radio stations might be worth considering. Many cable channels, for example, feature community activities and events as part of local programming. Announcements of and invitations to intramural activities could be included in these programs. For larger events, such as orientation, Winterfest, or a special fund-raiser, involving local broadcasting media can increase exposure and help to maximize participation.

Print

Print media typically includes magazines, newsletters, newspapers, and other publications. Like national and network radio and television, however, advertising in national print media will likely be too expensive. (Besides, advertising in national print media is not exactly reaching a target audience.) Local and student newspapers and other publications, however, are often excellent, low-cost advertising vehicles. In fact, some may be willing to run free advertisements for upcoming events, particularly if the event has a broad appeal. In the case of a community newspaper, such broad appeal may include an event for families, special instructional clinics for single parents, or a fund-raising event for a local charity. Student newspapers are less strict in requiring broad appeal for free advertising. They also offer quite affordable paid advertising. Best of all, their readership is precisely the group of people you're trying to reach.

There are other print advertising vehicles available, particularly at the college and university level. In addition to the regular college and university mailings, there are often smaller newspapers and newsletters. For example, try advertising in publications form various students clubs or those produced by fraternities and sororities. These are all opportunities to reach a wider target market by reaching the smaller groups on campus.

Computer

Like computer promotion, computer advertising is an invaluable resource for increasing program and event visibility. Plus, because it can be changed easily and at little or not cost, computer advertising is highly efficient. The intramural Web site and institution-wide or intramural-specific listserves also provide a great opportunity to advertise intramural events. With students' increased reliance on the computer for information, intramural directors would be wise to advertise activities and events on the computer.

The neat thing with computer ads is that the director can embed a link from the ad to the program registration. The students are attracted to the ad and can immediately go to the registration page without trying to find an office or a person. E-mails to specific people or groups can also be a quick way to disperse important information, but be careful not to overuse this tool or people will delete the message before reading it.

Calendars and Daybooks

As shown in figure 8.3 (see page 141), calendars and daybooks are excellent advertising vehicles. Students use these scheduling tools to stay abreast of school events, holidays, deadlines, and other important dates, and thus are in the habit of checking them regularly. A strategically located advertisement, ideally in the month or week of or prior to an event, will create huge visibility. Likewise, key intramural dates can be printed right on the calendar so that students will be aware of when activities are taking place.

Other

In effect, there are as many opportunities to advertise an intramural program as there are ideas for advertising. Ads placed on bulletin or sandwich boards strategically placed in high-traffic school hallways and other areas; place mats for cafeteria tables right before an event; posters advertising a specific activity just before the start of the season; T-shirts, hats, and other items used in a competition or event; intramural staff dressed up as basketball players the day before basketball sign-ups are due; soccer ballons hanging from the ceiling before soccer sign-ups; demonstrations of the next intramural sport in the front lobby—(for example, foul-shooting contests)—the possibilities are endless. Tried and true methods of promotions may work well, but remember, every tried and true method was used the first time once. Experiment and have some fun as you find new and exciting ways to promote your intraumral programs.

The Program

The intramural program itself is an invaluable promotional resource both in maintaining active participants and in recruiting new participants. Promoting and advertising future events will certainly help in this regard, but the program must also sell itself. Indeed, once participants show up, the program is the number-one selling characteristic.

If the program is well organized, satisfies students' needs (instruction, social interaction, and so on), helps participants become physically fit and feel better, provides opportunities for learning and leadership, and is enjoyable, participants will come back. Not only will they come back, but they will likely promote the program to others (word-of-mouth promotion) and encourage them to join in the fun. Unfortunately, the reverse is also true. An unorganized, unsatisfying, boring experience that teaches students little or nothing and leaves them feeling no better than when they arrived will discourage participants from coming back. What's more, people are much more likely to share complaints than compliments.

Promotional Activities

Finally, in addition to promoting specific intramural activities, games, and events, it's helpful to organize activities solely to achieve the intramural mission—in our case, fun and active movement. These promotional activities, while also a great boost to the intramural program in terms of creating visibility and providing the opportunity for specific activity and program promotion, should be large, high-profile events that everyone can enjoy. The events should not be typical sport events because that will limit participation to underrepresented populations such as females and minority groups. Chose some fun events that equalize abilities and that will appeal to all. They should provide a fabulously fun activity for students and remind them of the exciting goings-on in intramurals.

Intramural directors can capitalize on school scheduling by offering these promotional events and activities during opening registration, orientation day or week, and so on. The following sections describe some specific ideas for developing promotional activities. These are just a starting ground, however. Work with school administrators and other faculty to make the most of school schedules and develop other wonderful experiences that will get the word out that intramurals is fun.

Registration

At class registration, high school in some cases but more often at the collegiate setting, many schools provide tables and booths for different departments within the school and for corporations that wish to advertise to students. You, as an intramural director, should take advantage of this opportunity by staffing an intramural booth. This booth should provide information about specific activities and programming offered, certainly, but more importantly it should reflect the mission of your program: fun and active movement for all.

In other words, booth staff should be wearing intramural shirts, sweat bands, and hats. Staff should also show videos and have pictures on display of crazy and entertaining intramural events. You might even want to make the booth interactive, by having a few of last year's participants engage in an activity such as a tug-of-war or hackey sac rally (see how long a small group of people can keep a hacky sac from touching the ground). Finally, invite registrants to participate by offering a simple challenge (shooting a plastic hockey puck at a target) and offering a prize for anyone who participates or signs up for intramurals (an intramural T-shirt, hat, mug, pen or pencil, school folder or notebook, Frisbee, soccer ball, or other commemorative gadget).

Orientation

At a high school in Vancouver, intramural staff used the afternoon on the first day of school to get everyone organized for the upcoming intramural season and to welcome students back to school. Before they arrived at school, all students were assigned a house and a place to meet. The meeting and activities were mandatory for all students. At 1 p.m. on the first day of school, all students reported to their respective houses. At this meeting, under the supervision of a teacher, each house selected a team captain and team name (the blue team designated themselves the "Bluepers"). Students then created and practiced a team chant and designed a house logo.

After an hour, each team was introduced to the rest of the students, and everyone who wished to signed up for the first major activity of the school year: intramural soccer, which was slated to begin the following day. Then students were sent off on a quick treasure hunt. Following the signal to start, students were to report back at the gym and be seated with their team 15 minutes later. When all students were assembled after the hunt, teams delivered their chants and logos to the rest of the student body. Everyone voted for the best chant and logo, and then prizes were awarded to the winning teams. At the end of the day, students were able to participate in several mass games, including a penny hunt (500 pennies were tossed around the soccer field and the team that collected the most pennies won; 632 pennies came back), a team rally where each team lay on the field spelling out its name, and a huge four-corner soccer game using bladder balls.

An event like this can just as easily be held at the grade school and university levels. Organizing such events requires the cooperation of school administrators and teachers, but the effort is well worth it. The afternoon is a lot of fun, students are introduced to one another, new students quickly feel at home, and lots of eager participants are recruited for the intramural program.

Weekly Celebrations

Creating weekly celebrations gives students something to look forward to. These celebrations should be held in high-traffic locations during a busy hour. Recreation staff at Sir Sanford Fleming College, in Peterborough, Ontario, for example, hosts "Wild Wednesdays," a celebration in which students are challenged to partake in crazy games in the main foyer from 12:00 p.m. to 1:00 p.m. every Wednesday afternoon. Weekly games include golf putting, human knots (students hold each other's hands, but not the person's beside them, and try to unravel the know they are in), spoon passes (a relay in which a small team of 4 or 5 students carry, one at a time, a Ping-Pong ball on a spoon and run to a predetermined spot and back without dropping the ball), and free-throw challenges at portable basketball hoops. Winners get little prizes like water bottles and T-shirts. Weekly celebrations like these not only boost student morale but they

also enable personal interaction between students and recreation staff.

Demonstrations

Activities that students are not familiar with may intimidate them. Offering demonstrations is one way of to reduce intimidation and encourage students to try something new. The cafeteria at noon is ideal. Students are there anyway and are usually sitting around for a while, so it doesn't require any additional time. Main corridors before and after classes may also be effective, since students arriving early or late may have some extra time. Types of activities that are particularly suited to these demonstrations include kick boxing, Tae Kwon Do, fencing, Tai Chi, and step aerobics, although many other activities would work too.

Chapter Summary Exercises

An intramural program must be effectively promoted and advertised if students are to come out and benefit through participation. The following four exercises will help you review the components of effective promotion and advertising, and begin the process of formulating your own promotional campaign.

1. Get a sport magazine and flip through it. Notice your first impressions and try to identify what that compels you to look at various advertisements. Share your impressions with the class.

2. In small groups, discuss promotional campaigns and advertisements that you feel effectively communicate a product's benefits, create awareness, or encourage a change in behavior. What aspects of those promotions or advertisements are critical to their success?

3. Develop one of the following promotions for an upcoming intramural basketball tournament: presentation, P.A. announcement, poster, flier, or school newspaper article. Start with your audience, then plan your message. What should you highlight to appeal to your target audience? (Consider visual appeal if choosing a poster or flier.) What elements must you include (who, what, where, when, and why)? What is the most effective way to present those elements?

4. Before developing a Web site on the computer, it is helpful to organize the pages on paper first. If you had a maximun of 10 screens (Web pages) to work with, what would you put on these pages, and how whould they be connected with each other? Use the following two Web sites as a guide: www.ruf.rice.edu/~ims/, www.uwo.ca/campusrec/

References

Conlon, D., 1999. Fly on the wall. *The Leader.* 7 (4): 4.

Claris HomePage—the Basics. 2001. [Online]. Available: http://acomp.stanford.edu/acpubs/Docs/claris_homepage/

Mendelson, E. 2001. *Adobe Pagemill 3.0.* [Online]. Available: http://www.zdnet.com/pcmag/firstlooks/9804/f980423a2.htm

Velicer, W., J. Prochaska, J. Fava, G. Norman, and C. Redding. 1998. Smoking cessation and stress management: Applications of the transtheoretical model of behavior change. *Homeostasis* 38: 216-33.

Resources

Web sites

Carmel Clay School
www.ccs.k12.in.us/chs/intramurals/about.htm

A high school Web site with specific information such as rules and sign-up procedures for intramurals.

Clipart.com
http://www.gifworld.com/

Offers links (and rankings) to other sites that provide clip art.

Indiana University
www.indiana.edu/~recsport/

Hosts an excellent college Web site that identifies its various programs, how people can register, banners announcing new events, and links to pages with more information. Note how easy it is to move through the site.

University of Iowa
http://www.uiowa.edu/~commstud/resources/advertising.html

Features excellent print advertisements.

Periodicals

Ad Age
965 East Jefferson Avenue
Detroit, MI 48207-3187
Phone: 313-446-0450
Web site: http://adage.com/news_and_features/special_reports/commercials/

One of the leading advertising publications in the country. Also hosts a Web site featuring a collection of some of the best print advertisements around.

9

Awards

To never acknowledge people for something they did well would make for a sad and gray world. In the intramural setting especially, participants need to be acknowledged and rewarded, both to recognize their efforts and to keep them coming back for more. To give an award is to acknowledge someone's extra effort, unique contribution, or outstanding performance. The giving of the award is a celebration of that effort, unique contribution, or performance. In short, awards are celebrations of accomplishment.

As such, awards are a key component of an effective intramural program. As intramural directors, it will be your job to plan these awards by determining what and who will be rewarded, how, and when. This chapter is designed to help you do that.

Chapter Objectives

▶ Learn how awards can enhance the intramural mission.
▶ Explore how different awards contribute to the success of an intramural program.
▶ Understand how to develop an awards program and plan a celebration of the intramural season.

Importance of Recognition

All people are motivated by rewards. Some of these rewards are intrinsic and others are extrinsic. An example of an **intrinsic reward** is personal satisfaction and pride. In the intramural setting, intrinsic rewards would come from the satisfaction of participating in an event or activity. People who are intrinsically motivated would participate just for the fun of it, even if there were no prizes or awards. People who are motivated by **extrinsic rewards**, those who are extrinsically motivated, participate in intramural activities for the win, the prize, or the pat on the back from friends and spectators.

Ideally, intramural participants will participate for intrinsic rewards. Indeed, the literature suggests that when people participate in an activity for external rewards, their interest in continuing the activity is reduced (Deci and Ryan 1985; Amabile and Hennessey 1992). That said, however, a reward presented as a bonus afterward will not decrease a participant's interest or intrinsic motivation. In other words, most people do appreciate a bonus after doing something but do not appreciate feeling manipulated or bribed into doing it (Harackiewicz 1979).

The message for intramural directors, then, is that awards should not be large carrots dangled in front of participants' noses to get them to come out for an activity. Rather, awards should be celebrations of effort, participation, physical activity, and satisfaction. Indeed, this focus fits with the very mission of intramural programming: mass participation in fun and active movement. Thus, it is participants' contributions to the mission that should be acknowledged, celebrated, and rewarded.

The best reward in intramural involvement is being part of an exciting and fun program. When participants contribute to that excitement and fun, celebrate their contributions. One way to do that is holding an annual banquet at the end of a season or the school year. Another is hosting a small pizza (or other) party at the conclusion of various events. Awards can focus on team or individual contributions and can range from trophies to prizes to certificates. These and other types of recognition constitute the subject of this chapter.

Striking a Balance

Awards should not be viewed as ends in and of themselves. Awards can encourage students to participate and conduct themselves in the desirable way, certainly, but they should not be emphasized so much that they overshadow or undermine the mission. Particularly in competitive programming, awards tied to winning create incentives to win at all costs, which can hurt the intramural program. If the prize or trophy is substantial, teams will get serious about winning, hold regular practices, and push the rules and officials to the edge. In such cases, intramural activities turn into an athletic contest and the mission of intramurals is undermined.

The trick of using awards in intramural programs, then, is to strike a balance. Awards should spur participants' enthusiasm but should not be so prestigious or important that participants will do anything to win them.

Creating an Awards Program

As is likely obvious from all the mentions of "mission" so far in the discussion, the first step in planning intramural awards is revisiting your mission statement. On the basis of mission, awards should be developed that celebrate participants who contribute toward the successful realization of that mission. For example, the fair play team of the year might be a team that officials most often ranked high in fair play conduct. Such an award should be significant, like a large plaque that hangs in a conspicuous place in the gymnasium plus some tickets to get free pizza for the team at a local eatery.

The next step is considering the awards themselves, including how many will be presented and to whom. Awards should be specific enough that those who receive them feel special, recognized for a unique contribution, but broad enough that many participants can be applauded for their contributions. For example, each team decides, following a game, which player on the other team best exemplified the intramural spirit of fun and encouraging competition. The convener then provides each team with a gift to give that player (a water bottle, a shirt, or a can of juice).

The third step is designing and constructing the awards. What form will they take? Will certificates and prizes be awarded, or will trophies, merchandise, and commemorative plaques be included in the mix? Whatever the type of award, the construction of the awards should support the intramural program mission. That is, the trophy should be fun to look at, something like an old running shoe painted gold that is nailed to a piece of wood, or a metal ball sculpture with a happy face design on the front. It should also be fun to receive. Encourage the photography club to take pictures of the trophy presentations.

Note: Constructing the awards is a great opportunity to utilize the creative talents of staff and other students in school (in particular, those in graphics and art classes, woodworking or metal-working classes, and photography club).

The fourth and final step in designing an awards program is determining what the awards will acknowledge and how they will be distributed. The remainder of this chapter is devoted to this step, providing examples of the types of awards to give and how to present them. First, however, the display of awards is worth mentioning.

Award Display

People display memorabilia they are proud of. It should be no different in intramural recognition. A glass-enclosed display case be a wonderful place to archive awards of the past and present. Encourage participants and alumni to display their awards for all to see. Team pictures, trophies, and other prizes can be included in a display case. Participants will be encouraged to participate in fun, active, and fair intramural programs by looking at their fellow students, wondering who will get which awards this year, and recalling the award-winning game or ceremony. To hold their interest and keep them coming back to the display case, change the display from time to time. For example, to increase interest in intramurals at the beginning of the school year or intramural season, display team photos and trophies from years past. To recognize and reward current participants during the school year or intramural season, display this year's team photos and prizes.

Ceremonies

It is important to celebrate the highlights of an intramural program. Hosting an annual or seasonal awards ceremony is a great way to do that. These ceremonies can take place at a school assembly, an intramural breakfast, or a scheduled banquet (often combined with athletic team banquets). At Niagara-on-the-Lake High School, for example, an annual breakfast banquet is held in early June, before the first period of the day. Of course, banquets can also be held at noon and in the evening. Whatever the time or type of ceremony, take the time to enjoy the successes of the year or season.

As an intramural director, it will be your job to make the awards ceremony a special affair. The following components of successful ceremonies, along with useful ideas and suggestions, will help you do that.

▶ Theme. Start by choosing a theme. Themes might include Western days, March madness, the '50s, at the beach, Summer (or Winter) Olympics—anything that would be fun and appropriate. You can also encourage students to dress according to the theme. In fact, you can have some fun with a dress code. Some years it may be fun to have a formal banquet, while other years it might be more interesting to add a twist. Encourage attendees to go all out in their attire and award prizes to those who are best dressed.

▶ Decorations. Simply put, the livelier the decorations, the more festive the ceremony. If the ceremony has a theme, decorate the facility accordingly. In addition, you might want to add a festive atmosphere by using gold-painted running shoes from the lost and found to anchor helium-filled balloons on every table. Since the ceremony is a celebration and is meant to highlight the fun of intramurals, have fun with the decorations. For example, decorate the tables with newsprint and place crayons on the table so that attendees can doodle during the ceremony. Or on each table place small containers that contain deflated balloons, pipe cleaners of various colors, tinfoil pie plates, a roll of colored tissue paper, and so on. Then have the attendees at each table decorate one table mate using these items.

(The table with the best-decorated person gets a certificate or prize at the end of the evening.)

▶ Photographs. Be sure to take a lot of pictures throughout the evening, especially of those who dress up for the ceremony theme and those donning the table decorations mentioned in the previous paragraph. Team photos can be taken and given out to attendees or used in promotional materials. These pictures are excellent additions the intramural display case.

▶ Refreshments. Most ceremonies include some sort of refreshments, usually a meal or light snack, largely depending on the available budget. Sometimes a parent or student council may be willing to contribute some money to the event, or it might be possible to charge a small fee for attendance, although such fees may make it difficult for some to attend. Be creative in planning ceremony refreshments. For example, attendees could bring in some of the food (have a bake-off contest), or those interested could go out for pizza (dutch treat) after the ceremony. Likewise, ceremonies can be planned around low-cost refreshments. For example, pancakes at a breakfast banquet are certainly cheaper than steak or chicken at a supper banquet.

▶ Memories. Reminiscing should be big part of any ceremony. Highlights of the year (photographs and video clips from activities and events) can be compiled into an entertaining video or a slide show. Such presentations keep the ceremony moving, particularly during a meal. Encourage participants to share their own memories as well, making short presentations to the group or having an "open mike" for willing participants to come up and tell a story.

▶ Silly awards. You might also consider giving odd or unusual prizes throughout the celebration, supplemented by the story behind the prize or video clips and photographs of the inspiration for the award. For example, a player whose shorts ripped in the middle of a game could get a new pair of shorts.

▶ Pace. It is best to keep the ceremony moving. Particularly during the awards portion, banquets can easily become bogged down. Awards should be described briefly (the criteria of the award and the accomplishments of the recipient only), and award recipients should be encouraged to limit their comments to a few statements, or less.

▶ Fanfare. Award recipients should have their moment in the spotlight. It can be fun to approach the awards portion of the ceremony "Oscar" style. That is, announce the award, describe the criteria of the award, announce the nominees and a brief description of why they are nominated, and then read the winner from a card in an envelope ("And the winner is . . ."). To keep the pace moving, of course, you may want to limit the presentation and winner acceptance speeches to 30 seconds or less.

When all is said and done, ceremonies should be a highlight of the intramural season or school year. They are an important opportunity to reinforce your mission, acknowledge the people who have contributed to your program, and reward participants who deserve special recognition. Seize this opportunity. Take the time to enjoy the successes by celebrating with awards. Above all, the entire ceremony should reflect the primary mission of intramurals: having fun.

Annual and Ongoing Awards

The two types of awards discussed in this chapter are annual awards and ongoing awards. **Annual awards** are awards given in recognition of a unique contribution to the intramural program. These contributions can be a special one-time effort, such as putting a lot of work into an event or organizing and hosting the awards banquet, or a season- or year-long effort, such as refereeing the most games during the year or being the best sports. Annual awards are cumulative. That is, they are tracked throughout the year and presented at its completion.

Ongoing awards, the second type of award, are given throughout the year. Traditional ongoing awards include trophies and prizes for winning a tournament or competition or game, as well as sportsmanship trophies for the team or individual exemplifying the ideas of fair play. Less-traditional ongoing awards can reward such achievements as winning the most games in a league or sport season as well as being on a team

An Intramural Extravaganza

Ceremonies can be as simple or involved as you want them to be. The following exerpt illustrates the approach of Prince Edward School, in Prince Edward Island, Canada. They developed an intramural extravaganza night to wrap up their program for the year. They took the top 70 students from the intramural program and invited them to the event. The participants were divided into eight teams balanced by gender, grade level, and athletic ability. Each team was given the name of a country.

"The leadership class made medals with the extravaganza logo on them and painted them gold silver, and bronze. The logos are unique to each year and are created by the leaders. These engraved and painted medals are eagerly sought after. Teams receive points for a number of events and members of each team receive the appropriate medal. Other awards are also given out for individuals who demonstrated the best blooper play, best team play, best team player, and best sportsmanship.

"Originally each team was given a country and a team pinnie matching the country's flag color. The last few years they went with T-Shirts that students purchase. The T-Shirts are of various team colors but all have the extravaganza logo. Students appreciate these T-Shirts and wear them with pride long after the event—great promotions for next year's extravaganza.

"The events run from 6:30pm to 9:30pm sometime around mid-June. We run a round-robin style tournament with 20-minute games. The event goes on rain or shine, though it is scheduled to be in the gym if it rains, and activities include variations on softball, football, volleyball, basketball, bladder ball, ultimate Frisbee, Omnikin, and scooter hockey.

"The evening is concluded with an awards assembly. Parents are invited to watch. The top three teams are given medals, and individual award winners receive water bottles or other prizes donated by local businesses. Following a snack and drink, sold at a discounted price, students and parents leave enthused and happy after a great evening of intramural fun and excitement with a bunch of great people." (Howard, 1996)

Reprinted by permission of the Canadian Intramural Recreation Association. From B. Howard, 1996, "Intramural extravaganza," *CIRA Bulletin* 22 (1):11.

that accrued the fewest penalties, that was always dressed the best, and so on.

Ongoing awards provide the opportunity to celebrate regular highlights and achievements throughout the intramural program, including the type of participation you wish to support. For example, St. Thomas High School gives out a "tip-of-the-hat award" every week to a participant who offers a special contribution to the intramural program during a specific week. Criteria change from week-to-week. One week students may receive the award for a unique contribution (helping to organize the basketball tournament), and another week for an outstanding performance (winning a competition or exemplifying the standards of fair play). Many schools designate an intramural star or athlete

of the week, who receives a certificate and gets his or her picture and a brief write-up in the school or local newspaper.

Equipped with a clear understanding of the difference between annual and ongoing awards, then, let's move on to the two components of intramural awards—specifically, program awards and sport- or event-specific awards.

Program Awards

To promote participation in intramurals, it is a good idea to encourage individual and team participants as well as staff, volunteers, officials, and other program leadership. The best way to do that is to offer program awards. Program awards are traditionally presented annually (hence the "of the year" tagged onto most of the award names in this section), but they can also be presented at the end of a season, event, or special activity. The essence of program awards is that they recognize people for contributing to the program.

Before describing the various program awards used in intramural programs across North America, a caution is in order. Program awards, even fun or silly awards, can quickly be seen as a group of intramural staff congratulating themselves and their friends on their entertaining and funny experiences. In other words, when establishing your program award criteria, you must consider all program participants. Determine which awards best celebrate the mission of your program and the contributions of participants.

The following sections describe some specific program awards and provide suggestions for establishing award criteria. These awards are not the only options available, however. If people have done something special for the intramural program or conducted themselves in an exemplary way, create an award to celebrate their contribution.

Fair Play of the Year

This should be a significant award. "Fair play of the Year" is, perhaps, the most important award for an intramural program. It rewards sportsmanlike conduct, of course, but it also reinforces the very mission of the program. Thus, the recipient should be someone who best exemplifies the spirit of your mission and standards of fair play. That is, the recipient of this award should be someone who encourages fun and participation for all, even the marginalized populations at your school. He should be someone who participated in almost every intramural league or activity, from those he excelled at to those in which he was a novice. She should be someone who strove, in every game or event, to make new friends and make the activity enjoyable for all.

Best Ump (or Ref) of the Year

As described in chapter 5, officials get their share of criticism and insults—and then some. An award for best ump (or ref) of the year is an opportunity to publicly acknowledge an official who played a key role in ensuring safety and fun participation for all program participants. Criteria for this award should include officiating at a significant number of games throughout the year or season, exemplifying the characteristics of good officials (see chapter 5), being highly ranked on participant evaluations, and participating in further training to improve skills. Because some officials may only oversee certain sports, it may be a good idea to refine this award by presenting sport-specific "ump of the year" awards. For example, a separate award could be presented for hockey, basketball, and baseball leagues. You could also broaden this award by awarding the "best official of the year," which could include head and supervisory officials.

Top Team of the Year

At some institutions, an annual award is given for the top intramural team of the year. Selecting the top team is made easier when the house system is used because the same teams participate in all program events and leagues. Teams may gain or lose a few players, depending on the specific activity they are engaged in, but the core of the team and the team name stays the same for the entire year. In cases where the house system is not used, the top team of the year could be given to a team that stuck together for much of the year and most demonstrated and encouraged fun and fair play through their participation.

The basic design of this award is as follows: Teams are awarded points both for winning and for participation. At the end of the year, these points are totaled and the team with the most points receives the award. The underlying idea is that earning points will encourage team members both to play and to show up at games to support their team.

For example, at Confederation College in Thunder Bay, Ontario, each team can sign up a maximum of 15 participants per event. For small-number events such as three-on-three basketball, they can enter several teams (i.e., three teams of five students each). Different players can sign up for different events, but the core of the team stays the same. To encourage more students to come out for intramural events, teams earn extra points when they bring in a person not previously involved in intramural events: 10 points per person to a maximum of 250 points per semester or year. (Even if a team had a maximum of 15 people signed up for a previous league, a couple of those might not be interested in the next league, which creates and opportunity to recruit some new people to add to the team.)They also earn additional points for other events that promote intramurals or school spirit, such as entering a team float in a local parade or helping as a team for a local community project. Teams also lose points. For example, if they do not show up for a game, they lose 25 points for an individual event and 125 points for a team event.

Note: Having houses, or annual teams, makes organization easier and teams become part of intramural promotion as they seek out new players to earn extra points. If points are kept for the entire year, however, some teams may lose heart if they fall too far behind. Figuring they have no chance of winning the overall team event, many players may become discouraged and stop participating. This, of course, hurts the program. A solution is doubling the points in the second semester, which gives the underdogs an opportunity to catch up.

In the Confederation College and similar point systems used, points are recorded on a participation record like the one shown in figure 9.1. The first grid is an attendance record. It provides space for the names of all team members and a check-off grid to record their attendance (participation) on various game dates. Participant names are written in the left column and game or event dates are written at the top of each subsequent column. (There should be a separate column for each game or event.) Whenever a player shows up, he or she gets a checkmark for that game or event date. Each checkmark is worth one point. Thus, if all 10 teammates come out for five games, the team would get 50 points.

Points are tallied and totaled in the lower right table in figure 9.1. In the case of a league, attendance points are multiplied by five. In the case of a one-day event, attendance points are multiplied by 4. Then each team gets points for its final standing. Like total attendance points, the point total depends on whether the event involves league play or individual play (e.g., bad-

minton singles), or is a one-day event. For example, if the team places first in the league, that is worth 72 points. If the team places first in a one-day event, that is worth 54 points. And if it is an individual event, the individual competing earns 36 points for his or her team.

Working down the table, new-participant points are added. If a new person is brought in for a one-day or individual event, the team gets 15 points. If it is a league, the team gets 20 points for each new person. Finally, to discourage no-shows, points are deducted.

Top Participant of the Year

Rather than track participation points by team, some institutions prefer to use a point system for each participant. Every time a person participates in an intramural event the player is given one participant point. At the end of the year, the individual with the most participation points wins the "top participant of the year" award.

When using a point system for individual participation, try to ensure that it is equitable. That means, points should be weighted according to the type and duration of the activity. For example, participating in a one-day event should be worth more than participating in a half-hour event. Likewise, different points can be awarded for different types of participation. For example, award a different number of points for being a competitor, official, and scorekeeper. In addition, keep the criteria and scoring simple, and keep accurate records. To prevent misplacing or losing point totals halfway through a season, it is helpful to keep a master record in the intramural office and transfer individual event records to the master at the end of each event.

Other

The awards described in the previous sections are commonly used to acknowledge and reward intramural participants. In addition, consider the following awards:

▶ Fair players: teams nominated by the officials, program staff, and fellow participants for adhering to and encouraging the standards of fair play (more than one fair player award can be presented)

Team Participation Record

Name	Date									Total
1										
2										
3										
4										
5										
6										
7										
8										
9										
10										
11										
12										
13										
14										
15										
										Total

Participants new to intramurals
1
2
3
4

Participation points
- League team 5 X total attendance
- One-day team/individual event, .4 X total

Place in league	Place for one-day event	Place for individual events	
• 1st 72 points	54	36	
• 2nd 60 points	45	30	
• 3rd 48 points	36	24	
• 4th 36 points	27	18	

Bonus points for new participants (see left) X 15 for a one-day or individual event X 20 for a league	

Minus defaults	
League first time	−50
League second time	−100
One-day or individual first time	−25
One-day or individual second time	−50

Total points	

FIGURE 9.1   Sample intramural team participation sheet.

▶ Best departmental participation: Academic programs at universities and colleges are often departmentalized according to majors (business, nursing, computer science, English, and so on). The department with the highest number of students participating during the year receives the award

▶ Most physically active staff: the staff person who was most involved in physical activity during the year

▶ Outstanding official: the official who refereed many intramural games and whose evaluations were positive

▶ Team captain of the year: the team captain who contributed the most to the intramural program (this could also be a general team captains award and be presented to all team captains)

In the spirit of promoting fun in an intramural program, you might also want to include some silly awards such as the following:

▶ Deflated ball award: given to participants who accidentally broke some equipment

▶ Red face award: presented for the most embarrassing situations in an intramural event or activity

▶ Eager beaver award: presented to the participant who gives the most conscientious effort

Event Awards

Event awards traditionally included prizes and game trophies awarded at the end of a tournament, season, competition, game, or other event. In the interest of encouraging the mission of intramurals, however, intramural directors would be wise to consider offering other event awards that will celebrate unique and positive contributions made to leagues, teams, activities, games, and events throughout the year. The most common intramural event awards are listed in the following sections. This list is far from comprehensive. Use a little creativity to come up with more awards that will promote fun and active participation at every event.

Game Trophies

It is always helpful to recognize people for achievements. Winning a game or league is an achievement and deserves some praise. But remember that intramural competition is first of all about fun and active movement. At Redeemer University College, a stuffed dog on a wooden platform is given to the winning team. The winning teams keeps the trophy till the next event, at which point the trophy is passed on to the winner of that event. The trophy has some prestige to it, it acknowledges the winner but is also a fun trophy, and is less important that the awards given to the team that displayed the best intramural spirit.

MVP

Players who contribute the most to winning the game (i.e., score the most points) are usually dubbed MVPs (most valuable players). To promote the mission of intramurals, however, a better use of this award is recognizing the player who most contributes to a fun, inclusive atmosphere—sort of a best sport award. Likewise, in professional sports, MVPs are traditionally named at the end of a season.

Just as it is important to recognize sportsmanship in the overall program, it is also important to reward sportsmanship at each and every event. Like the program "sportsmanship of the year" award, event "best sport" awards should be significant. Indeed, they are perhaps the most significant awards presented at games and other events. And like the criteria for the program "sportsmanship of the year" award, the recipient of this event award should be the player who best exemplifies the spirit of play and fun, encouragement, and fair play. Best sport awards can be given after each game, after a tournament, at the conclusion of a league, and so on. The more often good sports are recognized and acknowledged, the stronger the emphasis on sportsmanship during play and in your intramural program.

At Calvin grade school, good sports are recognized with a weekly sportsmanship award. Recipients appear in the weekly newsletter and are announced every Monday morning over the P.A. system. The criteria for the week's best sport include

► winning or losing graciously;

► participating in all activities;

► cheering on all players, not just teammates;

► not criticizing anyone;

► following the rules; and

► demonstrating respect for the officials.

Participation Awards

Many schools reward every participant's effort. If they showed up and tried their best, they deserve some recognition. This is especially important for younger students in grade and high school, expecially nonathletes and students who struggle with certain activities. Consider offering T-shirts, balls and other sports equipment, and even miniature trophies to recognize players' efforts and willingness to participate. The affordability of these rewards, of course, will be determined by your budget, but a little creativity can go a long way.

Certificates

Certificates offer a low-cost alternative to participation awards. For example, to encourage fun in its intramural program, MacDonald High School gives out a "fair play" certificate after each game. Players from each team select someone on the other team who they feel deserves recognition and then presents a certificate to that person at the end of the game. Names of certificate winners are publicized on the school's daily announcements and recorded by the intramural director. At the end of the year, the students who receive the most certificates are eligible for a special prize. At MacDonald High School, these prizes are T-shirts with the logo "I played fair." But any recognition will do.

Certificates are inexpensive, and can often be generated on the computer. At John Darling Elementary School, students are given participation certificates after the first game. These certificates are filed in the principal's office. As students participate in each event, they are given stickers to affix to these certificates. At the end of the year, students receive their sticker-laden certificates to take home and enjoy all summer. An example certificate is shown in figure 9.2.

Prizes

Unlike trophies, plaques, and other traditional awards, prizes can be fun, creative, silly, and/or unusual. Indeed, prizes should reflect the mission of fun in intramurals. At Redeemer University College, for example, the winner of the competitive division gets the "Golden Muffy" award, a stuffed dog on a wooden base representing the poodle of the president's wife. The winner of the recreational division gets "Walley's chicken," a plastic chicken on a wooden base representing the maintenance person's pet chickens. In both cases, winning teams keep their award till there is a winner in a subsequent event. Silly prizes like these are not only fun ways to award participants but also a positive way to keep the support of important people on campus.

Of course, you are not limited to sport- or activity-specific criteria in awarding prizes. For example, provide a laughing machine for the student who laughs the most during intramurals or a pair of shoelaces for the person whose laces kept coming undone. You could also give a tie-dyed T-Shirt to the player who wears the craziest clothes to intramural activities or an intramural hat for the player who usually competes while wearing a hat.

Prizes can also be used as incentives. George Brown College, for example, created an incentive program to challenge students in the mileage club. All students are given "Husky Bucks" for participating, which they can redeem at the college store for merchandise. To prevent counterfeiting, these "bucks" are signed by intramural personnel and redesigned every year. Any intramural program can design their own program coupons (see figure 9.3). A similar incentive program can be easily developed. Instead of going to the expense of printing coupons or "bucks," simply keep track of participation points (see figure 9.1 on page 154) and then offer intramural merchandize or other prizes for accumulated points.

Prizes can vary from inexpensive gadgets and memorabilia to moderately priced and expensive merchandise. Carvings, glassware, pottery, clothing, free passes to a local facility or event, certificates for free food, water bottles, whistles, rackets and other sports equipment—anything participants might want can be used as a prize.

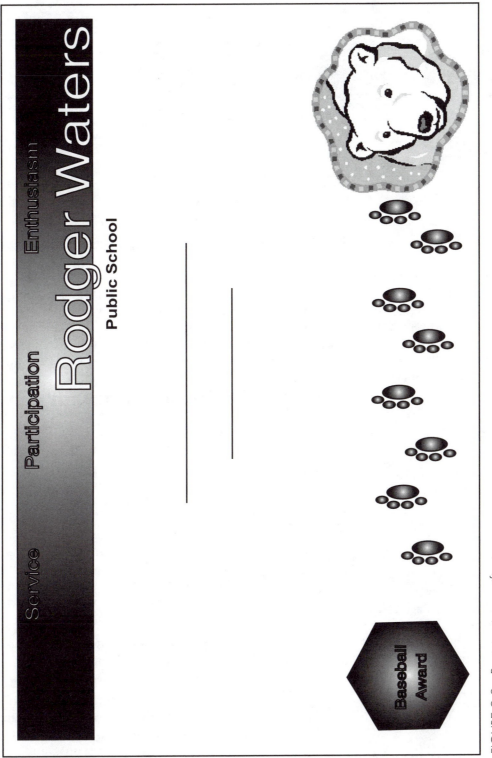

FIGURE 9.2 Participation certificate.

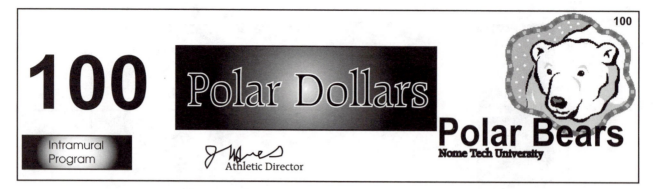

FIGURE 9.3   Polar Bucks. Program awards redeemable for prizes.

Since prize recipients' tastes might differ from that of the intramural director or staff person selecting the merchandise, it might be simpler to have a prize table that recipients can select their prizes from, although that may give rise to some squabbling among prize-winning participants. The simplest way to distribute prizes is to award the same prizes to everyone. In the collegiate setting, for example, appropriate prizes would include Frisbees, T-shirts, college sweatshirts, book bags, backpacks, and travel bags.

Surrey Middle School gives a "golden running shoe" prize to participants who complete 100 miles (kilometers) running or walking. Golden shoe holders keep the prize until the next person reaches the target (100 miles [kilometers]), and they continue running or walking their next 100 miles (kilometers). Several schools present the "rusty whistle award" (the prize is a rusty whistle) to teams that play a penalty-free game. At the end of the season, the names of all rusty whistle holders are placed in a hat, and the team whose name is drawn gets a certificate for a pizza dinner. Of course, trophies, certificates, plaques, and other merchandise can also be awarded for this type of individual and team achievement, but prizes such as these are a low-cost alternative and in many cases are quite popular with students.

Scoring as an Incentive

The literature suggests that people have a need to evaluate their personal abilities relative to those of others (Festinger 1954). One way this need is satisfied is by people comparing themselves with others in game activities. Scores in games and standings in leagues and tournaments serve as an award or incentive to keep some people coming out. Keeping scores and standings is a prize for some people. Without overemphasizing winning games, after all intramurals is about fun active movement, keeping score and standings provides a positive incentive for some people to keep participating.

Chapter Summary Exercises

Awards are an opportunity to publicly acknowledge participants' successes and achievement. As described in this chapter, achievement includes more than doing well or winning a game. Achievement in intramurals includes showing up, being a good sport, encouraging others to participate and become active, increasing everyone's enjoyment by emphasizing the spirit of play and fun, and celebrating the mission of the program. The following four exercises will help you review the material in this chapter and plan your awards program.

1. Look at the mission statement you developed in chapter 2. Think of specific awards that will further your mission.

2. Review the different awards listed in this chapter, and recall your own intramural experiences. Come up with a list of all the awards you want to include in your program. Be sure to consider ongoing and annual awards.

3. For three of the awards listed in number 2, develop the criteria for each award (who will receive it and how many) and the method of presentation. When and how will you present each award?

4. Considering your awards from number 2 and your method of presentation from number 3, plan an awards ceremony.

References

Amabile, T., and B. Hennessey. 1992. The motivation for creativity in children. In *Achievement and motivation*, edited by A. Boggiano and T. Pittman. New York: Cambridge University Press, 54-74.

Deci, E., and R. Ryan. 1985. *Intrinsic motivation and self-determination in human behavior*. New York: Plenum Press.

Harackiewicz, J. 1979. The effects of reward contingency and performance feedback on intrinsic motivation. *Journal of Personality and Social Psychology* 37: 1352-63.

Howard, B. 1996. Intramural extravaganza. *CIRA Bulletin* 22 (1): 11. Used by permission of the Canadian Intramural Recreation Association.

Resources

For two sites that note their awards programs look at:

CIRA-Ontario
www.mohawkc.on.ca/external/cira/awards.htm
University of Wisconsin – Stout
www.uwstout.edu/univrec/imaw.htm

The Budget

If an institution values an intramural program, then those in charge should provide adequate funding to support the program. In elementary schools and high schools, this funding often comes via the physical education department or from a parent council donation, and in universities students are often charged student activity fees, a portion of which is designated for intramural programming. Nevertheless, these resources are usually insufficient for a comprehensive campus recreation program.

In the face of too few funds for too many activities, as intramural directors, you will be charged with the task of using limited resources wisely and finding creative ways to increase financial support for your program—all the while satisfying your mission of fun, active, healthy participation for as many as possible. These are the topics of this chapter.

Chapter Objectives

▶ Understand the budgeting process.

▶ Identify the many sources of revenue for an intramural program.

▶ Identify the expenses of an intramural program.

▶ Explore various cost-saving measures to reduce intramural expenses.

▶ Learn how to use computer spreadsheets to calculate an intramural budget.

An Introduction to Intramural Budgets

Before discussing the specifics of financing and budgeting for an intramural program, there are some terms that need to be defined. First, there are *budget* and *budgeting*. A **budget** can be both a statement of financial position as well as the amount of money available for a particular purpose. **Budgeting** is simply the process of keeping track of the money coming in and going out.

Starting with the inflow, the money that is brought into the program is **revenue**. Intramural revenue (also called "income") is generated from student fees, participation fees, rentals, fund-raising, sponsorship, and advertising. The outflow, **expenses**, is money spent. Intramural expenses include program costs such as staff salaries, facility rental, equipment, office and event supplies, travel, and promotion.

Ideally, revenue and expenses should balance each other out. This is called a **balanced budget**. When out of balance a deficit budget or surplus budget is the result. In a **deficit budget**, expenses are greater than revenue and the budget has a negative balance ("in the red"). In a **surplus budget**, revenue is greater than expenses and the budget has a positive balance ("in the black"). To know what the numbers are, of course, you will have to keep track of them. Intramural directors can track budgets—on paper or on computer—with a **spreadsheet**, a document with many rows and columns.

Forecasting

If an intramural program has existed for some time, there is probably a fairly predictable cash flow coming in and going out, revenue and expenses. Grade and high school intramural directors usually receive their budgets at the beginning of the year, so they know what they have to work with right off the bat. At the university level, intramural directors are often given a budget to work with *plus* a portion of student fees. The amount from student fees will fluctuate slightly from year to year, but it is fairly predictable. These budgets are mainly composed of monies available for the program, or revenue. That is, the institution's governing body informs intramural directors how much money their programs will be allotted out of the entire school budget.

Using that budget, then, intramural directors go about the process of **forecasting**, which is the process of estimating program expenses and additional revenue they can generate. Based on predicted total revenue (school allotment plus additional revenue generated), intramural directors have a pretty good idea of what can be spent. By considering the activities and events planned and the costs of those activities and events, directors are able to forecast whether the program will end the year with with a balanced budget, a surplus budget, or a deficit budget. In the case of a deficit budget, intramural directors know that extra money will need to be generated.

Revenue

As everyone knows—with the possible exception of government, that is—to spend money, there must be money to spend. To turn a deficit budget into a balanced (or better yet, surplus) budget, intramural directors must have some way of generating revenue. Revenue generation can take a variety of forms, including charging student and participation fees and fund-raising. **Student fees** are flat fees students are charged by an institution (typically colleges and universities) for participating in intramurals, recreation, athletics, and other school programs. Intramural directors are allotted a portion of these fees to run intramurals. **Participation fees** are variable fees charged students for participating in a certain program or activity, such as aerobics classes or a volleyball league. **Fund-raising** is simply raising funds. Fund-raising activities typically include special campaigns and events that people pay to participate in.

Before getting into these and other specific types of revenue generation, which are explained in the following sections, a brief mention of program mission. As intramural directors, you will need to be clear about your intramural mission so that you do not end up compromising the integrity of your program for the sake of bringing in more money. If your mission is to encourage fun and active, healthy living, for example, accepting donated or sponsorship money from a cigarette manufacturer would likely compromise that mission. Likewise, if the mission is to promote mass participation, participation fees may decrease the opportunities for low-income students to become involved.

Participation Fees

Participation fees are the most common source of additional revenue for intramural programs in North America. Because they are so common, different institutions use a variety of names for these fees: activity fees, student activity fees, member or user fees, program fees, and so on. And, many institutions charge several of these types of fees. For example, some schools charge an annual student activity fee to all full-time students at the beginning of each semester to supplement the fixed budget allotted by the institution. In addition to annual student activity fees, they charge user fees for specific intramural activities.

When it comes to participation fees, the possibilities are endless. You can charge fees for certain events or activities and not charge for others. You can charge all participants a flat fee at the beginning of each season, league, or year. You can charge all participants for the use of some or all of your intramural facilities, or you can allow students free access and only charge community members. You can offer paid memberships, both to students and to members of the community. Or you can use a combination of all of these, not to mention others. When implementing participation fees, keep the following principles in mind.

- ▶ Heed your mission. The idea is not to make millions but to make enough to provide the best program to as many users as possible.

- ▶ Consider your competition. Fees should be commensurate with market conditions, that is, competing prices at other educational institutions, fitness clubs, and community health programs.

- ▶ Remember the fair play principle of equal opportunity. User fees can be discriminatory, particularly against the poor, so be careful that fees do not become excessive.

- ▶ Be fair. Do not discriminate by gender. For example, many institutions often do not charge for intramural league programs but do charge for aerobics. Since males typically engage in the former and females in the latter, this type of pricing discriminates against women.

Busy institutions sometimes also apply different participation fees for different times of the day. If, for example, the weight room is busiest in the late afternoons, you can raise revenue as well as reduce overcrowding by increasing the fee for the late-afternoon slot. Likewise, squash courts, which tend to be heavily used in the evenings and rarely used in the mornings, can be more expensive in the evenings to encourage users to come earlier. Be creative with your facilities. If squash courts are not used much during the morning, drop some golf nets from the ceiling, put a mat on the ground, and voila! You have an indoor driving range—another activity and another opportunity to generate revenue.

With the recent surge in weightlifting interest, weight rooms have become a moneymaking venture for many intramural operations. Indeed, some institutions charge as much as $100 per semester per student to use the weight room. Depending on how busy the weight room is, and the amount of the fee charged, schools can make a few extra dollars or hundreds of thousands of dollars from weight room user fees. Some institutions also offer weight room (or gym or fitness center) memberships to students and members of the community. Money generated from membership fees is used both to update the weight room and add more equipment and to supplement other intramural activities. Of course, there are trade-offs to be considered when it comes to community memberships. While they bring in additional revenue, if there are too many members, students may become frustrated because they do not have sufficient access to "their own" facility.

Many institutions (particularly large colleges and universities) charge parking fees. Intramural programs can get in on this revenue-generating action if the gym or other recreational facilities are near parking lots or ramps. This, too, involves a trade-off. Having to pay for parking each time they use the facilities can deter students from participating in intramurals. Thus, if possible, it may be wise to forego the revenue and try to make special parking arrangements (free or low cost) for fitness center (or gym or weight room) members and students who return to school at night to use the center or participate in intramural activities.

Rental

Your facility itself, particularly gyms and weight rooms, may be potential moneymakers. Indeed, most collegiate institutions generate a lot of revenue by renting their facilities to other sport organizations and groups that are hosting anything from a large garage sale to a fair or show. Fees depend on the size of the facility and its location, but typically gymnasium rental fees are between $400 and $1000 a day. The institution provides the gymnasium plus supervisory staff, regular secruity staff, and clean-up following the activity. Equipment is not usually included in these fees but can usually be arranged for extra costs.

Some institutions offer their facilities for physical and fitness testing. For example, fire, police, and security departments typically test recruits before hiring them. An arrangement like this not only brings people and dollars into the facility, but it can also provide fitness-testing equipment for the intramural program. How about trying a scaled-down version of a firefighter fitness test as a Winter Relay? Events include rope climbing, carrying a 150-pound dummy through an obstacle course, and getting fully dressed (including boots) and running through an obstacle course. This could be done as a relay with different member of the team completing different parts of the challenge.

Facility rental, too, requires a balancing act. Remember your mission. While the additional revenue is attractive, certainly, the aim of intramural programming is providing adequate and equal opportunity for students to be physically active. Not only that, if the institution charges student fees and/or if you charge annual student activity fees, the students have paid for this opportunity. It is now your obligation to provide it.

Fund-Raising

As introduced earlier, fund-raising activities typically include special campaigns and events for which people pay to participate. In the intramural context, this usually involves a service, class, or other intramural-related activity. While the primary goal of fund-raisers is to make money, intramural fund-raisers should also seek to satisfy the program mission. In other words, intramural fund-raisers should raise money by offering a chance to participate in fun and active movement.

The varieties of intramural fund-raisers are many, ranging from events such as a dance to contests such as a three-point shooting contest. Selling products such as refreshments and merchandise and offering services such as a school car wash also make excellent fund-raisers. Before discussing specific fund-raising ideas, it is important to understand the organization and effort required in hosting a fund-raiser. As intramural directors, you will need to know the following nine steps of effective fund-raising.

Step 1. Before getting too far ahead of yourself, you will likely need to check with your institution. State laws, local ordinances, and school policies may restrict certain fund-raising activities. For example, many public schools accept gifts but not money. If your institution has a fund-raising department, which is often the case at large universities and colleges, fund-raising personnel may be able to offer helpful advice. For example, they may ask that donors who have already given at a previous school fund-raiser not be approached this time around to avoid donor burnout.

Step 2. Once your have the OK from the institution, begin by setting your goals. This includes the purpose of the fund-raiser as well as how much money you want (or need) to raise. If you want the event to be successful, your purpose should have public appeal. Raising $1,000 to pay for a staff retreat, for example, is not nearly as motivational to potential donors as offering skill-development clinics, uniforms, and important recognition to program participants.

Try not to make your goals too restrictive, in case the money raised exceeds the amount needed. If, for example, you need $1,000 for uniforms and the event raises $3,000, what will you do with the extra money? On the other hand, remember that success, even a small one, is better than failure. Set your goals realistically high to be challenging but not so high that reaching them will be impossible and frustration will ensue.

Step 3. Once you have set your goals, it's time to think about the fund-raising event. To do this, you will need to create a budget. Raising money often requires money. That means, you will have to decide how much money you can afford (and want) to put up to raise additional funds. If you decide to hold a dance, for example, there will be costs for decorating the hall, the entertainment, refreshments, and staff. If you're holding a tournament or other competitive event, you'll need to pay for prizes. In considering these costs, weigh the risk. If the event is unsuccessful, you may lose more money than you raise.

In addition to the costs of the actual fund-raising event, you will also have to consider organization and promotion costs. After all, if no one knows about your fund-raiser, no one will show up. Think about the time and staff required. Take a golf tournament fund-raiser, for example. You will need people to organize the event, make necessary arrangements with the golf course, take care of sponsorships (see "Sponsorship" on page 167) and prizes for tournament winners, control the money, organize pre-registration, plan and oversee the playing schedule, design and print and distribute promotional materials, and so on. Unless you plan to do everything yourself, which is next to impossible for a large fund-raiser, you will need competent people to organize and run the event well.

Step 4. Also when considering the event, you'll want to ask yourself, Has this idea been tried before? And, the immediate questions that follow: Did it succeed? Did it fail? Will this event be on the same par? Timing is also a consideration, both the timing of the event (a chocolate heart run is perfect for Valentine's day but is not quite as suitable in November) and the amount of time available for preparation (a bake sale can be organized in a week or two, whereas a masquerade ball will take considerably longer).

Before getting too excited about your idea, you may also need to check with your institution's insurance provider that there is adequate coverage for the event.

Step 5. Once you have answered the questions in step 4 and have a good idea about costs (step 3), it is time to finalize the fund-raiser plan. Determine the type of event you will host and start making lists. Think through the details, including decorations, promotion, fund-raising goals, staff required, and so on. You will also want to come up with a name for your event. You may be able to tie a current fad or school tradition into the event. For example, was an event held last year that could be built upon this year? If that event was successful, participants may be ex-

pecting it to happen again this year. At this step in the process, also consider future fund-raising. For example, if you've come up with a fabulous idea for a new type of fund-raiser, perhaps you want to dub it the first of an annual event.

Step 6. With your fund-raiser plan in place, it is now time to set it in motion. Gather your people and assign duties. Get promotion staff working on promotion and advertising ideas. Have your finance people estimate attendance and then set entrance fees according to revenue-generation goals. And so on. A note about price setting: Setting prices can be tricky. Entrance fees and other pricing cannot be so high that they deter attendance, but they cannot be so low that the return will not be worth the effort.

Step 7. Hold the fund-raiser. If you have created a specific plan and covered your bases in step 6, this should be a relatively easy step. Last-minute problems may need to be handled, but otherwise, you should be able to relax and have a good time at your event.

Step 8. Immediately after the fund-raiser, get your people together and go over it, step by step. Think about the organization involved, evaluate individual tasks and assess the coordination and cooperation among your team. This should be an open, honest evaluation so that everyone learns from the experience and is prepared to do it better the next time. Particularly if the event was the first of what will become an annual fund-raiser (see step 5), this learning process will lead to a smoother operation in future years.

Step 9. Tally the money raised and celebrate your success, no matter how large or small. Thank all participants with thank-you notes, certificates of participation, posters and other announcements detailing the amount raised (including the original goal), and so on. Likewise, thank your organizers, donors, and sponsors, particularly those who contributed a lot to the event.

Now that you know how to hold an effective fund-raiser, let's explore the myriad fund-raisers available. The following have been tried by many institutions, some with more success than others, but this list is certainly not exhaustive. Rather, it is intended to stimulate thinking about what is possible. The revenue opportunities for these fund-raisers are as varied as the activities themselves. Some ideas: admission fees, betting on teams (check with state laws and school policies), sponsorship per mile, user fees, and so on. While going through these ideas, you may wish to jot down notes, variations on these ideas, your own ideas, and other successful fund-raisers you have attended or heard about.

Events:

- Socials: special dinners, social hours, dances, masquerade balls, and so on
- Shows: fashion shows, amateur nights, air-band contests, movie showings, and so on
- "A-thons": walk-a-thons, bike-a-thons, skate-a-thons, dance-a-thons, skip-a-thons, swim-a-thons, trash-a-thons, step-a-thons, and other activities in which participants earn so much per mile traveled, hours danced or skipped, laps swum, bags of litter picked up, or number of flights of stairs climbed
- Auctions: silent or public auctions in which goods and/or services are donated and the highest bidder gets the item

Contests:

- Guessing games: how many golf balls, gum drops, and so on in a large container (participants pay to submit their guesses)
- Sport and other tournaments: golf, pool, dart, and other tournaments in which competitors earn so much per hole, pocket, ball, point, and so on
- Races: bed races, three-legged races, flour-sac races, and so on
- Department or group competitions: students vs. faculty, psychology majors vs. chemistry majors, school vs. the local police department, and so on
- Cake walks and musical chairs: using participant-baked cakes or fancy cakes from local bakeries
- Shooting (or putting or dribbling and so on) contests: contests in which participants pay so much per shot, ball, and so on (In a three-point shooting contest, for example, contestants pay $1 for the chance to shoot 15 balls [five balls at three different stations] in 60 seconds; the winner gets half of all entrance fees and the rest goes to the intramural program.)

- Coin collections: any contest in which participants bring in coins (A penny-raising contest, for example, is held between classes or departments; the winning class [the class that raises the most money] gets a pizza party [Byl 2000].)

Products and services:

- Services: instructional clinics or ongoing classes (Tae Kwon Do, aerobics, and so on), fitness appraisals and health fairs, car washes, and sports equipment exchange. At the beginning of the skiing season, for example, people bring in equipment they want to sell and on a given day all the equipment is displayed and available for people to buy. Any items not sold are returned to the owner. The money received goes to the previous owner and the intramural program retains 10 percent for hosting the sale.
- Tours: walking tours of the city, hikes, cycling, bird watching, and so on
- Sales (charge per item, display/table, and/or a percentage of everything sold): community garage sales, community sports equipment (old and used) sales and exchanges, bazaars, farmers' and citizen markets (fruit, cheese, chocolate), recycling sales (used books, CDs and tapes, house fixtures, brooms, and so on), intramural clearance and rummage sales (pictures from last year's intramural program, old equipment, leftover promotional T-shirts and other gadgets), and so on
- Concessions: maintain school or community vending machines, operate a school snack bar, or staff refreshment stands at special events
- Publications: intramural cookbooks, know-your-town books, or school who's who directories, games books (students and participants make up fun recreational games), and so on

The council planned a variety of events to raise pennies, including penny carnivals (each game would cost between two and four cents; they didn't want to get any nickels) and penny challenges. One penny challenge was dubbed the "Battle of the Sexes." Boys were on one team and girls were on the other. Starting on Monday of

A Million Pennies

The intramural director at Lo Ellen Park Secondary School in Sudbury wanted to raise some extra money for intramurals. A member of the intramural council had heard about a local penny-raising contest and suggested it at the council meeting. While brainstorming ideas and setting goals for a penny fund-raiser some council members began to wonder what a million pennies would look like. The goal was set. They would try to raise one million pennies.

Reprinted by permission of the Canadian Intramural Recreation Association. From M. Harkness, 1998, "$10,000 jackpot," INPUT (December):6.

the week of the challenge, two empty bins were placed at the front door of the school. As they entered and exited school, girls would toss pennies into their bin and boys would toss pennies into theirs. At 1:00 p.m. each Friday, the pennies were counted and whichever team had the fewest pennies had to carry the winning team's books the next Monday.

It took seven years before the school reached its target of one million pennies. The pennies were stored in, and filled, a small room. It took several weeks to roll all the pennies into rolls. As a way to enhance school spirit and show their community what they had done, the students lined up from their school to the nearest bank and passed the 400 boxes of rolled pennies from the school to the bank. Each box weighed 16 pounds. By the time they were done, they had moved 6,400 pounds of pennies to the bank and raised $10,000 for intramural programming (Harkness 1998).

Sponsorship

Through sponsorship, businesses have an opportunity to support intramural programming in their communities. Corporate sponsorship usually comprises monetary donations, in-kind giving, or a combination of the two. While it is tempting to approach sponsorship from a giver-recipient standpoint, do not sell your program short. Corporations receive the following benefits in return for their sponsorship.

- Visibility and name recognition (corporate logos on signage, promotional materials, equipment, and so on)

- Public goodwill
- Increased sales (from visibility and public goodwill)
- Product preview and promotion (perhaps through special participant discounts—some equipment suppliers provide free use of equipment if you exclusively use their product)
- Improved company image (from public goodwill and visibility)

Above all, intramural sponsorship enables certain corporations to reach their target market: young children and parents, teenagers (with or without their parents), and young adults. In some respects, no other promotion delivers such a targeted group of potential customers. In other words, sponsorship is good business.

Of course, the benefits to the intramural program are the money, equipment, time, and other sponsorship you receive, as well as the opportunity to offer bigger, better intramural programming. The types of sponsorship available include the following.

- Money: A straight donation to the intramural program, though money gifts are often times given for a specific aspect of the program such as uniforms, increasing female participation, or helping with a specific event.
- Prizes: Food outlets are often willing to provide discount coupons that can be given to event winners to be used to purchase food a their restaurant. Sporting goods stores are often willing to donate

some equipment such as a goalie stick for the best goaltender in floor hockey, or a beach volleyball for the beach volleyball league or tournament winners, or a mountain bike for an annual draw for an active living contest.

▶ In-kind giving: One simple and visible sponsorship opportunity involves team shirts. For example, some schools give each team in an intramural ice hockey league a set of team shirts. The intramural directors in this situation often go to a clothing company to give the shirts to the program in exchange for placing the company's logo on shirts, schedules, and other printed material associated with the ice hockey league.

▶ Time: Time come in various forms. For example, a radio station may give free air time for an intramural program to promote its event, or a celebrity may be willing to donate time to make some official presentation at an intramural event.

▶ Equipment: Some suppliers are willing to provide equipment, like squash or racquetball racquets to the program, if they are given the frights to be the exclusive suppliers for their type of product to the on-campus store.

The process of seeking corporate sponsorship can seem daunting at first. It does not have to be so, however. Here is a simple six-step process to get sponsors for an intramural program.

Step 1. Start with your mission. Review your intramural mission statement and identify which businesses match your overall program goals and vision. Starting with your mission will also help if you are approached by a corporation wanting to sponsor your program or a certain activity. If your program is about promoting physical health, which it likely will be, then accepting sponsorship from a local brewery will present a conflict of interest.

Step 2. Determine what you need. Set realistic, but optimistic, goals for what you need. Remember that sponsors are more likely to give something specific. For example, going to a supplier and asking for money for an intramural softball league is not likely to meet with success, even though that is what is needed. By look-

ing for equipment or clothing sponsorships however, you are more likely to find sponsors for specific needs.

Step 3. Do your homework. Once you have identified corporations and businesses that match your mission and your needs for the intramural program, you must determine how to approach them. Most companies see sponsorship as an investment and, since they are in business to make money, they need a positive return. Ask participants where they eat out, shop, watch movies, and have their vehicles serviced. This information can be used as leverage when approaching potential sponsors.

In addition, you will have to find out what potential sponsors' sponsorship policies are, when their fiscal year begins, and what their application guidelines and deadlines are. Local firms are often more flexible and can sponsor an event only a few weeks away, while larger and national firms will often need a year or more to incorporate the event or program into their budgets. If your institution has an alumni directory, try to find an alumnus insider and speak to him or her in person. Having someone on the inside is helpful, particularly if sponsorship spending falls in the "flexible" category. If you must go in "cold," start with the marketing department.

Step 4. Submit a proposal. Most large and national corporations have formal requirements for sponsorship. These requirements usually start with a proposal. When submitting your proposal, keep it brief and to the point, but provide enough detail to explain your request. The following information should be provided to outline the potential partnership:

▶ Goals of the intramural program

▶ Total sponsorship goals

▶ Exactly what you are asking for (equipment, money, time, and so on)

▶ Potential benefits to the sponsor (see page 167)

▶ Term of sponsorship (how long you want the sponsor's support)

▶ What the activity or event is

▶ Activity or event length (how long the activity or event will last)

▶ Activity or event budget

▶ Who and how many will participate

▶ Who will benefit from the activity or event

▶ Community or student needs met by the activity or event

▶ Other necessary background information (staff and their expertise, history of the activity or event, and so on)

▶ A list of other sponsors

Step 5. Get it in writing. Documenting the terms of sponsorship ensures that both parties understand what they will "give" and what they will "'get" from the arrangement. This may require some negotiation, but once an agreement is reached, a formal letter or contract outlining the sponsorship is necessary. This contract or letter should contain a statement of thanks.

Step 6. Service the sponsor. Once the agreements are signed and the program, activity, or event is underway, keep the sponsor informed and involved, as appropriate. Keeping sponsors "in the loop" makes them feel appreciated, which is critical if you want to retain their support in the future. Far too often, the hours and effort spent finding sponsors and selling them on the proposal are lost because of lack of communication.

If you are clear on the sponsor's needs and requirements, make sure they are met. Every sponsor should receive a written final report that highlights their contributions and specifically describes the ways their sponsorship benefited the program, activity, or event. It is also a good idea to outline how the program, activity, or event benefited the sponsor. This report should include publicity (newspaper clippings), photographs (with corporate logos and signage clearly visible), and highlights of the activity. The report should conclude by encouraging the sponsor's continued support.

Step 7. Thank and re-sign. As important as servicing sponsors is, thanking them is even more important. Thank them when they agree to provide sponsorship, thank them during the activity or event (if they are present), and thank them at the conclusion of the partnership. This does not only apply to large, national, and formal sponsorships. Even local firms or businesses should be thanked as often as possible. Say, for example, that a local pizza chain has given you free soda and pizza coupons as prizes. Thank the manager when she agrees, thank her again when you pick up the coupons, and when you hand out the coupons to the winners, ask them to thank the pizza place for helping the intramural program. An article in a school or local newspaper highlighting a company's contribution can also be a nice "thank you." Finally, you might consider offering your sponsors some perks for contributing to your program. For example, you could offer free passes to your fitness center, parking passes, or invitations to an intramural banquet. Be creative. The more creative the "thank you," the more it is appreciated.

Likewise, the more frequent the "thank you," the greater your chance of re-signing that sponsor for next year's event or other intramural activities. The chance of re-signing is also given a boost by keeping your sponsors involved and updated throughout the program, activity, or event duration.

Advertising

As was explained in chapter 8, there are numerous advertising vehicles available. You can look at these same advertising vehicles whey trying to generate revenue for your program. Perhaps your department produces a newsletter, student calendars, or team and staff directories. By selling advertising space in these publications, you can turn each one into a moneymaking venture. Advertising can even be sold on team rosters and sign-up sheets.

Web sites can also be used to generate revenue, although not as much as was once thought. In the 1990s, many Internet companies were counting on making a lot of money by offering free services to clients and paying for their site through advertising. Many went bankrupt. One way Web sites generate revenue is through the sale of banner advertisements, those little squares and rectangles that offer free samples, low interest rates, and discounts for "clicking now" when you visit Web pages. **Banners** can also be offered as a "thank you" to sponsors who agree to partially or totally sponsor the program Web site. Some intramural departments so not make money on the banners but use it as another way to acknowledge a sponsor and, in so doing, increase the sponsor's satisfaction with their sponsorship, especially if the banner provide some links back to their company. Another source of Web revenue is the sale of merchandise, such as intramural clothing and memorabilia. Clothing items such as intramural T-Shirts, sweatshirts, and shorts are some of the items most commonly sold on Web sites. Selling merchandise on the Web does require providing a secure Web site and the ability to do your transactions through a credit card company.

Expenses

Revenues are necessary because there are expenses. In the world of finance, there are two types of expenses: direct expenses and indirect expenses. In the intramural setting, **direct expenses** are those resulting directly from the program or activity, for example, an aerobics instructor who earns $12.50 an hour or facility rental for a special event or particular intramural program. **Indirect expenses** are those not directly related to the program or activity, such as office supplies and training. Although indirect expenses are somewhat vague in nature and, thus, difficult to measure, they are important to consider when budgeting. If numerous enough, indirect expenses can turn a balanced budget into a deficit budget.

The rest of this section explains the principal expense categories in intramurals—the program as well as specific activities—including staff, facilities, equipment, promotion, office supplies, travel, and insurance.

Staff

Staff are usually paid according to the level of their responsiblility. Full-time intramural directors and other full-time staff are paid the most. Part-time staff, inlcuding conveners, officials, and instructors are usually paid less. Even within part-time staff, major officials have greater responsibilities than minor officials and therefore are usually paid more.

Benefits

Benefits are usually limited to full-time employees and added on top of the wages paid. Benefits usually relate to health benefits and cover such items a hospital coverage, drug costs, dental expenses, sick pay, life insurance, and retirement/savings account contributions. Clearly, wages and benefits, need to reflect going rates for these positions if an institution wishes to maintain or attract high-quality candidates to

fill the staffing needs of an intramural department.

With the high cost of staff, in some cases, it may be cheaper to hire someone outside the institution. For example, depending upon the pay scale in intramurals, it may be cheaper to hire off-campus officials. Even when the costs are the same the institution's cost for training officials are reduced when hiring off-campus officials. Some institutions also hire an event manager at orientation. When such people bring in their own equipment, the costs are less than an intramural department paying its own staff and renting equipment.

Training

Regardless of whether intramural workers are on staff or hired as contract labor, training is a necessary staff expense. And, training is not free. The costs of training typically include paying the employees (often at a reduced rate) and trainers for their time, facility rental, travel, and supplies. Refreshments, if they are offered, are also expenses of training.

► Employees. Salaried workers are paid their regular salaries, regardless of where they are at the moment. If they happen to be in a training session or at a staff retreat, they are still paid. The payment of part-time workers differs from institution to institution. Some pay regular wages for training time, while others figure that part-time workers will gladly donate their time in exchange for a great retreat, enlightening discussion or instruction, and delicious food.

► Trainers. Good speakers will typically require an honorarium plus travel expenses.

► Facility rental. Training ought to be special, something apart from the normal day-to-day operations, and distractions should be kept to a minimum. Thus, it's a good idea to hold training sessions away from the office or usual work environment. If you have a large campus, perhaps another school facility can be used for training. If not, you will likely need to rent a facility.

► Supplies. Training supplies can range from simple and inexpensive (like paper and pens) to elaborate and costly (like manuals, books, and clothing).

▶ Refreshments. Food and drink can often make or break a training session, so try to make your training as good as possible without being too expensive. Refreshments are, of course, necessary for lengthy training sessions, but even if the session is just a quick half-hour meeting, offering snacks such as cookies or fruit can help to warm up staff to the intramural program.

Staff travel is also included in this expense category. Officials, office staff, team captains, and sometimes volunteers may need to visit other institutions from time to time, for example, to learn how they do things. Attending training sessions and conferences may also involve travel. If staff members are required to attend these sessions travel expenses should also be budgeted.

Facilities

When facilities are too small or are not set up to accommodate particular intramural activities, there is often little that can be done—short of not offering that particular activity. Indeed, inadequate facilities are a primary concern of most intramural directors. They long for a larger gymnasium and equipment room, dream of larger and more elaborate weight rooms, and if they are really aiming high, hope to someday offer on-campus hockey, bowling, paintball, and so on.

Of course, most intramural directors proceed the best they can and try to be creative with what they have (see "Facilities" in chapter 3, starting on page 24). This often includes renting other facilities such as local gyms, ice rinks, bowling alleys, paintball facilities, and so on. In addition to regular intramural programming, special events often involve facility rental.

The name of the game in facility rental is keeping the price down. Many local facilities may partially reduce their prices to support their schools and students, and encourage active and healthy living. You may also be able to get corporate sponsorship to deflect the facility-rental cost for a particular or several off-campus activities and events.

Additional facility costs that need to be kept in mind include maintenance and cleaning. Maintenance costs include such expenses as painting, repairing broken doors, and replacing lights. Cleaning expenses include all the cost related to paying staff to clean the building as well as cleaning supplies.

Equipment

Like existing facilities, available equipment may be inadequate for certain programming, activities, or events. In these cases, equipment purchase or rental will be an expense. When selecting equipment to purchase, it is not always appropriate to go for the cheap stuff to save money. Equipment must be appropriate to the activity and safe. Volleyballs, for example, are hit with the soft part of the forearm. Thus, buying cheap volleyballs, which are usually hard, is not a good idea.

One way to get the best price for equipment is to prepare a specific list of equipment requirements and get competing bids from suppliers, called **tendering**. Tendering is process of getting bids from various competing companies for supplying equipment or the execution of work. In the tendering process, be sure to reserve the right not to go with the lowest price. The lowest price is worth something, but so is delivery time and customer support. If a local supplier's prices are close to the lowest bid, for example, its proximity to your institution may save you some time and may make it worth a few extra dollars.

Tendering is an opportunity to ensure both that you, the buyer, get value for your money and that all potential suppliers get an equal chance to enter bids. That means, you must compare the bids objectively to determine the best offer. The administration of the contract rests with the buyer, in this case you. The tendering process involves five steps.

Step 1. In order to receive tender submissions, you must first prepare tender documents. Preparation of tender documents includes:

▶ Letter of invitation to tenders

▶ Instructions to tenders

▶ Conditions of contract: how much equipment is needed and when

▶ Technical specifications: statement of comparison criteria, including price, service, guarantees, and so on

▶ Term of tender: the length of the tendering process (usually three to eight weeks)

Step 2. Identify which suppliers you will approach (those most likely to be able to supply you with what you need) and send out tender documents.

Step 3. Obtain tender offers. This step typically lasts three to eight weeks, but you can solicit offers for any length of time—as long as you specify the term in your tender documents.

Step 4. Evaluate tender offers. Use the comparison criteria stated in your tender documents, but remember that service is often as important as price.

Step 5. Award the contract to the best supplier.

Of course, purchasing equipment is not the only option. If the budget is tight, in addition to considering equipment rental, be creative in obtaining equipment. In intramural programs, not all equipment has to be traditional sport equipment. Unusual or quirky balls, discs, bats, sticks, and other objects can add considerable fun to the program and be inexpensive. For example, the bladder of an old basketball, volleyball, or soccer ball, which would normally be thrown out, is a free piece of equipment. Ball bladders move erratically, providing an entertaining and equalizing experience for all.

Equipment Control

Equipment distribution and control can be a nightmare for intramural directors in grade schools and high schools. Lost or damaged equipment adds up to a huge expense every year. Many of these schools encourage students to bring in their own equipment for recess play. Having students bring their own equipment reduces expense and supervision of equipment on the part of the school. However, it would be difficult to plan a league or other event relying solely on equipment that students bring.

Other schools assign equipment to every home room (usually a recess bag with Frisbees, skipping ropes, and play balls). The downside to this approach is that there is a lot of equipment "floating around" in the school that is not available for physical education classes. The upside to this approach is that the responsibility of caring for and monitoring the equipment lies with the home room teacher. The homeroom teacher is assigned the responsibility for ensuring the equipment is returned and properly cared for. He may delegate some of this responsibilty to the students by having an equipment monitor with a checklist sign out the equipment and ensure its return at the beginning and end of recess for lunch breaks.

Other schools store equipment in lockers at or near the intramural office, in the equipment room, or in the gym. These schools appoint or hire an equipment monitor to sign out (write down each borrower's name) or lend out equipment in exchange for collateral (a valuable such as an ID card, wallet, or watch). The idea behind exchanging equipment for a valuable is that students will be more likely to return their piece of equipment. If students do not mind being without their collateral for a couple of days, however, the equipment you planned to use for a class or activity may not available. And if the equipment is more valuable than students' collateral, you may never see it again. Another disadvantage to the sign-out approach is that if an anonymous valuable such as a watch or ring is offered as collateral, there is no way of tracking the student down.

Colleges and universities usually have the benefit of paid staff at a gymnasium equipment desk. At these facilities, equipment loss is less of a problem if the equipment is carefully monitored. Many of these institutions have computerized methods for equipment inventory and control. Students use their student ID swipe cards to sign out equipment. Then students are charged for equipment that is lost, damaged, or returned late.

Whatever your sign-out procedure, remember that kids will be kids. In the case of lost equipment especially, students will be quick to say they gave the ball to "so and so" to turn in. Unfortunately, "so and so" usually thought someone else was going to bring it in, and the ball was left outside and is now gone.

It may be best simply to rent or sell intramural equipment. These fees should be low enough not to deter students from participating but high enough to cover your cost. Ping-Pong balls, for example, break easily and are relatively inexpensive, so sell them at cost. Your decision to rent or sell equipment, of course, should depend on the age and economic status of your students. Young children in grade school will not have access to money for equipment unless their parents give it to them. In these cases, some schools have student government pay for equipment used in recreational intramural programs or allot a certain portion of student and program fees to equipment costs.

Finally, an efficient equipment inventory and storage system should be developed to keep your costs low. First, keep equipment visible so that staff can quickly detect loss. Having the equipment on the same shelves all the time or using see-through ball bags or fixed size ball bags will help with this process. Second, get an idea of how long certain equipment lasts by labeling everything. By putting the date of purchase directly on a ball (e.g., "902" would signify September 2002), for example, when the ball finally tears or bursts, you will know how old it is. This information is extremely helpful when budgeting equipment costs for the year. Third, repair equipment whenever possible to keep your costs down. Buying a repair kit and supplies to mend balls, racquets, nets, and other equipment saves money in the long run. Plus, repairing salvageable equipment as soon as it is broken increases the amount of equipment available and keeps the equipment and program looking crisp and professional. Fourth, be sure to take regular inventory. Count the number of balls, bats, and so on every week. Fifth, save your best equipment for important activities and games. Students will want to use the game balls all the time, so it is a good idea to store them in a secure place where they can be reserved for special games.

Promotion and Awards

Promotions and awards, including prizes and ceremonies, all cost money—unless, of course, a sponsor pays for or provides them (see "Sponsorship" on page 167). When it comes to posters, fliers, and other promotional materials, the primary expenses usually include design, materials, and printing. Again, having students from the graphic arts, design, advertising, and art departments create your promotional materials will save a lot of money, and will given these students valuable experience and portfolio samples. To save money on materials and printing, ask local printers to help out by providing paper and/or their printing services for free or at a reduced cost. (Then thank them by listing them as sponsors or acknowledging their support/donation on the promotional pieces themselves.) Do the same for other types of promotion, including Web sites, calendars, merchandise, and so on. (See chapter 8 for a complete discussion of promotion, including advertising and some low-cost promotion options.)

Awards ceremonies have several categories of expenses, including organizers' salaries, facility rental, speakers, supplies, and refreshments. These are discussed in the "Training" section earlier in this chapter. Two additional expenses of awards ceremonies are decorations and entertainment. Like prizes and promotional materials, corporate and other sponsorship can go a long way in reducing these costs. Perhaps a local party-supply company will be willing to donate some balloons, crepe paper, and table decorations. Perhaps a local television station wants to support local schools and would be willing to put together a "season's highlights" videotape for free or a nominal cost. Audiovisual faculty and students may also be able to help in this regard. If donations and sponsorship are not enough to cover the costs, you might consider charging an entrance fee. Because participants enjoy award banquets and season-end ceremonies, they will usually not mind paying an entrance fee to help defray some of the costs.

Office Supplies

Although a few pens, ink cartridges, paper, paperclips, and poster board are not all that expensive in themselves, they quickly add up and need to be accounted for. Like equipment, some of the higher-priced supplies (e.g., poster board, ink cartridges, and reams of paper) may have a habit of disappearing from the office. To keep office-supply expenses to a minimum, you may want to monitor ordering and inventory by designating someone to keep track. That person can be in charge of the office supplies, replacing staff's supplies when they run out and ordering from a local supplier. A less-formal tendering process can be used to get the best pricing. In this case, it could simply entail calling a few suppliers to get the best pricing.

While not considered office supplies by most accountants, office furniture, copy machines, and computers may also need to be replaced or repaired from time to time. The cost of these items and services is usually high and is budgeted differently at different institutions. At large and public institutions, service is usually contracted ahead of time, when the equipment is purchased, and the money comes out of the school's operating budget. Sometimes, however, these expenses are included in the program's operating budget, intramural directors would be wise to plan for such expenditures ahead of time. At small or private institutions, you may be on your own. It will be up to you to determine whether to buy a service contract or take a chance and pay for repairs as they are needed. The costs of repair and service typically include labor and materials, although some firms charge for travel time.

Travel

Although some high school and university students can arrange their own transportation to off-campus events and facilities, that is not the case for grade school and younger high school students. For lower-level grades, buses or vans (depending on the number of students participating) will need to be provided if the facility is not easily accessible from the school. The cost of such transportation usually includes vehicle rental and driver compensation, although some transportation companies provide the driver with the vehicle rental. A low-cost alternative to paid travel expense is carpooling. If this is not an option, however, you might be able to recoup transportation costs by charging an enrollment fee. To ensure fair play and satisfy your mission of fun and active movement for all, these fees should be set low enough so as not to deter participation.

Insurance and Risk Management

The school's operating budget typically covers insurance costs, so the intramural program does not usually have to budget for this. For special events, however, additional insurance may be necessary. For example, a rock-climbing outing, an overnight cycling trip, or an outdoor camp in the middle of winter involves higher risks for injury than typical intramural programs. Before entertaining these events, it is wise to discuss with the institution's insurance company the plans for the event and the adequacy of insurance coverage for those events. Certain fund-raising events may also require liability insurance. For example, any event that is a little bit out of the ordinary and involves some risk, such as a hay ride on a wagon behind a tractor, the use of large air-filled inflatables that students can climb and jump on, or bringing in amusement rides.

Whether in a special event, fund-raiser, or regular intramural programming, protecting the safety of all participants is important. Formulating and enforcing policies on fair play and safety (see chapters 6 and 7) will help in this regard. Likewise, safety audits should be conducted regularly (see chapter 7). Most importantly, these safety practices will ensure and safe and enjoyable experience for all participants. On the budget side, these safety practices may help to reduce the insurance costs to an institution. In addition, loss-control procedures are usually suggested by most insurance companies. When the insured implements these procedures, a better insurance rate or discount is offered.

Cost Savings

As introduced throughout this section, being frugal and creative can do a lot to keep expenses down. Charging enrollment fees and for equipment are two good ideas. If the event or activity is an exciting one, participants are usually willing to pay a fair price to take part. Shopping for the lowest price is also a good idea, but scrimping on expense should never threaten the safety of participants. When safety is at risk, cost savings are not worth it. There are other ways to save money, too. These involve on-campus and off-campus partnership.

On-Campus Partnership

As mentioned earlier in this chapter and in chapter 8, partnership with such departments as graphic arts, design, art, marketing, and advertising can be a win-win situation. The intramural program benefits by getting talented practitioners and fresh ideas. Design, advertising, and other students benefit by getting much-needed experience in and practice at their craft. Department faculty may also be a valuable resource, as they are experts in their fields and will likely offer assistance and advice.

Although not yet mentioned in this chapter, athletes and intramural participants do occasionally require the services of a doctor, physiotherapist, and/or masseuse. If your facility has the space and budget to provide these services, great. If not, mutually beneficial arrangements can often be made. For example, you could allow a physiotherapist to use an office or other recreational space in exchange for free services and use of the weight room for clients. If this arrangement is not suitable, you could offer a reduced facility-rental fee in exchange for discounted prices for students.

Off-Campus Partnership

In exchange for facility-rental fees, it may be possible to offer the members of these facilities access to and use of intramural facilities and equipment. For example, clients and members could use some of the school's fitness-testing equipment. There is no direct cost of this arrangement for the school, other than additional wear and tear on the equipment. Likewise, this access could be offered in exchange for reduced student rates. In this case, the students directly benefit from the arrangement because they have greater access to facilities that help them stay active and fit.

Some institutions have benefited by partnering with a municipality and jointly financing a separate facility. Neither a small town nor a small college in that town may individually have the money to build a swimming pool or ice arena, for example. If they pool their resources and share the costs, however, these facilities become a reality.

Tracking a Budget

Understanding the categories and fine details of intramural budgeting, then, how do you go about the process of developing and tracking a budget? The easiest way is with spreadsheets. Computerized spreadsheets, in particular, are powerful tools to efficiently prepare a budget and keep track of it. Using a spreadsheet and the revenue and expense categories presented in this chapter, an intramural director can easily project income and expenses for each event and activity (and, thus, the entire program) throughout the year.

From there the budgeting process simply needs to be monitored, or tracked. Actual revenue and expenses should be compared against projected revenue and expenses throughout the season or year, and after each event. At large institutions, budgets are tracked at least twice a month and usually weekly. At small institutions, seasonal and event budgets are usually scrutinized at their completion. If the numbers are far off projections, evaluation and assessment is needed. This involves identifying the discrepancies, determining what is contributing to these

discrepancies, and making necessary adjustments. Periodic evaluation is far better than finding out at the end of the year that the intramural program significantly overspent and is nowhere near a balanced budget.

There are two levels to intramural budgets. The first level is the overall program budget, which keeps track of major categories of income and expenses. The second level is the more detailed listing of income and expenses for each event or activity. The second level is the more detailed lists of everything from the number of registration fees paid to the number of balls purchased. The cumulative income and expense items are then brought forward to the overall program budget.

Spreadsheets

Financial spreadsheets are simply grids, containing columns and rows that separate distinct categories of revenue and expenses. They can be generated by hand or on the computer. Given that budgets are likely to change thanks to last-minute additions and changes, of course, computerized spreadsheets are the most efficient. The most popular spreadsheet programs are Excel and Quattro Pro. This section provides a general description of computerized spreadsheets, followed by a brief but specific example of tracking two activity budgets.

Let's start with spreadsheet navigation. On computerized spreadsheets, columns are vertical and identified by letter (A, B, . . . Y, Z, AA, AB, . . . AY, AZ, BA, BB, and so on), moving from left to right. Rows are horizontal and identified by a number (1, 2, 3, 4 and so on), moving from top to bottom. The point or area where columns and rows meet, called a "cell," is labeled by column and row. The first cell in column A, row 1, for example, is cell A1. The cell immediately to the right of A1, in the same row but in column B, is B1. The cell immediately below cell A1, in the same column but in row 2, is A2.

Now a brief description of what computerized spreadsheets can do. First, because they are on computer, spreadsheets can be changed easily. Rather than having to re-create the entire budget because an expense category was forgotten, for example, intramural directors can simply add a row or column to the existing spreadsheet. Second, numbers are added, subtracted, multiplied, and divided almost instantaneously as long as the correct formulas are used.

Let's look at an example. Suppose you were planning an awards ceremony and were preparing a budget for it. As outlined in chapter 9, ceremonies have many components: entertainment, decorations, refreshments, awards, prizes, and staffing. For argument's sake, let's say you come up with 20 expense categories. Using a spreadsheet, you would type "Expenses" in cell A1 (to designate that part of the budget) and "Ceremony" in cell A2 (to label the expense category). Then, in cell B3, you would type "Decorations." (Locating subcategories in the next column helps to make each visually distinct.) Then, starting in cell C4, you would list your decoration expenses: "Candles" in C4, "Candle holders" in C5, "Balloons" in C6, and so on. For your next "Ceremony" expense, you would type "Entertainment" in cell B10 (if you had six decoration expenses). Then, starting in cell C11, you would list your "Entertainment" expenses, perhaps a speaker or emcee, music, and so on. You would list the remaining 18 expense categories the same way.

Now for the fun part: inserting the numbers. First, you would want to label the number columns by adding headings. For example, in cell D1 you would type "Units," in cell E1 you would type "Cost" or "$," in cell F1 "Subtotal," and in cell G1 "Total." Then, in cell D4 (to the right of "Candles") you would enter "30" (the number of candles), in cell E4 you would enter "0.75" (the cost per candle, if you're using votive candles), and in cell F4 you would type the formula "(D4*E4)." This formula tells the computer to multiply the number in cell D4 by the number in E4 and provide the answer, $22.50, in cell F4. You would do the same for each item listed under each category on the spreadsheet. On the last row of expenses (let's say row 120), you would enter the formula "@SUM(F4..F120)" in cell G120 to tell the computer to add the subtotals in column F. This number, then, is your total cost of putting on the awards ceremony.

Back to what a computerized spreadsheet can do. If the total in cell G120 is too high, you will likely want to reduce your expenses. Perhaps you can do without the emcee, for example, or maybe you can get by without candles. In the latter case, you would simply go back to cell D4 (the number of candles) and enter "0." The spreadsheet will automatically recalculate that subtotal and the expense total in cell G120. With a few simple keystrokes, you have just saved yourself all the work of having to recalculate all the numbers by hand.

Chapter Summary Exercises

Sound financial planning, creative fund-raising, and careful control of expenses can go a long way in making a lasting, effective intramural program. The following four exercises will help you review the material in this chapter and lead you through the process of budgeting.

1. You are planning a turkey trot just before Thanksgiving. Identify the types of prizes you want to award and then decide how you might get them through corporate sponsorship. Write out a proposal.

2. You are planning to hold a semester-long fitness challenge. You would like to develop inviting and challenging posters to encourage students and staff to get involved, and you would like to provide some prizes as incentives. Identify some potential sponsors for the event and write out a proposal for two of them.

3. Create a budget on a computer spreadsheet for one intramural program event. Be sure to include staff time, equipment, facility rental (if necessary), and so on. Forecast anticipated attendance and decide how much revenue you will need to run the event "in the black." Be sure to use the correct formulas.

4. Your school needs to raise $2000 for a new piece of equipment. You've tried but cannot get the donation through corporate sponsorship. Plan a fund-raiser (including a budget) to raise the money.

References

Byl, J. 2000. Put your money on the edge. *INPUT* (March): 4-5.

Harkness, M. 1998. $10,000 jackpot. *INPUT* (December): 6. Used by permission of the Canadian Intramural Recreation Association—Ontario.

Resources

To consider eight different spreadsheet programs, look at the following Web site: http://www.knowledgestorm.com

The Program

Now that you have now generated your idea and planned many of the specifics of your program, it is time to prepare to implement your intramural programming. To do that, you'll need to consider exactly which activities and events to offer and the best time to offer them. This includes considering the best use of tournaments and leagues. You'll also need to consider the last-minute details and make sure they are covered. Finally, you'll need to have tools and procedures in place to evaluate your program and programming, both while it is running and at the end of the year. This evaluation will not only help you identify the successes that deserve celebration today but also help you improve your program for next year, when the whole process begins again.

This final part of *Intramural Recreation: A Step-by-Step Guide to Creating an Effective Program* involves every consideration, step, and topic outlined so far. It incorporates the discussions in parts I and II and leads you through the steps of actual implementation. The final chapter, "Putting It All Together," is the last step and is the culmination of our journey: creating your own, personalized intramural handbook.

Programming

Recreational activities, sports, games, and events, and competitive activities, sports, games, and events, not to mention instructional clinics, sport clubs (in some cases), contests, plus all of the above for alumni, faculty, and family members—these are the components of programming. In other words, intramural programming includes every type of activity or event offered to participants. It also includes the act of determining that programming. Most of the components of programming have been discussed up to this point in the book, some in more detail than others. Tournaments and leagues, two specific components of competitive intramural programming, are covered in the next chapter.

When it comes to programming, it is helpful to think of an intramural program as a business. Its participants are clients, or customers, and the programming itself is the product or service being offered. This mind-set will allow intramural directors and program staff and volunteers, in the process of programming, to focus on the primary task at hand: attracting as many customers as possible and providing them with something that will satisfy them and keep them coming back for more.

The first part of that focus, attracting as many clients as possible, is the first topic of this chapter, followed by the second part, providing them with something that will satisfy them and keep them coming back for more. This part of the chapter, having to do with programming, is broken into two separate sections (a distinction used so far in this book): activities and special events, because of the distinct nature of each. Finally, a sample intramural programming calendar, with plenty of specific programming suggestions, is outlined.

Chapter Objectives

► Consider who should, or could, be participating in intramural programming.

► Explore some of the myriad activities and events intramural programs can offer.

► Understand how to create an annual intramural programming schedule.

Who's It For?

We need to know whom it is that we are tying to include in intramural programming. Students are the primary clients of intramural programs, of course, but there are also alumni, families, and school staff to consider. Each group is discussed in the following sections, in terms of both how different institutions include them and how they participate. Regardless of which groups are included, however, eligibility rules will need to be clearly spelled out so that everyone knows who is welcome to participate. If alumni are permitted, that needs to be written out so that current students are not wonder what a nonstudent is doing participating in an intramural event.

Students

When it comes to attracting students, the first things to consider are age, fitness level, and developmental stage. As introduced in chapter 6 (see "Equal Opportunity, Age" on page 87), students of different ages have different interests and abilities. Thus, targeting your audience will vary depending on whether you direct a grade school, high school, or university intramural program. In all schools, characteristics such as skin color, race, gender, and disability should be considered as well (see chapter 6's "Inclusion" on page 86).

At colleges and universities, the target group (students) is typically larger and more diversified. For example, students who live in school residences live near the intramural facilities and can easily get involved in the evening. Students who live off campus and commute to school, however, are less likely to return in the evening to participate in intramural activities. These stu-dents need events during the day. Clearly, it is easy to select students as the primary group, but it is not as straightforward to plan for them because of different time preferences.

Alumni

Alumni are often participants in intramurals. Wanting to maintain a connection with their alma maters, these graduates stay involved with many school programs, and intramurals can benefit. Alumni add participation numbers to a program. Alumni come back to an institution's intramural program because they enjoyed it. This joy is likely to rub off through their participation. Maintaining positive relationships with alumni might bring benefits to the program through sponsorship opportunities. For example, various alumni may wish to seek ways of promoting their new careers (or places of business), and as a way of giving back to a program they so much enjoyed while at school.

Colleges and universities include alumni in different ways. Some institutions provide free access to campus recreation and intramurals, while others invite participation but charge a fee. Some schools include alumni in competitive intramural programs as if they were regular students; others restrict participation to a special alumni team. Still others do not allow alumni to participate in any intramural leagues.

In the spirit of promoting active living and in light of the benefits of including alumni, offering alumni some sort of access to intramural programming seems to be in the best interests of everyone. That said, certain restrictions may be necessary. To avoid a group of alumni ex-varsity basketball players getting a team together and dominating the intramural basketball league, for example, you could limit the number of ex-varsity or former competitive athletes per team. These restrictions should be noted in eligibility rules and posted at sign-up.

Families

In many cases, although most often at the collegiate level, intramural programming has an opportunity to serve the families of students, particularly adult students with young children. For example, you can include families in special events such as family bowling nights, skiing trips, and local hikes. During times when facilities are not used much, you can offer daycare services or fun activities that the children of students can enjoy while their parents are using the weight room or taking a yoga class. (If you charge a small fee, this type of programming could be a real moneymaker.) When students have older children, you can allow them to register for and compete in intramural competitions, although it is wise to limit this type of involvement to children who are 16 and older. For liability reasons, children should compete on the same team as their parents (who are participating).

To include families, it is important to have accessible parking and to provide varied programming that accommodates different skill levels. For single parents, in particular, it is helpful to create activities for the children while their parents participate in intramural programs. This often is the difference between it being possible or impossible for parents to attend intramural activities (Bulfin 1996).

Faculty and Staff

Getting faculty and staff to participate in intramurals is a wonderful opportunity to build institutional camaraderie and school spirit. When faculty participate, everyone benefits—the students, the program, and the faculty/staff members. Interaction between faculty and students in fun games is a great morale booster. Students like seeing their teachers outside of class and they appreciate the extra attention. The program can benefit from older, wiser eyes on and in the action of the game. And faculty members not only get to know their students better, which improves their teaching ability, but also get the opportunity to stay fit and have some fun, and get a much-needed break during the day.

There are many different ways to attract faculty and staff to intramural programming. For example, including them in fitness classes or as participants in a sport club. In addition, involve them in competitions by:

▶ forming an "all-star" staff team that competes against a team of student winners;

▶ forming a regular staff team that competes against other intramural teams;

▶ having a separate staff league and

▶ organizing a staff tournament after school.

Community

Community members should also be encouraged to make use of fitness classes, clinics, and weight room facilities. It is a good public relations gesture on the part of the intramural director and another means of raising revenue. The director should be careful to not allow too many community member or the students will not have enough time to participate in "their" facility.

Community leagues are another way to involve the community and diversify the program—not to mention a great way to generate some extra revenue. Intramural leagues are typically run exclusively for students of the institution, but in some situations, local high school or community teams are invited to participate as a means of filling out the league and as a source of revenue. For smaller colleges, which might not have enough teams to make up a league, the intramural director enters the intramural teams into an off-campus community league. Some intramural directors combine both methods, inserting intramural teams into community leagues that are held on campus. Community leagues are charged a facility rental fee for those league games that do not involve a college team. College badminton nights are also opened to community members at a number of colleges and universities.

Eligibility

We began this chapter with the question concerning who is eligible to participate in intramural programs. That question needs to be answered in general terms and in specific terms. For example, are alumni permitted to participate? If the answer is yes, then the next question is , how?

Questions such as the following help answer that question. Can they form a team made up completely of alumni? Are there rules about how many ex-varsity alumni players can be on one team? The answers to these questions need to be spelled out for participants to read at sign-up.

Activities

Now comes the second part of the intramural mission: providing clients with something that will satisfy them and keep them coming back for more. Intramural programming should provide plenty of opportunities for many different clients to get involved. The challenge for the intramural director is to understand the changing needs of clients and to meet those needs with fun and physically challenging programming. The two types of programming presented throughout this book, activities and special events, are explained in this and the next section respectively.

Although some schools enjoy success by offering the same activities year after year, it is far better to build on successful activities and modify less-successful activities by encouraging students to suggest and develop new ideas. Besides asking students for new suggestions, we can look at list of what other schools are doing and explore the internet to see what opportunities exist. Indoor cricket, anyone?

When we recently asked students in Ontario colleges, "What would motivate you to become more active in intramurals?" the responses were informative. More than half of all respondents wanted activities that were more fun and less competitive, including alternative activities such as kick boxing, martial arts, aerobics, aquatics, and self-defense classes. Accessibility was also an important factor for these students. Some of their concerns focused on the expense of events and the fact that existing activities were run at inconvenient times. For some students, a lack of privacy in weight rooms, locker rooms, and shower areas, and feeling intimidated as a beginner, also prevented them from getting involved. Finally, nearly 30 percent of all respondents found it helpful to exercise with a friend. Keeping this informal survey in mind, then, let's look at different types of intramural activities that can be offered intramural participants.

Sports

Most intramural programs offer traditional sports for their locale at both competitive and recreational levels. What is popular in one place may not be well known in another. Looking at the following list of sports activities should stimulate an intramural director's thinking about the many options available. An intramural director who offers ten sports may wish to add or replace one or more of these from time to time. By occasionally experimenting with new sports for their program, they may run across something that students take a real liking to. An intramural director can choose from among the following:

- ▶ Aerobics
- ▶ American football
- ▶ Archery
- ▶ Australian rules football
- ▶ Badminton
- ▶ Baseball
- ▶ Basketball (one on one, two on two, three on three)
- ▶ Billiards
- ▶ Bowling
- ▶ Broomball
- ▶ Canadian football
- ▶ Cricket
- ▶ Cross-country running
- ▶ Curling
- ▶ Cycling
- ▶ Dancing
- ▶ Fencing
- ▶ Field hockey
- ▶ Frisbee (ultimate and golf)
- ▶ Golf
- ▶ Handball
- ▶ Ice hockey
- ▶ Lacrosse
- ▶ Marathon running
- ▶ Martial arts (Tae Kwon Do, yoga, Tai Chi, and kick boxing)
- ▶ Net ball
- ▶ Orienteering
- ▶ Racquetball

- ▶ Ringette
- ▶ Rock climbing
- ▶ Rowing
- ▶ Rugby
- ▶ Skateboarding
- ▶ Skiing (cross-country and downhill/slalom)
- ▶ Snowboarding
- ▶ Snow shoeing
- ▶ Soccer
- ▶ Softball
- ▶ Skating (figure, speed, and in-line)
- ▶ Squash
- ▶ Swimming
- ▶ Table tennis
- ▶ Team handball
- ▶ Tennis
- ▶ Track and field (athletics)
- ▶ Triathlon
- ▶ Volleyball (beach, two on two, three on three)
- ▶ Weightlifting
- ▶ Windsurfing
- ▶ Wrestling

Despite the popularity of these sports, it is also important to offer some variety. Do not shy away from introducing new and silly games from time to time. Ultimate Frisbee, in fact, which is now a popular game worldwide, began as a creative high school activity and grew from there. Even when you do offer traditional sport games, consider altering the rules to maximize participation and fun. For example, instead of regular indoor soccer, try four-team indoor soccer for some extra fun and excitement. Place a soccer goal in each corner of the gym, and use bladders for balls. Using the bladders adds a craziness, safety, and equalizing factor that is sure to be enjoyed by all. Have five players per team on the floor at once, blow the whistle every 60 seconds, and (without stopping play) each team substitutes the players on the floor with those waiting on the sidelines.

Contests

In addition to hosting regular leagues and sporting events, which usually involve scheduled games that run for several weeks or longer, short contests can also be a lot of fun for participants. Contests usually involve nonsport games or challenges involving one aspect of a sport. Games like Murder Flag, or a variation of it known as "Gotcha" (Byl 2002), for example, are hosted by a number of schools. This game is a two- to three-day contest in which participants try, during regular class hours, to snatch as many socks away from other players as they can. To start, players write their names on a piece of paper and stick it inside a sock. Socks are then distributed. Players look at the name inside their socks and then try to steal that person's sock. If successful, players look at the name inside of the socks they just stole and then try to steal that person's sock. At the end of a predetermined time, the player who has stolen the most socks wins.

Other contests can be of a shorter duration. For example, hold a lunchtime free-throw contest or a volleyball-serve contest in the gym, a putting contest in a long or wide hallway, and so on. If participants will have quick and easy access to the outdoors, try a home run contest on a baseball diamond or in a batting cage, or a penalty-shooting contest on the soccer field. These types of contests can also be held for an entire day. Students need only register and show up to take their shots, and then you can announce the winners at the end of the day or the beginning of the next school day.

Fitness

Most colleges and universities offer intramural fitness activities, although there is no reason fitness classes and activities cannot be offered at grade and high schools as well. Traditional fitness activities include aerobics, fitness and health classes and clinics, kick boxing, Tae Kwon Do, yoga, Tai Chi, and other martial arts. But less-traditional fitness activities can also be offered, for example, walking and hiking clubs, rock-climbing fieldtrips, and so on.

There are two challenges in running these types of activities: getting certified instructors and maintaining adequate enrollment. From a safety perspective, it is important to hire insturctors for aerobics and other fitness courses that are properly trained and certified. These people can sometimes be difficult to find. Maintaining enrollment is challenging because lots of people sign up at the beginning of the semester, especially in January after making New Year's resolutions, but attrition rates climb in the months that follow. In addition, scheduling fitness classes can get tricky. Using an informal survey of students and recreation directors, it appears that the best times for these programs are (in order of student preference) (1) noon (some staff are permitted an extended lunch to participate in these activities but must add half of their missed time to the end of their day), (2) late afternoon, and (3) early in the morning. Although many of these programs are free, some colleges are starting to charge up to $50 a semester to cover program costs and prevent attrition in attendance.

Offering fitness testing and campus-wide health challenges is also helpful in encouraging students to become more active and get involved in intramurals. Fitness testing can be used to identify medical problems and user interest, to establish a baseline and personal goals, and to develop a personal exercise program. Campus-wide health challenges also encourage students to think about their fitness level and, hopefully, participating in intramurals. Hold a campus-wide walk around the facility (led by the school principal or president), or challenge everyone to take no escalators or elevators for a week. Participants would complete some kind of monitoring sheet to document their achievements. To generate interest in this type of activity, try to find some appropriate awards such as a gift certificate for a pair of running shoes at a local sporting goods store, and intramural T-shirt, or a free pass at a local rock-climbing facility. Likewise, consider hiring a massage therapist to give 15-minute massages (for $5 or $10) after fitness testing or a facility walking tour.

Active Living

According to a 1999 survey, students are busy with school, work, and other commitments. No big surprise there. In this particular survey, however, which polled 125 students from 17 Ontario colleges, respondents reported that they needed incentives even to snatch 10-minute intervals out of their days for physical activity—the goal being one active hour each day. Students were asked, "What major obstacle prevents you from becoming more physically active?" More than half identified lack of time as a major obstacle.

The students surveyed were committed to doing well in their courses, which makes sense when you consider the skyrocketing costs of a college education in Canada. Many were also committed to their work. Approximately 10 percent of respondents said they worked "a lot," but most had some sort of job. When asked how much they worked, many students reported 30 to 40 hours a week. That's in addition to a full class load.

The good news is, these obstacles to active living had nothing to do with what the intramural department was or was not doing. Indeed, the underlying challenge for most of the college students surveyed had to do with time management. While most intramural staff will not be equipped to educate students on managing their time effectively, you can do something to help. Namely, make it easy for students to incorporate physical activity into their lifestyles. Offer fun and active activities for those 10-minute snatches students talked about. For example, how about putting up temporary basketball hoops in the main foyer or cafeteria for a 10-minute game of one-on-one, or why not make jump ropes available in a main corridor and hold a rope-skipping demonstration?

The Ontario colleges participating in the survey were called to action. As a major component of its Active Living initiative, they developed a two-page flier and distributed it to all interested students. The front page, used as figure 8.1 (see page 130), grabs students' attention with a collage of colorful photos that feature active, happy-looking people. These images are meant to bring out the joy of being active and to entice students to turn the page. The back page, shown in figure 11.1, explains the initiative, including the rules, offers prizes ("free stuff"), and provides a log for students to record their activities. The hope is that participants will be active one hour a day, but the pyramid also allows for slow starters.

When students complete the pyramid, each box representing 10 minutes of activity, they submit the sheet to the intramural director and get a new flier. This is a great way to get students to

FIGURE 11.1   Active Living guide.
Courtesy of Ontario College Athletic Association, 1185 Eglinton Avenue East, Suite 505, North York, Ontario, Canada, M3C 3C6.
Phone: 416-426-7043. Art work by Kristine Verbeek.

come down to the intramural office, especially if they have never been there before. It is also an excellent opportunity for intramural staff to personally connect with students. The sheet itself is also an excellent source of evaluation information. Because students use symbols to identify their fitness activity (shown on the left side of the box pyramid), intramural staff will get to see which activities students are most interested in.

To hold students' interest and get them to turn in these sheets, prizes are awarded. The name of each student who submits a completed pyramid is entered into a drawing and names are drawn every three or four weeks. In addition, students who submit a completed pyramid are also entered into a grand drawing, held once a semester, which offers a weekend for two at a local hotel, a weekend for two white-water rafting, a new mountain bike, and/or other large prizes obtained from sponsors. (For more information on how you can get your institution involved in this program, contact the Ontario College Athletic Association, noted in "Resources" at the end of this chapter.)

Recreational Sport and Play

Not everything must be organized. Most colleges and universities have free gym time during the day for pick-up games. Some intramural directors find that they have 50 students playing pick-up basketball during these open gym times but have only 20 sign up for intramural basketball. The lesson: sometimes people prefer to organize an activity by themselves at a time that works for them. In other words, not all intramural activities need to be organized by the intramural department.

Scheduling open gym time can get tricky, especially when you have several competitive leagues. Large institutions, which usually have several gymnasiums, often reserve one gym for intramural league competition and use the other for free gym. If you are among the thousands of intramural directors who have no such luxury, consider other alternatives. For example, you might partner with a local facility for league play and reserve your own gym for unstructured activities and pick-up games.

Skill-Development Clinics

One of the difficulties that many participants face, especially underrepresented groups such as females, is not having the expertise to participate. Feeling unsure of the rules and/or awkward about looking stupid, these students do not participate. Offering skill-development workshops and clinics on the games and activities you offer is one way to help these students feel more comfortable and participate.

There are many other ways to encourage people to become or remain physically active. Instruction in other types of physical movement can be extremely popular among students. For example, yoga, Tai Chi, martial arts, and stretching classes are experiencing quite a resurgence at community gyms nationwide. You can also motivate people to stay active by offering courses that have little or nothing to do with intramurals but nonetheless encourage active and healthy lifestyles. For example, consider offering clinics on such topics as bicycle maintenance, gardening, and relaxation.

Sport Clubs

Yet another way to organize activity is to facilitate the formation of sport clubs. As introduced in chapter 3 (see page 28), in addition to promoting camaraderie among students with similar interests, sport clubs are a great opportunity for students to assume and develop leadership skills. What's more, they provide opportunities for students to get involved in activities that the intramural staff may have little or no expertise in, thus broadening the intramural program (Lore 1994). Sports clubs are run by students and are often self-financed, but some receive money from the institution or student government.

Before too many sport clubs spring up at your school and you lose all control, it is wise to set up some policies ahead of time. The first step is designating or hiring a sport club administrator. According to Shirley Cleave (1994), kinesiology faculty member at the University of New Brunswick and author of the 1994 book *Managing the Sport Club Program*, this sport club administrator should oversee or handle the following areas:

► Meet with institution legal advisors and safety officers to ascertain that appropriate procedures and guidelines are established to minimize the risk of both injury and liability.

- Regularly monitor the financial-management practices of the clubs to ensure that funds are being handled appropriately, especially if clubs receive school grants.
- Offer general advice with respect to programming ideas.
- Guard the clubs from being taken over by staff, coaches, or volunteers who are brought in by the club. A club is designed to be run by students for their members. Sometimes when a coach is hired, the coach begins to take control of the club and tell the members what they should and should not be doing, how they should be spending their money, and who is entitled to join. This is not the direction a club should take.
- Help with regular club evaluations and record keeping so that future leaders understand the history of the club.
- Encourage the development of a sport club council so that different sport clubs can learn from each other.

That leaves the intramural director and program with the following responsibilities, according to Cleave (1994).

- Establish clear guidelines outlining who has responsibility for making facility arrangements, providing equipment, and covering the costs involved.
- Adequately train student sport club leaders.
- Establish appropriate guidelines to ensure that club travel is conducted safely and that club members, as representatives of the institution, behave in an appropriate manner.
- Recognize sport club leaders through the intramural award program.

Special Events

Last but not least, special events are usually the icing on the cake of intramural programming. Intramural directors can take advantage of holidays and create other special days or times throughout the year by offering fun-filled, exciting, and unusual special events. In addition to the numerous examples of special events discussed throughout this book, particularly in

chapters 8 (promotional events) and 10 (fundraisers), four types of special events are described here, each with activity ideas: orientation, Winterfest, fieldtrips, and outdoor activities. Holidays and seasonal activities are discussed in the next section, "Sample Activities for the Year" (see page 189).

Orientation

Recreational games and activities at orientation welcome new students to the institution and welcome returning students back. First-year students, in particular, can "let their hair down" and begin to develop friendships and camaraderie with their peers. For campus recreation staff, orientation activities are a great opportunity to connect with students and introduce (and recruit) them to the intramural department..

Most orientation games are held on campus. They typically last a few hours on orientation day but can also be extended with activities offered throughout the entire first week of orientation. The intent is to build an academic family, so to speak, by using fun games in which students could laugh, get to know one another, and be silly. Institutions use such activities as climbing a greased flag pole, sliding on sheets of plastic with soapy water running over them, tugs-of-war, outdoor volleyball (on the grass, in the sand, or in the mud), dunk tanks, fitness testing, and massage stations. Henderson High School had an arm-wrestling station at orientation, but someone popped an elbow and the station was discontinued at future events.

In other cases, albeit a few, orientation games are held off campus. Loyalist college buses students to a local beach and has second-year students lead first-year students through a variety of activities. The games begin with icebreakers on the bus (introducing the person beside you, or playing concentration games). Once at the beach, students participate in tugs-of-war, relays, and group games. In one relay, student teams try to be the first to fill a 45-gallon plastic drum (with holes in it). A particularly popular game on the beach is the Great Escape. In this game, a circular area is roped off (shoulder height or 5 feet high). Teams stand inside the roped circle and must try to get out without touching or going under the rope (each team is given an 8-foot 4 x 4) (Byl 2002). The day ends with beach volleyball, a barbecue, and an informal dance.

Winterfest

Especially in northern climates, with winter come the winter blahs and cabin fever. Schools in these regions usually offer some sort of Winterfest activities. Winterfest can comprise a single winter-related event or several winter-related activites held over a day, week, or even a month. The best ingredients for an effective Winterfest are cold and snow, but activities can also be played indoors (e.g., a sock "snowball" fight). At many northern schools, Winterfest is scheduled to coincide with a citywide Snowfest or other winter festival, although some have found that city activities take students away from school events and schedule their winter celebrations at a different time. That way, students get to attend both.

Winterfest can accommodate any number of participants. Simply divide participants into teams of up to 10. (Be sure to have five males and five females on each team.) Following is a list of Winterfest activities commonly used at various school levels, but each activity could be modified to work at other grade levels.

Grade school:

► Inner tube races. Players sit in inner tubes while their partners push them around an obstacle course.

► Sleigh rides. Use a real horse and sleigh, or have players pull their teammates around on toboggans.

High school:

► Tugs-of-war. Have a traditional tug-of-war or four-way tug-of-war outside in the snow.

► Scavenger hunts. Have a one- or two-day scavenger hunt.

► Toboggan races. Hold toboggan or sled races and relays on a snow-covered hill near campus.

College and university:

► Toboggan pulls. Students pile on to a five-person toboggan and two students pull the toboggan from a start line to a finish line. If any of the players fall off, the whole team and toboggan must go back to the start line and start over. The fastest team wins.

► Toboggan-building contests. Participants build a sled or toboggan out of anything but steel. To qualify, toboggans must be large enough for one driver. Toboggans are judged on speed, originality, and detail (give different prizes for each category). For example some groups put a long skinny box on a snow-board (speed), while another wrapped a cardboard box in tin foil, complete with bouncy antennas (originality). Then hold races.

► Chili cook-offs. While the toboggan races and judging are taking place, other students can be preparing a batch of chili (using a school-provided recipe or their own). The team with the best-tasting chili wins a prize. When the toboggan races or other activities are over, everyone gets a warm chili lunch.

► Bonfires with hot dog roasts. If there is enough room for several fire pits, have student teams race to see who can build a fire first. Provide hot dogs and soda.

Fieldtrips

Don't confine intramural activities to the gym or other on-campus facilities. Off-campus fieldtrips provide students with an excellent opportunity to get to know their community, and make for a much more thorough and attractive intramural program.

The possibilities for exciting, fun fieldtrips are endless. They include, but are certainly not limited to, canoeing, kayaking, hiking, walking, downhill and cross-country skiing, snowmobiling, camping, bird watching, professional or community sporting events, and so on. Most schools provide the transportation but require students to provide their own equipment. If food and entrance fees are required, most schools try to negotiate a discounted rate and then charge students a fee to attend. For safety reasons, it is wise to limit participation according to the number of leaders, staff, or supervisors attending and the type of event. For example, 16 students would be a good size for two leaders, and that number works well for most camping facilities.

Fieldtrips can be day trips or overnight adventures. Day trips require less equipment and organization than overnight trips, of course, but overnight adventures provide more of a getaway for students and often enable them to get to know one other better. Participant age and maturity should be considered carefully when planning overnight fieldtrips, and participants should have their parents' permission to attend. In addition, students (or parents of students) participating in any fieldtrip should sign a waiver to protect the institution (see chapter 7).

Outdoor Activities

Likewise, do not restrict your special events to indoors. Outdoor facilities on campus may enable such outside activities as baseball or softball, parking-lot basketball games, Frisbee golf, pond or ice hockey, and beach volleyball (on sand). How about playing baseball with no force-outs (you can have as many players on one base as can safely touch it), or Frisbee soccer (like ultimate Frisbee but the Frisbee must pass through the soccer goal, there are no goalies, and no one is allowed inside the crease), or inch football (where everyone plays from their knees)? For complete rules of these and other fun games, see *Co-Ed Recreational Games* (Byl 2002). Outdoor events do not have to be limited to supervised activities either. At one college, students organized paint ball in the nearby woods.

Sample Activities for the Year

When planning intramural programming for the year, it is helpful to use the calendar. That is, plan events and activities by season, using holidays and seasonal sports to add excitement and hold students' interest. Overall it may be best to plan short, fast units (three to four weeks), interspersed with special events or shorter one-week units.

After four weeks of a basketball unit, for example, schedule a week of basketball-related contests such as 21 shooting, three-point shooting, or timed dribbling. In 21 shooting, two players compete at shooting foul shots. One player shoots from the foul line, scoring two points for each basket, until he misses. Then his opponent gets the rebound and takes a shot. If she makes this shot, she gets one point and then goes to the foul line to take her foul shot until she misses. The first shooter to reach 21 is the winner.

In three-point shooting, shooters get 75 seconds to take 25 shots from behind the three-point line: five shots from the baseline, five shots from halfway to the top of the arc, five shots

from the top of the arc, five shots from three-fourths of the way around the arc, and five shots from the other baseline. Each shot is worth one point, and the last shot of each sequence of five shots is worth two points. The highest possible score is 30 points. The opponent who gets the most points in 75 seconds is the winner.

In timed dribbling, competitors dribble a basketball through an obstacle course and are timed. Time is added (usually two seconds) if competitors hit one of the obstacles or fumble the ball. The fastest dribbler wins.

Annual Programming Schedule

Fall, winter, spring, holidays, and sport seasons lend themselves to intramural programming. The following list of activities has been structured around the typical school year, September through May. (If your school year runs through early June, "borrow" some activities from May.) As was the case with previous activity suggestions in this and previous chapters, this list is not exhaustive. Recall your own intramural experiences and talk to other intramural directors to come up with more great events.

September

September, sometimes including late August, is the time to get to know fellow students and the community. It is also soccer season and the end of the golf season. Try the following activities:

▶ Soccer shootout. One goalie is in the net and each participant gets five shots. For added fun and increased safety, particularly for young students, use a beach ball or the bladder of a soccer ball.

▶ Soccer keep-up. The object is to keep the soccer ball up in the air (as many consecutive hits as possible). Students scatter across the field and a soccer ball is tossed into play. Students may contact the ball with any body part but the arms and hands, and they count out each contact. To add fun, throw several balls into play. To "level the playing field" or modify the game for young students, use a bladder of a soccer ball.

▶ Bicycle rally. Students form teams and show up at school with their bikes. At the start, teams get a map and a list of items to find in the community. (Establish boundaries in a large community.) For example, a certain type of leaf, garbage (for a coordinated community trash pick-up), a business card from a local firm, and so on. The younger the students, the simpler the items should be. You may also want to staff some strategic checkpoints to make sure participants are cycling rather than driving.

▶ Golf. To shorten the game and promote camaraderie among student teams, play best ball: each player takes a shot and the next shot is taken from the spot where the best shot landed.

▶ In addition try basketball, floor hockey (outside), golf, and cross-country running.

October

October is the month of crisp fall leaves (if you live in a northern climate) and Halloween. It is also the time for the World Series. Try these activities:

▶ Home run derby. See how many home runs students can hit in 60 seconds (or five swings, or 10 pitches, and so on).

▶ Great pumpkin race. Hold relays such as carrying a greased pumpkin (have students wear garbage bags to protect their clothes from the grease) from a start line to a finish line or around an obstacle course, and have students decorate pumpkins.

▶ Special records day. Have students compete for the longest hula-hoop time (use two hoops for older students) as well as the longest time to balance a soccer ball on top of their heads, to spin a basketball on their fingers, and so on. Record these longest times and see if students can beat them in future years.

▶ Halloween crack-up. Pair up students and have them make frightening faces at each other until one partner smiles or laughs. Once eliminated, students help other players make their partners crack up. The last one not smiling or laughing is the winner.

▶ Broom balance. See who can balance a broom on his or her nose (or chin) the longest.

▶ In addition try football, soccer, and rugby.

November

November is the month of Thanksgiving, of course. It could also be a great time to organize some fieldtrips and outdoor activities (see pages 188 and 189). Try these activities:

▶ Turkey trot. Students run a specified distance (1 kilometer or 1 mile) and must predict how long it will take. The runner closest to his or her estimated time wins a chocolate or real turkey.

▶ Twin days. Participants try to look as alike as possible (clothes, hair color and style, glasses, and so on) and then play partner games and challenges such as a three-legged race, balloon toss (see which teams can throw a water-filled balloon the farthest without the balloon breaking; this activity is best done outside), or a game of two-on-two basketball or volleyball.

▶ Organize a billiards tournament. Have students compete as individuals and on teams.

▶ In addition, try marathon running, team handball, racquetball, and squash.

December

December brings the end of the semester, the official start of winter, and the full swing of the hockey season. December also marks several seasons and, thus, is a time for charity competitions. Try these activities:

▶ Hockey showdowns. These include a variety of games including shootouts, puck-dribbling contest (see who can dribble around a number of pylons the quickest; maybe add a bench or two that students must pass the puck through or over), and stick-balancing contests and relays (students balance a hockey stick on their noses or chins the longest, through an obstacle course, and so on).

▶ Charity pledges. Organize a hoop-a-thon (students get sponsors to pledge so much per basket or shot) or a tribute run (students get sponsored to run as a memorial to someone, perhaps dressed as Elvis Presley). Likewise, you can organize a fund-raiser (see chapter 10 for ideas) to raise money for a local charity such as a halfway house, food bank, or shelter.

▶ Inuit games. To celebrate the start of winter, try the Alaskan High Kick or the Finger Hang. The Alaskan High Kick begins with players sitting on a gymnastic mat with one hand on the mat and the other hand holding the opposite foot (see figure 11.2). The objective is to kick the target and then land without sitting back down on the mat. Each player gets three tries. Players who succeed in three tries move on to the next round, when the target is raised 2 inches (5 centimeters) and players get another three tries. Rounds continue until one player is left. In the Alaskan Finger Hang, players are required to sit cross-legged on a gymnastics mat while two people hold a broom handle over their heads. They grab the broom handle with the middle finger of one hand and grab that wrist with the other hand, hanging from the broom. The broom holders lift the player off the ground. The player who holds on the longest wins (Keewatin 1998).

▶ In addition, try fencing, dancing, or table tennis.

January

In addition to cabin fever, lots of sporting events are happening in January, including the Winter Olympics, perhaps, and the Super Bowl. Basketball season is also in full swing. In addition to the Winterfest events described earlier in this chapter (see page 188), try these activities.

▶ Basketball golf. See how many shots players need to make a basket from nine predetermined spots.(The first shot could be a foul shot, the second from the three-point line directly in front of the basket, the third a right-hand lay-up from the right side, the fourth a three-point shot from the right baseline, the fifth a baby hook in front of the basket, the sixth from the baseline behind the basket, the seventh from anywhere outside the key, the eighth a left-hand lay-up from the left side, and the ninth a three-point shot from the

FIGURE 11.2 Alaskan high kick.
Adapted, by permission, from the Teaching and Learning Centre-Kivalliq School Operations.

left baseline.) To "level the playing field," use a small teddy bear instead of a basketball.

- California beach volleyball. For students longing for the long, hot days of summer, there's nothing like some beach volleyball. Bring sand in to the main lobby (use a large tarp underneath) and set up a beach volleyball court. Pipe in Beach Boys music.

- Football accuracy throws. Hang a hula hoop from the ceiling or basketball hoop and pick a throwing line. The object is to see how many consecutive throws players can get through the hoop. To "level the playing field," use larger hoops and rubber fish instead of footballs.

- Indoor Winter Olympics. Hold "ski" races (players sit on two scooters and propel themselves around a small obstacle course using two toilet plungers) and "bobsled" races (players lie on three scooters and their teammates pushing them around an obstacle course).

- In addition, try badminton, curling, ice hockey, ringette, and some of the martial arts.

February

With Valentine's Day on the 14th, February is an ideal month to emphasize heart-related fitness. Try these activities:

- Heart tournament. Basketball would be fine, but any active game will do.

- Campus fitness challenges. Conduct mass aerobics for the whole school with the aerobics instructor(s) leading from the roof or from the balcony in a gymnasium.

- Indoor track meets. Use pool noodles for javelins, paper plates for discuses, beach or foam balls for shots, and so on. For the running events, have students sit on scooters and propel themselves with their hands and feet.

- Air soccer. Opponents (two teams) kneel on opposite ends of a Ping-Pong table (without the net) and try to blow a Ping-Pong ball into their opponent's goal (half the table, marked with cups).

- In addition, try basketball, broomball, handball, skating, skiing, snowboarding, and snow shoeing.

March

The arrival of St. Patrick's Day calls for green activities, and the March Madness basketball season is in full swing. Try these activities:

- Basketball madness. Hold basketball contests such as free-throw shooting (most baskets in 60 seconds wins) and fowl shooting (see how many foul shots you can score out of 10, using a rubber chicken instead of a basketball).

- Bump. Players line up behind the free-throw line. (The first three players each have a ball.) Player 1 (the first in line) takes a shot. If Player 1 misses, she retrieves the ball and goes for a rebound basket. Meanwhile, Player 2 (the second in line) tries to sink a basket before the Player 1 sinks the rebound. If Player 2 is successful, Player 1 is eliminated (bumped out) from the game. If Player 2 is unsuccessful, Player 1 goes to the back of the line (handing her ball to Player 4 on the way) and Player 2 retrieves the ball and goes for the rebound. Meanwhile, Player 3 tries to sink a basket before Player 2 sinks his rebound. And so on. When players are bumped, they give their ball to the next player in line and stand on the sideline. The last player left in line is the winner.

- March madness. Host crazy and unusual activities, such as dress-up relays (the first player puts on certain clothing, such as a pair of large overalls, large rubber boots, and a hat, and runs around an obstacle course; then comes back and removes the clothes and passes them on to the next person who puts them on and runs the obstacle course), musical balloon volleyball (have lots of balloons on each side of the net; players hit the balloons over the net while music plays; when the music stops, the team with the fewest balloons on their side of the net wins the point).

- St. Patrick's fun. Hold St. Patrick's Day activities such juggling contests (use green

Winter Olympics

In conjunction with the Winter Olympics, Alberton Consolidated Elementary School held its own Olympic celebration: "Olympic Fun on Ice." All classes took part, with different combinations of grades on different days.

Students in grades 1 through 4 took part in an Olympic torch parade (carrying an upside-down pylon with a ball on it) and then went through the following five stations, each of which matched Olympic events:

► Hockey (using "plastic hockey sticks, tennis balls, and a net; older students played a game, while younger students experimented with the sticks and balls)

► Slalom skiing (skating between pylons)

► Cross-country skiing (three skaters in a line with two skaters holding on the waist of the person in front of them through an obstacle course)

► Bobsled racing (players sat on scooters or chairs and their partners pushed them)

► Curling (using rubber chickens and a hoop)

Students in grades 5 and 6 were divided into teams of eight, each representing a different county. They took part in five relay races, corresponding to these five stations, except that cross-country skiing became ski jumping (jump/step over a stick on the ice). Each team also took part in the Olympic torch procession, complete with a large flag. Everyone had lots of laughs, especially since ability was not a major factor in these activities. Winning teams and students got first-, second-, and third-place ribbons, and everyone got participant ribbons. Gold and silver medalists also received chocolate coins wrapped in gold and silver tinfoil.

In the end, having these events in our school made the students more aware of the "other" Olympics going on, and since fun and sportsmanship rather than competition were stressed, we believe the true Olympic spirit shone throughout (Bolo 1999).

Adapted, by permission, from S. Cleave, 1994, "Sport clubs: More than a solution to shrinking dollars and growing demands," *NIRSA Journal* 18 (3):30-33.

construction paper) and a tug-of-war out on the grass.

► In addition, try indoor soccer, volley ball, rock climbing, weightlifting, and wrestling.

April

April showers present an opportunity for lots of indoor games. Early April, or perhaps late March, marks the arrival of Easter. And this is the month when students are getting ready for the warmth of summer. Try these activities:

► Hat day. Have students bring in hats (or provide them) and see how far they can throw them (highest, longest, and so on), how many times in a row they can throw and catch them. To add some challenge, get students to catch them on their heads and/or incorporate flips and spins into the throwing.

► Easter egg hunt. Deposit foil-wrapped Easter eggs around the school and, at the signal to start, students try to find as many as they can.

► Egg toss. Pair up students and have them toss an egg to their partner. The team that tosses the egg the longest (or farthest) without breaking it wins.

► In addition, try cycling, bowling, swimming, skateboarding, orienteering, and netball.

May

Summer has almost arrived. Track and field is in full swing, and students can enjoy being outside again. Try these activities:

▶ Frisbee golf. Set out nine targets that players will try to hit one after the other with their Frisbees. Players throw their Frisbee towards each target and throw again from where they pick up the Frisbee. Each throw counts as one stroke.

▶ Ultimate Frisbee. Players pass a Frisbee between each other in an effort to get the Frisbee across a goal line.

▶ Block golf. Have players try to putt a wooden block into a hole.

▶ Frisbee contests. Have students compete for distance and accuracy (it should land in one of several hoops on the field).

▶ Penny field hunt. Scatter a few hundred pennies ($1 to $5 worth) around a field. At the signal to start, students try to find as many as they can. (Offer a prize for the most pennies collected, or throw in a few quarters.)

▶ Track and field challenges. Average the total times and distances for all the members of a team in specified events, such as a 100 m sprint, a ball throw, and a standing long jump.

▶ In addition, try archery, cricket, field hockey, and tennis.

Chapter Summary Exercises

This chapter explained who should be involved in intramurals and suggested many activities that will attract them and keep them coming back for more. To better understand these concepts and to begin the process of developing your own exciting intramural programming, complete the following three exercises.

1. Sit in your school cafeteria (or ask permission to interview students from a local grade or high school) and ask at least 20 students the following questions.

▶ What major obstacle prevents you from becoming more physically active?

▶ What would help you to become more active?

▶ What would motivate you to become more active?

Compare your results with the results of other students in class. Then, as a group, determine the major obstacles and the most promising solutions for the age group you surveyed.

2. Select a major sport and come up with new rules that will make the game more challenging and fun for students with a broad range of skills.

3. Develop specific descriptions of three programming ideas you will use in your program and determine the best time to offer them. Each activity should support your mission, fit your budget, suit your staffing structure, and so on.

References

Bolo, C. 1999. Special intramural events. *The Leader* 7 (5): 1. Used with permission of the Canadian Intramural Recreation Association.

Bulfin, D. 1996. Family programming for fun and profit. *NIRSA Journal* 20 (3): 4-5.

Byl, J. 2002. *Co-ed recreational games.* Champaign, IL: Human Kinetics

Cleave, S. 1994. Sport Clubs: More than a solution to shrinking dollars and growing demands. *NIRSA Journal* 18 (3): 30-33.

Keewatin Divisional Board of Education. 1998. *Inuit games book.* Rankin Inlet, Northwest Territories, Canada, XOC OGO: Keewatin Divisional Board of Education. Used with permission. To order the book, call 819-645-2673 or fax your order to 819-645-2127.

Lore, J. 1994. A survey of selected collegiate sport club programs. NIRSA Journal. 19 (1): 32-35.

Resources

Journals

CIRA Bulletin
CIRA 740 B Rue Belfast Road
Ottawa, Ontario, Canada K1G 0Z5
Phone: 613-244-1594
Fax: 613-244-4738
E-mail: cira@intramurals.ca

Bulletin is included with a $45.00 annual membership ($25.00 for students).

NIRSA Journal
4185 SW Research Way
Corvallis, OR 97333-1067
E-mail: nirsa@nirsa.org

A valuable resource that is included with the cost of membership providing articles on many important intramural topics.

Books

Barbarash, L. 1997. *Multicultural games.* Champaign, Ill.: Human Kinetics.

Some great games from a variety of different cultures.

Doyle, P. 1997. *Activities for groups of 50 or more.* Hamilton, Ontario: CIRA-Ontario.

A great book when you are looking for mass games for large groups. Available from the Canadian Intramural Recreational Association-Ontario (CIRA-Ontario), c/o Student Life, P.O. Box 2034, Hamilton, Ontario, Canada, L8N 3T2. Phone (905) 575-2083. Web site: http://www.mohawkc.on.ca/external/cira/resource.html.

Doyle, P. 1998. *Awesome asphalt activities.* Hamilton, Ontario: CIRA-Ontario.

A great book for kid's games on the asphalt around the schoolyard. Available from the Canadian Intramural Recreational Association-Ontario (CIRA-Ontario), c/o Student Life, P.O. Box 2034, Hamilton, Ontario, Canada, L8N 3T2. Phone (905) 575-2083. Web site: http://www.mohawkc.on.ca/external/cira/resource.html.

Doyle, P. 1998. *Great gator games.* Hamilton, Ontario: CIRA-Ontario.

A great book of games using gator balls, which are soft foam balls. Available from the Canadian Intramural Recreational Association-Ontario (CIRA-Ontario), c/o Student Life, P.O. Box 2034, Hamilton, Ontario, Canada, L8N 3T2. Phone (905) 575-2083. Web site: http://www.mohawkc.on.ca/external/cira/resource.html.

Doyle, P. 1998. *Schlockey.* Hamilton, Ontario: CIRA-Ontario.

This is a book that explains the rules and construction of a schlockey game; a kind of a floor hockey game played by two people on a 4 x 8 foot sheet of plywood within wooden borders. Available from the Canadian Intramural Recreational Association-Ontario (CIRA-Ontario), c/o Student Life, P.O. Box 2034, Hamilton, Ontario, Canada, L8N 3T2. Phone (905) 575-2083. Web site: http://www.mohawkc.on.ca/external/cira/resource.html.

Doyle, P., and J. Berry. 1997. *Another games book.* Hamilton, Ontario: CIRA-Ontario.

A collection of great games for elementary school intramural programs and physical education classes. Available from the Canadian Intramural Recreational Association-Ontario (CIRA-Ontario), c/o Student Life, P.O. Box 2034, Hamilton, Ontario, Canada, L8N 3T2. Phone (905) 575-2083. Web site: http://www.mohawkc.on.ca/external/cira/resource.html.

Doyle, P., D. Schei, and B. McFarlane. 1994. *Not just another games book.* Ottawa, Ontario: CIRA-Ontario.

A collection of more great games for elementary school intramural programs and physical education classes. Available from the Canadian Intramural Recreational Association-Ontario (CIRA-Ontario), c/o Student Life, P.O. Box 2034, Hamilton, Ontario, Canada, L8N 3T2. Phone (905) 575-2083. Web site: http://www.mohawkc.on.ca/external/cira/resource.html.

Lichtman, B. 1993. *Innovative games.* Champaign, Ill.: Human Kinetics.

A great book of new and innovative games.

Lichtman, B. 1999. *More innovative games.* Champaign, Ill.: Human Kinetics.

A great book of more new and innovative games.

Midura, D. 1992. *Team building through physical challenges.* Champaign, Ill.: Human Kinetics.

A helpful book of games that encourage team building. The games could be used in leadership development or as part of intramural activities.

Midura, D. 1995. *More team-building challenges.* Champaign, Ill.: Human Kinetics.

More great games that encourage team building.

Morris, D., and J. Stiehl. 1999. *Changing kids' games.* Champaign, Ill.: Human Kinetics.

A great book for changing traditional games into ones that are better suited for younger children.

Strong, T., and D. LeFevre. 1996. *Parachute games.* Champaign, Ill.: Human Kinetics.

A collection of fun games using a parachute.

Williams, D., ed. 1995. *Zany activities with a rubber chicken.* Ottawa, Ontario: CIRA.

A book with a lot of fun ways to use a rubber chicken in intramural programs or physical education classes. Available from the Canadian Intramural

Recreational Association-Ontario (CIRA-Ontario), c/o Student Life, P.O. Box 2034, Hamilton, Ontario, Canada, L8N 3T2. Phone (905) 575-2083. Web site: http://www.mohawkc.on.ca/external/cira/resource.html.

Williams, D., ed. 1997. *Zany activities with panty hose, boxer shorts, and leotards.* Ottawa, Ontario: CIRA.

Some fun games using panty hose as a main part of the game's equipment. Available from the Canadian Intramural Recreational Association-Ontario (CIRA-Ontario), c/o Student Life, P.O. Box 2034, Hamilton, Ontario, Canada, L8N 3T2. Phone (905) 575-2083. Web site: http://www.mohawkc.on.ca/external/cira/resource.html.

Web sites

Canadian Association for Health, Physical Education, Recreation an Dance (CAHPERD) www.cahperd.ca/

Offers ways that grade and high schools can promote active living. Look under the "active living challenge" link.

Coalition for Active Living in Canada www.activeliving.ca/activeliving/

Offers information on promoting active living, including examples for grade and high schools, and colleges and universities. The Coalition for Active Living in Canada is a group of organizations and individuals working together to promote healthy, active living among all Canadians, enhance quality of life, and reduce the risk of illness associated with sedentary lifestyles. Its members (and lots of links) are also listed on the site.

National Federation of State High School Associations (NFHS) www.nfhs.org/rules.htm

Offers 16 different sport sections dealing with rule revisions, points of emphasis, comments on rules, related publications, signals, playing area dimensions, and instructions to major and minor officials—information that is extremely helpful in developing and implementing an intramural program. NFHS governs virtually all U.S. high school competition. Its rules-writing program, which stresses "grass-roots" input, was initiated for high schools, coaches, athletic administrators, and interscholastic officials to have direct influence in developing rules.

Ontario College Athletic Association (OCAA) www.ocaa.com

Sponsors the Active Living initiative discussed in this chapter (see figure 11.1 on page 185). For more information about this initiative, contact OCAA's executive director at exec-director@ocaa.com or 416-426-7043.

Purdue University www.purdue.edu/RecSports/im/rules/rule1.html

Provides a list of many institution-specific intramural rules.

Sonoma State University www.sonoma.edu/recsports/im/imrules.htm

Provides rules for intramural sports, including some not listed on the Southern Indiana site.

Virtual Resource Center for Sport Information www.sportquest.com/

A comprehensive site with information and links for practically every sport.

12

Tournaments and Leagues

In the last chapter, we reviewed who should be involved in intramural programs and we provided a lot of programming ideas. One of the best ways to organize competitions for the intramural participants is through tournaments and leagues. As introduced in chapter 11, tournaments and leagues are two components of competitive intramural programming. In fact, they provide the primary means of organizing intramural competitions at most schools. This chapter explores various tournament and league structures, a discussion that will assist you in selecting the best structure to further your intramural mission.

Chapter Objectives

▶ Explore the pros and cons of various tournament and league structures.
▶ Understand the role and implementation of seeding and byes.
▶ Understand how to use various extended tournaments.

Types and Progression of Tournaments and Leagues

Let's start with some definitions. To review, **leagues** are a competitive structure in which teams or individuals (called **entries**) compete for a week or more, perhaps an entire school year. **Tournaments** are typically shorter: one- or two-day events in which entries are scheduled to compete. If there are a large number of entries, the entries can be put into two or more pools in both leagues and tournament play. In both leagues and tournaments, players can also be placed in different levels: a competitive tournament/league and a recreational tournament/league. Dividing the participants creates a more positive experience for both the competitive and recreational players, and provides a safer playing environment for both. In addition to leagues typically running longer than tournaments, the other difference between a league and a tournament is that in a league everyone plays all the other teams in their pool. Tournaments will often have everyone play all the entries in their pool but sometimes will use a single or double elimination (explained more fully in this chapter) in which an entry is eliminated after one or two losses. Single or double elimination is never used in league play. Leagues will sometimes have everyone play all the entries two or more times, but this does not happen in tournament play. Although the sections in this chapter on single and double elimination apply only to tournaments, the sections on round robin tournaments, seeding, byes, and tie breaking apply to both tournaments and leagues. Building on those definitions, then, a tournament could be used to determine an overall league champion.

Before looking at the specific types of tournaments and leagues, there are some more terms that need to be defined: seeding, brackets, draw, and standings. **Seeding** is the process of ranking players according to their ability relative to other entries. A **bracket** is a graphic illustration of where entries advance when they win, and, in the case of double elimination, where the first-time losers go. The **draw** involves the placement of entries onto the tournament bracket sheet or league schedule. **Standings** refers to the final position that entries find themselves in at the end of the tournament or league play. The winner is first in the standings, the second-place fin-

isher is second, the third-place finisher is third, and so on.

The most common types of tournaments are single- and double-elimination, multilevel, and various round-robin formats. Each of these formats has distinct strengths and weaknesses, the identification and assessment of which will help intramural directors select the right format for each specific situation. Let's look at each of these.

Single Elimination

Single elimination is a tournament in which an entry must win to advance to the next round. If an entry loses once, that team or individual is eliminated from the tournament. The greatest appeal of the single-elimination tournament is its simplicity, as shown in figure 12.1. Losers are eliminated and winners advance to the next round until there is only one contestant remaining, the tournament champion.

Although eliminating losers is not desirable in most intramural contests (ideally, everyone should play the same number of games to encourage participation), the single-elimination tournament is valuable when the number of entries is large, time is short, and the number of playing areas is limited. Of all the tournaments, this one requires the fewest games. Half the entries are eliminated after one game, one-quarter remain after the second round, one-eighth after the third, and so on. When more extensive participation is important and more playing areas and time are available, however, using this tournament is not advisable. For one thing, if highly skilled entries have a bad game or are badly seeded in the draw and lose, they would be out of the tournament earlier than they should have been—and with no opportunity to get back in the game.

The best use for the single-elimination tournament is probably play-offs at the end of a league or following a longer tournament such as a split round robin, in which there are several pools (explained later in this chapter). The seeding for the single elimination is based on team or individual standings at the conclusion of the previous playing period. For example, the top-ranked team in the league should play the second-ranked team in the final game of the single-elimination play-offs. To ensure that happens, they are placed as far as possible from each other on the single-elimination bracket.

Round   1   2   3

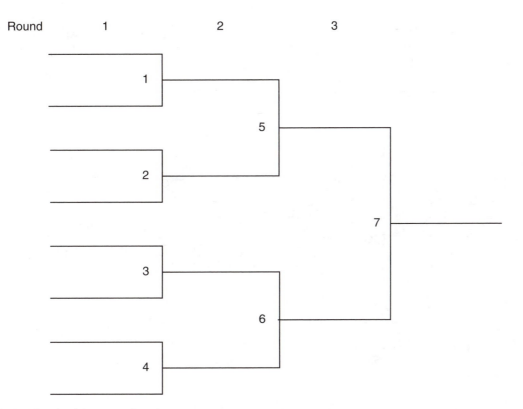

FIGURE 12.1   Single-elimination bracket.

Reprinted, by permission, from J. Byl, 1999, *Organizing successful tournaments*, 2nd ed. (Champaign, IL: Human Kinetics), 25. Copyright 1999 by John Byl.

Double Elimination

Double elimination, shown in figure 12.2, is like single elimination except that if entries lose once, they move to a loser's bracket. If they lose a second time, then they are eliminated. If they win every game in the loser's bracket, they come back to the winner's side and play the winner of the winner's bracket. Because it is awkward to have entries going in two different directions, figure 12.3 shows a double-elimination bracket but with all the winners moving to the right.

The double-elimination tournament was designed to address the problems inherent in single elimination. First, entries in double-elimination tournaments are not eliminated after only one loss, as they are in single elimination. Second, all entries get to play at least two games (they may only play once in single elimination). These strengths are often overrated, however. Double elimination also has weaknesses. For one, second- and third-seeded players play many games, particularly in the final rounds of the tournament, which requires many rounds of competition (number of games). Also, this tournament type often does not use available areas

efficiently. If, for example, the tournament consists of nine teams/entries and there are four playing areas available, the double-elimination tournament takes six rounds to complete, leaving many playing areas unused as teams wait for other teams to work their way through the loser's bracket.

Double elimination is best used when the number of playing areas is limited. It is important for everyone to know who the top teams are, and it is important that all entries play at least two games.

Multilevel

The **multilevel** tournament is also similar to a single-elimination tournament. In a multilevel tournament, however, entries are not eliminated after a loss but simply move down one or more levels of play into the consolation rounds. This downward movement continues until no other challengers remain. For an eight-entry multilevel tournament, for example, those who lose in the first round (of A) go to level C. In the second round, the losers of A go to B, and the losers of C go to D. In the final round, every entry is still

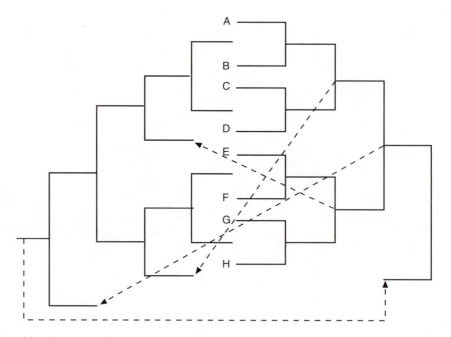

FIGURE 12.2 Double-elimination bracket.

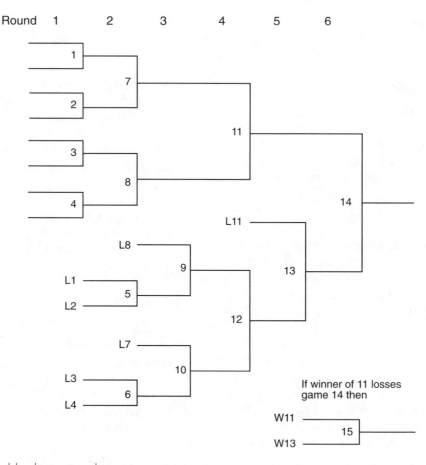

FIGURE 12.3 Double-elimination draw.

playing (see figure 12.4). This leads to the primary advantage of the multilevel tournament: all players play approximately the same number of games. Another advantage is that players are more likely to encounter others of their caliber in each round.

In the final round of single- and double-elimination tournaments, there is only one playing area in use, for the championship game. This is not the case in the multilevel tournament because there is less elimination. As a result, when sufficient playing areas are available, the multilevel tournament requires the same number of rounds to complete as the single-elimination tournament. The multilevel tournament is also advantageous because it takes half the time of the double-elimination tournament. If six playing areas are available and there are 13 entries

in the tournament, for example, single-elimination and multilevel tournaments will require four rounds, whereas a double-elimination tournament will require eight rounds.

Multilevel tournaments are an excellent choice when time is limited and when fairly even or comparable play, in terms of the number of games played and playing level, is important. Thus, the multilevel tournament is, perhaps, most useful in intramural or recreational settings where eliminating players is undesirable and final standings are of less significance.

Round Robin

In the **round robin** tournament, all entries play all other entries an equal number of times. Because of this equality, the round robin is usually

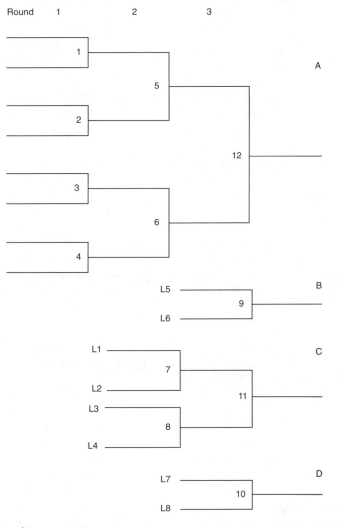

FIGURE 12.4 Multilevel bracket.

Reprinted, by permission, from J. Byl, 1999, *Organizing successful tournaments*, 2nd ed. (Champaign, IL: Human Kinetics), 45. Copyright 1999 by John Byl.

the tournament of choice for intramurals. Basically, a schedule is made up before the tournament/league begins in which everyone plays each other one time, regardless of whether teams win or lose any of their games. In fact, the round-robin format is used to create league schedules. One time through a round robin provides a complete league schedule.

The round robin and round robin splits (explained in the following sections) have fixed schedules. That is, all entries know exactly who they play and what time they play them, which offers some advantages in preparing for the tournament and upcoming games. In addition, seeding does not affect the outcome, because everyone plays everyone. When the number of entries is small and games are played quickly (as in table tennis, badminton, or volleyball), the round robin and split round robin are effective for a one-day tournament. When the number of entries is large and the games take longer to complete (as in hockey, football, or basketball), however, a round robin is problematic. For example, a tournament with 32 entries would take 496 games to complete using a round robin. This compares with 62 games in double elimination and only 31 in single elimination. Also, when there is considerable discrepancy in level of play, countless games will be frustrating to players because the outcome of most of these games will never be in doubt.

Round Robin Double Split

When a round-robin format is desirable but the number of entries is too large, splitting the entries into "pools" is a practical solution. When two pools are created, it is a **round robin double split**. Each pool follows the round robin format, but only the top two entries from each pool participate in the play-off game to determine the final standings. The obvious benefit, then, is that the number of games is halved. The drawback is that proper seeding becomes important. For example, if the top three seeds are placed in one pool and only the top two from each pool advance to the play-offs, then (if entries perform consistent with their seedings) the third seed cannot play in the play-offs.

The round robin double split is commonly used to structure league play. When lots of entries sign up for the league, intramural directors split the entries into two pools, called **divisions,** and provide a league schedule for them. Follow-

ing the regular league playing season, the top two teams from each division compete in the play-offs to determine final standings.

Round Robin Triple Split

The **round robin triple split** is similar to the round robin double split, except there are three pools. Because it would be awkward to have a single-elimination play-off with three or six finalists (top two seeds would not play in the first round of the play-off; this will be explained under "Byes" later in this chapter), however, using a round-robin format is more suitable. Such a format will require more games in the play-offs and, thus, is a satisfactory alternative to the round robin double split only when the number of entries is very large. The same thing would apply to leagues that have many entries and are then divided into three divisions.

Round Robin Quadruple Split

The **round robin quadruple split** is also like the round robin double split, except there are four pools. This format is useful only when the number of entries exceeds 11. Typically, the round robin quadruple split is used for one- or two-day tournaments and in leagues that run over a long period of time. The major disadvantage of this format is that when there are only 12 to 15 entries, the weaker entries might participate in only two games. For example, if there are 14 entries, there would be two pools of four and two pools of three. The entries in the two pools of three would only play two games. The two winners would advance into a play-off round, but the loser in each of those pools would be eliminated after only two games.

Tie-Breaking Procedures for Tournaments and Leagues

To determine final league standings or to choose who advances to the play-offs, a tie-breaking procedure needs to be set up before league or tournament play. There are two common methods to break a tie. Both begin with step 1: considering only the record of tied entries (entries with the same number of wins). Step 1 is followed through in the order presented. If there is still a tie after considering the three criteria for breaking ties in step 1, the tournament/league convener goes to step 2.

Step 1. Considering only the record of tied entries, give the highest rank to the entry that:

▶ has defeated the other(s) (e.g., if two entries are tied but one has beaten the other in play, the entry that won is placed ahead of the other);

▶ has the best win/loss ratio (e.g., in games such as badminton or volleyball, entries must win two out of three games or three out of five games); or

▶ has the best goals (points) for/against ratio.

A tie might still persist after step 1. For example, two entries may have played to a 1-1 tie in a soccer game and ended up tied in the final standings. Another example would involve three teams: Team A beat Team B 1-0, Team B beat Team C 1-0, and Team C beat Team A 1-0. Each team has beaten the other, has the same win/loss ratio, and team A has 1 goal for and 1 against, team B has 1 goal for and 1 against, as does team C.

The most common way to break the tie following these three criteria is to compare the records of the tied entries with the records of all the other entries. If the tie is for first place and all games and points factor into breaking the tie, then how these entries did against the last-place entry will come into the equation. However, if entries suspect that the final standings might be close, they may deliberately run up the score when playing against weaker entries. To have a weaker entry be outmatched is one thing, but to have the stronger entry try to score as many points as possible on a weaker entry is demoralizing (which is never desired in intramural competitions). Therefore, a second step for tie breaking was devised to minimize the importance of unevenly matched games.

Step 2. If a tie persists after step 1, considering the records of the tied entries with the records of entries immediately below or above them in the standings, give the highest rank to the entry that

▶ defeated the entry below or above if the other(s) did not,

▶ has the best win/loss ratio of games against the entry below or above, or

▶ has the best goals (points) for/against ratio with the entry below or above com-

pared with the other tied entries (Byl 1995).

If three entries (out of eight total entries) were tied, for example, the sequence for breaking a three-way tie is shown in the following grid. If three entries are tied for first, then the tournament director considers how each entry did against the fourth-place entry. If they are still tied, the tournament director considers how they did against the fifth-place entry. To use a different example, if a three-way tie exists for third place, then the tournament director considers how each tied entry did against the sixth-place entry, then the second-place entry, then the seventh-place entry, and so on.

Tied position (3 teams)	Sequence of entries to consider
1st	4, 5, 6, 7, 8
2nd	5, 1, 6, 7, 8
3rd	6, 2, 7, 1, 8
4th	7, 3, 8, 2, 1
5th	8, 4, 3, 2, 1
6th	5, 4, 3, 2, 1

Seeding and Byes

Seeding and byes are important concepts to understand in preparing a successful tournament. Ideally the championship game is between the two best entries. If they played earlier in the tournament, then the second-best entry would likely be out of the tournament and the best team would play the third-best team in the championship. This is undesirable in intramurals because the championship game is most exciting and the score is more likely to be close when the two best teams are there.

Ranking the entries and placing them on a tournament bracket in such a way as to avoid strong teams from being eliminated too early is what seeding is all about. Sometimes not all entries can play every round. If there are three entries in a single-elimination tournament, for example, two entries can play in one game but the other has to sit a game out. Deciding which entry sits out is what byes are all about. The following sections describe seeding and byes and provide suggestions for implementing them.

Seeding

Seeding, the process of ranking players according to their ability relative to other entries, takes place before a tournament begins. The main principle is that the top two entries should meet in the final game. The logical extension of this, then, is that the higher an entry is ranked, the closer it should come to the final game before being eliminated. A second principle is that entries of similar ability should encounter equal difficulties on the road to the championship game.

The higher the ranking, the lower the seed numeral. For example, the highest-ranked team is Seeded 1, the second highest is Seeded 2, and so on. If there were eight teams, the lowest-ranked team is Seeded 8. Seeding is most accurate when it is based on the standing at the end of league play or a round-robin tournament. Those standings are then used to seed for a single-elimination play-offs. If the teams have not played each other, then the tournament convener will need to seed on the basis of such factors as how teams have played against other teams, the strengths and weakness of certain players, and how these teams may have done in the past.

There are two philosophies on how to apply seeding. The first and most common seeding type is the **advantage seeding** approach, which gives Seed 1 a slightly easier schedule than Seed 2, and so on. For example, in the semi-finals Seed 1 competes against Seed 4, while Seed 2 competes against Seed 3. The second type of seeding, the **equitable approach**, gives Seed 1 as difficult a schedule as Seed 2, and so on. For example, in the semi-finals Seed 1 competes against Seed 3, while Seed 2 competes against Seed 4—both two seeds apart.

Figure 12.5 shows the advantage seeding approach for a single-elimination tournament with eight entries. Seeds 5 through 8 should be eliminated in the first round because they are the weakest entries. In the second round, the Seeds 3 and 4 should be eliminated, and in the final round Seed 2 should be eliminated, leaving Seed 1 victorious.

Byes

A **bye** is the position of a top-ranked tournament entry that advances to the next round without playing. When there are fewer entries than spaces on the tournament bracket, the top seeds

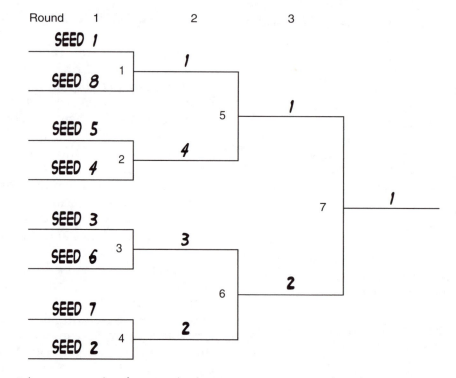

FIGURE 12.5   Advantage seeding for a single-elimination tournament with eight entries.
Reprinted, by permission, from J. Byl, 1999, *Organizing successful tournaments*, 2nd ed. (Champaign, IL: Human Kinetics), 25. Copyright 1999 by John Byl.

do not play in the first round and are given a bye. In figure 12.6, for example, which shows a single-elimination tournament with five entries, the top seeds do not play in the first round but automatically advance to the second round. Seeds 4 and 5, however, play each other to see which one will advance to the second round.

Byes are only used in round-robin tournaments/leagues when there are an odd number of teams, in which case each team will take one bye during the different rounds of play. The formula for computing the number of byes (in the single- and double-elimination and multilevel tournaments) is as follows:

1. Take the total number of entries (for example, 25).
2. Determine the exponential values of 2 that this number falls between (25 falls between 16 [2 x 2 x 2 x 2] and 32 [2 x 2 x 2 x 2 x 2]).
3. Choose the higher exponential value (32).
4. Subtract the number of entries from that number (32 - 25 = 7).
5. The difference is the number of byes (7; the top seven entries will get a bye).

Tournament/League Selection

Clearly, there is a lot to know and consider when choosing a tournament or league format. Do not pick a format simply because you are familiar with it. Rather, you should try to understand the advantages and disadvantages of each, and select the format(s) that will enhance your intramural goals and mission. There are five important variables to consider when planning a tournament/league.

▶ Number of rounds/games required to complete the tournament/league
▶ Equality of playing opportunity (how many games each entry will get to play)
▶ Tournament/league completion time (vs. time available)
▶ Competitive level (how close most of the games will be)
▶ Importance of seeding accuracy

As shown on table 12.1, these variables are helpful in evaluating tournament formats. If you were pressed for time and had only one playing

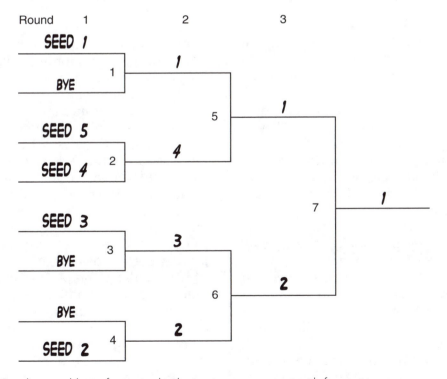

FIGURE 12.6   Seeding and byes for a single-elimination tournament with five entries.
Reprinted, by permission, from J. Byl, 1999, *Organizing successful tournaments*, 2nd ed. (Champaign, IL: Human Kinetics), 22. Copyright 1999 by John Byl.

TABLE 12.1	Tournament Selection Guide				
	Number of of games	Equal number of games	Tournament completion time	Number of close games	Accuracy of seeding
Single Elimination	Very few	Very poor	Short	Many	Very important
Double Elimination	Few	Poor	Long	Few	Important
Multilevel	Few	Good	Short	Very few	Very important
Round Robin	Very many	Very good	Very long	Many	Not very important
Round Robin – Double Split	Many	Good	Long	Many	Important
Round Robin – Triple Split	Many	Good	Very long	Many	Important
Round Robin – Quadruple Split	Few	Good	Long	Many	Important
Extended	Optional	Possible	Optional	Many	Not very important

Reprinted, by permission, from J. Byl, 1999, *Organizing successful tournaments*, 2nd ed. (Champaign, IL: Human Kinetics), 5. Copyright 1999 by John Byl.

area, for example, the single-elimination format will always be the fastest way of completing a tournament. If you have many playing sites available, however, that time advantage is minimized. Given that single elimination ranks "very poor" for equal playing opportunity, which is key in intramural leagues and tournaments, however, a single-elimination tournament would not be the best choice. In principle, the best tournament for intramurals will almost always be a round robin (or a split round robin if there are too many entries). It ranks "very good" for equal playing opportunity, has "many" close games, and seeding is "not very important."

Table 12.2 identifies how many rounds each tournament type requires based on the number of entries and available playing areas. Various assumptions are built into the numbers used. For each tournament, it is assumed that the seeding works out perfectly. For round robin splits, the top two entries from each pool/division advance to the play-offs and one more game is held for third and fourth place. Using these assump-

tions, the playoff round requires four extra games for the round robin double split, six extra games for the triple split, and eight games for the quadruple split.

As is evident from table 12.2, single-elimination and double-elimination tournaments use multiple playing sites least effectively, round robin splits use multiple sites reasonably well, and multilevel and round-robin tournaments use multiple sites most efficiently. If there were eight entries and only one playing area for a tournament, for example, single elimination would be the quickest tournament. With four playing areas, however, it takes just as long (three rounds) to complete a single-elimination tournament as a multilevel tournament, and only two more rounds (five) to complete a round robin double split. Thus, the round robins can be completed in just slightly longer time but offers a balanced number of games to all participants, which is an advantage in intramurals where mass participation is encouraged.

TABLE 12.2 Rounds to Complete Tournament

	Number of playing areas							
	1	2	3	4	5	6	7	8
Two entries								
SE	1							
Three entries								
SE	2							
DE	4							
RR	3							
Four entries								
SE	3	2						
DE	6	4						
RR	6	3						
Five entries								
SE	4	3						
DE	8	5						
RR	10	5						
Six entries								
SE	6	4	3					
ML	7	4	3					
DE	10	6	6					
RR	15	8	5					
RD	10	5	5					
Seven entries								
SE	6	4	3					
ML	9	5	3					
DE	12	7	6					
RR	21	11	7					
RD	13	7	5					
Eight entries								
SE	7	4	4	3				
ML	12	6	5	2				
DE	14	8	7	6				
RR	28	14	10	7				
RD	16	8	6	5				
Nine entries								
SE	8	5	4	4				
ML	14	7	5	4				
DE	16	9	8	7				
RR	36	18	12	9				
RD	20	10	8	7				
RT	15	8	8	8				
Ten entries								
SE	9	5	4	4	4			
ML	15	8	5	4	4			
DE	18	10	8	7	7			
RR	45	23	15	12	9			
RD	24	12	9	7	7			
RT	15	9	7	6	6			

(continued)

TABLE 12.2 (continued)

	Number of playing areas							
	1	2	3	4	5	6	7	8
Eleven entries								
SE	10	6	5	4	4			
ML	17	9	6	5	4			
DE	20	11	9	8	8			
RR	55	28	19	14	11			
RD	29	15	11	9	7			
RT	21	11	8	7	6			
Twelve entries								
SE	11	6	5	4	4	4		
ML	20	10	7	5	5	5		
DE	22	12	10	8	8	8		
RR	66	33	17	14	11	11		
RD	34	17	12	10	8	7		
RT	24	12	9	8	7	6		
RQ	20	10	8	6	6	6		
Thirteen entries								
SE	12	7	5	5	4	4		
ML	22	11	8	6	5	4		
DE	24	13	10	9	8	8		
RR	78	39	26	20	16	13		
RD	40	20	14	11	10	9		
RT	28	14	11	9	8	7		
RQ	23	12	9	7	6	6		
Fourteen entries								
SE	13	8	6	5	5	4	4	
ML	28	14	10	7	6	6	4	
DE	26	14	11	9	9	8	8	
RR	91	76	31	23	19	16	13	
RD	46	23	16	13	11	9	9	
RT	32	16	12	10	9	8	8	
RQ	26	13	10	8	7	6	6	
Fifteen entries								
SE	14	8	6	5	5	5	4	
ML	28	14	10	7	6	6	4	
DE	28	15	12	10	9	9	8	
RR	105	53	35	27	21	18	15	
RD	53	27	19	15	12	11	9	
RT	36	19	13	11	9	8	8	
RQ	29	15	11	9	8	7	6	
Sixteen entries								
SE	15	8	6	5	5	5	5	4
ML	32	15	10	8	7	6	5	4
DE	32	17	12	10	10	9	9	8
RR	120	60	40	30	24	20	18	15
RD	60	30	21	16	14	12	10	9
RT	41	21	15	12	10	9	8	8
RQ	32	16	12	9	8	8	7	6

Tournament Panacea: The Double Elimination

Susan was the intramural director at Fair Glen High School and any time she organized a league, she used the double-elimination tournament. She was used to this type of tournament because it was the one used at her high school and university. She liked it because it assured everyone at least two games. Since intramurals is about including everyone, Susan considered a two-game guarantee a real plus.

However, some of her participants were complaining that the schedule was unfair. They complained that some teams were getting a lot more games. Susan took a look at the schedule. The last activity was a volleyball tournament five teams played on two courts. The players who complained had finished fifth, playing their guaranteed two games and that was it. Some of their buddies were on the team that finished third. When Susan looked at the schedule for the third-place team, she noted that they had played four games—twice as many.

Susan realized that the students had a point, but she only had five days to complete the tournament. A colleague suggested she consider a round-robin tournament. In the round-robin tournament, the colleague said, "everyone plays everyone" and therefore everyone plays four games. But wouldn't that take more days? Susan wondered. She wrote the schedule out and, to her surprise, found that the round robin also took five days, just as many as the double elimination, but everyone would end up playing the same number of games.

Susan was gracious enough to admit to her students that there was a better way. Next time, she promised, she would choose a league format that better met her students' goals for intramurals—namely, getting to play.

Extended Tournaments

Like the elimination, multilevel, and round-robin tournaments, extended tournaments provide another option for intramural directors considering league and tournament schedules. **Extended tournaments** can carry on indefinitely and can often be self-monitoring. Typically they involve players challenging others of slightly higher ability. Should the challenger win, the winner and loser exchange places. They can last an indefinite amount of time or be limited to a week, month, or other period of time. Extended tournaments, including ladder tournaments and pyramid tournaments, are especially useful for entries competing in racquet sports.

A **ladder tournament**, is an extended tournament in which players are aligned in a ladder formation, one on top of the other, with the strongest entries on top and the weakest entries on the bottom, Players challenge others of slightly higher ability. Should the challenger win, the winner and loser exchange places. In ladder tournament entrant names are written on tongue depressors or similar objects and placed on a "ladder," a wooden board with pegs or something similar. Entries can challenge any entry within a couple rungs of theirs. If the lower entry wins, the two entrant names are switched on the ladder. The major benefits of this type of tournament are that it is self-monitoring and enables evenly matched entrants to compete. Its major weaknesses are twofold: First, players challenge each other and, therefore, some players may not play as much. Second, because of the challenge system, the ranking at the end of the tournament may not be accurate.

A **pyramid tournament** is an extended tournament in which players are aligned in a pyramid formation, one level on top of the other with the strongest entries on top and the weakest one the bottom. Players challenge others of slightly higher ability. Should the challenger win, the winner and loser exchange places.

Both the ladder and pyramid tournaments replace a league structure, saving an intramural director time and giving players more choice in when they play. On the other hand, extended tournaments often start well, but players lose interest when they are not assigned games and when they end up playing the same opponents regularly.

Tournament Administration

One of the main purposes of this chapter is that you understand various tournament formats well enough that you will not have to choose a format because of its simplicity or because you are familiar with it. Rather, you should select the format that best satisfies your mission. Tournament administration can be tricky, as the following example illustrates.

At Redeemer University College, different types of extended tournaments were tried to accommodate intramural squash players. A league would not have worked because there were too many different levels of ability, and a small difference in ability in squash often accounts for a large difference in the score. Fifty students and faculty signed up, and a ladder tournament was selected because it easily accommodates many people. Rather than allow students to monitor the tournament themselves, however, the intramural director scheduled each week's play—who would compete against whom—for the entire semester. At the end of each week, winners were moved up and losers down accordingly (Byl 1990).

When midterms rolled around, this format did not work very well. At the end of the semester, when papers were due and finals were around the corner, this format did not work at all. One week was simply too short a time. Many entrants did not play their games and players became frustrated.

Wanting to accommodate the players, the intramural director set up a pyramid tournament to give everyone more time. There were five people to a pool, and they were to play each other once during a four-week period. At the end of each month, the director would move the winners to a higher pool and the losers to a lower pool. Students and faculty, being who they are, procrastinated till the last week and then could not get all their games in. One month was too long a time period; it, too, led to many defaults.

The director then went to smaller pools, three entrants per pool, ranking each pool above or below the others. This meant that entrants would have to play two matches in two weeks, after which time winners would move to the pool above, losers would move to the pool below, and those in the middle would stay where they were. This play schedule worked for most participants, but those on the bottom of the ladder, looking at the 40+ entrants above them quickly lost hope of advancing up the ladder and started not playing their games.

The intramural director then switched to a side-by-side round robin ladder. Participants were grouped in pools of three or four players and expected to get their games in within two weeks. These pools are in a group of ladders with the top pool being identified as AAAA, the next group of ladders as AAA, then AA, and finally A. Rather than place these groups above or below one other, the director places them slightly below and to the right of the stronger group. Entrants in each of the different levels compete to move up in their respective ladder, then on to the next one.

This approach seems to be working . . . for now. The round robin ladder appears to have provided the right incentives for participants at all the levels to stay involved. The director posts a signup sheet beside the tournament draw so that new people can sign up (they are automatically on the bottom), and current participants can withdraw if they choose to after the current round of play. If entrants do not participate for two full rounds of play, the director eliminates them from the tournament and simply moves lower entries up one rung.

The solution to keeping everyone meaningfully participating in this squash tournament involved some creativity and flexibility in working with and combining different tournament types. You should be prepared to do the same as you undergo the process of tournament and league administration. Choose the format that will best accommodate your participants and will best satisfy the mission of your program. You can get some help in this regard from the computer and/or by hiring a tournament or league administrator, which are discussed in the following sections.

Note: The pool sheets used at Redeemer University College are shown in figure 12.7. They are all set up for the AAA group. To produce sheets for the other groups, simply photocopy these pages and erase one of the letters. Players in the AAAA pool challenge the three other entries during the two weeks alloted to them. They record their scores on the appropriate sports on the grid. Based on wins and losses, the players are ranked from first to fourth. When making up a new draw, the top two finishers of pool AAAA go to postitions "a" and "b." The third and forth place finishers go to the top of the

respective BBBB pools, while the top finishers in the BBBB pools go to the "c" and "d" position of the AAAA pool, as indicated on the pool sheets. The rest of the BBBB and CCCC pools follow a similar pattern.

From there, the process of tournament administration involves the following four components.

AAAA						
Names	A	B	C	D	Wins	Place
A		a – b	a – c	a – d		
		a – b	a – c	a – d		
		a – b	a – c	a – d		
		a – b	a – c	a – d		
		a – b	a – c	a – d		
B	b – a		b – c	b – d		
	b – a		b – c	b – d		
	b – a		b – c	b – d		
	b – a		b – c	b – d		
	b – a		b – c	b – d		
C	c – a	c – b		c – d		
	c – a	c – b		c – d		
	c – a	c – b		c – d		
	c – a	c – b		c – d		
	c – a	c – b		c – d		
D	d – a	d – b	d – c			
	d – a	d – b	d – c			
	d – a	d – b	d – c			
	d – a	d – b	d – c			
	d – a	d – b	d – c			

FIGURE 12.7 Pool sheets.
Reprinted, by permission, from J. Byl, 1999, *Organizing successful tournaments*, 2nd ed. (Champaign, IL: Human Kinetics), 145. Copyright 1999 by John Byl.

1. Promotion. Many promotional ideas can be learned from chapter 8. Tournament/league conveners need to use promotional techniques to get people to sign up and to inform them of upcoming games and the results.

2. Monitoring. As the tournament/league is proceeding, the convener should monitor the games to make sure no problems are developing and find solutions when problems do develop. For example, if a team misses a game, the convener needs to find out why. If players were not aware there was a game, then clearly the problem was in the promotion of the games. If the team didn't feel like playing that night, then the problem is with the team and they need to be reminded of their responsibilities, and perhaps fined for missing a game.

3. Results tracking. As games are completed, the convener needs to keep track of the scores, and wins and losses. At the conclusion of the league/tournament, the final standings need to be determined.

4. Reporting. The convener should write a final report to the program convener or intramural director detailing the success and challenges of the tournament/league. The report should have a particular focus on recommending improvements should the event be offered again. The report should include the areas of promotion, playing results, participation records, summary of awards given, a financial report, safety considerations/problems, and recommendations for next time. Some of this material is covered in greater detail in chapter 14.

Computerized Tournament/ League Administration

Thanks to the popularity of the Internet, particularly in collegiate recreational programs, there are numerous Web sites that allow intramural directors to schedule leagues, record the results, communicate to Web site users, create announcement and rule pages and much more. The advantage to having computerized tournament and league administration, of course, is that students can easily check schedules, results, and standings on their own. In addition, these sites can be part of or linked to the intramural Web site.

The most comprehensive of these Web sites are www.sportsstandings.com and www.sportspilot.com. You can list the entries, choose the tournament/league type, and select the dates and times for the competitions, and the Web site program will automatically create a schedule or bracket. (You can edit these schedules and brackets if necessary.) Sportsstandings does charge a registration fee per entry, but the time you will save (you won't have to make a schedule and enter in each individual game), particularly when it comes to leagues with many entries, will more than make up for the fees charged. A similar site, albeit only for tournaments, is www.tournamentwizard.com. This site is free but charges a fee per tournament for web publishing your tournament.

At the other end of the spectrum is www.esportsdesk.com. This Web site allows intramural directors to create leagues and tournaments online for free. The catch is that you must first create the entire schedule by hand and then enter every game into the computer. In between lies itsportsnetwork.com. This Web site is a bit more developed than esportsdesk, offering some services for free and others for a fee.

Tournament/League Administrators

People who administer tournaments and leagues need to understand tournament and league mechanics, be organized, and have the time to continually stay on top of the event. Even the best organized tournament/league runs into difficulty, and the administrator often needs to make quick and wise decisions (problems such as a referee being late because of car trouble, an electrical problem with the scoreboard, or a mixup with security and the gym is opened a half hour late). But an administrator who is well organized, stays on top of the event, and delights in ensuring that the experience is a great one for the participants will most often satisfy her goals and improve the intramural experience for all.

Chapter Summary Exercises

The best practice for organizing a tournament is to run one. The following exercises will help you practice what you've learned in this chapter and gain some practical knowledge in implementing a tournament/league. The first step is to find an institution or organization that would like you to organize and run a tournament/ league. Then follow the three steps below.

1. Plan and implement a tournament or league. Review the implementation process on figure 12.8. Use *Organizing Successful Tournaments* (Byl 1999) or www.tournamentwizard.com to create the schedules. Or visit www.esportsdesk.com or itsportsnetwork.com and plug in the schedule.

2. Run the tournament or league. Running the event involves several components, including making sure that all the teams and officials are aware of the schedules and playing rules. When things are up and running, the tournament/league convener needs to make sure things continue to run smoothly and solve problems if they arise.

3. After you've run the tournament or league, have the intramural director or tournament supervisor complete an evaluation like the one in figure 12.9. Read through this evaluation, particularly the director's or supervisor's comments, to see how well you implemented your tournament. Return the evaluation form to your instructor.

References

Byl, J. 1990. Formalizing a ladder tournament. *NIRSA Journal* 15 (1): 41-43.

Byl, J. 1992. A round robin pyramid. *NIRSA Journal* 16 (2): 41-42.

Byl, J. 1994. A round robin ladder tournament. *CAHPER Journal* 60 (2): 25-27.

Byl, J. 1995. Tie-breaking: Minimizing the blow-outs. *NIRSA Journal* 20 (1): 53.

Byl, J. 1999. *Organizing successful tournaments.* Champaign, IL: Human Kinetics.

Resources

Books

Byl, J. 1999. *Organizing successful tournaments.* Champaign, IL: Human Kinetics.

Implementation Process

Tournament/league project

Objective: to propose, implement, and evaluate a 10-hour tournament/league.

Step 1. Discuss a proposal idea with prospective tournament supervisor.

Step 2. Discuss a proposal with Professor _____.

Step 3. Prepare a proposal that includes:
- what you plan to do,
- when you plan to do it,
- how you plan to do it, and
- where you intend to do it.

Note: Description should include the activity, projected participation, advertisement, monitoring, costs, tournament type, awards to be used, who will officiate, and so on.

Step 4. Have the proposal signed by Professor _____.

Step 5. Have the proposal signed by the tournament supervisor.

Step 6. Implement your proposal.

Step 7. Prepare a report on the tournament. When the tournament is completed, compile a copy of all letters, score sheets, memos, financial statements, and so on, plus a one-page evaluation of the tournament and the procedures you used.

Step 8. Submit your report to Professor _____ within four days after the conclusion of the tournament.

FIGURE 12.8 Tournament and league implementation process.

Evaluation of Student Work
by Athletic/Intramural Director

Student Name: _____

Please evaluate the student's work on the scale below, circling the appropriate number.

1 = Unacceptable	4 = Good
2 = Poor	5 = Excellent
3 = Satisfactory	N = Not Applicable

1 2 3 4 5 N   Pre-tournament advertising

1 2 3 4 5 N   Selection of tournament type

1 2 3 4 5 N   Monitoring participants

1 2 3 4 5 N   Monitoring officials

1 2 3 4 5 N   Monitoring games

1 2 3 4 5 N   Keeping participants aware of tournament results

1 2 3 4 5 N   Reporting on and evaluating tournament

Additional comments: _____

_____

_____

Director name: _____

Title: _____

Institution: _____

Date of evaluation: _____

FIGURE 12.9   Tournament implementation evaluation.

Offers in-depth explanations and examples of seeding charts, schedules, and photocopy-ready brackets of other team structures.

Organizations

For a listing of the online tournament/league organizers discussed in this chapter see:

itsportsnet.com
58 Panorama Hills Circle NW
Calgary, Alberta, Canada T3K 4T5
Phone: 1-877-226-7726
www.itsportsnet.com

SportsPilot, Inc.
2514 Tarpley Road, Suite 104
Carrollton, TX 75006
Phone: 972-416-8657
www.sportsstandings.com
www.tournamentwizard.com
www.sportspilot.com

Recreation Sports Management
#101-1001 West Broadway, Suite 112
Vancouver, British Columbia, Canada V6H 4E4
Phone: 604-258-2276
www.esportsdesk.com

Ensuring Success

By completing the previous chapters in this book, you are now armed with a solid understanding of how to plan and implement effective intramural programming that will be fun for all. The final two steps—what to do on the big day and what to do after the activity or event is over—are the subjects of this and the next chapter. Even with great ideas, solid planning, and thorough preparation, there are still lots of details to work out on the day of each intramural activity and event. Considering and being prepared to handle these details will help intramural directors make intramural events and activities run smoothly.

Chapter Objectives

▶ Explore the various "day of" details for implementing an intramural event or activity.

▶ Define specific "day of" responsibilities and identify who is responsible for each.

▶ Understand the sign-in process.

▶ Learn how to establish no-show procedures and solve last-minute problems on the day of an intramural activity or event.

The Day Arrives

The big day arrives. A game, contest, tournament, special event, league, or other component of intramural programming has been conceived and planned, and everything should be ready to roll. To ensure that it runs smoothly and will exceed participant expectations, it is time to double-check that all the *i*'s have been dotted and the *t*'s have been crossed. Specifically, it is important to check that the following criteria have been met, each of which is reviewed and/or discussed in detail in the following sections.

▶ Sign-up sheets/registration forms have been prepared and are on hand.

▶ Officials are lined up and ready to go.

▶ Promotions are complete.

▶ Sponsorship and partnership commitments have been honored.

▶ Facility and equipment are available, safe, and suitable for use.

▶ Other event- or activity-specific necessities are ready to roll.

Sign-up Sheets

The first item to check are sign-up sheets, also called "registration forms." In younger grades, particularly at the elementary school level, sign-up sheets are not typically used; anyone who shows up participates. At the high school and university levels, however, teams and individuals usually sign up ahead of time. Most high schools and colleges have students sign up as a team, except in the case of individual events. Students choose the activities they most enjoy and select teammates they most enjoy being with. Because students at this age often want to hang out with their friends (see the discussion on age characteristics in chapter 6), if their friends are competing in a game, they will be more likely to participate. This reduces the likelihood and number of no-shows, which will be discussed later in this chapter. Students submit their own team lists identified by a name they choose. (Note: some team names may need to be scrutinized.)

A team sign-up sheet is shown in figure 13.1. (See figure 7.3 on page 112 for an example of another team sign-up sheet.) Some of the items on this sheet merit discussion here. First, the team captain's name, telephone number, and E-mail address must be filled in. Should the intramural director or event convener need to contact the team for scheduling changes or other reasons, the team captain is the liaison. Second, if the activity or event is available only to students of the institution, as opposed to alumni, faculty, and other community members, student ID numbers are important because they ensure that the player is a student at the institution. Third, note the waiver at the bottom and the small "agree to waiver" in each signature box. This waiver (see chapter 7) can also be on the back of the signup sheet.

Some institutions also include space on the registration form for participants to note when they are available. Based on this information, intramural directors (or their assistants) are able to design a schedule that will accommodate participants, as much as is possible. Scheduling competitions and events around participants does not always work out perfectly, but it helps to reduce no-shows.

Individuals who wish to play on a team but cannot find a team to play on are often referred to as **free agents**. These individuals sign up as free agents and either wait to be drafted by a team (who is looking for additional players can select one or more from a list of available free agents) or are assigned to a team by the intramural director. (See the top of figure 13.1.) If there are enough free agents signing up for an event, some schools combine them into their own team. In order to prevent team **stacking** (teams drafting or otherwise selecting strong players from other teams to strengthen their own team) before the play-offs, most schools limit the use of free agents: teams are allowed to **draft** only one free agent and drafting must occur within the first few weeks of the league schedule.

At some schools, intramural directors have everyone sign up as individuals and then assign teams. This approach is common in ice hockey. Players list their experience, competence, and the position they play on the registration form. This information helps the director or team captains create fair teams from a pool of players they may know little about. Based on the information provided, those who indicate a desire to be a team captain are invited to a closed-door draft to select their teams. Figure 13.2 is an example

Intramural Sports Program
Team Registration

Sport/Activity:_____

Team Name: _____

Team Captain: _____

Program: _____

Will you take others as spare players?

☐ Yes ☐ No

Telephone Number: _____

Email: _____

#	Signature	First Name (Print)	Surname (Print)	Student #	Phone #
1					
2					
3					
4					
5					
6					
7					
8					
9					
10					
11					
12					
13					
14					
15					

Participation in athletic and recreation activities involves the risk of personal injury. The use of equipment, facilities and premises of _____ college (The College) by persons participating in athletics and recreation activities shall constitute acceptance of that risk regardless of the nature of the injury. The College, its officers, employees and agents shall not be liable for any injury, loss or damage sustained or suffered by persons participating in athletics or recreation activities on or off college property, whether caused directly or indirectly by conditions that may be aggravated by participation in this event (Examples: epilepsy, heart conditions, joint problems, a state of poor physical fitness, etc.) should check with their physician before entering Intramural programs.

PLAYERS NOT ON TEAM ROSTERS AT TIME OF REGISTRATION MUST REGISTER WITH THE RECREATION DEPARTMENT TO BE ELIGIBLE TO PLAY.

YOUR SIGNATURE GIVES THE ATHLETIC/RECREATION DEPARTMENT PERMISSION TO VERIFY YOUR ENROLLMENT FOR ELIGIBILITY AND TABULATION OF INTRAMURAL POINTS.

OFFICE USE ONLY

DATE RECEIVED _____

AMOUNT _____

PAYMENT BY _____

OFFICE SIGNATURE

FIGURE 13.1   Intramural team sign-up sheet.

Intramural Ice Hockey Registration Form

Name: _____

Age: _____ Height: _____ Weight: _____

Phone: _____ Answering Machine: ☐ Yes ☐ No

Playing Experience

Have you ever played before: ☐ Yes ☐ No

If yes, where: _____

Position Played: Defense _____ Forward _____ Goalie _____

Any other playing experience: _____

Would you be interested in being a team captain? ☐ Yes ☐ No

If you are a goalie, do you have your own equipment? ☐ Yes ☐ No

Can you play another position if necessary? ☐ Yes ☐ No

Participation in athletic and recreation activities involves the risk of personal injury. The use of equipment, facilities and premises of _____ college (The College) by persons participating in athletics and recreation activities shall constitute acceptance of that risk regardless of the nature of the injury. The College, its officers, employees and agents shall not be liable for any injury, loss or damage sustained or suffered by persons participating in athletics or recreation activities on or off college property, whether caused directly or indirectly by conditions that may be aggravated by participation in this event (Examples: epilepsy, heart conditions, joint problems, a state of poor physical fitness, etc.) should check with their physician before entering Intramural programs.

PLAYERS NOT ON TEAM ROSTERS AT TIME OF REGISTRATION MUST REGISTER WITH THE RECREATION DEPARTMENT TO BE ELIGIBLE TO PLAY.

YOUR SIGNATURE GIVES THE ATHLETIC/RECREATION DEPARTMENT PERMISSION TO VERIFY YOUR ENROLLMENT FOR ELIGIBILITY AND TABULATION OF INTRAMURAL POINTS.

_____
Signature

FIGURE 13.2 Individual sign-up sheet for ice hockey.

of an individual registration form containing all relevant information (name, age, personal characteristics important to ice hockey such as height and weight, and contact information), including a liability waiver (see chapter 7) to warn participants of the inherent risks and protect the institution.

When individuals sign up as free agents or in the case of individual signup, as in the previous ice hockey example, they should be informed at least two days before the first play date of their team name, the location and time of the first game, and who their team captain is. (Hence the importance of getting their contact information at signup.) This communication is also a good time to answer any questions they may have. Thus, free agents and players who signed up individually should be reminded on the signup form that it is their responsibility to contact the intramural department if they have not heard anything within two days of the event or league start date. Placing the responsibility on their shoulders will prevent players from slipping through the cracks in the all-too-typically hurried and disorderly registration process.

Officials

The next item on the list is confirming that officials have been scheduled and notified of game times (with a phone call and/or schedules given to them) and that officials' schedules are posted at the event, so that everyone knows who should be officiating the games. Along with this goes making sure that copies of the rules are available for reference before and during the game. Scorecards should also be ready for the officials, as should any other items involved in officiating and scorekeeping, such as stopwatches, pens, scorecards, and whistles. If officials will be evaluated by the players (see figure 5.6 on page 81) and/or if the officials will be rating players for adherence to fair play standards (see chapters 5 and 6), be sure those evaluation sheets are also available.

A scorecard is simply a player roster with a place to keep track of the running score, as shown in figure 13.3. It contains the names, ID numbers, and emergency contact information of all players, as well as game details: the type of game being played, whether it is a league or other type of competition, date and time of game, and player contributions (goals scored and penalties received). Near the bottom of the scorecard, the winner and final score are noted, plus the names of all officials. (Also note the "safety check" checkbox at the top, as well as a place where the official responsible for the safety check can sign.) At the bottom of the scorecard, there is room for the officials to make comments about the game as well as space to record the results of the players' official evaluations (see figure 5.6). Finally, emergency procedures and/or first-aid information should be listed in case there is an injury or accident.

Promotion

Of course, if no one is aware of the event, the chance of it being a success is low. Thus, the next item on the list is making sure that promotion has been planned and that promotional materials have been distributed. The goal here is to ensure that no one is left out. It may also be helpful to review the event promotion in properly preparing for the event. For example, if promotional materials specify specific prizes to be awarded at the event, the intramural director or convener should make sure that those prizes are on hand and that the criteria for distributing them are posted and are understood by all participants. If points will be tallied and tracked for weekly, seasonal, or annual awards, necessary scorekeeping materials should also be on hand. Likewise, if the event was promoted as offering a strenuous workout, then the convener needs to make sure that the event will be physically demanding. The time of implementing the programming, the big day, is the time to outperform promotion. It is in your best interest, then, to make sure the event will live up to its hype.

In addition, be sure all the promotional vehicles used contain accurate and up-to-date information. If posters were produced months before the event but the location or time changed, for example, you will want to let participants know ahead of time. Use the intramural Web site, bulletin board(s), and other promotional vehicles to advertise the change. You may also want to print up special bulletins or announcements (distributed through student mail) or take out a special ad in the school newspaper. If other participants such as community

Scorecard

Game or activity _____

Gender: Men Women   Co-ed Open

League _____

Date _____ / _____ / _____   Time _____ a.m. p.m.

Safety check (circle one)   Yes   No

Official's name _____

Signature _____

Running Score

Home team	Visiting team
1 2 3 4 5 6 7 8 9 10 11 12 13 14 15 16 17 18 19 20 21 22 23 24 25 26 27 28 29 30 31 32 33 34 35 36 37 38 39 40 41 42 43 44 45 46 47 48 49 50 51 52 53 54 55 56 57 58 59 60 61 62 63 64 65 66 67 68 69 70 71 72 73 74 75 76 77 78 79 80 81 82 83 84 85 86 87 88 89 90 91 92 93 94 95 96 97 98 99 100	1 2 3 4 5 6 7 8 9 10 11 12 13 14 15 16 17 18 19 20 21 22 23 24 25 26 27 28 29 30 31 32 33 34 35 36 37 38 39 40 41 42 43 44 45 46 47 48 49 50 51 52 53 54 55 56 57 58 59 60 61 62 63 64 65 66 67 68 69 70 71 72 73 74 75 76 77 78 79 80 81 82 83 84 85 86 87 88 89 90 91 92 93 94 95 96 97 98 99 100

No.	Name	I.D.	Score	Penalty	No.	Name	I.D.	Score	Penalty
1					1				
2					2				
3					3				
4					4				
5					5				
6					6				
7					7				
8					8				
9					9				
10					10				
11					11				
12					12				

FIGURE 13.3 Intramural game scorecard.

No.	Name	I.D.	Score	Penalty	No.	Name	I.D.	Score	Penalty
13					13				
14					14				
15					15				
16					16				
17					17				
18					18				
19					19				
20					20				
21					21				

Winning team _____

Score _____ to _____

Officials 1 _____

          2 _____

          3 _____

Game comments: _____

_____

_____

_____

Officials' evaluations: _____

_____

_____

_____

Emergency procedures: _____

_____

_____

_____

Injuries (list and describe): _____

_____

FIGURE 13.3   (continued)

members, faculty, and alumni will be participating, you may want to take out an ad in the community newspapers and bulletins to let them know of the change.

On the other side of this item lies the chance for future promotion. If the event or activity is sure to be a hit, make sure that cameras are available to take pictures or video and make sure staff or participants have been designated to monitor the event for picture-taking opportunities. Likewise, if something noteworthy happens during the game that deserves mention in the student newspaper or later discussion, it is a good idea to have notepaper and pens on hand to jot down notes so that the details aren't forgotten.

Sponsorship and Partnership

If sponsorships or partnership arrangements have been made, it is important to make sure you are in a position to follow through. Double-check the contract or formal letter of agreement (see chapter 10) to be sure you or your institution has lived or is ready to live up to its part of the agreement. For example, is the signage proper (what was agreed to)? Have sponsor and partner logos been printed on programs and other promotional materials? Have sponsor display banners been hung?

In addition to confirming the program's adherence to the agreement, it is also important to follow up with sponsors and partners. Send a letter confirming the agreement up to a month before game day. Repeat the details of the agreement, including term of contract, sponsorship or donations agreed to, and so on. If part of the agreement will be satisfied on or after game day (e.g., product samples and awards), confirm the specifics: when products or awards should be delivered, who the intramural staff liaison is, and so on. Finally, ask that sponsors and partners acknowledge receipt of the confirmation, either with a phone call or fax. You might also consider sending the letter registered mail.

Facility and Equipment

The next item on the list is making sure facilities and equipment have been reserved and are ready to go. First, the intramural director or conveners must make sure facilities have not been double booked. For example, an intramural

event may be planned for a Friday afternoon and a large athletic event for Friday evening, but the gym needed to be closed at noon on Friday so that there would be sufficient time to prepare the facility for the athletic event that evening. These conflicts create unnecessary animosity between intramural and athletic programs, but they can be avoided by having a master schedule. It helps to have a central place to record facility bookings. This can be done using a traditional calendar or a more sophisticated computer program like Human Kinetics's Sport Director CD (2001). If the facility is off campus and is being rented, be sure to get the agreement in writing. Everyone is fallible, even a reservation clerk at a large facility. Few things are worse than arriving with busloads of students only to learn that the facility is double booked, and another group has an event already in full swing.

Once the availability of the facility has been confirmed, the facility should be checked for safety. The specifics of safety were discussed in chapters 5 and 7. Intramural staff conveners and officials should use the facility safety checklists in figures 7.6, 7.7, and 7.8 (see pages 121-123) to evaluate the safety of the facility.

Finally, the proper equipment must be ready and in good condition to play with. Practice balls or other equipment should be counted and then distributed to players for pre-game practice; when returned before the start of the game, practice equipment should be returned and counted again. Game balls should be given to the officials to care for until game time. If equipment needs cleaning, although it should have been cleaned before storage, clean it before or during (if alternate equipment is available) practice time. (Following the game, all equipment should be cleaned and properly stored.) If equipment needs repair (and wasn't spotted at the end of the last game or practice), it should be put to the side and brought to the attention of the appropriate staff. (Also see discussion on equipment inventory in chapter 10.)

Other Necessities

Last on the list are other event- or activity-specific necessities that should be handled. These, obviously, will vary according to the type of activity or event being offered. If the event will be held after regular school hours, for example, be sure security and janitorial personnel are notified. They may need to unlock rooms that are normally locked and may need to rearrange their clean-up schedule or provide extra services. If the event will be held outdoors at night, lighting may need to be set up. And so on. Basically, this item on the list is the catchall: anything that has been planned should be double-checked, and any last-minute details should be nailed down.

Setup

On the day of the activity or event, it is a good idea not to leave things to the last minute. It often takes longer to set things up than one would expect. Get to the facility early and have sufficient staff on hand to make sure the activity or event will start on time. The following sections explain who does what to set up an event or activity.

Staff and Volunteers

It will largely be the program staff's or volunteers' responsibility to make sure the event is ready to go. These staff members will need to make sure that the facility is open, the equipment is ready to be used, the officials are present, and the event starts on time. Once the event is rolling, these or other staff members will need to supervise, making sure the event runs smoothly and is run in such a way that it will support the mission of the intramural program. This, of course, may require some problem solving as situations develop.

As mentioned earlier in this chapter, program staff should be responsible for obtaining and distributing copies of game rules. Rules should be given to officials as well as team captains and posted prominently at the event. Program staff who will be attending the event should also keep a copy in case a question arises.

Officials

Depending on the type of game, officials should arrive at least 15 minutes prior to game time. Usually 15 minutes will be enough time to perform setup duties. As explained in chapter 5, these duties include

▶ checking the facility (see figures 7.6, 7.7, and 7.8 on pages 121-123) and equipment to make sure it is ready and safe;

▶ double check that necessary score sheets (see figure 13.3 for an example of a scorecard) are on hand;

▶ checking with minor officials to be sure everyone is clear on the rules and is knowledgeable enough to complete the necessary forms;

▶ observing the warm-ups to get a feel for participants' skill levels, their perceived importance of the game, and any tension that might exist between opponents;

▶ calling team captains together to explain last-minute details (such as special rules or game modifications), to remind them about the mission of intramurals, and to alert them about when the time will start; and

▶ meeting with other officials to delineate responsibilities.

Team Captains

As listed in the previous section, team captains should meet with officials before the game to go over special rules and game modifications. In addition, team captains should

▶ make sure all team members are present before a game;

▶ repeat officials' instructions, including game details and rule changes, to all team members;

▶ encourage their teammates to adhere to safety and fair play rules and standards (they should also monitor their teammates for this adherence during the game); and

▶ promote and courage the spirit of intramurals, including the program mission.

Sign-In

When players show up, they should be checked off on the official participant roster. This roster can be printed up separately or simply a copy of the team or individual registration/signup sheet. Better yet, have students place a checkmark "4" next to their names, indicating that they plan to participate. You can add a column on the team signup sheet (see figure 7.3 on page 112) and registration form (see figure 13.1 on page 217) for students to check. Place this column next to the to the signature columns to remind them that they have agreed to the waiver. Or, to keep things simple and eliminate unnecessary paperwork, use figure 13.3 (see page 220) to sign in players as they arrive.

Last-Minute Signup/Registration

The more formal the event or activity, the more problematic last-minute registration. In free activities and informal events, students can sign up right to the last minute. If an informal chicken toss is being held with grade 3 students at noon, anyone who shows up at that time can participate. In team and formal or competitive events, when participants must be assigned to a team or be paired against opponents of similar ability, however, last-minute signups create chaos.

Still, it is better to allow last-minute registration so that no-shows do not result in game cancellation. (No-shows are discussed later in this chapter.) The cancellation or delay of games and activities is extremely frustrating for participants who showed up on time and will do nothing to help the intramural program. Say, for example, a volleyball match is scheduled. All 10 members of one team show up and are ready to play, but only five members of the opposing team are there by game time. Rather than cancel the game (and require the five-player team to forfeit) or modify the game to four-player volleyball, or modify the game to six-player volleyball and require two teammates from the other team to play for their opponents (one player and one substitute)—this would certainly be an unpopular option if the game was competitive or part of a league!—last-minute signups could be used and the game could be played. In the case of a competitive match or league play, you might give the five-player team the option of rescheduling or forfeiting the game if they grouse about having to use last-minute signups.

Problem Solving

No matter how well organized an intramural activity or event, problems will crop up. Program staff can plan for the predictable and some of the more common situations, but they will still have to solve other problems as they arise. In

the event of an injury, for example, an emergency action plan should be in place (see chapter 7). What happens if severe weather happens before or during an event? (Also see chapter 7.) Or what if players get their signals crossed and, following an old play schedule, show up a half-hour (or day) after game time? Or what do you do if participants complain about the scoring? Scheduling problems, no-shows, scoring, and suspensions are discussed in the following sections.

Less-common problems will require creative, wisdom, and fast thinking. For example, what should be done if there is an electrical problem and half the gym lights don't turn on? What happens if a referee does not show up? What happens if you left your keys at home and you cannot get the equipment out of a locked equipment room. Clearly, it would be an exercise in frustration to plan ahead for such occurrences. For one thing, these situations are rare. For another, there is no set answer or best solution for every situation. These types of problems will have to be solved at the playing site when the problem occurs.

Scheduling Problems

Because student's schedules vary, particularly at the collegiate level, some institutions try to avoid scheduling problems by forming intradepartmental leagues. This method of organization is helpful because students in certain programs have similar breaks and testing periods in their schedules. If no nursing classes are offered Wednesday afternoons, for example, nursing majors will likely be available at that time. Perhaps the engineering faculty are scheduled to meet every Monday morning. That will likely mean engineering students will be available then. Trying to schedule competitions between these two departments would be difficult, to say the least. If nursing students had a league of their own on Wednesday afternoons and engineering had a league of their own on Monday mornings, however, most entries would be able to make their games. Then, at the end of league play, winners from each department could compete in a tournament to determine the school champion.

Defaults and Forfeits

As introduced in chapter 1, there can be confusion when it comes to defaults and forfeits. For our purposes, a **default** is when a team declares ahead of time that it is unable to be present at the scheduled time of their game. Defaults result when a team notifies the intramural office (or league convener) ahead of time (usually 48 hours but up to a full week in advance) that it will be unable to play in the game. Advance notice enables appropriate staff to contact opponents and officials, thereby saving them the trouble of showing up for nothing.

Forfeits, on the other hand, are more severe. A **forfeit** occurs if a team does not show at the time of the event and has not given adequate advance notice. Sometimes intramural programs allow teams a 10-minute grace period. Because this is often abused (teams do not show up until eight or nine minutes after game time), however, it is common to have a "game time is forfeit time" policy. Meaning, if all (or enough) players are not present when the clock starts, that team forfeits the game. A team using an ineligible player (someone who is not a student, or a member of a different team) also forfeits the game.

Defaults and forfeits can pose a problem from time to time, depending on the institution and situation. Sometimes defaults and forfeits are due to lack of player commitment, but other times (particularly around midterms and finals) school and students' schedules make it impossible to meet their commitments. Players should be encouraged toward defaults and away from forfeits. One way to do this is with the use of monetary penalties.

At many institutions, league entries are required to post a bond when they register. Individual entries typically pay smaller bonds than team entries, both because teammates can pool their money to come up with the bond and because more people means more chances for no-shows. Then, if entries forfeit a game, they lose half of that bond. If they forfeit two games, they lose the entire bond and are removed from the league. (Forfeits are not usually a problem in tournaments because a tournament lasts only one or two days.) If entries show up for every game, the bond is returned in its entirety, although some institutions retain a certain percentage of the bond as an administrative fee. If the bond was $50 and 20 percent ($10) was retained for administration, for example, then entries would lose $20 for each game they forfeited. A portion of the bond may also be withheld if the team captain (in the case of team entries) is not present at team captains' meetings, or if entries have disciplinary action taken against them (e.g., for violent conduct).

The amount of these bonds varies, but bonds typically range from $20 to $75 per entry. In ice hockey leagues, where ice time must be rented, the bond can be as high as $200 per team. Some intramural directors avoid the bond altogether and simply remove forfeiting entries from the league—assuming, of course, that schedules are posted ahead of time (usually within the first two weeks of the league)—and produce new schedules after every forfeit. Clearly, this option is more time consuming, in terms of revising and posting new schedules. Thus, it is probably a good idea to give entries one "warning forfeit" before throwing them out of the league.

Scoring

Because fairness is such an integral part of intramural programming, it is best to think about and plan for scoring problems ahead of time. A scoring system that over emphasizes winning would be a problem for an intramural program whose purpose is mass participation. However, a scoring system that overemphasizes participation may be a disincentive for players to come out, since they feel there is inadequate attention given to competition. Developing a scoring system is a balancing act between rewarding competitive performance and participation. There are different options for scoring the outcome of a game, contest, match, or other competitive event. The three most common ways are listed below. The first focuses purely on the score and the final two focus on participation.

Scoring option 1: Points system. The first option for scoring the outcome of a contest focuses exclusively on the score. This scoring method provides an incentive to win and not to forfeit but does not provide an incentive for participation. Participation is, of course, a large part of what intramurals is about. Points-system scoring is as follows:

Win	3 points
Tie	2 points
Loss	1 point
Forfeit	2 to 0 points

Scoring option 2: Participation system. This method is similar to the points system but emphasizes participation by adding one point for every member that comes out for the event. This scoring is as follows:

Win	5 points
Tie	3 points
Loss	1 point
Forfeit	1 point
Participation	1 point per participant

If the wining team (win = 5 points) in a basketball game has only five players show up for the game (1 point per participant = 5 points), for example, the team would get a total of 10 points. If the opposing team had all 10 players (1 point per participant = 10 points) show up but nevertheless lost (loss = 1 point), that team would get a total of 11 points. This method encourages some healthy competition by awarding more points for a win, but it places significant value on participation. Of course, the size of teams should be limited so that everyone gets to play and participation points are fair to everyone.

Scoring option 3: Sportsmanship system. The third way to score competitive matches is to use either option 1 or option 2 and then add bonus points for the team that best demonstrates sportsmanship rules and standards (see chapter 6). Sportsmanship bonus points are either awarded by the referee or attending official, or are given to the teams with the fewest penalties

The Spirit of the Game

"The new Sports Centre was created to encourage students to be active and increase their well-being by being healthy, having fun, and relaxing in a safe environment. The leagues will follow this same rule. It focuses on participation and fair play while maintaining a competitive spirit. Students often play in a strained environment where their only focus is victory. That environment becomes more enjoyable when the focus is shifted to fun and relaxation.

"We have taken some measures to ensure that the competitive spirit remains moderate. They include a points system. . . .

Points for competition (9 points maximum)

- ▶ Win — 3 points per meet (a total of 3 meets)
- ▶ Tie — 2 points
- ▶ Loss — 1 point
- ▶ Forfeit — 0 point

"Points for fair play (9 points maximum)

- ▶ Participation (4 points maximum per meet). One half-point per attendance. The player is not considered present if he/she arrives after the first game.
- ▶ Attitude (5 points maximum per meet). One point lost per major penalty or misconduct.

"Bonus points
Players have the opportunity to win bonus points. An impartial jury will award points to the teams having the best costumes, the best college yell, and best team choreography during a theme week (Halloween during the fall term, and Valentine's Day during the winter term)" (Dion 2001).

Reprinted by permission of the Canadian Intramural Recreation Association. From E. Dion, 2001, "Spirit and game philosophy," *CIRA Bulletin* 26 (3):4.

in the game (Tower 1995). Each team earns bonus points according their adherence to sportsmanship rules and standards using the scale listed here (although it can be modified according to the number of teams or players participating).

Excellent	3 points
Very Good	2 points
Acceptable	1 point
Unacceptable	0 points
Poor	1 point

Suspensions

Players and teams can be suspended for a variety of reasons. Intramural directors typically suspend players, and an entire team in some cases, if they get involved in a fight. Likewise, suspensions can result from harassing another player, team, or official. Suspensions, while unpopular with players, are meant to enforce the spirit of fair play (see chapter 6) and protect everyone's right to participate.

Because players will likely object to and may even argue against being suspended, it is wise to have formal suspension procedures in place. This includes having a formal fair play policy, which players are required to read before participating, as well as devising suspension criteria and formal suspension procedures. Players who are suspended should receive a notification of suspension outlining the incident and their infraction or violation, the length of their suspension (including the date said suspension will be lifted), and any other necessary comments, as shown in figure13.4. Comments might include certain actions players can take to shorten the suspension, such as attending an anger-management class, and when the suspension will be lifted if those actions are taken.

From the time of suspension notification, students should be given the right to protest a suspension. Suspended players with qualifying grievances are generally given 24 hours after receiving notice. For grievances to qualify, students' appeals must involve misinterpretation of game rules and regulations (not an official's or referee's judgment), and questions of player eligibility.

Chapter Summary Exercises

As explained in this chapter, there are lots of details that can contribute to the overall success of an event or activity and, thus, can help to satisfy mission of the intramural program. Complete the following three exercises to apply these little details to your intramural program.

1. Develop a signup system. Prepare complete forms that you would use for team and individual signup. Describe how you will deal with free agents.

2. Come up with a way to deal with defaults and forfeits. For example, will you impose automatic forfeits? Will you allow a 10-minute grace period? Will you institute a policy of forfeits and defaults? Outline your policy and state your rationale.

3. Develop a scoring system for your events. Will you use the points system, the participation system, or the fair play system? Or can you come up with a different system that will better satisfy your mission?

References

Dion, E. 2001. Spirit and game philosophy. *CIRA Bulletin* 26 (3): 4.

Human Kinetics. 2001. Sport director. [CD.] Champaign, IL: Human Kinetics.

Tower, A. 1995. Consider a "spirit of competition" and a rating system for your intramural-recreation programs. *NIRSA Journal* 20 (1): 46-47.

Resources

Rice University
www.ruf.rice.edu

Offers a good example of free agent signup and other policies (see www.ruf.rice.edu/~ims/freeagent.html) as well as an effective way to list available free agents and implement other policies (see www.ruf.rice.edu/~ims/agents00.html).

University of Western Ontario
www.uwo.ca/campusrec/

Offers another example of how to deal with free agents and implement other policies. Use the "search the site" button and type in "free agents."

Suspension Notice

To:_____

Student ID: _____

cc: Disciplinary committee
   Intramural committee
   Team captain

From:_____

Date: _____

Activity or event: _____

Description of the incident:

_____

_____

_____

_____

Incident witnessed by:

_____

Incident reported by:

_____

Length of suspension:

Starting _____ at _____ o'clock

Ending _____ at _____ o'clock

Comments:

_____

_____

_____

FIGURE 13.4   Suspension notification form.

Evaluation

After all is said and done, the mission identified and stated, staff and volunteers and officials hired and trained, the programming and awards planned and promoted with care, the policies defined and written, the budget determined, and the "day of" details nailed down and dealt with, it is finally time to complete the last step in the process of creating an effective intramural program. Now you need to know if it all worked.

In evaluating the program, there are several questions to ask. Questions such as: What successes can be celebrated? Should the same event(s) occur again? What can be improved for next year (or the next season)? These questions, which constitute the bulk of the evaluation process, will be discussed in this chapter.

Chapter Objectives

▶ Understand the importance of evaluation.
▶ Learn the key components of effective evaluation.
▶ Explore various methods of program evaluation.
▶ Explore various methods of activity and event evaluation.

The Evaluation Process

Basically, the process of intramural evaluation includes five steps: (1) considering the mission and goals of an intramural program, (2) looking at the results, (3) measuring the difference between intention and reality, (4) explaining the differences, and (5) considering revision to either the mission or the implementation of the intramural program. This is the process of formal evaluation, which constitutes the bulk of this chapter, but informal evaluation is also useful in many situations. As defined in chapter 4, formal evaluation is the systematic collection of data for the purposes of measuring performance and making improvements—in this case, to the intramural program. Informal evaluation is the nonsystematic collection of data for the purposes of measuring performance and making improvements to the intramural program.

Informal evaluation occurs at many different levels and in many different ways. It happens when the aerobics instructor senses that the pace of the class is too fast and slows down to accommodate the participants. It occurs when the head official notices that officials are missing or having difficulty making some calls and holds a training meeting. And it happens when the intramural director glances at the schedule and has the feeling that there are not enough events to hold students' interest and, thus, starts planning more. In each of these three cases, data was collected in a nonsystematic manner (sensing, noticing, glancing), performance was measured (too fast, missing calls, and not enough), and adjustments were made or considered (slowing down, holding a meeting, and planning more events). This ongoing informal evaluation is very important to the success of an intramural program. In fact, it is crucial. All program leaders need to constantly evaluate and make adjustments where appropriate, or at least consider making those adjustments.

Formal evaluation should also be conducted to ensure the success and well-being of an intramural program. By definition, formal evaluation is more structured and, thus, more thorough than informal evaluation. Indeed, even the evaluation instruments themselves are evaluated in formal evaluation. To ensure a complete, thorough, and accurate formal evaluation, the first step is collecting all relevant information.

Information Gathering

Programs can be evaluated externally or internally. External evaluation typically involves hiring professionals and experts from outside the institution. These experts can be consultants who specialize in intramural programming and programs, or they can be colleagues from other institutions with a comparable intramural program. Either way, someone from the outside looking in brings greater objectivity and a fresh perspective to an evaluation.

Internal evaluation is typically conducted by intramural directors and staff. This type of evaluation is just as useful, if not more useful, than external evaluation. Why? Because those working on the front lines have the most access to information.

The sources of information available to intramural directors and staff are many and varied, from the program participants themselves to computerized participation tracking overseen by an intramural administrator. Some institutions place intramural suggestion boxes around campus and near the intramural office so that students can randomly make suggestions or raise concerns about intramural programming. Institutions that have an intramural Web site often provide online suggestion boxes so that students can vent their frustrations and make positive suggestions. While this information is always helpful, however, frustrations usually constitute the bulk of it. Thus, this type of information will not necessarily represent the feelings of all participants but perhaps only those who are frustrated at something.

Important information can be gathered from various sources. Numeric participation statistics can be gained by counting the number of teams and individuals participating in an event. Some of this numeric analysis also goes on at an informal level by (1) watching attendance, defaults, and forfeits, and (2) trying to determine why attendance is at the level it is, and why defaults and forfeits are increasing or decreasing. These numbers can be compared to previous years' statistics to determine any patterns.

Meetings and discussion groups are also helpful. These meetings can be very informal, such as going to the school cafeteria, sitting with a group of students you do not know, and asking them if they are willing to discuss their concerns and suggestions for the intramural program. These meeting can also be a little more focused by inviting select member from teams (perhaps team captains) to evaluate a program or a portion of a program such as officiating, promotion, sign-ip procedures, or general administration of a league/tournament.

Some methods will be more accessible to some intramural directors than to others, of course, given budget, time, and other constraints. The most effective method of information gathering that will be accessible to all intramural directors is **polling**, which for our purposes is simply asking specific questions to get feedback, suggestions, opinions, answers, and so on for purpose of evaluation. Polling can be conducted over the phone, via E-mail and listservs, on the program Web site, in face-to-face meetings, and with questionnaires, surveys, and evaluation forms. A sample of each is provided at the end of this chapter. These surveys can be adapted for use in meetings, phone interviews, E-mail surveys, and so on.

When gathering information, there are two components to consider: (1) who to approach for the information and how to approach them, and (2) what information to get. One of the most important sources is the student body, the primary participant group. Other important sources of information are staff and volunteers. These groups and the type of information they can contribute are discussed in the following sections.

Participants

To get information that is representative of participants' feelings about and views on intramurals, a systematic approach is required. Students should be polled from time to time during the semester and at the end of each activity, event, tournament and league. As most people do, students appreciate being asked for their input. It makes them feel valued, and when decisions are based on that input, they feel acknowledged and respected. All students can be asked to complete an evaluation form or questionnaire, or a sample of participants can be approached to save the cost of printing and distributing hundreds (if not thousands) of questionnaires and to save time in having to count and evaluate them.

To get a random sample, try giving an evaluation form to every fifth participant listed in the intramural directory or every fourth player on intramural team and league lists. If you want a more selective sample, you could limit the polling to team captains or one representative from each team. When limiting the amount of data you collect, be sure to have at least one representative from each team or competitive unit complete an evaluation.

The types of information participants can offer vary from program to program and from participant to participant. The following areas should be addressed in participant polling, whatever the vehicle may be (questionnaires, Web site surveys, and so on):

1. Programming
   ▶ Are participants satisfied with activities and events?
   ▶ Are activities and events run well?
   ▶ If given the chance, what programming would participants add or remove? What would they change?
   ▶ If last-minute problems occur, do event and conveners know what to do?

2. Budget
   ▶ Is the cost of activities reasonable?
   ▶ Is there something that the intramural department should be spending more money on?
   ▶ Is there something that the intramural department should be spending less money on?

3. Promotion
   ▶ Do participants know about activities and events? Enough ahead of time?
   ▶ Are promotional materials clear and understandable? Do they inspire participants to get involved?
   ▶ Is the program Web site useful?

4. Awards and prizes
   ▶ Are the intramural awards and prizes positive incentives for wholesome participation in intramural events?
   ▶ What parts of the intramural program should awards and prizes be added to?
   ▶ What current awards and prizes should be improved? How?

▶ What current awards and prizes should be diminished in importance? How?

5. Officials

▶ Are officials effective?

▶ Are they objective and fair?

▶ Do they contribute to the fun of the activity or event, or do they strictly enforce the rules?

6. Mission

▶ Do participants know what the intramural mission is?

▶ Do the intramural department and activities represent and fulfill that mission?

▶ What should be the prime goals of intramurals?

7. Tournaments and leagues

▶ Is the structure effective?

▶ Is it fair?

▶ Does the schedule work?

8. Leadership

▶ Are program staff helpful and informative?

▶ Are they available?

▶ Are they well informed about the activities and events?

9. Policies

▶ Do participants know about the program policies?

▶ Are they fair?

▶ Which areas of intramurals should have policies to encourage broader and more postive participation?

Staff

Staff can also provide important feedback on the intramural program, especially if they complete an evaluation of their own areas of responsibility. Staff should submit reports at the end of each school year as well as after each event, league season, ongoing activity, and so on. These reports should include some input from participants (what staff members have heard or observed during activities and events) but also each staff member's own observations and recommendations for the next event or year. These recommendations are important because they

may help to identify procedures that will improve the event or program the next time around.

In addition, staff reports should include the following:

▶ Description of the activity or event (facility; league, tournament, or other; whether it was a women's, men's, coed, or open event, and so on)

▶ Length of the event or activity

▶ Total number of participants

▶ Successes (things that went well)

▶ Failures (major problems)

▶ Difficulties (minor problems)

▶ Injuries

▶ Suspensions that resulted (and appeals/protests made)

▶ Changes made this year based on last year's recommendations (did those changes work?)

▶ Recommendations for next year

▶ Additional comments

Finally, staff should also be asked about their job satisfaction. Remember, part of creating or running an effective intramural program is keeping staff happy. Poll staff members about the following areas:

▶ Management and supervision

▶ Compensation

▶ Schedules and time management in the department

▶ Workload

▶ Working climate between members of the intramural staff

▶ Ideas for improving staff performance and enjoyment

▶ Staff training suggestions

▶ Innovative ideas to improve the intramural program

▶ Competency in dealing with emergencies

Officials

Officials, of course, are in the middle of the action. Thus, their input will be valuable—perhaps more valuable than that of participants. Particularly in the grade and high school settings, officials will likely be more mature and/or objective, and they may have expertise from officiating other intramural activities and events at your school or at other institutions. In addition, officials are the intramural staff who are probably most aware of the fair play and safety policies and procedures. Thus, they should be polled frequently for feedback and information on these components of the intramural program.

As outlined in previous chapters, scorecards and game sheets should include areas for officials to note their comments. Should they have additional concerns or feedback, intramural directors and staff should maintain and communicate an "open door" policy, where officials (and other participants, staff, and volunteers) can come to talk at any time. In addition, you may want to develop specific official surveys and questionnaires that report on the following:

- Officiating competency
- Officials ability to relate with participants, spectators, and colleagues
- Suggestions for improving officiating
- Clarity of rules and policies
- Adequate support for officials from administration

Volunteers

Volunteers typically participate in a program because they agree with the mission of the program and want to contribute to that mission. Their input is valuable in terms of improving the intramural program and enhancing volunteers' experiences. Both formally and informally they need to be asked about the program:

- How do they feel intramurals is going?
- Are there areas that need improvements?
- Are there areas that are outstanding?

In terms of their own experience, they need to be asked:

- Are you satisfied with your intramural experience? Why?
- Were you adequately prepared and trained for the volunteer work you do?
- Are there ways the intramural program can make the volunteer experience more positive?

Others

The main source of other information comes from parents. Students typically share the highlights of their school day with their parents (both the high experiences and the low experiences). If parents do not hear anything positive from their children about intramurals, then either the program is not very exciting, or the children of the parents you are contacting do not participate in intramural programs, or the parents are not aware of which programs and events are sponsored and run through intramurals. If the parents do not report on any low experiences, then either your program is doing well or their children do not participate in the program. It is helpful to ask parents the following questions.

- Do you know if your child participates in the intramural program?
- What are some of the positive things you hear about school lunch and recess activities?
- What are some of the negative things you hear about school lunch and recess activities?
- What skills or sponsorship could you contribute to the intramural program?

Evaluation Criteria

Armed with the information you've gotten by polling participants, officials, volunteers and staff, and others involved in intramurals, now it is time to use that information to evaluate your program. Whether you are evaluating the entire intramural program or specific activities and events, the evaluation criteria are essentially the same. The only difference is that event or activity evaluation should be specifically related to that program or activity, whereas program evaluation should encompass all activities and events as well as each component of an intramural program discussed in this book.

The following key questions are geared toward an overall program evaluation, but each can be fine-tuned to apply to the evaluation of an activity or event.

- Is the intramural mission being satisfied?
- Has the program stayed within budget?

- ▶ Could more revenue be raised?
- ▶ Is participation high?
- ▶ Is participation inclusive?
- ▶ Are promotions effective?
- ▶ Are intramural policies and procedures working well?
- ▶ Are sport and activity rules effective?
- ▶ Have there been any injuries?
- ▶ How can safety be improved?
- ▶ Is fair play evidenced throughout the program?
- ▶ Do officials handle players satisfactorily?
- ▶ Is the programming calendar effective?
- ▶ Are employees happy in their jobs?
- ▶ Are people volunteering to help out?
- ▶ Are officials satisfied with the program?
- ▶ Are last-minute problems bogging down events and activities?

Going through these questions, a pattern begins to emerge. The best way to evaluate an intramural program is to revisit each component of the program, one at a time. Here are the steps of evaluating an intramural program.

Step 1. Revisit mission. Look back at the purpose or mission of the intramural program. If the program mission emphasizes fun, then one of the program characteristics to evaluate is whether all those involved—the participants as well as staff, volunteers, and officials—are indeed having fun. Likewise, if the mission emphasizes mass participation, consider the total student population and determine the participation ratio. If participation is high and/or growing, that means you're achieving your mission. If participation has dropped however, you'll need to determine the cause and what can be done to change this negative trend. The key in this step is knowing your mission and measuring all program components accordingly.

Step 2. Revisit budget. Examine the financial records to determine whether you ended up with a balanced, surplus, or deficit budget. Then look at each activity or event budget and compare revenue to expenses to determine which programs made money and which ones lost money. Finally, evaluate the budgeting process itself to determine if any improvements

can be made. For example, are tournament conveners aware of how much money they are able to spend? Does the convener know what to do when registration fees are given to her (or should conveners accept no money and direct all payments to a specific person) and how she will pay for things such as officials and prizes? Are those people who are in charge of budgets aware of the components of a budget?

Step 3. Revisit fair play. Look at your participation and leadership statistics. Intramurals should be for everyone, regardless of gender, age, race, skin color, and so on. It is important here to consider typically underrepresented populations as well. For example, are girls coming out for football? Are boys coming out for aerobics? Are African Americans coming out for hockey? Determine how you can include these groups in all activities. Likewise, you need to consider sportsmanship. Are participants getting in fights regularly? Is the spirit of play present at all games and contests, or are players trying to win regardless of the cost? Sportsmanship is such an important aspect of intramurals that it must be considered carefully when evaluating the program. It is not simply the respect participants show for the rules, officials, and each other, although that is a significant part of it. It is also the spirit of play and fun that must be communicated and perceived throughout the program.

Step 4. Revisit promotion. Consider your promotional campaigns for various events as well as the intramural program itself. Are the promotional vehicles you are using effective? Are you generating a lot of interest and traffic at the intramural office? Are students regularly stopping at the intramural bulletin board or surfing the Web site to see what's going on? It is a good idea to keep copies of all promotional materials, including posters, signs, announcements, videos, and so on. That way, when you're evaluating promotion, you can evaluate the materials themselves. Perhaps a poster, for example, was visually appealing but didn't contain the necessary details about an event. In other words, it was nice to look at but did little to increase participation or interest in the program. It may also be a good idea to get some staff and participants together to evaluate these materials at a year- or season-end meeting.

Hockey Could Learn From Intramurals

"In light of all the discussions over the state of hockey in our country, it is interesting how often I've heard, 'We have to put the FUN back into the game.' Competition, winning, more games, quick advancement, parental pressure, $$$, $$$, and more $$$ seem to be at the root of the problems related to our national winter game.

"As I think about hockey and the challenges facing the sport, I can't help but self-evaluate my intramural program from last year.

▶ Competition was downplayed and in its place was more participation. Scores were seldom kept since the emphasis was on fun and the object of all games was to 'score, not to keep score.'

▶ Winning became a secondary issue. The real issue was to produce an atmosphere of FUN. No one advanced or was eliminated. Participants only returned for more of the same FUN.

▶ All ages, genders, and cultures were included in the program. No one was excluded.

▶ The kids told their parents what a blast they were having during lunch hours in the gym. They couldn't wait for their next hour of FUN.

▶ Intramurals were FREE fun.

"Ah! Another passing grade. The state of intramurals at John Darling Public School is healthy. Everyone likes to have FUN. Fun in your programs overcomes ALL obstacles" (Doyle 1999).

Reprinted by permission of the Canadian Intramural Recreation Association—Ontario. From P. Doyle, 1999, "Hockey could learn from intramurals," *INPUT* 18 (8):2.

Step 5. Revisit policies. If there were problems during the past year, did the policies and procedures help to deal with them effectively? Or were too few participants and staff aware of them? Such problems may have to do with harassment, inclusion, and safety. If there were several "special circumstances" or situations that were more specific than the policies you have in place, you may need to broaden your policies to apply to all situations.

Step 6. Revisit rules. This step is fairly specific, more so than the other steps so far, but it is important. You will need to know if game, activity, and event rules were effective. In some cases, the rules themselves are fine but the problem may have been in communicating those rules to the participants. In other cases, the rules may need revision. Perhaps they need to be spelled out in more detail. Or perhaps a demonstration is in order, as is often the case in new sports and activities or when lots of new students sign up.

Step 7. Revisit safety. The main question when evaluating safety is, of course, Were there any injuries? The natural follow-up question: If so, what was the cause? The safety of participants is of utmost importance in intramurals and should be considered carefully. Evaluate every program component that may affect safety. For example, are officials doing their jobs? Are officials, team captains, and event staff apprised of and trained in basic medical care and program safety procedures? Is the competitive nature of games causing injuries? If so, should the focus be switched from winning to having fun? Are the mission and promotion and rules communicating this?

Step 8. Revisit programming. This step involves the evaluation of not only the specific events and activities, including leagues and tournaments, but also the programming calendar itself. A poorly attended event may be a good event, but it may need to be offered at a different time of year or a different time of day. Look at the types of activities offered and when they were held. Also, consider the length of time devoted to each activity. Was it sufficient? Finally, look at the entire programming schedule. Are activities and events diverse enough to achieve high participation for the entire program? Are students' needs and wishes being met?

Step 9. Revisit leadership. The last step in the evaluation process is looking at yourself and your employees. How are you doing as a manager? Are staff and volunteers satisfied in their work? Does the departmental structure help or hinder your mission? How effective are staff and conveners? Do things in the office run smoothly, or are staff members constantly rushing to put out fires? Do event and program details slip through the cracks, or does everything get done in an orderly, relaxed fashion? What is the mood in the intramural office? If your program relies on volunteer help, do you have an adequate pool of candidates wanting to join the team, or are you left shorthanded throughout the year? Finally, look at the official component of your program. Are officials satisfied with their intramural experiences? Are participants satisfied with them?

Sample Evaluation Forms

Now that you understand the evaluation process, including where to gather information as well as what should be evaluated, it is time to look specifically at different types of evaluation forms. Many institutions post these forms online for participants, staff, volunteers, officials, and so on to complete on their own time. This works extremely well. Online evaluation forms are effective not only because they are easy to assemble and update but also because they are easy to tally and assess, assuming you have the software to do that (see "Resources" at the end of this chapter). If the intramural department is not yet online, however, evaluation forms can also be printed and handed out. To help you create an effective evaluation form, the rest of this section is devoted to the topic, including several examples of different types of evaluation forms.

Figure 14.1 shows a questionnaire that would be useful in a high school setting, either mid year or at the end of the school year. It asks students—both those who participate and those who do not—to describe their involvement in

intramurals. Those who participate are asked which activities they most enjoy. Those who do not participate are asked why. Finally, students are asked for their suggestions on improving the intramural program, including specific activities they would like to see added or dropped. This type of questionnaire, then, should be distributed to all students, not just intramural participants. It is important to understand non-participants if we want to include them in the program.

Angela Lumpkin, dean of education at West Georgia State University and the author of several books on Physical Education and sport, and Samuel Halstead (1995), have come up with a simple survey that could be used to analyze the program in general or specific components of the intramural program, shown in figure 14.2. Primarily composed of statements participants can agree or disagree with, its main focus is determining the degree of participant satisfaction with the program. The statements on this survey are more general in nature, but they can be made specific fairly easily. If you were interested in a specific activity like a basketball league, for example, you could simply replace "intramurals" with "basketball league" or a similar modification. Likewise, to determine specific demographics, questions about gender, marital status, ethnicity, grade level, level of intramural involvement, and any other relevant questions could be added to the bottom.

Figure 14.3 shows the third and final sample evaluation. Adapted from a format used by Jim Kestner in *Program Evaluation for Sport Directors* (1996), this evaluation form seeks more specific information than the survey in figure 14.2. Rather than being asked to classify their degree of agreement, individuals are asked to circle either "yes," "no," or "not sure." Tabulating the results of this type of survey, then, is a bit simpler. So is the process of filling it out. To make sure that respondents are able to provide more information if they wish, each statement has room for comments or further explanation.

Chapter Summary Exercises

This chapter explained the importance and process of the last component of an effective intramural program: evaluation. To help you build formal evaluation into your program, the following exercises will get you started on that process.

Intramural Survey

Please answer the following questions as best as you can.

1. Grade: _____

2. Sex: ☐ Female ☐ Male

3. Do you participate in intramurals? ☐ Yes ☐ No

If you answered no to #3, please explain why and then go to question 4.

_____

_____

If you answered yes to #3, how many times did you participate in intramurals during the past four months?

☐ 1-10 times ☐ 11-20 times ☐ 21+ times

If you answered yes to #3, which activities did you enjoy the most? _____

_____

4. Do you feel that the intramural department offers an activity for everyone? ☐ Yes ☐ No

Explain: _____

_____

What activities would you like to see added and which would you like to see dropped?

Please add   Please drop

_____   _____

_____   _____

How do you think we can improve intramurals at our school? _____

_____

_____

FIGURE 14.1 Sample intramural program questionnaire.

1. Develop a participant evaluation tool that will help you assess the success of a particular activity or event. Create the questionnaire and describe the method of distributing and collecting it.

2. Review this chapter's section on information gathering and list three types of evaluation that will be effective for your program. If the budget is low and you don't have an intramural Web site, for example, online surveys are probably not an option. Likewise, if most students are participating in intramurals, face-to-face interviews would probably be more time consuming than effective.

3. Using your three evaluation methods from number 2, list the pros and cons of each method in surveying participants, staff, and officials.

4. Review the evaluation criteria discussed in this chapter and the sample evaluations in figures 14.1, 14.2, and 14.3. Design a program questionnaire for one of the following groups:

Intramural Survey

For each question or statement below, please check the appropriate box.

1. How did you learn about intramurals? (Check one.)
   - ☐ Physical education class
   - ☐ Program publicity
   - ☐ Intramural staff
   - ☐ Communication with students
   - ☐ Other (please specify) _____

2. Indoor facilities are adequate for intramurals. (Check one.)
   - ☐ Strongly agree
   - ☐ Agree
   - ☐ No opinion
   - ☐ Disagree
   - ☐ Strongly disagree

3. Outdoor facilities are adequate for intramurals.
   - ☐ Strongly agree
   - ☐ Agree
   - ☐ No opinion
   - ☐ Disagree
   - ☐ Strongly disagree

4. Intramural competitions are well organized.
   - ☐ Strongly agree
   - ☐ Agree
   - ☐ No opinion
   - ☐ Disagree
   - ☐ Strongly disagree

5. Intramural activities and events are managed competently.
   - ☐ Strongly agree
   - ☐ Agree
   - ☐ No opinion
   - ☐ Disagree
   - ☐ Strongly disagree

6. Management levels (competency) of student personnel in intramurals are appropriate.
   - ☐ Strongly agree
   - ☐ Agree
   - ☐ No opinion
   - ☐ Disagree
   - ☐ Strongly disagree

7. Recognition of efforts and accomplishments in intramurals is adequate and appropriate.
   - ☐ Strongly agree
   - ☐ Agree
   - ☐ No opinion
   - ☐ Disagree
   - ☐ Strongly disagree

Adapted, by permission, from J. Kestner, 1996, *Program evaluation for sports directors* (Champaign, IL: Human Kinetics), 45-52.

FIGURE 14.2   Sample intramural satisfaction survey.

Intramural Survey

Date distributed: _____

Please return to: _____

Please return by: _____

Because we feel it is essential to monitor the breadth and depth of our intramural program, we are requesting that you take a few moments to provide feedback about our program offerings. Your responses will be kept confidential.

To complete the form, circle the response that best describes your opinion for each statement. If you are not familiar with a particular aspect of our intramural program or are unable to render an opinion, circle "Not sure."

In the space below each statement, labeled "Comments," write a brief explanation of your response.

Thank you.

Intramural program offers a good variety of choices.   Yes   No   Not sure

Comments: _____

_____

Intramural program offers affordable opportunities for all individuals.   Yes   No   Not sure

Comments: _____

_____

Intramural program provides equal opportunities for males and females.   Yes   No   Not sure

Comments: _____

_____

Intramural program provides opportunities for individuals with disabilities.   Yes   No   Not sure

Comments: _____

_____

Intramural program offers opportunities for individuals of all races and ethnicities.   Yes   No   Not sure

Comments: _____

_____

Intramural program provides opportunities for individuals interested in high levels
of competition.   Yes   No   Not sure

Comments: _____

_____

Intramural program provides opportunities for individuals interested in fitness and fun. Yes   No   Not sure

Comments: _____

_____

FIGURE 14.3   Sample intramural evaluation.

Intramural offerings are safe for participants.	Yes	No	Not sure
Comments: _____			
_____			
Intramural program encourages lifelong fitness and health.	Yes	No	Not sure
Comments: _____			
_____			
Intramural program emphasizes individual development over winning.	Yes	No	Not sure
Comments: _____			
_____			
Intramural program is a valuable part of students' educational experience.	Yes	No	Not sure
Comments: _____			
_____			
Are there any activities you would like the program to add?	Yes	No	Not sure
If yes, list them here (provide an explanation if appropriate): _____			
_____			
Are there any sports you would like to see discontinued?	Yes	No	Not sure
If yes, list them here (provide an explanation if appropriate): _____			
_____			

Please indicate your   Gender_____   Grade/year_____   Major_____

Adapted, by permission, from J. Kestner 1996, *Program evaluation for sports directors* (Champaign, IL: Human Kinetics), 67-69.

FIGURE 14.3   *(continued)*

► Participants
► Officials
► Staff
► Volunteers

References

Doyle, P. 1999. Hockey could learn from intramurals. *INPUT* 18 (8): 2. Used by permission of the Canadian Intramural Recreation Association-Ontario.

Kestner, J. 1996. *Program evaluation for sport directors.* Champaign, Ill.: Human Kinetics.

Lumpkin, A., and S. Halstead. 1995. North Carolina State University intramural-recreational sports program participants' satisfaction survey. *NIRSA Journal* 20 (1): 26-27.

Resources

Survey Documentation and Analysis (SDA)
http://csa.berkeley.edu:7502

This Web site offers programs for the documentation and Web-based analysis of survey data.

University of Pudget Sound
www.ups.edu/pe/imquestionnaire.html

Offers a detailed online intramural questionnaire.

University of Western Ontario
www.uwo.ca/campusrec/

Offers an example of an online intramural questionnaire. Click on "intramural sport," then "evaluation."

15

Putting It All Together:

The Handbook

You now understand all the components of an effective intramural program. As promised at the beginning of the book, this final chapter involves pulling all those components together to create your own personal intramural handbook. An intramural handbook will serve as a useful guide both as you get started and throughout your tenure as an intramural director. And the best part is, by completing the chapter summary exercises at the end of each chapter, you've already started creating it!

▶ Review the components of an effective intramural program.
▶ Construct a comprehensive intramural handbook.

A Comprehensive Handbook

An intramural handbook is a great resource in several regards. For starters, having a comprehensive handbook will mean that do not need to reinvent the program every year. For example, having relevant activity and event documents—including rules, registration/signup policies, forms, promotional materials, and so on—provides a readily accessible resource the next time that activity or event is run. Planning and implementation simply involve going to that activity or event, reviewing the procedures and documents, and revising as necessary.

Another benefit is that a comprehensive handbook gives an intramural director a broad as well as a detailed overview of the entire program before it begins. This builds confidence in program implementation and makes life easier during the school year when daily pressures can quickly crowd out long-range planning.

Finally, having a comprehensive handbook provides a great resource for evaluation. If too many participants are getting injured in a specific event, for example, you may need to revise the policies or procedures of that event, modify the rules to make it less competitive, or better communicate the standards of fair play and safety to event participants. By having all these materials in one place, organized by event, doing this will be a snap. If the event itself is simply too dangerous, and you have to drop it from the programming calendar, in the handbook you can simply note the problems associated with that event and reasons for dropping it. Then, if and when the same event is suggested or considered in future years, you (or your replacement) will be able to assess quickly whether the event should be reconsidered.

This handbook will be of most use, of course, if you keep it up to date. Thus, in designing your handbook, it is a good idea to allow for future modifications. If signup sheets and other forms are compiled into a three-ring binder or other folder, all you need to do is take each sheet, form, or promotional piece and tweak it as necessary. If these documents were included as part of a printed manual, on the other hand, each revision would require reprinting the entire manual (or at least a chapter). This can be time consuming and expensive. *Note:* When it comes to promotional materials, it is a good idea to keep a sample of everything used in prior years or events. That way, your promotion will not look the same year after year.

The rest of this chapter is an assignment: create a comprehensive intramural handbook that will serve you and your staff well in the current intramural season and future seasons in the years ahead. In performing this assignment, you will be able to review the contents of this book and integrate your dreams for an intramural program. At the completion of the assignment, you will have a program that you can implement with confidence and ease.

The Assignment

The process of creating an intramural handbook parallels the structure of *Intramural Recreation: A Step-by-Step Guide to Creating an Effective Program*. That is, each part of the assignment coincides with each part of the book. In addition, many parts of the assignment directly coincide with the chapter summary exercises at the end of each chapter. That is, if you have completed these exercises, you are done (or partially done) with that part of the assignment.

Now for the assignment. Start by selecting the type of intramural program you will be directing: grade school, high school, or college/university. (If you've developed grade- or school-specific materials in the chapter summary exercises so far, you will probably want to use the same school level for this assignment.) You may choose an existing school or develop a hypothetical but realistic institution. The forms and suggestions throughout this book can be modified to work in your situation.

Part I: The Idea

1. Briefly describe the school you have chosen. Include such information as the student population, number of staff, intramural program history, and other information that may be relevant to the program.

2. What is your mission statement?
   ▶ Look back to the chapter exercises at the end of chapter 2 (see pages 18-19).
   ▶ How do you plan to communicate, implement, and evaluate this mission?

3. What key benefits do you want to develop in your program?

▶ Start with the benefits you listed in the chapter summary exercises in chapter 1.

▶ Are there other benefits you want to add?

Part II: The Plan

4. How will you structure your program? Be as creative as you were in answering question 1 of the summary exercises for chapter 3. Complete the following.

▶ Describe your existing available facilities.

▶ Identify suitable off-campus facilities and plan how to use them.

▶ Describe how you will organize events and activities. Specifically, outline how you will use the following:

Leagues and tournaments
Special events
Sport clubs
Competitive playing units
Open participation
Houses
Team and individual signup

5. Who will lead and/or be involved in implementing your program? To answer this question, complete the following steps.

▶ Look back at your answer for chapter 4, summary exercise 2. Develop a detailed flowchart for your program (see figures 4.1 and 4.2).

▶ Develop a job description for each paid and volunteer position (see figure 4.5).

▶ Outline the role of volunteers in your program.

▶ Create a volunteer contract and confidentiality agreement (see figures 4.3 and 4.4).

▶ In terms of positions that need to be filled, explain how you will recruit, hire (see figure 4.6), and train your workers. Also develop management strategies to increase job satisfaction and evaluate personnel (see figures 4.7 and 4.8).

6. Explain how you will structure your officials program, including recruiting, hir-

ing (see figure 4.5), and training them (some of this you may have already done in answering chapter 5, summary exercise 3). For example, will you provide checklists for them to use (see figures 5.2, 5.3, 5.4, 7.6, 7.7, and 7.8)? How will you train officials to handle injuries and accidents (see figure 5.1)? How will they ensure safety (see figures 5.2, 7.6, 7.7, and 7.8)? Will you establish a code of ethics to ensure their competence and commitment as well as increase their job satisfaction (see figure 5.5)? Finally, how will you evaluate officials (see figure 5.6)?

7. How will you ensure fair play? Develop a fair play policy that identifies specific standards and procedures for each of the following (also see your answer to chapter 6, summary exercise 3):

▶ Inclusion (meaningful participation for all) (see Table 6.1)

Age
Gender (see figure 6.1)
Disability (see figure 6.2)
Fitness and skill level
Race, skin color, and ethnicity

▶ Sportsmanship (see figure 6.3), which requires that players

respect the rules,
respect officials and their decisions,
respect opponents, and
maintain self-control at all times.

Then come up with an effective way to communicate your fair play policy to all involved (see figure 6.4).

8. Develop a safety policy with standards and procedures for enforcing those standards. Will officials or activity staff be provided with safety checklists (see figures 7.6, 7.7, and 7.8) to check for hazards and appropriate precautions before the start of each event or activity? Devise separate policies for each of the following areas or include them in one comprehensive safety policy:

▶ Attire

▶ Mixed competitive levels

▶ Injury procedures (see figure 5.1)

▶ Lightning and blood policies

▶ Violence

▶ Suspensions (see figure 13.4)

▶ Alcohol

▶ Facility vandalism

▶ Facility audits

Develop liability releases (see figure 7.1) and waivers (see figures 7.2, 7.3, and 7.5) for all participants and describe how/when they will be used in your program. (See figure 7.4 if children under the age of 18 will participate in program activities and events.)

9. How will you promote your program, including events, activities, games, contests, leagues, tournaments, and so on?

▶ How will you use the following types of "live" promotion?

Presentations
Word of mouth
P.A. announcements
Videos

▶ How will you use the following types of print promotion (see chapter 8, summary exercise 3)?

Posters (see figure 8.1)
Bulletins, newsletters, and fliers
Student and local publications

▶ How will you use bulletin and sandwich boards?

▶ Will you publish daybooks and calendars that promote your program (see figure 8.2)?

▶ How will you use the following types of advertising?

Radio and television
Print media including student and local newspapers
Agenda books and calendars (see figure 8.3)

▶ How will you use the computer for promotion and advertising?

Web sites
E-mail

▶ Will you hold promotional activities such as the following?

Orientation
Demonstrations
Weekly celebrations
Registration

▶ Develop two promotional pieces for your program (a poster [see figure 8.1], flier, video, advertisement [see figure 8.3], and so on).

10. Explain in detail your awards program. Will you offer annual awards, ongoing awards, or both? (You should find it helpful to first review your responses to chapter 9 summary exercises) Answer the following award-related questions:

▶ Which awards do you plan to use? Why those awards?

▶ What criteria will you use to give those awards?

▶ Who will select the award recipients? How?

▶ Who will distribute the awards? When?

Now plan your awards ceremony or banquet, including the following components:

▶ Theme (if desirable)

▶ Decorations

▶ Refreshments

▶ Fanfare

▶ Memories and season highlights

11. Formulate a computerized budget (using a spreadsheet) for your program (see figure 10.1). *Note:* You will need to create budgets for each activity and event before you can do this. Your responses to the chapter 10 summary exercises should have given you a great start—just see if you want to add, delete, or change anything.

▶ List your sources of revenue and forecast amounts for each. For example:

Participation fees
Facility rental
Fund-raising
Sponsorship
Advertising

▶ Forecast your expenses:

Staff (including benefits and training)
Facilities and equipment
Promotion and awards
Office supplies
Travel
Insurance

▶ Describe some cost-saving strategies you will implement, such as partnerships on and off campus.

▶ Insert relevant formulas to calculate your subtotals and determine the bottom line.

Part III: The Program

12. Describe your programming and how you will implement it. Your responses to chapter 10 summary exercises should have given you a great start. Now take what you have learned and expand it to the whole program.

▶ First, determine which activities and events you will offer. Choose from the following:

Sports
Contests
Fitness (see figures 8.1 and 11.1)
Recreational sport and play (see figure 11.2)
Skill-development clinics
Sport clubs
Special events
Fieldtrips
Outdoor activities

▶ In terms of tournaments and leagues, which do you plan to use (see figures 12.1 through 12.7 and tables 12.1 and 12.2)? When? And for which activities?

▶ Now determine how you will implement those activities by

defining eligibility rules, include a copy of the game and playing rules for each activity, and developing an annual programming schedule.

▶ Finally, how will you ensure successful events and activities? Consider the following questions:

How will you ensure that everything is ready for the big day?
Will you use formal signup/registration forms (see figures 13.1, 13.2, and 7.3
Will scoring procedures and forms (see figure 13.3) be created? For example, will you use the points system, the participation system, the fair play system, or a different system? Who will decide?
How will you handle last-minute signup/registration?

How will you train your activity and event staff to think on their feet and solve problems?
How will you handle suspensions (see figure 13.4)?

13. Devise a formal evaluation process for your program. Your responses to chapter 11 summary exercises should have given you a great start. Now take what you have learned and expand it to the whole program.

▶ What components will you evaluate? Why or why not?

▶ When (annually, monthly, after each event)?

▶ How will each component be evaluated?

What information-gathering tool will you use (see figures 14.1, 14.2, and 14.3)?
How will it be distributed and collected? To whom?
How will it be analyzed?

For Professors Assigning the Intramural Handbook

If you used this book as a textbook and used the assignment of preparing an intramural handbook as outlined in this chapter, then the student-prepared handbook will need to be evaluated. The chart below is intended as a template, to help you evaluate the student's work.

The marking template covers all the areas discussed in this book. Each area is weighted to account for the anticipated time it would take to complete each section. For example, it is expected that developing a mission statement will take half the time of developing the leadership component of the handbook or the promotion section. Each section is graded on thoroughness and clarity of presentation. Use the blanks to fill in each student's score, out of the total possible score presented in parentheses "( )".

_____(2) Description of school (population, number of staff, program history, and other relevant information)

_____(5) Mission statement (clearly written, comprehensive and inspirational, with a clear plan of how to communicate, implement, and evaluate this mission)

_____(3) Benefits (clearly written and documented benefits for the program)

_____(5) Program (comprehensive description of available facilities, and a detailed plan of how students will be organized for the intramural events and activities)

_____(10) Leadership (detailed flowcharts, job descriptions, contracts, recruiting strategies, hiring policies, training sessions, and evaluation tools and procedures for intramural staff and volunteers)

_____(5) Officials (detailed explanation of recruiting, hiring, supervising, training, and evaluation of officials)

_____(10) Policies on fair play (detailed policy statement on the specific standards and procedures to implement a fair play policy that encourages inclusion [age, ethnicity, gender, disability, fitness level, skill level] and sportsmanship [respecting rules, officials, and opponents, and maintaining self control])

_____(10) Policies on safety (develop facility safety checklist and participant waiver forms; policies dealing with attire, mixed competition levels, injury procedures and blood, lightning, violence, suspensions, alcohol, facility vandalism, and audit concerns)

_____(10) Promotion (explaining how live promotions, print promotions, the computer, and events will be used to promote intramurals [two pieces should be included])

_____(5) Awards (detail the criteria, the construction, and the distribution of awards, including and awards ceremony or banquet)

_____(10) Budget (a comprehensive computer spreadsheet detailing the income and expenses of a one-year intramural program)

_____(10) Programming (a detailed calendar of events, along with the rules for the various activities)

_____(5) Evaluation (a detailed explanation of what is evaluated and how, along with relevant sample questionairres)

_____(10) Overall presentation of the handbook (organization and presentation)

_____(100) Total points possible

Glossary

actual damages—Costs directly related to an injury (medical expenses, lost wages, and so on).

advantage seeding—A type of seeding that gives the best ranked seed a slightly easier schedule than the second seed, and so on. For example, the semi-finals, Seed 1 competes against Seed 4 while Seed 2 competes against Seed 3.

administration—Running or operating specific programming components. For example, league administration involves promotion, budgeting, preparing playing schedules, organizing the officiating, tabulating results, and evaluation.

advertising—A specific tool for raising people's awareness about an intramural program or activity that typically involves media. Advertising is a component of promotion.

annual awards—Awards given in recognition of a unique contribution to the intramural program. These contributions can be a special one-time effort or a season- or year-long effort. Annual awards are cumulative. That is, they are tracked throughout the year and presented at its completion

appellant—Someone who loses in court and appeals the court's decision to a higher court.

appellee—Someone who wins in court and against whom the appellant appeals.

assumption of risk—Voluntarily assuming responsibility for risks inherent in an activity.

athletics—A game in which players are more committed to winning than to the spirit of play. Athletics usually takes the form of formalized competition between schools and involves practices, coaches, rulebooks, and so on.

balanced budget—A budget in which expenses equal revenue.

Banner—A small sign on a Web page that is typically used as advertising space for a company.

bracket—A graphic illustration of where entries advance when they win and in the case of double elimination, where the first-time losers go.

brainstorming—A method of idea generation that involves such things as solving specific problems and developing new ideas through unrestricted participation in discussion.

budget—A statement of financial position or the amount of money available for a particular purpose.

budgeting—The process of keeping track of revenue and expenses.

bye—The position of a top-ranked tournament entry that advances to the next round without playing.

campus recreation—An umbrella term that includes intramural and extramural programs.

claimant—The person filing for compensation in a legal action.

consent form—An authorization, usually signed by a parent or guardian, permitting a child to participate in some activity.

contests—Activities that are interspersed throughout the year to generate interest in an intramural program and to attract students who might not normally participate in competitive leagues and tournaments. Contests usually have a competitive element to them (trying to sink a basket or putt a ball into a hole), whereas something like a special event usually does not (get a bus load of students to go skiing or watch a professional sporting event).

convener—An official who is responsible for running an event, including special events, leagues, and tournaments.

defamation—Spoken (slander) or written (libel) communication that is false and holds the subject of the statement up to public ridicule.

default—This is when a team declares ahead of time that it is unable to be present at the scheduled time of their game. Defaults result when a team notifies the intramural office (or league covener) 48 hours ahead of time.

defendant—Someone who is being sued and must defend against the plaintiff's claims.

deficit budget—A budget in which expenses are greater than revenue and the budget has a negative balance ("in the red").

direct expenses—Costs that result directly from the intramural program. For example, an aerobics instructor's hourly wage of $12.50 is a direct expense.

dismissal—When a judge refuses to hear further evidence about a case because it is fraudulent or specious on its face.

divisions—Separate pools of tournament and league entries that are sometimes divided by area (the engineering division) or by playing level (junior and senior division, or a recreational and competitive division).

double elimination—A tournament like single elimination, except entries keep playing until they lose twice.

draft—The process of team captains selecting from eligible players who have registered to participate.

draw—The placement of entries onto a tournament bracket sheet or league schedule.

employment contract—A formal letter or document that commits a hiree to perform his or her work responsibilities and outlines the role of the institution and program staff.

entry—Teams or individual scheduled to compete in a tournament or league.

equal opportunity—A component of inclusion that involves ensuring everyone an opportunity to participate.

equitable seeding—A type of seeding in which the top seed's schedule is as difficult as the second seed's, and so forth. For example, in the semi-finals Seed 1 competes against Seed 3, while Seed 2 competes against Seed 4—both two seeds apart.

expenses—Money spent for the program, including the cost of salaries, facility rental, equipment, office and event supplies, travel, and promotion.

extended tournament—These tournaments can carry on indefinitely and can often be self-monitoring. Typically they involve players challenging others of slightly higher ability. Should the challenger win, the winner and loser exchange places. Ladder and pyramid tournaments are common types of extended tournaments.

extramural programs—Organized recreational activities that take place off campus. Typically, extramural activities involve informal competition between schools.

extrinsic reward—A prize, trophy, pat on the back, or other external motivation to participate in intramurals. People who are extrinsically motivated seek the win, the prize, the pat on the back from friends and spectators, and so on.

facility audit—A regularly scheduled and thorough site review to evaluate facility safety hazards and protective equipment.

fair play—A way of thinking that incorporates concepts of friendship, respect for others, and always playing within the right spirit.

forecasting—The process of estimating revenue and expenses.

forfeit—This occurs when a team does not show at the time of the event and has not given adequate advance notice.

formal evaluation—The systematic collection of data for the purposes of measuring performance and making improvements to the intramural program.

formative evaluation—Any evaluation that is used to help a person improve.

free agents—Individual intramural participants who wish to play on a team but cannot find a team to play on.

fund-raising—The activity of raising money. Fund-raising activities typically include special campaigns and events that people pay to participate in.

game—An activity in which participants attempt to accomplish a specific task by agreeing to overcome unnecessary obstacles.

gross negligence—Conduct so reckless as to demonstrate a substantial lack of concern for whether injury results.

harassment—One or a series of bothersome comments or conduct that is known or might reasonably be known to be unwelcome or unwanted, offensive, intimidating, hostile, or inappropriate.

head officials—Officials responsible for successfully recruiting, training, managing, and evaluating officials.

house—A competitive group to which participants are assigned by dividing the student body equally in several large groups. When a house is scheduled to compete, anyone from that house is welcome to participate.

inclusion—A spirit in which everyone feels encouraged to participate regardless of such personal characteristics as ethnicity, age, gender, disability, fitness level, and so on.

indirect expenses—Costs not directly related to an intramural program, for example, training.

informal evaluation—A nonsystematic collection of data for the purposes of measuring performance and making improvements to the intramural program.

intentional wrongdoing—The intent to do harm.

intramural council—A group of students (volunteer or recruits) who help with the leadership to and implementation of intramural programs at many institutions. Intramural councils operate under the leadership of the intramural director.

intramural program—The entire intramural program, including both the programming and the staff, volunteers, and procedures responsible for implementing that programming.

intramural programming—All organized recreational and physical activities for students and other participants that take place on campus (also called "campus recreation"). Intramural programming can include anything from team sport competitions and recreational games to fitness classes and special intramural events. The term also refers to the act of determining that programming.

intramurals—See intramural programs.

intrinsic reward—Personal satisfaction, pride, and other internal motivation feelings that motivate participation in intramurals. People who are intrinsically motivated participate just for the fun of it, not for prizes, trophies, and other awards.

ladder tournament—An extended tournament in which players are aligned in a ladder formation, one on top of the other, with the strongest entries on top and the weakest entries on the bottom. Players challenge others of slightly higher ability. Should the challenger win, the winner and loser exchange places.

leadership—Stimulating and aiding groups to accept, formulate common goals and to carry out effectively the measures leading to the attainment of those goals.

league—A competitive structure in which teams or individuals compete for a week or more, perhaps an entire school year.

liability—Legal responsibility for injury or damage to another. If found guilty, the defendant may need to pay or make restitution.

mission statement—A precise statement of what an institution wants its intramural program to be.

multilevel—A tournament similar to a single-elimination tournament, except that entries are not eliminated after a loss but instead move into consolation rounds.

negligence—doing something a reasonably prudent person would not do, or not doing something a reasonably prudent person would do, under similar circumstances. In other words, it is the failure to provide an ordinary or reasonable standard of care. Negligence is the most common violation brought against intramural professionals.

ongoing awards—Awards given throughout the year to celebrate regular highlights and achievements throughout the intramural program, including the type of participation an intramural director wishes to support.

open event—An event that is open to either male or female participants (teams are not required to have a specified number of males or females).

open participation—This approach specifies a grade level that the activities are geared for, and attendance is open to anyone from that grade level who wishes to participate.

participation fees—Monies charged students for participating in certain programs or activities, such as aerobics classes or volleyball league.

peer officiating—An intramural volunteer program in which team members officiate other teams' games.

physical education—In-class instruction of physical activity.

pick-up game—An informal game between a few participants who agree on the game and decide to play.

plaintiff—One who was injured and files a claim in court. Also called "claimant."

play—A voluntary activity intended to be pursued purely for the fun of the moment.

playful game—A game in which opponents are more committed to the spirit of play than to winning. An example of a playful game might be one-on-one basketball where players don't keep score and try odd or unusual shots.

play-off—A tournament structure in which the highest-scoring teams or individuals compete to determine an overall champion.

policies—Formal, written declarations, based on the mission statement, that define the parameters necessary to achieve the program's goals.

polling—Asking specific questions to get feedback, suggestions, opinions, answers, and so on for purpose of evaluation.

professionals—Those who participate in a field for material or other gain or for their livelihood.

programming—See intramural programming.

promotion—Any activity or result of that activity that raises awareness about the intramural program, including specific intramural activities and the benefits of participating.

punitive damages—A court's award to punish a defendant and prevent the violation from being repeated.

pyramid tournament—An extended tournament in which players are aligned in a pyramid formation, one level on top of the other, with the strongest entries on top and the weakest entries on the bottom. Players can challenge others of slightly higher ability. Should the challenger win, the winner and loser exchange places.

revenue—Money brought into the program from such things as student fees, rentals, fund-raising, and sponsorship.

risk management—The process of limiting dangerous, harmful, and hazardous situations.

round robin—Basically, a schedule is made up before the tournament or league begins in which everyone plays each other one time, regardless of whether teams win or lose any of their games.

round robin double split—A round-robin tournament in which two pools of entries compete.

round robin quadruple split—A round-robin tournament in which four pools of entries compete.

round robin triple split—A round-robin tournament in which three pools of entries compete.

safety audit—A regularly scheduled and thorough site review to evaluate safety hazards, protective equipment, safety procedures, and staff preparedness for dealing with emergencies.

seeding—The process of ranking players according to their ability relative to other entries.

settlement—A reward or solution both parties agree to before or during a trial.

single elimination—A tournament in which an entry must win to advance to the next round. If an entry loses once, that individual or team is eliminated from the tournament.

special events—An event that celebrates something or promotes the intramural program, or an event in which students do something out of the ordinary. Special events are typically one-day events.

speculative damages—Costs the injured party will likely suffer as a result of the injury (future income, medical costs, and so on).

sport—A game in which participants are equally committed to the spirit of play and to winning.

sport club—A group of individuals who join together voluntarily, in a more or less formal organization, for the purpose of participating in a particular sport. Sport clubs in educational institutions are typically student initiated and operated, and largely self-financed.

sportsmanship—Showing fairness and equity to others in play and competition.

spreadsheet—A document with many columns and rows useful for keeping track of budgets.

stacking—teams drafting or otherwise selecting strong players from other teams to strengthen their own team.

standard of care—The basic standard a reasonably prudent individual would expect under the same or similar circumstances.

student fees—Flat fees charged by an institution (typically colleges and universities) for participating in intramurals, recreation, athletics, and other school programs. A portion of these fees are usually allotted for intramural programs.

student intramural association—A student-run group that plans and implements an intramural program or activity. Also called an "athletic association," these groups are usually self-financed or funded through student fees.

summary judgment—judgement made on the case when there is no dispute about the facts of the case and, therefore, case law is directly applicable.

supervision—In the context of intramural safety, the keeping of order in a game or activity, stopping of fights and other hazardous conduct, and general protection and assurance of safety for all program participants.

surplus budget—A budget in which revenue is greater than expenses and the budget has a positive balance ("in the black").

Target audience—a group of people with shared characteristics at which promotions, speech, organizational structure, and activities are aimed. The intent is to get more of the target audience involved in intramural programs.

tendering—The process of getting equipment bids from various competing companies for supplying equipment or the execution of work. The process of tendering involves five steps: (1) preparing a document of the specific supplies or work required; (2) identifying appropriate suppliers; (3) obtaining tender offers; (4) evaluating tender offers; and (5) awarding the contract.

tort—Injury to a person or to property, which is compensable under the law. Categories of torts include negligence, gross negligence, and intentional wrongdoing. To justify a legal tort claim, an act (or inaction) must satisfy four elements: (1) There must be a legal duty of care to another person and (2) a breach of that duty; (3) the claimant must have suffered damages; and (4) the damages must have been proximately caused by the breach of duty.

tournament—A competitive structure in which teams or individuals are scheduled to compete over one or two days.

varsity athletics—A voluntary program that offers highly formalized, between school competitions that are oriented toward winning.

waiver—An agreement to waive the right to seek damages from the intramural department, its staff, and the institution should an injury occur while participating in an intramural activity or event.

Bibliography

Academy of Leisure Sciences. 2001. White paper #2: Leisure apartheid. [Online]. Available: www.eas.ualberta.ca/elj/alswp2.html

Alsager, D. 1977. Intramural programming in Ohio high schools. Unpublished manuscript, Miami University, Oxford, Ohio.

Amabile, T., and B. Hennessey. 1992. The motivation for creativity in children. In *Achievement and motivation*, edited by A. Boggiano and T. Pittman. New York: Cambridge University Press, 54-74.

Americans with Disabilities Act. 1990. Public law 101-336, July 26, 1990, 104, Statute 327. [Online]. Available: http://janweb.icdi.wvu.edu/kinder/pages/ada_statute.htm.

Antons, J. 1999. The intramural experience. *CIRA Bulletin* 25 (3): 11. Used by permission of the Canadian Intramural Recreation Association.

Appenzeller, H. 1994a. College student injured on obstacle course. *From the Gym to Jury* 6 (1): 6.

Appenzeller, H. 1994b. Student tackled during flag football awarded $99,000. 1994. *From the Gym to Jury*. 6 (1): 6.

Bailey, D. 2000. Is anyone out there listening? *Quest* 52 (4): 344-50.

Balady, G. 2000. *ACSM's guidelines for exercise testing and prescription*. 6th ed. Philadelphia: Lippencott Williams and Wilkens.

Bancroft, E. 1917. *Jane Allen of the sub team*. Akron, Ohio: Saalfield.

Bancroft. E. 1918. *Jane Allen: Right guard*. Akron, Ohio: Saalfield.

Barbarash, L. 1997. *Multicultural games*. Champaign, IL: Human Kinetics.

Bolo, C. 1999. Special intramural events. *The Leader* 7 (5): 1. Used with permission of the Canadian Intramural Recreation Association.

Boyles, M. 1996. On officials, fair play, and otherwise sunny days. *CIRA Bulletin* 22 (3): 3-5.

Brudney, J. *Fostering volunteer programs in the public sector*. San Francisco: Jossey-Bass, 1990.

Bulfin, D. 1996. Family programming for fun and profit. *NIRSA Journal* 20 (3): 4-5.

Byl, J. 1990. Formalizing a ladder tournament. *NIRSA Journal* 15 (1): 41-43.

Byl, J. 1992. A round robin pyramid. *NIRSA Journal* 16 (2): 41-42.

Byl, J. 1994. A round robin ladder tournament. *CAHPER Journal* 60 (2): 25-27.

Byl, J. 1994. Coming to terms with play, game, sport, and athletics. In *Christianity and leisure: Issues in a pluralistic society*, edited by P. Heintzman, G. Van Andel, and T. Visker. Sioux Center, Iowa: Dordt College Press, 155-63.

Byl, J. 1995. Tie-breaking: Minimizing the blow-outs. *NIRSA Journal* 20 (1): 53.

Byl, J. 1999. *Organizing successful tournaments*. Champaign, IL: Human Kinetics.

Byl, J. 2000. Put your money on the edge. *INPUT* (March): 4-5.

Byl, J. 2002. *Co-ed recreational games*. Champaign, IL: Human Kinetics

Byl, J., and J. VanderWier. 1995. Encouraging fair play in college intramurals. *CAHPERD Journal* 61 (2): 26-27.

Cai, S. 2000. Physical exercise and mental health: A content integrated approach in coping with college students' anxiety and depression. *Physical Educator* 27 (2): 69-76.

Canadian Parks and Recreation Association. 1997. *Benefits catalogue*. Ottawa: Canadian Parks and Recreation Association.

Cappadonia, P. 1970. Evaluation of vandalism during leisure time in all junior high schools of Utah County, Utah. Master's thesis, Brigham Young University, Provo, Utah.

Carroll, L. 1960. *Alice's adventures in wonderland*. New York: New American Library.

Chandler, T. 1988. Building character through sport, and striving to win in sport: Values at odds or in concert? In *Persons, minds and bodies*, edited by S. Ross and L. Charette. North York, Ontario: University Press of Canada, 161-69.

Claris HomePage—the Basics. 2001. [Online]. Available: http://acomp.stanford.edu/acpubs/Docs/claris_homepage/

Cleave, S. 1994. Sport clubs—More than a solution to shrinking dollars and growing demands. *NIRSA Journal* 18 (3): 30-33.

Cobb, C. 2001. Recognizing impact of sports not rocket science: Common sense dispensed after national summit. *National Post* (April 30), A1.

Cohen, A. 1991. Crime and punishment. *Athletic Business* 15 (10): 31-35.

Coleman, D., and S. Iso-Ahola. 1993. Leisure and health: The role of social support and self-determination. *Journal of Leisure Research* (25): 111-28.

Conlon, D., 1999. Fly on the wall. *The Leader* 7 (4): 4.

Cooper, N. 1997. Will the defendant please rise: How effective is your risk management plan? *NIRSA Journal* 21 (2): 34-41.

Cotton, V., W. Kelley, and W. Sedlacek. 1999. Situational characteristics of positive and negative experiences with same race and different race students. [Online]. Available: http://www.naspa.org/resources/complete.cfm?ID=1&display=full.

Csikszentmihalyi, M. 1975. *Beyond boredom and anxiety: The experience of play in work and games.* San Francisco: Jossey-Bass.

Deci, E., and R. Ryan. 1985. *Intrinsic motivation and self-determination in human behavior.* New York: Plenum Press.

Dewey, J. 1916. *Democracy and education.* New York: Macmillan.

Dion, E. 2001. Spirit and game philosophy. *CIRA Bulletin* 26 (3): 4.

Doyle, P. 1997. *Activities for groups of 50 or more.* Hamilton, Ontario: Canadian Intramural Recreation Association-Ontario.

Doyle, P. 1998. *Awesome asphalt activities.* Hamilton, Ontario: CIRA-Ontario.

Doyle, P. 1998. *Great gator games.* Hamilton, Ontario: Canadian Intramural Recreation Association-Ontario.

Doyle, P. 1998. *Schlockey.* Hamilton, Ontario: Canadian Intramural Recreation Association-Ontario.

Doyle, P. 1999. Hockey could learn from intramurals. *INPUT* 18 (8): 2. Used by permission of the Canadian Intramural Recreation Association-Ontario.

Doyle, P., and J. Berry. 1997. *Another games book.* Hamilton, Ontario: Canadian Intramural Recreation Association-Ontario.

Doyle, P., D. Schei, and B. McFarlane. 1994. *Not just another games book.* Ottawa, Ontario: Canadian Intramural Recreation Association.

Drowatzky, K., and J. Drowatzky. 2000. Physical activity and bone mineral density. *Clinical Kinesiology* 54 (2): 28-35.

Dudenyhoeffer, F. 1997. Life before NIRSA: A brief history of women's intramurals in the 20th century. *NIRSA Journal* 21 (2): 3-7.

Ellis, Susan J. 1994. *The volunteer recruitment book.* Philadelphia: Energize.

European Cultural Co-operation of the Council of Europe. 1992. *Code of sports ethics fair play: The winning way.* Europe of Cultural Co-operation. [Online]. Available: www.culture.coe.fr/Infocenter/txt/eng/espcod.htm.

Fabian, L. 1982. Leadership development through intramural sports. *NIRSA Journal* 6 (3): 18-22.

Fair Play Canada. 1994. *Fair play—It's your call!* Ottawa, Ontario: Fair Play Canada.

Flanery, T., ed. 1999. *National Federation of State High School Associations 1999-2000 rule book for soccer.* Indianapolis: National Federation of State High School Associations Publications.

Froelicher, V., and E. Froelicher. 1991. Cardiovascular benefits of physical activity. In *Benefits of leisure,* edited by B.L. Driver, P.J. Brown, and G.L. Pederson. State College, Pa.: Venture Publishing, 59-72.

Gaskins, D. 1996. A profile of recreational sports student employees. *NIRSA Journal* 20 (3): 43-77.

Geiger, J. 1997. "Count it!" Officials that don't miss the call. *NIRSA Journal* 21 (3): 12-14.

Gobhai, X. 1996. Thoughts on intramurals. *CIRA Bulletin* 21 (7): 10. Used by permission of the Canadian Intramural Recreation Association.

Graham, P. 1994. The old and the new, the past, present, and future of the NIA. *NIRSA Journal* 17 (1): 21-22.

Hanniford, G. 1992. Our past: Our heritage. *NIRSA Journal* 17 (1): 24.

Harackiewicz, J. 1979. The effects of reward contingency and performance feedback on intrinsic motivation. *Journal of Personality and Social Psychology* 37: 1352-63.

Harkness, M. 1998. $10,000 jackpot. *INPUT* (December): 6. Used by permission of the Canadian Intramural Recreation Association-Ontario.

Helm, E.J., W. Sedlacek, and D. Prieto. 1998. The relationship between attitudes toward diversity and overall satisfaction of university students by race. *Journal of College Counseling* 1: 111-20.

Herzog, A., and W. Rogers. 1981. The structure of subjective well-being in different age groups. *Journal of Gerontology* 36: 472-79.

Howard, B. 1996. Intramural extravaganza. *CIRA Bulletin* 22 (1): 11. Used by permission of the Canadian Intramural Recreation Association.

Human Kinetics. 2001. Sport director. [CD.] Champaign, IL: Human Kinetics.

Human Services Institute. 1992. *Trying to play together: Competing paradigms in approaches to integration through recreation and leisure.* Cambridge, Mass.: Human Services Institute.

Hunter, G., M. Gamman, and D. Hester. 2000. Obesity-prone children can benefit from high-intensity exercise. *Strength and Conditioning Journal* 22 (1): 51-54.

Hurtes, K., L. Allne, B. Stevens, and C. Lee. 2000. Benefits-based programming: Making an impact on youth. *Journal of Park and Recreation Administration* 18 (1): 34-49.

International Paralympic Committee. 2001. Goalball. [Online]. Available: www.lboro.ac.uk/research/paad/ipc/goalball/goalball.html.

Iso-Ahola, S., A. Graefe, and D. La Verde. 1989. Perceived competence as a mediator of the relationship between high risk sports participation and self-esteem. *Journal of Leisure Research* 21: 32-39.

Jandris, T. 1980. Possibilities and potentials: High school intramurals. *Journal of Physical Education and Recreation* 51: 48-50

Johnson, M. 1999. The intramural experience. *CIRA Bulletin.* 25 (3): 11. Used by permission of the Canadian Intramural Recreation Association.

Johnson, O. 1912 (Reprinted 1968, 1997). *Stover at Yale.* New Haven: Yale Bookstore.

Keewatin Divisional Board of Education. 1998. *Inuit games book.* Rankin Inlet, Northwest Territories, Canada, XOC OGO: Keewatin Divisional Board of Education.

Kelly, J. 1983. *Leisure identities and interactions.* London: Allen and Unwin.

Kensington High School Intramural Department. 1980-1981. Kensington intramurals. Unpublished handbook, Burnaby, British Columbia.

Kestner, J. 1996. *Program evaluation for sport directors.* Champaign, IL: Human Kinetics.

Kleiber, D., and C. Kirshnit. 1991. Sport involvement and identity formation. In *Mind-body maturity: Psychological approaches to sport, exercise and fitness,* edited by L. Diament. New York: Hemisphere.

Kraus, R. 1985. *Recreation leadership today.* Chicago: Addison-Wesley.

Lam, L. 1999. The intramural experience. *CIRA Bulletin* 25 (3): 11. Used by permission of the Canadian Intramural Recreation Association.

Lee, M. 1986. Moral and social growth through sport: The coach's role. In *The growing child in competitive sport,* edited by G. Glesson. London: Hodder & Stoughton, 248-55.

Lichtman, B. 1993. *Innovative games.* Champaign, IL: Human Kinetics.

Lichtman, B. 1999. *More innovative games.* Champaign, IL: Human Kinetics.

Lore, J. 1994. A survey of selected collegiate sport club programs. *NIRSA Journal* 19 (1): 32-35.

Lumpkin, A., and S. Halstead. 1995. North Carolina State University intramural-recreational sports program participants' satisfaction survey. *NIRSA Journal* 20 (1): 26-27.

Lundy, K. 1999. *Community vs. elite sport: The elusive balance.* Sydney, Australia. [Online]. Available: http://www.katelundy.dynamite.com.au/access&.htm.

Mann, T 1999. Volunteer recognition. *Recreation Saskatchewan* 26 (8): 3.

May, S. 2000. Volunteering—Back to basics. *Profile* (June/July): 3.

McGregor, I. 1997. Emergency response planning: Are you prepared? *NIRSA Journal* 21 (3): 24-25.

Mendelson, E. 2001. *Adobe Pagemill 3.0.* [Online]. Available: http://www.zdnet.com/pcmag/firstlooks/9804/f980423a2.htm.

Midura, D. 1992. *Team building through physical challenges.* Champaign, IL: Human Kinetics.

Midura, D. 1995. *More team-building challenges.* Champaign, IL: Human Kinetics.

Morris, D., and J. Stiehl. 1999. *Changing kids' games.* Champaign, IL: Human Kinetics.

Mullin, B., S. Hardy, and W. Sutton. 2000. *Sport marketing.* Champaign, IL: Human Kinetics.

Murray, C. 1995. Dealing with conflict. [Online]. Available: www.lin.ca/lin/resource/html/bramp3.htm.

National Collegiate Athletic Association. 1999. *NCAA soccer rulebook.* Indianapolis: National Collegiate Athletic Association.

National Collegiate Athletic Association (NCAA). 2000a. *Guideline 2H: Blood-borne pathogens and intercollegiate athletics.* [Online]. Available: http://www.ncaa.org/sports_sciences/sports_med_handbook/2h.pdf.

National Collegiate Athletic Association (NCAA). 2000b. *2001 men's and women's basketball rules and interpretations.* Indianapolis: The National Collegiate Athletic Association.

Nova Scotia Department of Education. 1978. *Intramural programming: A public school guide.* Halifax: Nova Scotia Department of Education.

Paffenbarger, R., R. Hyde, and A. Dow. 1991. Health benefits of physical activity. In *Benefits of leisure,* edited by B.L. Driver, P.J. Brown, and G.L. Pederson. State College, PA: Venture Publishing, 49-57.

Parks and Recreation Ontario. 1999. *Together with youth: Planning recreation services for youth at risk.* Toronto: Parks and Recreation Ontario.

Peng, S. 1997. The leadership challenge. *The Leader* 5 (4): 1. Used by permission of the Canadian Intramural Recreation Association.

Perry, H. 1999. *Call to order: Meeting rules and procedures for non-profit organizations.* Owen Sound, Ontario: Big Bay Publishing.

Phillips, M. 1992. The experience of disability and the dilemma of normalization. In *Interpreting disability: A qualitative reader,* edited by P. Ferguson, D. Ferguson, and S. Taylor. New York: Teachers College, 213-32.

Pratt, M, C. Macera, and G. Wang. 2000. Higher direct medical costs associated with physical inactivity. *Physician and Sportsmedicine* 28 (10): 63-70.

Proescher, L. 1996. Participant satisfaction in intramurals. *NIRSA Journal* 20 (3): 20-24.

Queens Intramurals. 2000. *Intramural program overview.* [Online.] Available: http://www.phe.queensu.ca/athletics/recreation/intramurals/intramurals.html.

Reich, J., and A. Zantra. 1981. Life events and personal causation: Some relationships with satisfaction and distress. *Journal of Personality and Social Psychology* 41: 1002-12.

Riley, R., and N. Cantu. 1997. *Title IX: 25 years of progress.* [Online]. Available: www.ed.gov/pubs/TitleIX/part5.html.

Robert, H., S.C. Robert, W.J. Evans, eds. 1991. *Robert's rules of order newly revised.* 9th ed. New York: Perseus.

Schwartze, A. 1899. *Vassar studies.* New York: G.P. Putnam & Sons.

Smith, S. 1995. Personal meaning in intramural basketball. *NIRSA Journal* 20 (1): 36-44.

Statistics Canada. 2001. *National longitudinal survey of children and youth: Participation in activities.* Ottawa: Statistics Canada.

Stein, E. 1985. The first organized intramural event (1869): Princeton University's cane spree. *NIRSA Journal* 9 (2): 42-43.

Strong, T., and D. LeFevre. 1996. *Parachute games.* Champaign, IL: Human Kinetics.

Suits, B. 1973. The elements of sport. In *The philosophy of sport: A collection of original essays,* edited by R.G. Osterhoudt. Springfield, IL: Charles C Thomas, 46-63.

Tennessee Tech. 2001. Handbook. [Online]. Available: www.tntech.edu/www/acad/honors/handbook/chap6/chap6.html.

Tharp, L. 1994. The effect Title IX has had on intramural sports. *NIRSA Journal* 19 (1): 29-31.

Tower, A. 1995. Consider a "spirit of competition" and a rating system for your intramural-recreation programs. *NIRSA Journal* 20 (1): 46-47.

Tudor-Locke, C., R. Bell, and A. Myers. 2000. Revisiting the role of physical activity and exercise in the treatment of type 2 diabetes. *Canadian Journal of Applied Physiology* 25 (6): 466-91.

U.S. Department of Health and Human Services. 1996. *Physical activity and health: A report of the surgeon general.* Atlanta: U.S. Department of Health and Human Services, Centers for Disease Control and Prevention, National Center for Chronic Disease Prevention and Health Control.

Vanden Boor, M. 2000. Ultimate medical dodgeball. *CIRA-Ontario Input* (March): 6.

Vandyke, R. 1980. Aggression in sport: Its implications for character building. *Quest* 32 (2): 201-8.

Varley, J. 1994. Campus recreation protest and conduct board. *CIRA Input* (December): 7.

Velicer, W., J. Prochaska, J. Fava, G. Norman, and C. Redding. 1998. Smoking cessation and stress management: Applications of the transtheoretical model of behavior change. *Homeostasis* 38: 216-33.

Wilhite, B., and D. Kleiber. 1992. The effects of Special Olympics participation on community integration. *Therapeutic Recreation Journal* 26 (4): 9-20.

Williams, D., ed. 1995. *Zany activities with a rubber chicken.* Ottawa, Ontario: Canadian Intramural Recreation Association.

Williams, D., ed. 1997. *Zany activities with panty hose, boxer shorts, and leotards.* Ottawa, Ontario: Canadian Intramural Recreation Association.

Index

About the Author

John Byl, PhD, is a professor physical education and the intramural director at Redeemer University College in Hamilton, Ontario, Canada. He directed physical education programs and coached various sports for 23 years at the community, high school, and college levels. He is a national board member of the Canadian Intramural Recreation Association, and executive member of the Ontario College Committee on Campus Recreation, and vice president of the Canadian Intramural Recreation Association-Ontario.

Byl received his PhD in organization, administration, and policy, specializing in the social-foundations division, from the State University of New York at Buffalo. He earned a master of human kinetics degree from the University of Windsor and a bachelor of physical education degree from the University of British Columbia.

Author of *Ongoing Successful Tournaments, Co-Ed Recreational Games,* and *Minor Games Manual,* Byl has also contributed chapters to several other books and has published many articles and proceedings on sports and physical education.

*You'll find other
outstanding recreation
and leisure resources at*

www.humankinetics.com

In the U.S. call

1-800-747-4457

Australia	08 8277 1555
Canada	800-465-7301
Europe	+44 (0) 113 278 1708
New Zealand	09-523-3462

HUMAN KINETICS
The Information Leader in Physical Activity
P.O. Box 5076 • Champaign, IL 61825-5076 USA